Cover and layout design by Alyssa Hardinger

Ring of Luck

A Novel of the Founding of the American Spirit at Jamestown, Virginia

Sarah Sue Hardinger

ii

Acknowledgements

For their faith in this project and their technical knowledge:

Dr. Bly Straub
Anne Conkling
Carl Lounsbury
Terry Marr

For reading the manuscript and moral support:

Carla Beaver
Sarah Nodine
Ron Mortenson

For layout and cover art:

Alyssa Taylor Hardinger

Forward   The Historical Archeology Record

Up until 1998, the scientific community and local lore both held that the original fort built at Jamestown had been washed away by erosion from the James River. The guides even pointed out a dead cypress tree a short way out in the river and said that was most likely the site of the first fort.

Absence of hard evidence to the contrary, the few reports of lazy gentlemen colonists bowling in the streets instead of growing food for the fledgling colony were generally believed. Indians, except for the blessed Pocahontas, were believed to be unsophisticated and violent. Death by starvation was held off only by the benevolence of the Virginia Company. The handful of artifacts displayed at the site mostly came from later in the settlement.

In 1998, modern archaeologists decided to defy convention and go looking on land for the 1607 fort. In almost twenty years of study, Dr. William Kelso and his team have found exactly what they were looking for in exactly the place they expected. What they have found has reversed almost all of what we thought we knew of the first permanent English colony in America. If you are ever in eastern Virginia, do go to Jamestown and look around. Until then, you can see a great deal at the Jamestown Rediscovery website.

I have had the privilege of visiting Jamestown many times and have incorporated many of the artifacts they have recovered into this narrative. Dr. Bly Straube has been most gracious in allowing me to see many of the artifacts close up. The other side of historical archeology is the written record and recently there have been new finds in this area as well. We have a very new picture of life in the first years of Jamestown. This is the first fictional retelling of the Jamestown story to paint that picture.

Preface

A story that faithfully follows history, includes documented quotes as dialog, fills out the characters with physical details and additional dialog and incudes a few fictional characters to facilitate the movement of the action has recently been referred to as fictionalized history or "faction." This book is the fictionalized history of the first twelve years of the Jamestown colony based on recent archaeology and recent document findings.

There are only two major characters that are not in the historical record by name, Josiah Tucker and Bridget Malone. However in every ship and fleet that came to the Virginia shores in the first years of the colony, there were those whose names appeared on a passenger list and then there were people listed simply as "diverse others." Josiah and Bridget are names I have given to two of those diverse others.

Events in which Josiah or Bridget is the central figure are compiled from fragments of other events or imagined. All the other significant events in this story are true, even the ones that seem implausible or impossible. I have given voice to these events with dialog, of which there is no record, but the events themselves are duly recorded in contemporary journals and reports or books based on that material. The first three years of the colony are very well documented. The next nine less so, but still a body of material survives.

The story we now know of the first years of Jamestown is much more compelling and amazing than the history textbooks, the movies or the myths. Please, enjoy reading the truth.

For background on the artifacts mentioned in this book and a wider discussion of early European settlements, visit Ring of Luck on Faceboook.

Dedication

For my descendants, current and future.

Those who do not study history are doomed to repeat its errors.

CHAPTER 1
The Virginia Company

Thief! Where is he, where is that thief?!

A girl of thirteen had been watching the proceedings from the shelter of a doorway. When the crowd picked up the cry of "thief" and began to check out all the boys who were alone and without purpose, she moved quietly to the side of the tall, roughly dressed boy and locked her arm in his.

"Just keep walking slowly and sometimes look down and talk to me."

Josiah Tucker still gawked at the people and buildings of London. He gawked at this young girl. Fifteen and recently arrived from the country, Josiah had come to seek his fortune, however it may come his way. Today fortune came in the form a jeweled snuffbox he had picked from the waistcoat pocket of a pudgy merchant while the man was busy sneezing.

"Wh...why should I be concerned about walking slowly much less talking to you?"

"I saw you put your hand in that man's pocket. Matters not to me, but any boy alone and not in livery is suspect right now, so I made it so as you are not alone."

"Well, thank you, I guess. Yes, sorry, thank you."

"Go round that next corner. That should be far enough."

They turned right entering a smaller street that showed none of the commotion of the theft. The girl withdrew her arm and stopped.

Speaking very softly she said, "You should be safe from here."

Mimicking the highborn manner he had heard in London, he said, "Thank you, again. My name is Josiah ... Josiah Tucker. I've just come from the country. Looks like I have some things to learn about the city."

"Indeed."

"And what, if I may ask, is your name?"

She hesitated, wondering if he could locate her only by her name. Deciding he could not, she said, "Bridget Malone."

She was very young looking, flat chested and pale, but the black curls tumbling from beneath her cap were lovely and her eyes were so blue. Josiah thought he would play the gentleman and asked, "May I walk you home, Miss Malone? Seems the least I can do for my rescuer."

"Thank you, no. I have errands for my mistress and now I am running behind. Have a good life, Mr. Tucker, and goodbye."

She turned like a dancer and strolled back the way they had come.

Josiah realized his mouth was gapping. He closed it sharply and looked around to see if anyone else had noticed. A fifteen-year-old ego bruises easily.

To cover his discomfort, he moved with purpose to the nearest pub and entered boldly. The room was lit brightly from two large diamond-paned windows in the front, diminishing into near darkness in the back. A small bar occupied the side of the room that was over-warm with the heat from a dozen bodies plus waves of delicious steam from the back room. Earlier thieving efforts had netted Josiah a little coin, so he indulged himself in a tankard of ale.

Standing at the bar, he surveyed the room. A group of three men were at a table nearest the door. The shortest man was doing all the talking and seemed to be trying to persuade the others of something. Josiah moved closer to where he could hear everything the little man was saying.

The man had the way of a soldier about him. He sat with a straight back and often moved his left hand to the hilt of his sword. His voice was powerful and Josiah imagined he was accustomed to giving orders. He was talking about gold. Then he mentioned a voyage to get this gold, a voyage to the other side of the world. One of the men listening was getting restless at the talk of the New World. He was shifting about, getting ready to rise from his seat and Josiah moved a bit closer thinking he would sit down when the man left.

So Josiah was actually standing in the main walkway when a boy about his age burst into the pub on a beeline for the bar. The boy was wearing some sort of emblem on his weskit identifying him as a part of some business. As he passed, he bumped Josiah's shoulder causing a large part of his ale to spill down the front of his coat and shirt.

Josiah spun around and grabbed the boy by his arm turning him back. "Hey, look what you did!"

"Do not bother me, boy. I am on my master's business and have only a moment to slake my thirst. Barman!" He tried to shrug off Josiah's grip.

Josiah was having none of it. He held on tight, carefully placed his ale mug on the bar and pulled the boy toward him. "Apologize, boy."

The city boy looked a bit older than Josiah, but working on a farm all his life, Josaih had built up strength much beyond that of the city boy. A look of doubt flashed across the face of the city boy, but the die had been cast between young men and there was no going back. Superiority must be proven.

The boy gave Josiah a sturdy blow in the ribs that made him lose his grip and take a step back. But that just put Josiah in a better position to feign with his left and fell the boy with a full right to the side of his neck. The boy crumpled and wisely stayed down.

"Now apologize and buy me a fresh ale, my employed friend."

The boy gathered himself in a crouch and made a successful dash for the door.

The older men had all stopped their conversations and watched the youngsters, remembering the days of proving their meddle. The short man spoke up, "Well done, young sir. Taught him what for!" and the whole room laughed in appreciation. Josiah checked their faces to be sure no one was laughing at him. Satisfied, he joined in.

"Care to join us?" the short man asked.

Josiah retrieved the remainder of his ale and took the seat the nervous man had since vacated.

"I heard you speak of gold and a voyage to the New World. Are you going there?"

"Just as soon as we can fill out our company. Might you be interested...?"

"Josiah, Josiah Tucker. Speak on, I just caught the last."

The short man introduced himself as John Smith, Captain of His Majesty's army and head of the military part of the expedition. His Majesty James the First had sanctioned the Virginia Company and this was to be the first of several planned voyages to the New World. The plan was to leave as soon as three ships could be provisioned and a full compliment of planters be gathered. The roster of gentlemen was complete, but there was still need for laborers and boys to serve the gentlemen during the voyage and to do the heavy work once the group reached their destination. Everyone in the company would be provided with food and clothing by the Virginia Company and all would share in the wealth taken from the New World.

Josiah had a wandering streak. It was what had taken him from his family farm to London and now it was luring him to the other side of the world. He also had dreams of great wealth. The hardscrabble living of a small farmer did not appeal to him at all. He liked the look of fine things and fine women and that was what he wanted out of life.

"Will you be looking for more men, then, Captain Smith?"

"Yes, I will be visiting several establishments around the wharfs."

"Would you mind if I just sort of come along?"

"I would be delighted for your company, Mr. Tucker." And so Josiah Tucker and Captain John Smith went out in search of a few young men of adventure.

Captain Christopher Newport, leader of the fleet, was, by all accounts, a tall, handsome man even though he had but one arm, with the wiry strength born of a life at sea. He had been born in the poor section of London called Limehouse and had shipped out very young as a cabin boy. He was experienced in Atlantic crossings and even in some parts of the North and South American coasts. In fact, one crew had abandoned him in Brazil. Several years later, the Earl of Cumberland had rescued him and brought him back to London to return to active sailing. He had made two voyages to the North American mainland and had spent a great deal of time in the Caribbean. He was trusted and even liked by his men, perhaps because he maintained an atmosphere almost like a privateer, or, as the opposition called him, a pirate.

Captain Bartholomew Gosnold would command the Godspeed and be vice-admiral of the little fleet. At 35, he was one of the few married men on this expedition. He had attended Cambridge, the Middle Temple, but chose a life of adventure. He sailed with the infamous Sir Walter Raleigh, had been to New England in 1602 and met a member of this expedition, Captain Gabriel Archer, on that voyage. Gosnold had explored parts of Virginia in a voyage in 1603 and then promoted another voyage that resulted in the charter for the Virginia Company from James I. He personally recruited Smith and others from the 1602 voyage. He also got the support of a prominent pastor, his friend, Reverend Richard Hakluyt.

Captain John Ratcliff, a stocky man with thin, fair hair, was in charge of the smallest ship, the *Discovery*. Captain Newport would command the largest ship, the *Susan Constant* and also be Admiral of the fleet, in charge of the whole voyage. Newport knew and trusted Gosnold, but Ratcliff was an untested captain and Newport could find out very little about him even through his less than savory contacts around the shipyards.

One hundred forty-three people were to cross the Atlantic in these three ships. The *Susan Constant*, a one-year old 120-ton galleon, 95-foot mast, 76 feet at the waterline, a deck area of about 82 by 24 feet, and a draft of 11 feet 9 inches, would carry 71 passengers and crew as well as most of the supplies. The *Godspeed*, a 40-ton flyboat, 71½-foot mast, 48 feet at the waterline, a deck area of about 65 by 17, and a draft of 7 feet, would carry 51 passengers and crew. The *Discovery*, a 20-ton pinnacle, 59-foot mast, 38 feet at the waterline, a deck area of 50 by 14, and a draft of 6 feet 6 inches, would carry 21 passengers and crew. Food, baggage, weapons and a disassembled ship were also wedged into these tiny floating islands with 3000 miles of open water before them.

One hundred eight men and boys had made their way from the heart of London across the Isle of Dogs, a peninsula that made the Thames wrap some distance south, east and then north before continuing on to the sea. At Blackwell in Wapping, the headquarters of the expedition was a tavern sometimes called the Sir Walter Raleigh House, a Tudor half-timber structure with two peaks on the front over two stories of stucco and wood. This building would be the final home for these men and the image of it would be carried in their minds as the very picture of home.

Just outside this tavern was a set of wooden steps down to water level. On the morning of December 20, 1606, the planters for the Virginia Company descended these steps and walked across the gangplanks on to their various ships. The three raised anchors and headed down the Thames toward Greenwich.

Josiah leaned against the port rail as the ship glided past Deptford with the tide. "Captain Smith, do you see that ship tilted in the mud? It looks as if it once was a queen of the sea."

"You've a good eye, lad. That's Raleigh's *Golden Hind.*" Smith craned his head back trying to catch sight of the Tower of London where Raleigh was still a prisoner. "Let's hope we fare better than that ship and her master."

"I am sorry, sir, but I know few details of the great Sir Walter's fate."

Smith looked wistfully into the distance, "It is a story of great success and sad failure. Mostly it is a story of the pride of aristocrats. Raleigh financed the voyages he sponsored. He took the *Golden Hind* to the New World in search of "El Dorado." His did not find the City of Gold. And his failures continued when he founded the ill-fated Roanoke Colony. He was a favorite of the great Queen Bess, but his heart led him to marry in secret and between his failures and what she saw as a personal betrayal in his marriage, he lost her favor. She threw him into the Tower of London for a time but let him go privateering again. His capture of the Spanish treasure ship *Madre de Dios* regained him enough of her pleasure to keep him out of the Tower, but his influence was never to be restored.

"As soon as the good Queen died, his enemies implicated him in a plot against the new King James and he was back in the Tower where he now sits. Many say he does retain his influence in the management of the Virginia Company, but I am not certain that is true. I believe Sir Walter has good sense about colonizing the New World. Between you and me, my young friend, I cannot always say as much of our sponsors.

"So Sir Walter rots in the Tower and his beautiful ship rots in the Thames. Such is the fate of some great men."

Josiah felt this remarkable tale demanded some response. His choice impressed Smith, "Let us, then, not strive to be great men."

On the first leg of the journey, the ships sailed only as far as the Downs, near the mouth of the Thames. The wind fell and the ships were becalmed. Often the only sound to break the stillness was the bleating of the goats that were tethered to carved wooden belaying pins stuck through the rails of the ship. Whenever possible, larger animals were kept tied on deck, as this was the best way they had found to confine the animals yet keep them healthy.

The weather was typical for December, foul. It was cold and wet and there was little change for over a month. There they sat, moored to await favorable winds. This extra month on board depleted their supplies and frayed their nerves.

There were no diversions for the men except drinking and gambling. Fights were inevitable. Not all gambling debts were fully paid. When the men were finally signaled to set sail there were new friends and new enemies. When they should have been half way to America, they finally left England.

Few of the passengers had any real idea of what to expect of an ocean voyage. Though the crew had experience in the waters of the Atlantic, most had been coastal sailors and the idea of crossing the ocean was also new to them. Nearly every map ever made showing the ocean also showed at least one monster the size of a country lurking at what was thought to be the edge of the world.

The captains of the three vessels used the discipline of normal shipboard activities to settle the nerves of the crew. The young adventurers at first volunteered to take on some of the chores to relieve their boredom. Later it became expected that they would assist in storing and securing cargo. A few took to coiling ropes and repairing nets and sails. But the running of the ship, like handing the sails, cleaning, steering and gun drills, was the responsibility of the sailors. One day, as they moved a bit further down the Thames, the sluggish movement of the ships changed abruptly as the outgoing tide of the estuary took hold of the ships. The hulls creaked at the increased strain and a when the sails were unfurled the masts sang in counterpoint. The orders of the captain and the repeated calls of the officers added voices to the symphony of ships in full sail.

Most who suffered from *mal de mar* when the ships wallowed in the river found the discomfort gone once the sailing ships came into their own world. For a sorry few, the reverse was true, but, by the second week, everyone had found a way to deal with the now familiar motion. When they first boarded, each man had picked out a spot to call his own. Adjustments to the motion caused some of these positions to change, but after only a few days of this easy sailing all the passengers had created the nest they would call home for at least two months.

Besides the spots each man claimed below decks, each one found one or two spots on deck they preferred. Josiah and Smith tended to lean on the port rail near the bow of the *Susan Constant*. Perhaps they subconsciously wanted to be the first to sight land. Certainly the southern exposure was more comfortable for a winter crossing.

The gaming and gambling among the young gentlemen continued on board ship, on pleasant days on the hatch cover. Boredom dilutes good spirits and by the third week, arguments and near fights were a daily occurrence. Newport, finding this behavior disrupting, simply outlawed it. The young gents got heir first taste of the absolute power of a ship's captain. Some bridled under the rules, but none challenged it so much as to suffer the stated penalty of flogging.

They sailed south traveling west of Spain and Portugal. Changing their heading to southwest to catch the Canary Current, they joined a well-traveled sea road across the Atlantic toward the West Indies.

After ten weeks of fairly clear sailing, a winter front moved over the little fleet. The clouds thickened. The winds dropped. Mist and fog surrounded the ships. Even the current seemed to slow. The front was wide and stalled for over a week. The sailors grumbled about the lack of progress, but those who had never been on the ocean began to panic saying with increasing fear, " God has abandoned us." "We've sailed into hell." "We are all doomed."

The supplies were being consumed and the ships seemed to be going nowhere. Even the most optimistic were loosing hope. Then the fate feared by all men on the sea came to pass.

The shout of "Man overboard!" came from an able-bodied seaman who had been working near the starboard rail.

No one knew how it happened, but one of the boys from London had fallen over the rail of the *Discovery*. The mist and fog made it difficult to see the boy, but his pitiful cries were clear. "Help, please!" Silence. "Help me, God!" One of the sailors threw a float in the direction of the sound. A full minute of painful silence passed. It was as if the vessel itself stopped breathing. Then a thin sound broke the quiet.

"Got it!"

Everyone who could reach a part of the rope began to haul in the float. The sides of the pinnacle were quite shallow and many hands reached down to pull the youngster up onto the deck. The chill of the January sea had permeated his thin, adolescent limbs and he looked an inhuman color of blue.

Someone brought a blanket. It was a challenge to wrap it around him because he was curled up tightly, rocking and raving.

"Monster... huge monster... eat us...eye...aargh...arms... so many arms...huge eye....aargh...monster..."

Even the most experienced sailor believed that there were monsters in the sea. They recalled the maps with the humped green dragon-like beasts at the edges of the known world. Pieces of enormous sea creatures had washed up on various beaches. Ships had been lost with no trace. No one really doubted there were monsters in the deep and now one was near their tiny ships.

At first it only sounded like the men were repeating the boy's words to those out of hearing. Within minutes it was the cry of a small mob. Fifteen terrified men can make a lot of noise and the men on the *Godspeed* heard the commotion. One passenger yelled to a friend on the *Godspeed*.

"Dru, Dru! Take a care! There is a monster under the ship!"

The reaction on the *Godspeed* and the *Susan Constant* was like a shot in a crowd. Everyone moved at once. Some sought the protection of below decks. Some moved to calm others. Some moved just because they could not control the fear surging through their bodies.

On the *Godspeed*, Dru Pickayes moved too, first one way and then another. He was terrified of monsters of any kind, especially sea monsters. His older brother had tormented him with tales of monsters coming to grab him as they played on the beach as children.

When young men are afraid, they do mean things they would never do otherwise in order to relieve their own tension and fear. One tool is to make the weak member of the group the scapegoat and boast of their bravery by making him the butt of their jokes. Jeremy Ailcock was afraid and he became the ringleader of poking fun at Dru Pickayes. "Ay, men, look at ol' Dru. Looks like his foot is nailed to the deck and he is running in circles. You will not get away from the monster that way, Dru, me boyo!"

All the young gentlemen nearby on the *Godspeed* laughed. They laughed loud and long. They gave him the nickname "Circle Dru" and found it funnier as the story spread. Each time he heard that laughter, Dru Pickayes' hatred for Jeremy Ailcock grew a little more.

The Captain of each vessel knew that this type of mindless panic could lead to disaster, so they assembled their officers near them and yelled to quiet the crowd. Three men yelling was better than a hundred, but the dissonant noise in the fog was unsettling.

Once the shouting became a murmur, Gosnold addressed his men. "Calm yourselves! We must have calm and quiet to determine the truth of the situation. Return to your duties and I will deal with this."

The crew reacted immediately. The passengers were slower to let go.

Newport sounded the signal for the Captains to gather on the *Susan Constant*. Rowboats were lowered and Gosnold and Martin transferred to Newport's flagship. They moved to the Captain's cabin and the conference began in minutes.

Newport began, "Captain Ratcliff, what happened?!"

Ratcliff was brief, "A boy fell overboard. When he was retrieved he was raving about seeing a monster with many arms and huge mouth. Word spread very quickly."

"What is the condition on your ships, gentlemen?" Newport asked.

Gosnold volunteered, "My crew is stable, but I fear the passengers are very restless."

"My passengers are milling around wanting to take some action but not knowing what to do. I have seen a few crewmembers with their heads together as well. I would say the situation is explosive," said Ratcliff.

John Smith, who had remained near Newport's cabin door spoke up. " I agree with you, Captain Ratcliff. This is an explosive situation. The weather has everyone tense. Any threat could result in an all out panic. Captain Newport, I would suggest we treat this with a military response and get everyone busy to distract them."

"But what should we do about the monster?" pleaded Ratcliff. No one laughed.

Smith had a ready answer, "I do not trust the word of one drowning boy that there is a monster, but, to comfort the men, we can put them to work preparing weapons."

Newport was decisive, "Captain Smith, I do not fully agree with your assessment, but I do think directed activity for everyone is the best course. Please work through the First Mates to organize whatever actions you feel will have good effect. Gentlemen, return to your ships."

Smith arranged for every hand to be busy at some chore that seemed directed at fighting the monster. Some sharpened already sharp bladed weapons. Some kept watch. Others checked every foot of rope for frays. Still others collected items that could be used as medical supplies. Decks were scrubbed over and over on the grounds that men could slip on a dirty deck.

Men still met in twos and threes to discuss the terror below, but the work did its job and kept the panic at bay. Two days later, the weather finally changed, the sun shone and the wind and current combined to move the ships away from the "monster's lair".

Newport called another conference. "Gentlemen, I believe the crisis has passed. Thank you, Captain Smith, for your efforts. Let us stand down from this unnecessary preparation and return to normal."

"Sir," Smith interjected, "I respectfully disagree. I feel we must keep the preparations going. Groups are still gathering and feeding the fire of fear. And there could be another incident at any time."

"Thank you, Smith, but we will stand down."

"No sir, I do not agree."

"Smith, I have decided. Arrange to have the weapons stored and the medical supplies put in a safe place. Dismissed."

Smith said no more. Life returned to normal on the *Godspeed* and *Discovery*, but Smith did not pass on the Captain's orders to the First Mate on the *Susan Constant*. He quietly continued to give direction to the passengers to check ropes and sharpen weapons. He did not countermand the rotation to watch for monsters.

Newport was occupied with calculating their position now that the sun and stars were visible. It was almost two days before he noticed two gentlemen checking rope.

"Mr. Martin, Mr. Ford, why are you examining that rope?"

"Captain Newport, Captain Smith assigned us this duty to be ready for the monster."

"And you have had no orders to stop in the last two days?'

"No, sir."

"Mr. Bales," Newport called for his First Mate.

"Aye, sir."

"Bring Captain Smith to my quarters."

"Aye, sir."

"Captain Smith, did I not order you to stand down from these extraordinary measures?"

"You did, sir."

"Why are they still in effect?"

"I thought it expedient, sir. Once men have sensed panic, they may...."

"Captain Smith. That was a direct order. I do not care what you thought expedient."

"Sir, I am in charge of the military aspects of this expeditions and this was in that realm. In military matters, my opinion...."

Smith's arrogance was beyond what Newport was willing to tolerate. "So long as we are afloat, Sir, your opinion has no weight. You will...."

"No, sir, I feel that…"

"Mr. Bales!", Newport yelled. Bales appeared at the door.

"Captain Smith you will not say another word or you will find yourself in the brig."

Smith opened his mouth. Newport leaned foreward menacingly. Smith backed down, but a precedent of distrust was set.

March of 1607 found them passing through the Indies. Newport chose to stop at Melvis (Nevis) Island. This was an inhabited island and the natives had clearly met Europeans before. They knew a few Spanish words, but no one in this expedition except Newport understood the meaning of the words and he knew only some. However, the natives who called themselves Kalmago, seemed very willing to assist in restocking supplies.

Smith was ordered to take a small party and go with the Indian guides to fetch fresh water. Smith selected his favorites, Calthrop, Robinson and Tucker. A smiling native led them to a spring only a hundred paces into the trees. Each of the four men filled two buckets. Knowing they were not expected back so soon, Smith proposed that they take advantage of the cool shade and the fresh water pool to clean up a bit. Conversation moved from the pleasant surroundings to the wisdom of extending this stop for some time and recuperating from the prolonged crossing.

The spring was in sight of a native village and Smith motioned to their guide that he would like to go there. Leaving the heavy buckets, Smith's party walked a gentle path to a small gathering of huts, basically interwoven palm leaves over a frame of sticks. One of the palm-covered structures had no sides. It was clearly the storehouse for it held bunches of long yellow fruits, piles of red and green fruits, baskets of large green and yellow vine vegetables, white grain, and dark red beans. To have that much fresh looking food in storage at the end of winter meant that the food here must be very plentiful.

Smith had heard that Captain Bartholomew Gilbert of Plymouth visited this island in 1603, spending two weeks to cut a large quantity of lignum vitae wood. Gilbert had been *en route* to Virginia to seek out survivors of the

Roanoke settlement but found no one alive. See no sign of such wood in the area, Smith reasoned that it must grow father up the volcanic center of the island. Investigating this source of timber was another good reason to stay and explore. By the time they returned to the ship with the water samples, Smith's mind was made up. He considered it militarily important to rest and restock supplies and to discover what other useful products were available on this island and its neighbors.

Unwisely setting aside his previous fateful interaction with Newport, Smith marched directly to the Captain.

"Captain Newport, the water on this island is sweet and plentiful. I observed many fruits or vegetables stored in the native village and even some still alive on trees. I would recommend an extended layover here to allow the men to rest and resupply our food."

Smith's attitude was completely unwelcome. Newport had already decided this would be a short stop, but he would have opposed Smith even if he had not.

"Mr. Smith, we will be leaving as soon as the water barrels are refilled. Not that I need explain myself to you, but we are only days from our destination so there is no need to resupply." While speaking, Newport had sampled the water in one of Smith's buckets. "You will work with Mr. Bales to arrange a bucket brigade. That is all."

"But, Captain, …", Smith began.

"Mr. Smith, do you recall my previous promise? If you open your mouth again, you will be in the brig."

Smith thought quickly and decided what he needed to do was to get the other Captains on his side first and then have them approach Newport. He nodded curtly and left to go in search of his companions. He had sent Calthrop to Gosnold on the *Godspeed* with a water sample and Robinson to Marin on the *Discovery*. The two young men were both back on the flagship talking with Tucker by the time Smith got back on deck.

"Captain," Calthrop nearly shouted when Smith came toward the group, "the men on the *Godspeed* want to go ashore and get some fresh food. So many took a cup of water from the bucket as I walked along the deck that there was fair little left to show the Captain."

"Same is true on the *Discovery*, sir," said Robinson. "Some of my friends said they would like to stay here until spring and follow along when the weather is better."

Smith looked at Tucker. "I guarded these other buckets, sir. No one on this ship but the Captain has tasted them, though I did tell a few men about the food we saw."

Smith was about to tell them what Newport had said, but he happened to look toward the other two ships at anchor and saw rowboats bringing both Captains to the flagship.

"Well done. It appears the other Captains may want to encourage Newport to stay a while. Go about your business for now. I will find you later."

With hopes that his plan was working already, Smith moved to the opening in the ship's rail to greet the two Captains.

He stood at attention and formally greeted each one. "Captain Gosnold, sir. Captain Martin."

Gosnold took the lead, "I hear there are good provisions on this island, Smith."

"Yes, sir. Excellent and in great abundance. The natives are very welcoming and I believe this is where Captain Gilbert cut good lumber for repairing his ship. We do not know what kind of wood we will find in Virginia."

"Good thinking, Smith. Come with us to see Admiral Newport, in case he has questions."

Smith thought that might be a bad idea, but Gosnold and Martin had already moved toward the Captain's cabin and they expected him to follow. He hung back at the doorway wanting Gosnold and Martin to press the issue without being involved directly.

Gosnold was settling into his chair and Martin opened the topic. "Captain Newport, we hear there are good victuals on this island. It might be a good place to stop for a few days and restock."

Smith hopes of staying out of the discussion ended immediately. Newport's stare went not to Martin but straight to Smith with a glare that should kill.

"Smith, have you been spreading rumors about this island?"

"No, sir. I have told no one and they are not rumors, it is true about the food."

Shifting his gaze to the two Captains, Newport said calmly, "Gentlemen, I have told this man that we will be leaving as soon as the water barrels are filled. We are only a few days from our goal and there is no point in wasting time here. Please prepare bucket brigades from each of your crews. I expect to leave with the evening tide."

Then to Smith, "Smith, have you found Bales and formed our brigade?"

"No, sir, these gentlemen ….."

"No excuses, Smith, hop to it." Newport was trying to belittle and embarrass Smith as much as possible in front of the other Captains. Smith knew it.

"But, Captain …"

"Smith, I told you before, one more word and you would be in the brig."

"BALES! BALES!" Newport shouted for his first mate.

Bales appeared in the doorway peering over Smith's shoulder.

"Bales, get two men and take the Captain below." Newport paused and checked the faces of Gosnold and Martin for agreement. They were not on his side yet. One more step should push them over. "Put him in irons."

The faces of Gosnold and Martin were easy to read now. They would not oppose Newport on this point or any point in the future.

"Captain Newport! I must protest!" but Smith got no further. Two large sailors grabbed his arms and dragged Smith out and into the hold where a leg iron affixed to one of the ribs of the ship by a four-foot chain was locked on his left leg.

Smith was so surprised he did not even fight the men. In the space of three minutes he had gone from being the military leader of a great expedition to a prisoner locked alone in a damp hold.

Hours passed and Smith grew thirsty and hungry. He could not imagine Newport meant this to be more than a temporary exercise of power. Smith could see light through a hatch and the day was fading. He was swinging between rage and despair when he heard footsteps coming his way.

Looking against the last of the sun's rays, he could not make out who had come until he spoke.

"Captain, it's Josiah, Josiah Tucker."

"Right, lad," Smith's voice was hoarse from lack of water.

"Sir, I went to the First Mate and asked if I could bring you food and water."

"Then he means to leave me here?!" Smith was embarrassed by the note of panic in his own voice.

"I think so, sir. He told me no more than to bring you food and drink tonight."

"Damn him, damn the man! Who does he think he is to treat me like this!"

Josiah had no answer.

True to his word, Newport left on the evening tide. They continued through the channel by the West Indies islands and then headed north to find the Gulf Current that ran along the coast of America. A good deal longer than a few days, in fact three weeks later, eighteen weeks after leaving London, the expedition was off the Virginia coast, but not yet in sight of land.

CHAPTER 2
Point Comfort

"Curse the equinox! I cannot remember a spring equinox without a storm. Are the *Godspeed* and *Discovery* in sight, Mr. Bales?"

"They were before the clouds closed in, Cap'n."

"If they keep afloat, we should all end up reasonably close when it blows out. Take precautions, Mr. Bales. I will be below with the charts."

The wind slowed after one day, but the rain stayed for three more. On the morning of March 25th, the sun finally came with the dawn. So did the birds. Everyone was on deck chattering, moving from group to group and all watching forward. Birds meant land.

The *Godspeed* and *Discovery* were not in sight.

"Good Morning, Master Wingfield."

Master Edward Maria Wingfield, was one of the major investors in the Virginia Company. He was irascible, unpopular, and at 56, the oldest of the party. He was the only investor to actually come to America. He stood at average height, had receding reddish hair and temperament to match. A gentleman and member of Parliament, he had good contacts among aristocrats and influential people.

Wingfield had some military experience. Most recently, he had fought with his brother for the Dutch in the Low Countries against the Spanish. He had been taken prisoner and held captive for several months by the Spanish until he was finally exchanged. He was a distant cousin of two men on this voyage, Captain Bartholomew Gosnold and his brother, Anthony.

His piercing brown eyes were again puffy and red this morning, but he was in good humor.

"Great Morning, Captain, we should be on land by nightfall.   It has been more than a fortnight since we were in the West Indies. I am sure everyone will be glad to be on land. Personally, I am looking forward to a long drink of fresh water."

By noon the groups had broken up. At two o'clock the gentlemen were served dinner in the mess. The sailors ate in shifts throughout the day. The gentlemen did their best to maintain the routine of home and therefore ate their larger meal at two, or as near as reasonable. A few passengers stayed near the bow all afternoon but most returned to their usual pursuits.

Josiah was one of those who stayed on deck and watched for land. Late in the day, off the port side, there was a brief sighting of land. Through the ropes of the ship he could see a dark line that resolved in some places into individual trees. Some trees were nearly twice as tall as their neighbors and the line stretched south forever. Then the ship seemed to pass the land and they tacked to port.

As the sun set into the water, the enthusiasm of the morning had faded among the passengers, but the crew knew that land was not far away. In fact, the *Susan Constant* entered the mouth of the Chesapeake Bay while all were asleep, except the night watch. The bay was so wide, it was hard to tell they were no longer in the ocean.

Bartholomew Wingfield, perhaps feeling the responsibility of being the leader of the colonists, was up before dawn. Pulling at the hem of his embroidered waistcoat and straightening his shoulders, he again approached Captain Newport, "We will need an exact point at which we leave the ocean? Our orders say to go 100 miles up river from any sea lane."

"Sir, we are no longer in the ocean. We entered this bay at about four this morning. Near as I can reckon from that Spanish map, it is called something like our word Chesapeake. We are heading for that point on the southern shore where we can wait to see if the other ships will catch up."

Newport took the ship toward a flat beach on the northwestern side of the point. There the depth changed rapidly and the lookout spotted an excellent place to pull in that allowed the ship to sit freely in twelve feet of water next to a sandbar covered by only a few feet of water.

Francis Magnel, a sailor who had recently joined Newport's crew, and his partner, simply known as "Tarman" for the tar he kept on his hair queue, climbed down a rope ladder and into the rowboat. Magnel pulled along a rope and, when they had reached the beach, he tied it to a half buried tree snag as an anchor. The ship settled gently against the steep sandbar. Another sailor jumped into the shallow water and planted a beach anchor to steady the ship.

Edward-Maria Wingfield yanked down his waistcoat again, straightened his shoulders and took his first official action. "Captain Newport, we must name this point in honor of our liege lord. We will name this point for his son, Frederick Henry, Prince of Wales. Please come with me."

The two leaders, along with most of the gentlemen aboard, went down the ladder and were rowed to shore while the other more adventurous souls jumped onto the sandbar. Near the snag, the group assembled in a rough circle around Wingfield and Newport. Wingfield drew his sword and, plunging it into the sand, he announced, "I claim this land in the name of James the First of England, Ireland, Scotland and Wales and name this place Point Henry, in honor of his heir, the Prince of Wales."

Only a few moments later, the lookout still on the ship sang out, "Ship ahoy, Captain!"

"Can you see who it is, Mr. Alcott?"

"Looks to be the *Godspeed*, sir, unless there is some Spanish ship like her in these waters."

Within the hour, the *Godspeed* had joined the *Susan Constant* and thrown her tie ropes over to the *Susan Constant*. The Godsppeed could come closer to the flat beach since she drew only seven feet of water, but her crew also put out a gangplank into the shallows.

Captain Newport called up to Bartholomew Gosnold, " Captain, good to see you. Do you know the whereabouts of Captain Ratcliffe and the *Discovery*?"

"Good to be with you again, sir. Quite a blow! I have not seen the *Discovery* since about an hour after the storm took hold."

Newport looked out toward the mouth of the bay, "I am sorry to hear that. *Discovery* is a small, light vessel and not really meant to withstand a storm like that. I pray she is well."

Newport closed his eyes for a moment, perhaps in prayer, then spoke in a loud voice, "We will stay here for the rest of today and anchor close off shore tonight. With or without the *Discovery*, we will start into the interior tomorrow."

The men broke up into small groups and made their way back to the two ships. Captain Archer led one group and was just heaving himself into the rowboat when an arrow passed just inches in front of his chest, grazing the backs of both hands, before landing in the side of the boat. He called out in pain and then in warning, "Awwww, Attack men! Look to yourselves!"

Savages had crawled up through the seagrass on the beach holding their bows in their mouths. Once they loosed one flight of arrows, they charged the men who were still on land. Men on the ships started firing at the natives. In only a few moments, this loud and strange weapon frightened the Indians and they ran across the sand and into the scrub on the dunes. As all trained warriors, they left a few men to cover their retreat and these braves fell upon the sailor who was loosing the rope from the snag. Two braves had cut him with knives before a final volley of musket fire chased them off. This beautiful, welcoming world had taken on a new face.

Once the ships moved into deeper water, the natives were not seen again and the tension raised by their attack was overcome by the comfort of a hot meal and calm water. Sleep came easily. March 27th brought a glorious dawn. Safe anchorage for the night had put everyone in a fine mood. They had looked briefly for fresh water at Point Henry, but there was only brackish water, part fresh and part salt. Today they would venture inside the bay and see if they could find one or more of the rivers that must feed it.

The bay was huge. First they sailed north to find the opposite shore. Sir George Percy, Son of the Duke of Northumberland and a soldier who had served with the Dutch in the Low Countries against the Spanish and in Ireland, was a well-traveled and educated man. He held the highest social rank of any colonist. On this day, he wrote in his journal that he was "almost ravished" by the sight of this land of "faire meaddowes and goodly tall Trees." Poetry aside, the size of everything in this new world impressed everyone.

The mouth proved to be sixteen miles wide and the bay opened up even further inside the opening. Then second day, they turned south again to find the best channel. The deepest channel seemed to be close to Point Henry, so they turned west from there. The deep channel pointed not west but northwest and their orders had said to find a river and "*make choice of that which bendeth most toward the North-West for that way you shall soonest find the other sea*". They traveled about eight miles along this channel and saw nothing new. The shores were still miles away and no land appeared ahead of them. By mid-afternoon, Captain Newport determined that they should return to the mouth of the bay in hopes of uniting with the *Discovery*.

Six miles down the channel, a sail made red by the rays of the setting sun was spotted just inside the mouth of the bay. The *Discovery* had survived the storm.

With all three ships together again, the senior members gathered aboard the *Susan Constant*. The Captain's cabin was filled to the walls. The air was stuffy and smoke of the oil lamps added to the fug. No one wanted to be in the close room but no one would miss the opening of the orders from the Virginia Company.

The orders covered where the company should land, how they should deal with the "naturals" and other items, but the topic that brought in the crowd was the naming of the Council members. Those who had been in the know in England expect to hear thirteen names. Newport, still being in charge of the expedition on water, read out the names.

"The Council shall consist of Captain John Martin, Captain George Kendall, Captain John Ratcliff, Captain Bartholomew Gosnold, Master Edward Maria Wingfield, myself, Captain Christopher Newport and as *ex officio* advisor the Reverend Doctor Robert Hunt, our honored preacher. John Smith is also named."

Smith was not in the room as he was still being held in irons below deck. Several of the gentlemen present thought highly of John Smith and were never content with his incarceration by Newport. The insult to Newport of reading his name separately and without his formal title irritated them and they expressed their displeasure among themselves. If Newport had wanted to exclude Smith, why read his name in public at all? No, the point was to insult the Captain, even in his absence, a dishonorable act indeed.

Newport continued, "With all due speed, the Council shall elect from among their number a President for a one year term. Said President shall have two votes rather than the one each of the other members."

"So, gentlemen of the Council, I suggest we proceed with the election of our President."

Smith's supporters called out negative remarks, "No..Unfair..Nay Nay…" Even those who did not strongly favor Smith expressed the thought that the wishes of the Virginia Company owners should be respected and that Smith should be brought up and included. Wingfield, being one of the four major investors in the Virginia Company, ended the muttering.

"Speaking for my fellow owners, I agree with Captain Newport that we should proceed with the election. Smith has relinquished his right to be here."

"Thank you, Master Wingfield. And let me propose that, by virtue of that ownership, you are the best man to be our first President." George Percy, though not a member of the Council, used his aristocratic rank to essentially end the nominations by agreeing with Newport that Wingfield be the first President. Martin, Ratcliff, Gosnold and Kendall added their assent, leaving only Robert Hunt who neither voted nor did not. He seemed more comfortable holding on to his *ex officio* status so that he did not have to agree or disagree.

Newport reported, "Hearing no dissention, I declare that Master Edward Maria Wingfield is elected the President of our plantation. Sir, I transfer to you the leadership of this community in all maters save those dealing with these ships and any voyages."

At this anticlimactic announcement, the room began to clear. Men took the dinghies back to their respective ships and regrouped there to revisit events. Those who stayed on the *Susan Constant* also gathered in small groups according to their loyalties.

Josiah Tucker, who had been listening from outside the cabin joined with no group. Instead he made it his business to inform his mentor John Smith of the appointments and election.

There was still a bit of evening light spilling into the hold. Josiah took a pitcher of fresh water and a biscuit he had saved from dinner with him.

"Captain Smith? Are you awake?"

"Yes, son, though I have no reason to be. What brings you here at this hour?"

"Sir, I just heard the reading of the orders for the Virginia Company."

Josiah hesitated not knowing quite how to break the news.

"You have something to tell me, Josiah, and it is not good news. Go ahead. Just tell me what the orders were."

Josiah decided to start with the one bit of good news. "Sir, you were named to the Council."

Smith had expected no less, but he was surprised Newport had let it be known. Josiah was quiet and shuffled his feet. "What else, son?"

"Well, sir, there were only seven names, not the thirteen agreed up on before we sailed. And Doctor Hunt, though he is set apart somehow. I think the word was "eggs official." The others are Master Wingfield, Mr. John Martin, Captain Gosnold, Captain Ratcliff, Captain Kendall and Captain Newport. Then Captain Newport read out as how they were to elect a President and he wanted to do it right away. Some of your friends said it was wrong, but Captain Newport said the owners would want Master Wingfield elected. So that is what happened."

Josiah barely got the last words out. He had told the bad news all in a one burst and had run out of breath. Smith smiled gently at Josiah's effort. Smith was not a particularly kind or understanding man, but even he could see how much being the bearer of this news had cost Josiah and he was grateful.

Smith turned the discussion away from himself. "So our Master Wingfield is to be President. What do you think of Master Wingfield, Josiah?"

"I ... I know him very little. I have heard ... I have heard that he gave gallant service to Her Majesty. ... But Henry Tavin told me some of the men who fought with him said the part he played was small and of little worth in the war. I see him pull at his waistcoat all the time. It is a silly habit."

Smith was chuckling now. Josiah thought he would go farther.

"He is so puffed up and full of himself. When he pulls on that shiny weskit he looks like a preening partridge."

Smith laughed outright.

Josiah laughed too. Then he continued, "We have been on this ship together for four months and I am sure he does not know my name. He only talks to the other gentry. I think he will favor the gentlemen and use the rest of us."

The reunited fleet patrolled the bay for two weeks. They sailed 40 miles north and mapped five major rivers that flowed from the northwest. There were other rivers, but they flowed from the north and northeast.

Occasionally they found a small spring that had good water, but every spot on this bay was accessible to marauding Spaniards. The owners must have understood this since they ordered the plantation to be set at least 100-miles up some river. Now they needed to go up those rivers.

Not knowing how quickly the rivers would become too shallow for the sea-going ships, Newport decided, " I believe it may be time to break out the packed long boat. Mr. Bales, please assemble a cargo crew to bring the parts of the shallop to shore. Mr. Black, take us to that point to the north."

The other ships followed the *Susan Constant* as they had for months now. All three ships came up on the western side of the point (a point that would later carry the name of the Senior Captain of the expedition, Newport News, Virginia). Each approached the coast as closely as their draft would allow,

The *Susan Constant* farthest from shore, then the *Godspeed* and the *Discovery* which drafted only six feet and so was very close.

Newport took many safety precautions in unloading the parts for the disassembled boat. The parts were put into cargo nets and gently handed from the *Susan Constant* to the *Godspeed* and then to the *Discovery*, where her passengers and crew climbed into the water and carried the parts to shore. Such care was taken that no part of the disassembled boat touched the water. In less than an hour the open hull, benches, rudder, mast and sail of a dismantled boat had been transferred to the sand. No matter how routine a procedure, Captain Newport insisted on safety. He had sailed to the new world before and clearly understood the implications of loosing a piece of equipment or a man, neither of which could be replaced until they returned to England.

Once the boat parts were on shore, the passengers and most of the crew of all three ships worked their way to shore, some by rowboat, some by swimming and some were close enough to walk. Newport sent several small groups up into the trees to look for water, food and savages. Some of the crew and passengers had heard about the savages only from people who were promoting this venture. They had characterized the locals as friendly and welcoming, ready and happy to help the newcomers. The encounter at first landfall caused these men to doubt what they had been told. Those of the party who had been to the new world before, or had talked with someone who had, were wary of the natives to begin with and even more so since that first encounter. Tales of the fate of the Roanoke Company had not spread too far, but those who had heard them knew it was possible to disappear without a trace in this strange new land.

Newport continued his orders, "Captain Gosnold, if you please, select four of your gentlemen for the boat crew. I will send for Captain Smith. We will supply two carpenters and three men to man the craft once the sail is in place.

"Mr. Bales, release Captain Smith from his irons."

"Aye, sir. Should I keep the irons out?"

"No, it is time for the Captain to earn his keep."

31

Bales pointed to two of his crewmen indicating they should help him row the dinghy back to the *Susan Constant*. Tucker saw him and quickly worked his way around the edge of the crowd to meet Bales at the little boat.

"Mr. Bales, may I go with you?"

Bales had noticed the strong young man during the voyage.

"So long as you help row, lad."

Bales ordered one of his men back and pointed at Josiah to take his place at the oar. They pushed off and were at the flagship in minutes. They tied the dinghy to a line hanging from the ship and the three crawled up the rope ladder. Bales spoke to the head of the watch and then led the way to the hold. He knelt on one knee and unlocked Smith's leg irons.

"Captain Smith, Captain Newport says you are to come to shore and join the foraging party on the shallop."

"Mr. Bales, at this point, I do not care if I am to swim to Araby. Anything that will get me out of this hold is welcome."

Josiah was pleased to see that Smith's spirit had not been broken by his confinement. Bales and his mate left quickly without waiting for Smith. Josiah was glad for it because, having had no chance to stretch his muscles in weeks, Smith was clearly having some difficulty standing. Josiah stepped over to Smith and said, "Captain, let me dust off your back. This place is filthy."

Under the guise of dusting Smith's clothing, Josiah took Smith's arm and steadied him while he gained his balance. Smith appreciated the help. He thanked Josiah and accepted his help for the first few steps. By the time Smith emerged on deck, he had complete control of himself.

"Mr. Bales, please give me a few moments to collect my belongings."

"Certainly, sir." Now that Smith was released, Bales gave him the respect due a military Captain. The four men descended the rope ladder and headed for shore.

The shallow, single-masted vessel had been brought along to allow the explorers to navigate the shallow shore waters and to enter rivers as seemed useful. It held about 24 and had benches situated so that fourteen men could row the boat in case speed was required.

Newport, Wingfield and Gosnold stood together. Newport nodded to Gosnold. Captain Gosnold, brown wavy hair blowing in the constant breeze, took a few steps to the edge of the water, "Gentlemen, your orders are to reconnoiter along the shore for a good source of fresh water and whatever food this land provides. Return to the ship no later than sundown. Mr. Black is in charge of the boat and Captain Smith is charge of any land or military action. Is that clear?"

"Aye, Sir," said Black and Smith sharply. The remainder of the crew nodded. Gosnold gave the crew one of his easy, wide smiles. With no further ceremony, the small select crew boarded and the single-masted shallop was launched.

Black and Tarman unfurled the sail and the little craft moved slowly along the port side of the Godspeed. Smith's friend Stephen Caltrop threw the last hauling rope into the shallop shouting, "Smith, find us a good spot to rest tonight!"

"Right, Stephen, that is my first concern, a cozy spot for you to sleep."

The shallop had moved too far for any more banter to be heard, but the friends exchanged a quick wave for luck.

For two more weeks, the shallop explored part way up each of the four rivers. The crew of the shallop changed from day to day, but Captain Smith as military leader, was always along. Smith wanted every opportunity to be out and moving and to be away from Captain Newport. Newport knew the value of a trained military man, so he had released Smith when he needed him, but Smith would not forget or forgive Newport for his treatment on the voyage.

The shallop entered each of the four northwest-pointing rivers but named only the southern two. The northern one they named the Prince Henry then they changed it to the Charles, and finally settled on the York, and the most southern they named for the king himself, the King's River. It was the

King's River that caused the most interest. They had gone far enough in the shallop to know that all three ships could navigate that river for many miles.

The commission from the Virginia Company had been to find a site 100 miles from the ocean that would have a safe port in the entrance of some navigable river. As noted in the charter, they should make a choice of a river that "bendeth most toward the North-West for that way you shall soonest find the other sea…" So the captains met and decided a small party should take the shallop up the King's River, which was now often called the James, as far as they could. The three larger ships would explore the bay further and map the area.

Captain Newport, George Percy, and Gabriel Archer headed a group of 24 who left the three larger ships and explored this key river for eight days covering about 45 miles upstream. Newport took all of those who had muskets and swords, perhaps expecting trouble from the natives.

On April 26, about 35 miles up the river, they encountered a fork in the river where both channels were equally wide. Not knowing which would be the main channel, they decided to go up each a short way. As they entered the northbound channel, they saw the first signs of the natives. The sand had been disturbed not just by the flotsam, seaweed and shells stacked in the shape of waves, but by the feet of men. Looking out toward a point, they could see the trunks of dead trees tall as a mast still upright in the gentle tidal surf. And between the ship and those trees was the remains of a campfire. Pulling near the west shore, they heard voices.

"Oi, oi," was the first sound they could recognize as a word. As there seemed more greeting than threat in the word, Newport ordered them to row to shore.

Half a dozen men in deerskin leggings and breechcloths appeared and trotted to the water's edge. One waved his hand toward the shallop and three of the men waded into the water to catch the prow of the boat and guide it to rest on the sand and gravel. Recognizing fellow sailors, two men from the boat jumped into the water carrying an anchor line to shore. The five men worked in efficient and companionable silence to drive stakes into the sand and secure the lines. As soon as the task was complete, a new shyness seemed to overtake the men and they each stepped back a pace or two to make a bit of space between the Englishmen and the natives.

At this tender moment, a small party of braves emerged from the tree line. Seeing the strangers so near their brothers, they assumed the worst and fired arrows toward the boat. Pandemonium broke out. The leader of the Indians shouted at the hunting party and gestured for them to stop. Some Indians rushed toward the party to prevent further misunderstanding. The English still in the boat ducked for what little cover there was and started to bring their muskets to bear on the offenders. Some of the English on land fell to the ground while other more aggressive fellows grabbed the nearest Indian as hostage.

Josiah was one of those who attacked and charged into a young brave, knocking him to the ground. They rolled back and forth in the sand punching with harmless short jabs while their elders restored order. Newport, keeping a cool head, let the leader of the Indians deal with the newly arrived braves. The leader told one of the party to stay with the welcoming group and sent the rest back the way they had come.

Once the man who had loosed the arrow was standing calmly beside the Indian leader, Newport motioned broadly for the musketeers to lower their weapons, but he told them to stand ready.

Josiah and his adversary were still tussling in the sand. As one, Newport and the Indian leader shouted one word at the two. Newport had shouted, "Stop!." Clearly the Indian had done the same but in his language. This common bond of command caused the two men to stare briefly at each other and then smile slightly. The smile may have meant, "We are not so different, new friend," or it may have meant, "boys will be boys." Whatever the intention, the bond was unmistakable.

The young men stopped, shoved once more at each other and then rose to stand near their commanders. Each man spoke quietly to his charge and each boy nodded the least bit toward the other to acknowledge a draw.

The practical matters having been attended to, it was time for the official greetings. The leader of the natives spoke first.

"Greetings, you are in the land of Wowinchopunck, weroance of the Paspaheghs." He paused clearly expecting a return statement from the leader of the newcomers.

Newport, having encountered other languages unknown to him guessed that the man was introducing himself and picked out the longest word as the most likely to be his name. Wanting to respond formally, Newport placed his fingers on his chest and said, " I am CAPTAIN Christopher Newport and I give greetings to Wo-win-cho-punck."

The Indians nodded among themselves and seemed pleased at the mention of the familiar name. The leader responded, "Cap-tane is welcome. He will come to the village of the weroance and make himself known."

Newport recognized that the Indian had assumed his name to the word he had stressed, Captain, and rather than cloud this first encounter, he let the misunderstanding go for now. Nothing in what the leader had said gave him any clue as to what the next step should be. After a brief pause, the leader motioned for the Englishmen to come ashore. Newport reacted immediately, "Mr. Bales, you and Tarman will stay with the boat. Mr. Small, stay with them and the two of you keep your muskets at ready. Everyone else with me."

Newport moved back toward the leader of the natives and waited for his group to form up behind him. "In good order, gentlemen, we want to make a good impression."

The leader turned to the man on his right and said something quietly. The man started into the trees at a long and steady lope. Newport assumed he had been sent ahead to announce their arrival, but being a cautious man, he knew the runner might also be arranging an ambush. "Look sharp, men, they know we are coming." He nodded toward the leader as he said this and gave him a big smile. The leader nodded in return, and set his face in a pleasant form though nothing you would call a smile. At this exchange, the leader turned and started toward the trees clearly expecting the newcomers to follow. Newport and his group of 20 marched behind the leader and the other three natives brought up the rear.

The trees looked solid from the shore, but as they got closer, there was a definite path, three, in fact. The trees were mostly oak here, different from those in England, but familiar enough to give the men pangs of homesickness. The path changed from river sand to gray dirt just inside the tree line. The man Newport thought of as Wo-win-cho-punck took the left path. Once in the trees, the path opened a bit and there was no trouble walking two abreast with muskets at port arms.

The leader set a quick pace consistently west and in less than hour the party reached a large clearing in which there were a dozen huts. They were made of vertical logs and thatch with a single door. The thatch came so close to the earth that the walls were clear for only about three feet. One hut was somewhat larger and more decorated that the rest and it was to this structure that the leader led the party. A man, somewhat older than the leader but still very much in his prime, emerged from this hut. The leader stopped immediately and inclined his head slightly toward the older man. He spoke without being acknowledged by the older man.

"Wo-win-cho-punck, I bring you Cap-tane who has come up the Chickahominy to the land of the Paspaheghs in a strange canoe."

His deep, dark eyes surveyed the group for a long moment. Newport seemed to be getting ready to speak but Wowinchopunck slowly raised his hand and Newport stayed quiet.

No stranger to meeting with people who spoke other languages, Wowinchopunck opened the conversation with a similar motion to the one Newport had used. Putting his open hand on his tattooed chest, he said, "Cap-tane, Wowinchopunck gives you greetings."

This uncomplicated statement cleared up to whom the name belonged and Newport picked it up immediately. However, that meant he now had no name for the leader.

Wowinchopunck continued, "You are in the land of the Paspaheghs" as he moved his arm in a wide arc. Newport took this to mean that the place was called Paspaheghs, but things were becoming clearer. Wowinchopunck motioned toward a long-established fire ring with logs around it and said, "Let us sit." The weroance moved to his usual place at the head of the ring and sat. Newport, Percy, and Archer occupied one of logs while the armed members of the party moved into the most strategic positions they could while staying near the fire circle.

Slowly, with hand signs and recognition of a few words, Newport answered the weroancer's questions about where he had come from and what his purpose was. The answers were simple, the English came from far away over the big water to meet the people who were already here and to look for something. Not finding this threatening, Wowinchopunck gave Newport a small smile and a gift, a few shells threaded on to a thong of deer hide. The weroance wore several of these talismans on his chest plate that was made of quills, shells and a few beads. Newport knew a return gift was expected so he pulled one of the silver buttons from the cuff of his coat and presented it to Wowinchopunck who was very pleased.

Wowinchopunck then called for refreshments to be brought and, while they all waited, there was a disturbance at the head of the trail. Several new Indians appeared and the Englishmen brought up their weapons into a ready position. Wowinchopunck showed no surprise when the new party appeared but he did look alarmed when the English moved their weapons. Newport judged the situation and motioned for the soldiers to lower their arms.

The leader of the new group, a man past his hunting years, dressed in formal regalia of feathers, beads, animal tails and a large carved walking stick, addressed Wowinchopunck. "Weroance of the Paspaheghs, greetings. I come to see who has brought this strange craft to our shores."

"Well you might wonder, weroance of the Quiyoughcohanocks." Indicating Newport, "This is Cap-tane of the Eng-lish. He and his people have come far across the big water to visit with us and look for something they do not possess in their home land."

There being no protocol to introduce one individual to another in their culture, Wowinchopunck left his new guest to address Newport as he would.

Gosnold, a keen observer of human nature, leaned over to Newport and said quietly, "I believe these chiefs have a rivalry and no matter who we may have encountered first, the other would be jealous of the honor. We must take care not to offend either." Newport gave him the least nod of comprehension.

Newport expected the weroance of the Quiyoughcohanocks to address him but instead the man on his left spoke to Newport. Pointing first at Newport, then including all of his company and then pointing with the other hand back down the trail the man indicated that he wanted the Englishmen to leave this place and come with him back toward the river and, presumably, to the village of his weroance. Newport thought a moment and noticing the failing light, he pointed at the setting sun and shook his head. The spokesman seemed to understand and asked his leader what to do now. The weroance said a few words and the spokesman then indicated the East and moved his hand up bit. He said only two words that Newport gathered meant, "Then come tomorrow." Not knowing how to deflect this invitation and remembering Gosnold's warning about not offending either chief, he agreed.

The weroance said something that must have been a farewell to Wowinchopunck and he and his men started back down the trail. Wowinchopunck muttered something under his breath and spit in the direction of the trail. Gosnold and Newport exchanged a knowing glance. Rivalry, indeed, these men hated each other.

Young men and women of Wowinchopunck's people then came to Newport and his men and indicated that they should join the Pasphaheghs for food and sleep. Newport told the now nameless leader they had first met that he needed to send word to the men he had left at the ship. The leader directed that food be taken to those men and he sent two of his young men with two of Newport's men to the ship. The four men returned in about two hours and the village of eight huts settled in for the night.

The village, about forty warriors, with as many women, a dozen older people and children too mobile to count, awoke with no alarm shortly after dawn. Breakfast was cornmeal baked on flat stones and a thin beer-like liquid. Just as the meal ended a deputation from the Quiyoughcohanocks arrived to escort the English to their camp. The escort had beached their canoes farther up the river than Newport had landed and so they came from the opposite direction. The group walked only a few minutes to reach the canoes the escort had brought to ferry the colonists across the river. While Newport was in the canoe with the head of the escort he had the chance to point repeatedly at the water asking the name of the river. The escort, who identified himself as Oschahanocks, said they called the river Powhattan because it ran through the land of Powhattan, the head weroance. This was the first they had heard of the head chief and it peaked Newports's interest. The village of the Quiyoughcohanocks was up an inlet on the south side of the river and the escort was able to beach the canoes only half an hour's walk from the village.

This village was much larger that that of Wowinchopunck. There were over a hundred warriors in evidence and the women, children and elders moved in such a large area that they could not count them. There were huts of three sizes; most were small, a few were larger and one was quite large and arranged more as a meeting place than a living place. In this structure, the English were brought before a most impressive figure. This was the same man who had visited the camp of the Pasphaheghs but now he was enthroned on a low shelf covered in hides of many kinds.

The man had the build of a warrior but he was no longer young. His body was painted all over crimson except his face that was blue with sprinkles of what appeared to be silver ore. He wore beaded leggings and had a cape of painted deer hide. He had a chain of beads at his neck, long loops of pearls hung from his ears and each ear lobe was pierced with a bird's claw wrapped in metal that was either copper or gold. His hair mostly hung loose down his back but a small part was made stiff and groomed up into a knot that was crowned with hair from a very red deer, plates of copper and two long feathers that stood up as if a pair of horns. Most amazingly, the chief was playing a kind of flute.

The braves who were escorting the English formed up in a row and stood in attendance until the chief was finished. The natives did not applaud but commenced a slow chant that sounded like, "Oi, oi, oi." The chant continued and Percy eventually joined in followed by all the English. The chief laid his flute aside and the chant ended.

The weroance said nothing directly to the Englishmen. Only the man on his left, the same who had been with him the day before, addressed them. He already knew where the visitors had come from and why, but he asked the same questions. He did inquire further about what it was the English had come in search of. Percy, believing the metal in the chief's ears to be gold, spoke up at this point and indicated the bird claws. The second in command and the weroance looked at each other looking confused. Why would people come all that way for a bird claw. Surely they had birds in their land. Then Percy pointed at the king's crown. Another warrior who stood to the side of the chief said a word, " *Dalonige*,"meaning the color yellow.

The spokesman repeated the word and both Percy and Newport said, "Yes, dalonige." They both thought the metal was gold and this word must mean gold. They thought they had reached their goal and that the long promised gold would be quickly found and shipped back to the investors.

The interview concluded almost immediately. The purpose seemed to have been more to impress the English than to gain information, but the mention of copper or gold brought a halt to the meeting. The English were dismissed and the escort rowed back all the way to where Newport's shallop was anchored.

The three men who had been left with the boat were very surprised to see their mates coming from a different direction and by water not land. They readied their weapons fearing an attack. Newport waved at the shallop assuring the men that all was well. Four canoes beached upstream from the anchored shallop and the passengers moved quickly to board and make ready to leave.

The nameless brave who had first greeted Newport stepped from the trees. He waited until the escort from the other tribe had left and then walked to the edge of the river. Either he had been waiting all morning or the communication network among these natives was impressive.

Newport and the warrior stood on the beach for a moment. The two men had developed a connection. They were both sorry to part company. They had each learned a few words of the other's language and they seemed to know there was much more they could learn from each other. Newport wanted to be sure he knew that they knew each other's names. Newport again touched his fingers to his chest and said, "Captain,' and then shook his head, a symbol that the English shared with the natives for "no." Then he said, "Newport" and the Indian repeated the name pointing at him, "No-port." The Captain thought that was close enough and nodded and said, Yes."

The native copied Newport's motion, putting his fingers on his chest and said, "Michono." Newport repeated, "Mi-ca-no." Newport extended his arm. Michono copied him. Newport took hold of Michono's arm and brought the two together in the traditional European warriors handshake. They both smiled slightly, nodded once more and parted.

Newport was very quiet on the shallop. He had never known an individual native before. He was sure they were on the verge of a real breakthrough, a way to actually realize the dream of the expedition.

"Percy, was that gold or copper?"

"Gold, my man, I'm sure of it."

"Did you see it anywhere but on the chief?"

"No, come to think of it, only that bit covering the ghastly bird claw and the one plate on this head."

"There must be gold here, but if that is all the chief of a large village has, it must be hard to come by."

"Perhaps it is not such a large village. Perhaps he is only a small chief. I think we must meet this Powhattan."

"Indeed. We must ask after him at every opportunity."

Back in the bay, the mapping was going well. There had been no rain since the storm in March, but on the second day after the shallop left, they did have a brisk wind from the south. They decided to take advantage of the wind and see how far north the bay ran. The sailors were amazed at the size of the bay. After nearly a hundred miles the water was still open to sailing. They encountered two large rivers going even further north. If they had been sailing northwest instead, they would have considered planting at that point. But the orders had been quite clear, so they turned around and tacked their way back south toward the point where they entered the bay.

On April 30th, just at the entrance to the James, a crew led by Jonas Bales was put aboard the shallop and they sailed north up a river where they had located fresh water before. They filled several kegs, and returned to the ships.

As soon as Jonas Bales' foot landed on the deck of the Susan Constant, Captain Newport marched from his cabin.

"Mr. Bales, what news?"

" It is an excellent river, Cap'n, The land was hospitable and the sailing was very comfortable."

"Comfortable, Jonas? I never thought of a river as comfortable. Ha, that will make a good name to mark this spot, Point Comfort."

Some laborers and the carpenters had gone ashore at one of the stops and felled two good-sized trees. The trees were huge. No one in England had seen trees this size in generations. The great forests of England had been felled for the ships needed to battle the Spanish Armanda a hundred years before. Here was another great forest ripe to supply the ship building industry of England.

The two carpenters who were with the colonists and the ships carpenters put all their skills into crafting two of the trees into a stately cross. It stood tall to be seen from afar, almost 40 feet, with a crosspiece of 25 feet. The cross was covered with carvings to honor the king especially St. George's cross which King James had recently combined with the cross of St. Andrew into the new flag of England. There were vines and leaves and an overall look of the bark of the English oak. Somewhat hidden among the leaves were the Tutor rose, the White Dragon and the three Lions of Richard the Lionhart in homage to earlier monarchs.

When the shallop returned from its explorations, the crew boarded the larger vessel and the small boat was hauled up on to the deck. The leaders of the James River expedition made a formal report to the other leaders, the sailors talked among themselves, and the commoners spread their version of events. Within a day, everyone on the ships was talking of nothing but the encounter with the natives and the first sighting of gold.

The day after the shallop returned, the three ships returned to Point Henry. In an intermittent drizzle, they held a prayer service and planted the cross to mark the spot of their first landing. As had happened the last time the company was at this point, Indians approached them as they were reboarding the ships. Everyone was alarmed and grabbed weapons expecting another attack.

This time was quite different. These five warriors seemed nervous and came forward slowly. Newport gave the signal to not fire on the small group and, after a short pause, he spoke with the natives. They invited the newcomers to visit their village at Kecoughtan. This proved to be very near, so Percy, along with a small number of gentlemen, followed the Indians and spent three hours being entertained by even the "chiefest of them." This tribe was small, only about seventy-five people, and their wereoance was a young man named Pochins, one of Powhatan's sons. Percy, believing that Powhatan must be the one who could lead the to gold, was excited by this contact with Powhatan's family.

Percy remarked on their fashion of wearing what looked like chicken bones through their ears. He further described the men of the tribe in his journal.

> "They shave the right side of their heads with a shell, the left side they wear long tied up with and artificial knot, with a many fowl feathers sticking in it. They go altogether naked, but their privities are covered with Beasts skins beset commonly with little bones or beasts teeth."

One more night they rested anchored just off shore and the next day, they began their convoy up the James. Slowly they moved up river. First moving southwest, they rounded the point where they had landed earlier and set a course northwest. There was a strong feeling among the gentlemen of the party that they were now definitely on their way to the passage to China. Conventional wisdom in Europe said that it could be no more than a few days journey across this land mass. Maps that had been circulated for a century confirmed this. The atmosphere was one of celebration for all, except the few who were concerned about the motives of the natives.

Smith, who was responsible for the safety of the colonists, and Gosnold, who had been to the northern part of the American coast in 1602, kept a close watch on the shores as they passed. The first friendly encounter seemed promising, but the stories of Roanoke were still vivid in their minds. Those natives had seemed friendly at first too and yet the colonists had disappeared without a trace.

Almost immediately they encountered a canoe. Seeing no sign of hotility, they tossed a rope down to the men in the canoe and invited them aboard. The Indians politely refused, but invited the ships to anchor and come ashore on the north bank. They repeatedly used the word Kecoughtan. Newport conferred with Wingfield.

"Mr. Wingfield, we should be heading on, but I believe local custom considers it an insult to refuse an invitation."

"I will bow to your judgment, Captain. Let us go ashore."

The village was only a short distance from the shore but completely invisible to anyone passing by. The visit turned into a three-day affair. There was feasting, hunting, games, and conversation. Smith had made contact with the some of the five Indians who had been brought back to England by George Wyemouth in 1605, so he had a very rough knowledge of some basic Indian language. Gifts were exchanged and the English who had never met an Indian before came away reassured as to the friendly nature of the naturals.

The first day back on the river, there was an unusually steady wind and the ships made good time. About 30 miles up the river, the party met a canoe coming from a tributary river. Word seemed to have spread along the river about the newcomers and the canoe approached the ships waving and calling out. With a few hand signals, the warriors in the canoe invited the group to follow them. Just out of sight of the main river, there were lovely cornfields surrounding a small village. The channel became shallow quickly and the big ships had to stop. The Captain of the third ship, the Discovery, lowered a small boat and took three men with him to land on the sandy beach.

One of the warriors ran ahead to alert the village. He returned with a party of six men including a grey-headed man with several feathers tied in his hair with red beads. Captain Ratcliff took several small knives to trade and the weroance was pleased. He explained that his people were called the Paspihe or Paspahegh and were part of Powhatan's people. This Powhatan must be a person to be reckoned with. Ratcliff did his best to explain that the river was too shallow and that they would have to leave. He was not sure the chief understood, but after only a short time, he and his party returned to the Discovery and the three boats managed to back out enough to turn around and reenter the main channel of the James.

The next day another emissary approached the ships, this time from the Rapahanna on the south side of the river. Gosnold chose to lead a small group to shore and accompany the emissary to the Rapahanna village. This visit took the remainder of the day and Gosnold was able to depart only by appealing to the setting sun.

Three days later and almost 60 miles from the ocean, the convoy stopped at a rocky beach where a likely stream suggested fresh water. They had tested the water in the James, but it had proved to be quite salty this close to the ocean, so refilling their water casks at every opportunity seemed wise. The particular area seemed to be a prime watering hole for animals as well and the hunting proved good. The musket men had good luck bagging deer and it was decided to take some time to dry the meat over a smoky fire to add to their provisions.

A small party of warriors entered their camp on the second day asking about the loud sound they had heard while they were hunting. The musket men proudly displayed their arms and even shot off two rounds to complete the demonstration. The natives who had identified the area and themselves as Apamatica, were clearly frightened of the noise and the effect of the guns when large dead branches fell from the target tree, but, being warriors and representatives of their people, they did their best to hide their terror. However they left rapidly and did not visit again in the three days the English stayed ashore.

Having reached the highest navigable part of the river, still nearly forty miles from the hundred-mile recommended distance, they turned around and went back downstream. The downstream current, urged on by run off from a two-day storm on top of the out going tide, brought the ships back 30 miles by May 12th. The ships rounded a large point on the south shore and saw a small cape extending from the north bank. The landing looked very promising. It was reasonably far from the ocean routes and, with a lookout on the opposite shore, the plantation would have long notice of any approaching ship. There was a good stream with fresh water and the area required but a little clearing to be easily defended. Captain Gabriel Archer argued strongly to make this the site of the settlement, so strongly that Captain Newport named the place Archer's Hope. The only drawback was that the deep channel did not run very close to shore so the ships would have to anchor out in the river and the passengers and gear would have to be ferried by small boat to shore. Considering that this was to be a main port for all of Virginia, this was a considerable impediment.

A small group surveyed the area for most of a day, but in the end, they decided to move back up river. The river turned due south for a few miles just past Archer's Hope and they spent the next morning checking the south shore. After midday they again turned northwest and sailed past what appeared to be an island. The island had the same advantage of early warning from a lookout just across the river. It was very flat and the deep channel ran very close to the south shore. This looked like a place worth exploring, but the light was failing and the ships dropped anchor in the channel for the night.

The Captains and Master Wingfield gathered in Newport's cabin to discuss the landing options they had seen.

Wingfield liked the look of this island. "It is the most defensible location we have considered, being an island with natural water barriers. This river goes a long way inland as recommended and if what we saw this evening holds true, it appears to have a good deep channel close to shore and safe natural harbor."

Martin protested, "But it is not nearly a hundred miles from the sea and the river at this point is almost a mile wide, much too far for a musket to fire across in.

Gosnold spoke up for a different location, "the place we just left was excellent. Yes, neither location is a hundred miles from the ocean, but from what we saw going up river, I doubt any river in this area goes so far without a waterfall to stop shipping. And of those we looked at from Chesapeake Bay, none were narrow, certainly not the 200 yards across that would allow musket fire to reach the opposite shore. However, yesterday's location was dry and high and had a good fresh water supply. Unless this swampy-looking dot of land surprises me, I doubt we will find as wholesome an environment here.

Martin again took the negative side, "But Bartholomew, the channel was so far from shore there. We would have to build a jetty dock of some kind to allow for unloading of goods. No one in our party has that expertise."

Newport, as usual, had the last word. "This geography is not as the Company expected. That is clear. There is no place that will meet all of their recommendations. Our first priority is to make a plantation. For that I would favor safety over comfort. Unless this place holds unwelcome surprises, I like the natural defenses and the close channel more than the high ground and streams of Archer's Hope."

Martin had one more objection, "But what about the Indians?"

Newport looked at each man and then said, "There are Indians everywhere. Our chance of finding any waterway that is not claimed by some tribe for a hundred miles from the sea is slim to none. We will just have to make peace with the naturals, or not, as fate provides."

CHAPTER 3
A Wholesome and Fertile Place

THUNK! The flagship grounded on the riverbed.

The abrupt stop nearly knocked Josiah off his feet. Josiah had never been much of a sailor. He was listed as gentleman's servant on the ships manifest, but he had grown up a farmer and he had never fully gotten his sea legs during the 3-month voyage. Each time they had landed in the last weeks had been moments of heaven for Josiah. He realized he loved the smell of the foliage and the dirt itself.

He had signed on not to farm, however, but to dig for gold. Gold was what the owners of the Virginia Company wanted, so gold is what the ships were sent for. The ships were leaving England and that is what Josiah wanted to do too - an adventure, a chance to make his fortune. Anything was better than his lot in England and the same old life he had always known. So farmer Josiah Tucker would dig for gold. Anyway, he figured one kind of digging was pretty much like another.

The pine scent of the forest nearly overwhelmed Josiah. He thought of the sap rising, it being spring, and he wondered at the tall pines that must be over a hundred feet.

"Make fast!," Captain Newport shouted.

"Cap'n, there is no room to drop an anchor. We are right next to the trees."

"Then tie her to the tree, Mr. Bales, and see about getting a plank to shore."

As always, those who felt they had rank debarked first. A little cluster of well-dressed gentlemen gathered in the center of a small field of long grass. Much of the land was covered in large trees. The forested areas gave way to bushes and then marshy grasses to the north and east. The western shore was not marshy, but had a shallow pebbly beach. The south side where they had landed had a steeper drop off toward the west that tapered to nearly flat in the middle of the island and into marsh at the east end.

The day was mild and beautiful, certainly a good omen for the place. Men of all ranks wandered over the middle and west end of the land. No one ventured near the marshes. This peninsula had several ridges. The group tended to gather on the third ridge from the west, the highest point of land on the island. The line of sight down river was excellent.

There was no formal decision, no proclamation. Wingfield, as President, simply took charge and started to give direction as to how the men were to disperse the goods in the open area. Apparently, this was to be home.

It took the better part of the day for the laborers and sailors to transfer the baggage, trade goods and remaining provisions to land. They were stacked willy-nilly in the open area. There was a rough division between company property and personal belongings, but beyond that, there was no good order in spite of Wingfield's command.

The leaders gave no further thought to the dispersement of the goods except to have several of the smaller crates placed in the shade of a large oak tree. There the gentlemen would attend to the government of the new plantation. Newport asserted his authority and collected five of the other six men named to the Council.

"Gentlemen," he began, "we need to be about the swearing in of the Council."

Robert Hunt, the preacher who had been named *ex officio* advisor to the Council, asked, "Where is Captain Smith?"

Wingfield, tugging on his waistcoat, was quick to answer, "We will not be needing him. Due to his egregious behavior on the voyage, he will not be taking a seat on this Council."

"But President Wingfield," Hunt protested, "the commissions were clear."

"I am well aware of the contents of the Company orders, sir, but they clearly could not know of Smith's character to have so mistakenly named him to a position of leadership. I shall advise them of their error when I return. As of now I have no intention of granting him the honor of sitting in this Council," said Wingfield with a brisk tug on his waistcoat.

And so, Captain Newport duly swore Captain John Martin, Captain, John Ratcliff, Captain Bartholomew Gosnold, Captain George Kendall, Master Edward Maria Wingfield, and *ex-officio* advisor Robert Hunt into office with no audience and without the presence or knowledge of Captain John Smith.

Hunt left the Council group almost immediately and sought out Captain Smith. He found him usefully employed in inventorying the weapons as they were taken from the ships. After hearing what had transpired Smith was determined to confront Newport and challenge his ruling, but Hunt begged Smith to let the matter lie for a day or two.

"John, not one of them spoke up for you. Captain Newport and Wingfield seem determined to make a show. Give it a little time, a day or two at least."

"Despot. Tyrant. Who does he think he is going against the Company's written orders!

"Well now it is not just Newport but Wingfield too. There is no one to appeal to, John. No higher secular authority on this side of the ocean and I am afraid Divine Authority will not help much in this case."

"If we were in London I would be in the Company office before you could blink an eye, but here, you are right. What can I do?"

Fires were built and a rough stew was served all around. The dark came late and everyone enjoyed a gentle evening. The sailors mostly chose to return to their bunks aboard ship for the night and most of the passengers opted to sleep on solid ground. A few chose to dig a shallow pit in the ground and cover it with a blanket or canvass while others built lean-tos of sailcloth and branches. Except for the rage stirring in Smith, all was at peace for this night.

About midnight, the sentry west of camp by the river set up an alarm. He had sighted Indians in canoes coming down the middle of the mile-wide river. Word spread quickly and the noise was growing when Smith took charge and silenced the men.

"It is better if we meet them on our terms in the daylight than to be caught here in the night. Quiet everyone. Block the light from the banked fires so they cannot be seen from the river. William, go quietly to the ships and tell them to black out all light. There were clouds covering the moon. With any luck, the dugouts would float right past on the current.

In another five minutes, the canoes were past the camp and moving down river. Smith breathed a sigh of relief and stepped from the shadows just as President Wingfield arrived. He had taken time to dress properly before being seen. His personal pride and arrogance had probably saved the day because he roared into the group shouting, "What's the problem, men?"

Captain Archer, who had been sleeping near Smith spoke for the group, "Nothing, sir, just a false alarm."

"Check these things out, men, before disturbing the whole camp. Back to sleep now, everyone."

And with that, the camp resettled and the crickets reclaimed the night.

The next day the colonists began the business of the Virginia Company. Gosnold and 20 men went to the "high ground" to dig for minerals. The "high ground" was a ridge wrapping around the northwest end of the island that was about 8 feet higher than the open grassy field. There was no reason to think there would be ore in that ground except the reports that had come to England that gold was everywhere in the New World. By midday, there was a hole every three or four feet all over the higher ground. No hole was more than two feet deep. No gold had been seen. The group was already becoming disheartened. This finding gold was going to be more difficult than they had been led to believe.

Clearly Gosnold did none of the digging, but he would have claimed anything valuable that was found. That was the right of a gentleman to take the fruits of the labors of those who work for him. The feudal system introduced into England by the Norman French with the invasion of 1066 had relaxed in some ways but the strict class mentality that was essential to its success was still very real.

The monarch was the top of the social pyramid with the royal family at the next level. Anyone with a blood relation to the royal family, which was most of the aristocracy, came next and then those who had the right to have a coat of arms, but no royal blood, the gentry or gentlemen. Those who did not fall into one of these categories were called commoners. A lord of any level thought himself superior to any commoner and the large majority of commoners thought themselves to be lesser beings than the lords. In the feudal system, serfs were actually the property of their lord. Serfdom had been abolished, but the culture still said that the fruits of the work of a commoner were owed to the lord who ordered or allowed the work to be done. It had been that way for generations and the instinct of these men was to bring that pattern into the new world. Gosnold certainly was ready to take his share. His share for this day would be nothing.

Some men began to clear land for a garden and the sailors and a few settlers went fishing. Archer headed a crew to create some defenses. Some threw up shallow earth ramparts and others cut small limbs and saplings to begin making a semi-circular brush fort. Archer was not the only one conscious of possible danger. Ratcliff and Martin assigned a few men to watch and guard the area. They chose gentlemen who were not accustomed to discipline and preferred to chat among themselves rather than keep a lookout.

The second day Robert Hunt went to find John Smith again. Smith's sense of injustice had not abated, but grown, and he was ready to go and challenge Newport. This time Hunt suggested Smith leave the company for a time, go out and prove his worth, so to speak. Smith recognized the wisdom of the course, not so much to sway Newport and his friend but to build support among the company. So he and Hunt approached Councilman John Martin and proposed an expedition inland to find the village of Powhatan. Martin agreed that knowing more about the neighbors had advantages, so Smith selected a small group and started out.

He selected three gentlemen, Richard Dixon, Stephen Calthrop and Jeremy Ailcock. He took five of his friends from his home county of Lincolnshire, John Herd, William Laxton, Robert Fenton, John Dods, and Nathaniel Pecock, and one young boy, also from Lincolnshire, James Brumfield aged 9. Three brothers from London, George, Thomas, and William Cassen and young Josiah Tucker filled out his exploration team.

The three bothers were difficult to tell apart from the back. Each was of average height; broad shouldered and short legged, with a shock of brown hair, cut like a bowl. However, from the front Thomas Cassen stood out among the three brothers. His eyes were just slightly crossed giving the impression that he was staring at your nose. He was definitely the most articulate of the three. He would form a sentence if forced. The other two brothers mostly stood mute and let Thomas speak for them all. Perhaps, as a balance to their silence, the three brothers were excellent men of action, the best of the crew in a tight situation.

Smith had met the brothers in London. They were the center of a tavern brawl with half a dozen toughs and they were winning. Smith had watched the fight evaluating the skills of the participants. He was looking for some strong men who would be good soldiers. The Cassen boys were excellent candidates.

"Well done lads," Smith began. "Do you often take on uneven odds in a fight?"

Thomas paused then answered, "Yes."

"Having you ever considered turning your fighting talent into a career."

Thomas looked at one brother and then the other and said, "No."

"I think we should talk. Can I buy you an ale?'

The three looked at each other and Thomas said, "Yes."

Over three ales each, Smith explained the expedition and successfully recruited them as general laborers. The soldier training could come later.

The seven walked in single file through the savannah. Within thirty minutes they had crossed a clear Indian trail. They turned onto the trail. There were Indian signs everywhere that Smith saw but no one else did. The Cassens watched everywhere at once. Smith congratulated himself again on his choice of settlers.

"Can you see the signs?"

"Signs of what, sir," asked Josiah.

"The Indians, son, all the Indians who have passed this way."

"What, sir? I see nothing."

So Smith began lessons for these chosen few, lessons in what he knew of the land, the natives, weapons, dealing with enemies and potential enemies. He taught them to look for broken twigs and turned over stones and to tell the difference between the track of an animal and that of a man. Having studied everything written on Virginia, he could show them where to find food in the Virginia woods. He taught them how to read a map and how to find their way in new territory.

He demonstrated how to fight with one blade and with two. The Cassens actually did much of the teaching in hand to hand fighting. They were all apt pupils and by the third day Smith had the beginning of a reasonably competent fighting team.

By chance, Josiah walked most of the time next to Stephen Calthrop. Stephen was a gentleman, meaning his family had the right to have a coat of arms, but they were not of the nobility. Stephen was classically handsome, like a Greek statue. He was a close associate of Smith and was accused of mutiny along with Smith in his decision to keep the "monster watch" going on board the ships. As a gentleman, he avoided punishment, however he thought Newport's actions toward Smith had been horrible and he had taken note that this young boy of the streets had stayed loyal to his hero, Smith. In spite of the difference in their status, they became friends. Stephen saw Josiah as a younger brother.

During a particularly dull part of the walk, Stephen decided to find out about Josiah's background. "You came on the *Constant*, right, lad?"

"Yes, sir. Cap'n Smith asked me to come so I stayed near him."

"And how did the Captain happen to find you?"

"In London, near the wharfs. I had a ... disagreement with a fellow in a pub where the Cap'n was re-kruet ... well, he was looking for men for this expedition. I had not been long in London, having come from my father's farm seeking my fortune. And I thought to myself, Josiah, this is a good way to go."

Stephen noted that Josiah was open and trusting and very talkative for a youngster in the company of a gentleman.

"Glad to have you with us," Stephen said to somewhat reestablish the line between a gentleman who was part of the company and a mere common boy who was there as a servant.

Following the Indian trail that was about two feet wide, they came to a spot in the forest that looked no different, but here three slightly smaller trails branched off. None went in just the same direction they had been traveling and all looked to be equally used. All were covered in the long pine needles that had fallen from the white pines and all continued into stands of trees that looked much alike. Having no true idea of where he was headed, Smith randomly chose a fork.

Late on the third day, the laughter of children broke through the monotonous blanket of trees. It had been months since any of them had heard that unmistakable sound. Children were happily running through the forest. The whole troop stood transfixed for a moment. Then Thomas quietly said, "Village," and pointed to the left.

Smith signaled them to stand still and wait. They watched for several minutes and, seeing no adults, Smith said, "Walk deliberately, keep your weapons down and smile." Then he led off in the direction the children had run.

In less than five minutes, they crossed an unmarked line into a small village. Smith quickly counted nine structures, more houses than tents, looking very permanent. Women were standing or sitting in front of each house, not just one woman per house but two or three in most cases, and all engaged in some type of work. Children seemed to be everywhere. They moved much too fast for Smith to count them, but he estimated about twenty. Few adult males were evident but two older men immediately noticed the English and approached them.

"Stand calm, fellows. Weapons close but keep them down," said Smith.

The two men, who Smith thought of as chiefs, walked with both hands held in front of them, palms up and open. Smith imitated the gesture. They spoke one word followed by a short phrase. Smith assumed it was a greeting and a request for information. He could not tell them why they had come, so he chose to tell them his name.

Moving his right hand to his chest, he said, "Smith." He patted his chest and repeated, "Smith."

The universality of this combination was understood and the older man touched his chest and said, "Manotua. Manotua." Then he touched the chest of the other man and said, "Sassomacu. Sassomacu," adding a few more words that must have been more identification of Sassomacu.

Smith wondered whether to try to name all the men in his party and decided that could be confusing. Instead he honored the two men by learning their names, "Man-o-tua," nodding at the older chief and "Sas –so-ma-cu," nodding toward the other.

Both men smiled and, in turn, said, "Smeeth." Smith smiled.

Sassomacu began speaking rapidly in what were clearly questions, but Manotua held his arm in front of him and said what must have been "no" or "stop." Manotua motioned to Smith and his men to follow him. Sassomacu left the group briefly apparently to arrange some refreshment for he spoke to one of the women who stood and started giving orders to other women and girls.

Manotua led them to a large house and indicated they should all sit in a circle on the ground outside the door. Josiah and young Brumfield were not interested in sitting and listening to talk they could not understand. The Cassens also looked uneasy. Smith pointed at these five and swept his arm around to indicate the whole of the camp. Manotua nodded and said, "E-ow, e-ow."

"The chief has said you can look around, but keep out of the houses. Keep in earshot and if you hear me raise my voice, rush back."

Archer, Dixon and Calthrop chose to stay with Smith. Archer had a way with languages and Dixon and Calthrop always stayed near Smith. The other five stayed close but chose not to sit in the circle. Sassomacu returned and brought a somewhat younger man with him, making the number of representatives nearly equal. Several women arrived with food on a wooden platter and a potter jug of a sweet liquid. Food and drink was passed around and everyone had a bite and drink before talk recommenced.

The Indians sat far back on their haunches with their knees drawn up close in front of them. Balanced in this fashion, they could sit for hours. This position left their hands and arms free for work and allowed them to reach the floor in front of them where the platters were finally placed. The Englishmen did the best they could to sit comfortably on the ground and eat, but after a short while they began to fidget. Just to save his legs from falling asleep, Smith would stand and move about while gesturing. It did seem to make communication easier.

They talked of where the English had come from and why they had come. Smith used signs to say "over the big water" and pieces of trade copper to indicate their goal. Manotua conveyed that he knew of the big bird ships from many years before. He used the word "uttasantasough" for that group of English visitors. Several times, Manotua asked 'Casa Cunnakck, pya quagh acquinta uttasatasough?" (In how many days will more English canoes come?) Smith misinterpreted the question to mean, "How did he get to the camp?" and replied by indicating the trails they had followed to reach Manotua's village. The Indians assumed he meant more English were coming right now and, for a moment, they were concerned. But then a pair of braves walked out of the woods on the trail Smith had indicated and the three Indians laughed. Smith felt foolish and, having a good memory for sounds, vowed to write down Manotua's question in his diary until he could find out what it really meant.

One of the young braves decided Smith needed better directions, so he reached into a pile of discarded pieces of deerskin, pulled a bit of charcoal from the edge of the fire and made a rough map showing the location of the village, the island on which the English had landed, which the Indian called by its old Spanish name, *Guandape*, and a much more direct trail between the two. The three English studied the map, looked at each other in disbelief and also laughed. By following the many hunting paths, they had gone nearly three times as far as needed to reach this village. Conversation continued to general topics, mostly pointing at belongings and learning their names and uses.

As the older men talked and the younger English explored, the young men of the village started coming home in ones and twos and threes. There were fifteen young men and nine middle aged braves. They first went to their houses to deposit the food they had gotten that day and then gathered in a larger ring around the elders and guests to listen. Individuals wandered in and out at will, always silent and respectful.

The Cassens stuck together first circling the village and then quartering it to judge its size and to be sure they saw everything. The women looked at them and went back to work. One little girl of about six started following them and soon they had become the Pied Pipers with all the children following along. After they had covered the entire village, they sat down in a shady spot and William pulled out a whistle and started playing for the children. Brumfield heard the music and joined the children. They were all delighted. Some of the older ones ran to their houses and brought back little drums and wooden whistles and other noise-making instruments. Music and children worked their magic and by dinnertime, there was no barrier left between the children and the three brothers.

Josiah took off in a different direction. He checked every house and working structure going as near as he could without actually entering the buildings. He studied the structure of the huts and made some rough measurements. He noticed all the young women and a two or three noticed him. They did no more than smile slightly, but their eyes followed his movements. His pickpocket's eye picked up many items that would be very easy to take. He was not in need of anything and there was no way to turn any of these things into money here, but instincts are powerful and when he saw a fringed pouch with colored designs on it hanging on the upright of a drying rack, he lifted it and put it in his shirt before he even thought.

As he walked slowly away from the frame, someone shouted. Josiah turned and saw a brave a bit younger than him pointing at the rack and at Josiah. He knew he had been seen. His reaction was to bluff it out.

He walked toward the boy with his hand open as he had seen Smith do saying, "What? What do you want?"

Again the young man pointed at the rack and at Josiah. He came to within reach of Josiah and made to reach inside his shirt. Josiah batted his hand away. The boy took another step closer. One thing led to another and the two ended up wrestling in the dirt. A woman's voice called out and four young braves and a father-type Indian appeared. The young braves pulled up the two combatants and held them while the father spoke sternly to the Indian boy. Josiah knew he was explaining that his pouch had been on the drying rack and that he had seen Josiah take it. The father asked one more question. The boy said, "E-ow," which Josiah had learned meant "Yes."

The father gave his son a friendly slap on the back and declared something called, "Catun catua." The father and braves smiled, let out little whoops, ruffled the young boy's hair and, keeping him in the center of the group, walked good-naturedly away. The father turned toward Josiah and repeated, "Catun catua." And held out his hand. The braves were gone and the father seemed happy, so Josiah thought he had better cooperate. He pulled the pouch from his shirt and handed it to the father. He turned the object over as if to assure himself it was the pouch that belonged to the boy. He nodded and handed the pouch back to Josiah. He moved away back in the direction of the elder's group shaking his head in wonder and muttering, "Catua, Catun catua."

Josiah had no idea what a "catua" was or what to "catun" a "catua" was, but it apparently was something that gave prestige to the one who did it and made the one to whom it was done the object of fun. It must have something to do with taking something from someone even though they were watching. If that had been true in London, he could have made his fortune there. He might learn to like this new land.

Josiah worked his way back toward the central action. He saw the Cassens entertaining the children and decided to sit near them. Before long, Manotua rose and declared dinner be served. Everyone ate well. The adults, who appreciated William's whistle as much as the children, played more music. The occasion turned into a party with dancing around a large fire. The English were invited to stay in three of the houses. There were sleeping racks along the walls. The racks were lined with grasses covered with deerskin. They were private and comfortable and the men slept well.

The next day was taken up with a good breakfast and a short hunting trip. In the afternoon, races were arranged. The braves won all the heats, but George Cassen came very close in each of his tries. For his effort, he was awarded a decorated eagle feather, an obvious sight of his fleetness. He and the overall winner were given the first choice of meat at dinner and were seated with the elders.

After another good night's sleep, the English departed early in the morning. With the new map to follow, they would be back at their camp by mid-afternoon.

Robert Hunt had walked with Smith as far as the edge of the forest. Once the last of Smith's party had disappeared into the trees, Hunt turned around and surveyed the site. It was depressing. Of the 104 people who had come to this new world, twenty were digging up a hill, 7 were off looking for Indians, a score of gentlemen were lounging in the shade of a large tree, a handful of men were preparing food, a party of a dozen had gone out in search of trees suitable for clapboard, several were repairing nets, and the rest were sitting about in small groups doing absolutely nothing. Well, four of these young gentlemen were playing at bowls, but that accomplished nothing.

If it had been a Sunday, this lack of industry might have been excusable, but it was Saturday and there were still many hours of daylight left. Tomorrow, they would have a church service and there should be a proper place for worship. Among the long grasses there were a few areas where the ground rose a bit and spindly trees and bushes grew. Hunt thought the most prominent of these would make a suitable site. Hunt strode off with resolve toward a group of gentry.

"Cloville, Eustace Cloville. We must prepare a place for worship on the morrow. Let us gather a few good men and see what can be done."

The two creases between his caterpillar eyebrows deepened as Eustace concentrated, "Pastor Hunt, I am not sure what we can do on such short notice. What did you have in mind?"

"See that small rise in the meadow with the largest trees. There is something of a natural apse about that arrangement. I was thinking of clearing the grass there and leveling a spot big enough for a table, if possible, or at least a pulpit, then a roof and naturally a cross. I will use my own Bible. Let me talk with the Council to see if we should have a Communion Service. Could you get some men to start clearing out this area?"

Cloville had no clear idea what an apse was but he could see the trees grew in a semicircle. He turned to his friends and said, "Alright boyos, we need a table, some pews, a cover and a cross. Any thoughts?"

Henry Adling, a friend from Essex, suggested, "Where they are felling trees for clapboard, I saw some discarded logs. They might do for seats. No idea what to use for a roof on short notice."

The activity had attracted the attention of Tarman and Francis Magnel who were nearby.

"A roof, young sir, is that what's wanting?"

"Yes, a roof. Do you happen to have one handy?"

"Well, young sir, I just might. There are some bits of torn sail on the *Susan C.* None of the pieces are enough to do much good on a ship, but they might serve right well for a roof."

"Excellent, Tarman. Do bring it straight away."

Excited by the prospect of having something to do, Adling gathered more than a dozen various men, both gentle and common, and headed for the tree cutting area. They found fifteen large bent limbs that would not do for clapboard and dragged them, branches and all, to the little knoll.

Tarman returned shortly with three rolls of dirty cloth wrapped around a board. Several of his shipmates came with him to see what the commotion was about.

Soon there was nearly a party atmosphere as two-dozen men worked on the rough little church. They stretched the cloth between the trees, overlapping the pieces to make the water shed away. They lined up the rough logs in two rows to make pews and an aisle. They nailed the board between two trees to make a sort of table. In all the excitement, the requirement for a cross was completely forgotten.

As Adling and Cloville started on their tasks, Hunt walked over to the shade tree where the remaining Councilmen were gathered.

"Gentlemen, I have asked Mr. Cloville to prepare a worship space. I was thinking to have a full Communion Service to honor the Lord for our successful landing. What think you?"

"Capital idea," volunteered Wingfield, tugging on his waistcoat. "Definitely the thing to do."

George Kendall more helpfully asked, "Doctor, what do you need from us?"

"Your support, gentlemen. And your attendance, of course, as a model for the men. Oh, and can any of you think of a proper table to use for an altar?"

Gosnold took his clay pipe from his mouth and started to point it in the direction of his ship, the *Godspeed*, but Kendall rose at the same time and Gosnold's pipe stem broke against Kendall's sword hilt. "God's blood, man, watch what you are doing. These pipes don't grow on trees. It will be months before we get a new supply from London. Say, do you supposed there would be a way to make them here? Now that would be a bit of a coup, eh? Sending pipes to London instead of buying from there. Ha! I would like that!"

To bring the group back to the subject, Hunt said, "Gentlemen, a table?"

After some muttering and head shaking, it was determined there was no table to be had and that Communion was at Hunt's discretion. Since no one seemed interested in continuing the discussion, Hunt felt himself dismissed. He gathered his dignity, nodded to punctuate an end and turned with head held high.

When he returned to his chosen site for the first church in the settlement, Hunt found Cloville with a crew of gentlemen, craftsmen, laborers, and sailors. Hunt stared. They had lashed a board between two trees for a pulpit, pulled up logs as pews, and strung a dirty and holey discarded sailcloth as a roof. Cloville came proudly up to Hunt.

"There you are, Doctor. A tidy spot for tomorrow."

Hunt was appalled, but Cloville seemed so proud of his work he could not bear to tell him how awful it was. His Christian kindness took over and he complimented Eustace and the men.

"Well done, fellows. The Lord will be pleased."

He had a hard time keeping a smile on his face. This world was not what he had hoped it would be.

The members of the Council approached the little knoll.

"So this is your little church, eh, Doctor?" said Wingfield.

Newport added, "Interesting you should have chosen this spot, Hunt. We were just discussing that this would be a good place to put that first demilune. Men, as long as you are all feeling crafty, join Archer's team and go get some supple, long twigs. Weave a screen and thatch it. We can keep out of sight behind it and it should stop most arrows."

So the church builders became fort builders. Twigs were collected that day. Sunday was a day of worship in the odd little church and then a day of rest. Monday, the first movable fortification was finished.

By nightfall on Tuesday a tidy settlement was shaping up. With the inspiration of the church and first fortification, the Council had laid out a plan for the settlement. A main street was cut from the long grass with the fortification at one end and the President's tent at the other. They directed that tents that had been brought from England be erected in lines facing this main street. The little church knoll sat at an angle to one side of the President's tent. The plan called for more fortifications on each side of the camp, earthen berms and brush fortifications. But before any further work was done, company came.

The inattentive guards were surprised on Wednesday morning when two naturals suddenly appeared next to the council area. They came only to deliver greetings and to say that their weroance would come soon with the gift of a deer.

Four days later the weroance of the Paspahegh came to the fort with a hundred well-armed braves and no deer. He indicated that he would give the colonists as much land as they wanted, so long as what they wanted was Jamestown Island. The meeting was friendly until a warrior who had wandered away from the main group, pulled a hatchet from a soldier's belt.

Though being merely an expression of curiousity among the natives, this act was considered aggressive by the English. The soldier retaliated, a struggle ensued, and the warrior's arm was hurt. It was a short fight but it angered the weroance. No one mentioned the promised deer.

On the morning of the 6th day, the weroance of Paspahegh made good his promise and sent forty braves to visit the newcomers. They came with gifts of a deer, deerskins, early squash, and bushels of dried corn. They indicated that they wanted to see everything around the site and on the ships. Newport and Wingfield led the Council in greeting the visitors. Newport used the few words of native language he had learned. Wingfield escorted their leader and nine others, while Newport, Martin, and Kendall each took a group of ten each.

They visited the net making, the clapboard making, and those out fishing. There was a brief discussion among the Council about whether or not to show them the digging site and it was decided to show them as a way to open the subject of gold.

The Indians understood the net making and the fishing, though they thought the technique was odd. They could see that the trees were being turned into something regular and presumably useful. They could not understand the purpose of the digging. There was nothing to be planted or buried. They seemed to be looking for something, but what could you hope to find in just an open field?

They were fascinated with the muskets and the cannon and even the belaying pins stuck in the rails of the ships. They were very interested in the clothes the men wore. Indians wore leggings, so the pantaloons were recognizable. Indians wore skins shirts, so the linen shirts were familiar though amazing for their color and thinness and for the ruffles. What the Indians could not identify were the coats. They were neither shirt nor blanket and they were much decorated. Even though the day grew hot, the new men did not remove these coats. That day, they newcomers gained a new name, the "coat-wearers."

None of these Indians were wearing gold ornaments or even copper, so there was no way to point to the metal as a way of asking for it. The English tried pointing to their gold rings. The Indians had nothing like the English jewelry so they took the pointing to be a show of wealth.

Wingfield thought it best to demonstrate, not only the English possessions, but also their superior military power. He had a leather target set up and invited the Indians to shoot at it. An arrow pierced the leather and continued a foot beyond. Then he had an old steel breastplate set up. Again he invited the Indians to shoot an arrow that shattered on impact. There was a great deal of chatter among the braves. The settlers were cheering. Both sets of leaders did their best to calm the uproar. After a long day, both sides were somewhat more familiar with each other, somewhat frustrated – and hungry.

Being a practical man, the Doctor had instructed those preparing food to make a great deal more. To honor the guests, they included the corn and the squash as ingredients for the dinner. Unfortunately, they simply threw them in the pot with salted beef and roots that were their standard fare and boiled them into an unrecognizable state. However, the Indians felt it was a sign of good manners to eat what was put before them and so Robert Hunt's diplomatic attempt went unnoticed.

The Indians had been told to "stay in the English camp,' though there really was no accomodation that could hold forty additional people. So it was decided that some of the company would move outside the tents for the night so that some Indians could have the novelty of sleeping in the English tents. A few of the braves were even adventurous enough to want to sleep on the deck of the ships.

The English were none too content to have Indians staying in their camp. Few slept well that night. Newport was also uneasy and so doubled the guard for the night.

When the English awoke, the Indians were gone. Suspicion ran high as they settlers came together that morning. They checked their belongings to see if anything was missing. Finally someone shouted, "There is smoke on the west beach.

A few grabbed weapns, but most of the company simply rushed toward the beach. The smoke was from new fires that the Indians had built. They had all risen before the sun and used some of the remaining corn to make corn cakes on hot stones as their people had done for centuries. They had also pulled water from the swamp and boiled it thoroughly in clay pots. Of course the English did not know they had done this, they only knew the Indians had provided sweet water and delicious corn cakes for breakfast.

There is nothing like good food to cement a friendship. Shortly after breakfast, the Indians made their farewells and prepared to head out. They had invited the English to visit them. Now they stood in a group just waiting. No one seemed to know what to do. Luckily it was at this moment that John Smith and his party returned from their short expedition. The party emerged form the forest not far from where the Indians waited expectantly. Smith slipped up beside Hunt and quietly said, "They expect gifts in return for whatever they brought you."

Hunt, in turn, suggested to Wingfield, "Gifts, Mr. Wingfield, I believe we should give them gifts of value similar to what they gave us."

This stirred the Council into quick action. Newport told Magnel to bring several belaying pins from the ships. Kendall went to get penny whistles and beads. This was not trading in the sense the English understood it from home, so no one had thought to use the trade goods in this manner. When the goods arrived and Wingfield ceremonious presented them to the leaders of the group, the Indians were happy and satisfied and left quickly.

As the English started back to their various tasks, Captain Newport walked slowly with head down toward Robert Hunt and John Smith.

"Doctor Hunt."

"Captain Newport."

"Smith. Thank you. That was becoming a bit .. awkward. Glad you got back. I intend to leave in a day or two for an extensive expedition upstream. You ... will be part of that company." Newport gave a nod of farewell to Hunt and headed back toward the area the Council had claimed as their own.

With a look of surprise on his face, Hunt turn to Smaith and said "Well, what think you of that, John?"

"Hmmmph. I save his face and he commands me to work, does not ask, simply commands. But, it is better than being in irons. And maybe it means he is recognizing my worth. Come, Doctor. Let's find some ale."

Fully loaded, the *Susan Constant* held 71 passengers and crew. Since they were only going up and down a river, tying up overnight, they could manager with a crew of 6. Newport chose a company of thirteen besides the sailors. He took Captain Gabriel Archer and George Percy. He took his favorite gunner, Robert Tindall. Robert Small, a carpenter, was chosen so he could evaluate the timber they would see. Robert Fenton and Nathaniel Pecock brought their muskets. Josiah Tucker, William Laxton, John Dods and the three Cassens came to do the rough work. And Smith finally took his rightful place as military commander of the expedition.

The goal was to take up to two months to explore the river up as far as it was navigable by a ship the size of the *Susan Constant*. They knew they were going into the prime territory of Powhatan, the senior chief in the area. They had hopes of meeting with Powhatan and, as always, hoped they would discover a route to the Western ocean and China.

Wingfield and the Council as well as some of the senior gentry were gathered in another insipid drizzle to see the expedition off.

"We wish you a successful trip, Captain Newport. Take our greetings to the chief Powhatan. Perhaps he will know how far it is to the western sea. Oh and we will be needing supplies soon, so get the native men going on planting corn. … And keep an eye out for pipe clay."

Captain Newport respectfully acknowledged his orders, "Yes, sir. And we look forward to seeing the fort you are planning upon our return. Raise anchor, Mr. Bales."

They went slowly. The wind twenty miles from the ocean was not strong from the east. They had been this way a month before, but now they evaluated the passing land for game, pipe clay and gold. They stopped each night, sometimes quite early so they could explore some distance from the river.

On the second evening, they dropped anchor and a few took the dinghy to shore. By the time they landed, a small party of Indians had appeared from a nearby wooded thicket. There was no ceremonious greeting. The men simply made a gesture of peace and indicated that the Englishmen should follow them. They had been sent to bring the newcomers to meet Parahunt, a son of Powhatan and chief in his own right.

There was some confusion as to whether this man was Powhatan himself or a sub-chief. He was tall, but somewhat stoop-shouldered and a not particularly impressive person. Newport estimated he was about forty years of age. The village was tidy and contained fifteen houses. All indications were that this was not the Emperor of the Algonquin nation. However, he was a chief and gave many hints that he spoke to, if not for, the high chief.

The English hoped this was a sort of test they had to pass in order to meet Powhatan himself, so when Parahunt offered to have two of his scouts go upriver with Newport, the Captain readily accepted.

The crew showed no anxiousness anticipating many days on this journey. The native scouts acted differently. On the second day out they gathered their few belonging and stood near the bow from midday on. About an hour after they took their post, the keen ears of some of the sailors picked up the sound of rushing water.

Tarman, one of Newport's most trusted men, said, "Captain, that sound is a lot of moving water. I see no sign of flood to make rapids that fast but something is ahead of us."

Archer, who had picked up more words of the native language than most, asked the scouts about the moving water. They had a special word for it, but Archer had no idea what it meant. They seemed easy about whatever it was, almost happy to be approaching it.

In another hour, everyone understood their attitude for before them was a beautiful waterfall. It was not very high, but there were several in a row and the noise and the spray was impressive. They moored downstream far enough that the current caused by the falls was not too strong. They had reached the highest navigable point in the river, not in two months, but in four days. As the sun set, the spray of the falls became a jeweled field of rainbows.

The next morning, everyone but a skeleton crew went ashore. The scouts took them around the falls on the north side. There was good water above the falls but the river definitely narrowed. The land above the falls looked to be excellent farmland. There were small fresh streams feeding the river frequently. As always, the sailors refilled their barrels with the pure water.

When the explorers returned to the falls, Parahunt and a large party were waiting for them. A few canoes were pulled up not far from the *Susan Constant*, but not nearly enough for all the Indians who were there. Clearly most of them had walked to this point in about the same time it had taken the English to sail. Either there was a fine trail or else these men had run a good part of the way.

They had already started several fires and had something cooking. Parahunt looked very pleased with himself. Perhaps he was teaching these newcomers that this was Indian land. Parahunt was making it clear that the Indians had complete control of their environment and that the English had a lot to learn from them. Newport did not disagree.

The two groups stayed together for the night sharing what the Indians had cooked. Newport brought out a keg of rum to add to the celebration. He was sparing in the amounts he gave to the Indians, but they reacted dramatically. There were a lot of sore heads the next morning.

Parahunt invited the English to visit again on their way back down river. Newport had planned to mark this spot by the falls for the King of England. He wisely waited until Parahunt had left for his village. He planted a cross at the base of the falls inscribed with "Iacobus Rex and Newport 1607." Martin led the group in prayer and called out three cheers for the king and then three more for Newport. The noise they made was enough to alert the Indians and Parahunt and his "court" returned to see what was going on.

Newport had to quickly come up with an explanation that would not offend Parahunt. Through Archer, Newport explained that the cross represented Powhatan and himself and their unity. He said the shouting was a reverence for Powhatan. Parahunt apparently accepted this. Newport hoped this explanation would reach Powhatan and impress him.

On the way back, they stayed with Parahunt's people for two days. Newport gave some penny knives, sheeres, bells, beads, and glass toys to each man and instructed them to trade when they could and give them as gifts when necessary. Cementing their friendship with this key group was very important.

The trade goods were very popular. Each man had made friends with one or two families. Josiah found a brave about his age and shared his trade goods with his family. Josiah could not resist trying to better some of his trades and the young brave, Koheno, caught on to what he was doing. The two nearly came to blows, but Archer happened to be nearby and came over to mediate the situation. Archer gave Josiah a stern talking to about his repeated fighting and about cheating the Indians. Either could undermine the efforts to create a tight friendship with Powhatan and his many peoples.

On the second night, Newport shared *aqua vitae* with the natives. The unrectified alcohol was not as popular as the rum had been and the men who had not been at the falls to taste the rum became jealous. Newport thought about bringing out the rum again, but first he tried sharing more trade goods to mollify the vocal braves. This seemed to work, so Newport left the rum on the ship.

Parahunt told Newport about another tribe whose village was across the river a little downstream. He suggested they stop there and named the king as Arrohattoc. Parahunt sent one of his runners to the other village to let them know the English would be coming by.

The runner must have told Arrohattoc a great deal about the visit of the English because the king and only a small court were standing on the shore as the *Susan Constant* approached. Newport, Archer and three others rowed into shore. The king's right hand man was ready with the words "aqua vitae." Newport offered penny knives, belles, and beads, but all they wanted was liquor. Newport gave in and had the bottles brought from the ship. The king and his court wanted seconds and thirds and Newport obliged. By the time Newport left the king was not looking well.

The trip downstream with the current in what they were now calling King James' River went very fast and the party was back at the camp in only seven days arriving on May 27th.

As they slowed and readied to drop anchor, Smith and Archer were standing together at the rail, "Gabe, something is not right."

"What do you mean, John? Both ships are here, the camp looks about the same. Most of the men must be out and about at this time of day."

"I cannot say quite what is wrong. But it is too quiet. Let Newport know I am going to take the Cassens, Tucker, Fenton and Pecock off first and look around."

Smith landed and deployed his men in a semicircle as they approached the camp. Smith drew his sword and the muskets were primed. Just as they reached the edge of the first tent, Doctor Hunt and a group of four laborers came from the area of the church headed toward the west wall of the fort.

"Doctor!" Smith shouted.

"Oh, Smith, am I glad you are back."

"What is wrong, Doctor? I can see something is amiss. What are you about?"

"It is a grave digging detail, John. Oh John – the day after you left - the Indians came."

CHAPTER 4
Cabbages and Kings

"Thomas, you are blocking the opening. You have to go outside before any of the rest of us. It is much better when it does not rain overnight and some of us can sleep outside. We are packed in here like sardines in a tin."

"Now, Rich, it is sort of cozy, sort of reminds me of ……"

A rip appeared in one side of the tent and then the opposite side.

"Yeow! What was that?!"

A third rip appeared and this time an arrow stuck in the tent pole.

All six men were up and out of the tent in seconds. They went about three steps and heard someone yell, "Get down!" They dove face first into the dirt.

"Anyone with a gun, get to the barricade." Two men came and fired random shots toward invisible targets in the woods.

"Keep down." "Find cover." "They are all around!"

Wingfield and the rest of the Council had gathered at the barricade. Since it was made of woven twigs and reeds, it stopped very few arrows. Martin was hit first. An arrow gazed his arm.

"John, we should get you out of here."

To where? Nowhere is safe. We have no defensible place."

Gosnold spun around and fell with a cut along the side of his head. Wingfield instinctively jumped up to go to his cousin and an arrow passed right through his beard.

Kendall spoke up, "We need to show our power. We have nothing here on land, but the cannons might serve. I will go signal the crews to fire."

"God go with you, George."

Kendall ran bent over dodging through the tents and around men cringing on the ground. He got to the edge of the sand and shouted out to the two ships, "Load and fire! Load and Fi …", but he was cut off as an arrow hit his leg and another hit his shoulder. He fell and was still.

Richard Mutton and Roger Cooke had been friends in London.
Roger was apprenticed to the bricklayer William Garrett, so when Garrett signed on to go to Virginia, Roger went with him. Rather than break up their friendship, Roger helped Dick find a gentleman who needed a servant. Thomas Gore engaged Dick as his personal servant and the boys had both come aboard the *Godspeed*. Now they lay side by side thinking they would be dead soon. They saw Kendall fall.

"Roger, we should pull him off the sand and back into the grass to have some cover."

"Looks like he is dead already, Dick. I am not ready to die to save a dead man."

"I do not think I can move him alone."

"Alright, but if they shoot at us, I am running for cover. On three. One, two, three!"

They ran the twenty feet to Kendall. Each grabbed an arm and they headed back to the grass. When they got two steps into the grass, Dick dropped his side and all three fell forward.

"We did it Roger! I cannot believe it, but we did it. … Rog? Roger!?"

Dick stretched over Kendall's limp body to where he could see his friend. An arrow had pieced his leg from side to side and his shoulders and neck were bent oddly.

Dick sat back and started to cry. When an arrow flew right over his head, he remembered to lie down. The tears ran from the corners of his eyes, down the sides of his face and onto the damp ground.

Kendall's message had been received by the crew on the *Godspeed*. One of her cannons roared carrying small shot into the trees. When Ratcliff heard the screams of the Indians, he jumped up and cheered. He was immediately hit. Two arrows cut through this coat and a third hit him in the side.

The second cannon fired hurling bar shot. The split cannon ball attached by chain was designed to snap the mast of an enemy ship. Today, it shattered the trunk of a large tree fifty feet into the forest. Thirty feet of solid wood came crashing down behind the shooters. They had never seen anything like it and they scattered.

Once the Indians had left, Gosnold went in search of Kendall. He found him unconscious and Dick still weeping over the body of his friend. Gosnold called for help to carry Kendall back but Dick personally carried Roger. Dick led the procession back to the President's tent. The Doctor saw them and joined them in the tent.

"President Wingfield, I implore you, this boy must be given a descent Christian burial – and soon."

"Doctor, I understand the need. Our orders specifically say we should not reveal any sickness or death to the natives. We will need to bury him inside the camp."

Doctor Hunt thought a moment. It was not a good plan, but better than holding on to a dead body in the heat of summer.

"Then, sir, I propose that I consecrate a bit of ground on the edge of camp to be used as a temporary cemetery until the crisis has passed."

"Inside the camp, you say. Is that wise? I have always heard bodies must be buried far from the living."

"Apparently, we cannot get the poor man far from the living, so next best is to put him in the ground here. Perhaps that open area to the west?"

"Alright, Doctor. Do what you must. You will explain it to anyone who asks."

Once again Wingfield showed he wanted the authority without any of the responsibility. Even Doctor Hunt was thinking a new leader was needed.

A small group gathered in the open space. The Doctor said the proper prayers to consecrate the ground, since a Christian should be burried only in hallowed ground, and the crew began to dig a proper grave. Hunt returned to the President's tent and he and Wotton readied the corpse. The practical Albertson had removed Roger's clothing and shoes. Leather and clothing were scarce. Burying them seemed a waste. Young Roger was wrapped in a bit of old sailcloth and buried, as was proper, with his head to the west. His was the first grave, but it would not be the last.

"We collected over a thousand arrows, John. There must have been two hundred savages. In a way, we were lucky. Other than the four Council members, only ten men were wounded. Kendall is alive. He was not too seriously hurt. Roger Cooke, his savior, is the only one who died."

"We have been here almost two weeks, Robert, and we have no defenses. What has the Council been doing? Has there been no training of the men with the weapons we brought?"

"Perhaps they were waiting for you, John. I do not know. They dig for gold. The young gentlemen play games or do some light hunting. They give orders to the others to cut clapboard and cook. Nothing has been accomplished, John, nothing."

"We need to fix this quickly, Doctor. Where is Wingfield?"

When Smith entered the President's tent, Newport, Archer, and Percy had just arrived. They had picked up the general news as they walked through camp. Wingfield was just giving them the causality count and Gosnold stood by watching.

"… seventeen wounded. We thought we had lost Edward Brinto as well as the boy, but he came into camp this morning. He had been up the stream looking for clay for pipes. Claims he can smell the right kind of clay first thing in the morning. He heard the fight and decided to stay away until he was certain it was all over. He fell asleep and could not find his way back in the dark."

He turned his attention to Smith.

"Captain Smith, you are our military expert about Indians. I thought we had made friends of these people. We cannot let this happen again!"

"No, sir, we cannot. We need a proper fort, a palisade."

"Right," Newport agreed. "I will have my crew pitch in and we can have a curtain wall up in a few days. It is … regrettable, this was not done while we were exploring."

Wingfield caught the implication and gave Newport a hard stare. Newport stared right back. Wingfield had been incompetent and Newport could not tolerate unsafe behavior.

Smith broke the stalemate, "Doctor Hunt said you collected a thousand arrows. Might I see them?"

"I told some boy to burn the devilish things, but he may not have done it yet."

Smith gave Newport a knowing look. Men who had fought enemies knew how much you could learn from their weapons, sometimes even turn them back on the enemy. To destroy them without examination was an amateurish thing to do. "I will see if I can locate this boy," said Smith and left.

The rest of Wednesday was devoted to mending tents, treating minor scrapes, and preparing to start the fort. Thursday morning brought the sound of many axes felling young trees with trunks of eight to ten inches in diameter. Sailors were used to this type of work, having to repair ships when they were out of port. Having the sailors' help made all the difference. The Company orders had specified that only twenty men be put to the task of building the fort. It was amazing how much twenty young men who were not accustomed to this heavy labor accomplished in only nineteen days. This small crew cut 610 trees. There were a few trees in the open space chosen for the fort, but most of the 400 to 800 pound trees had to come from a hundred yards or more away. They divided the trunks into lengths of twelve to fifteen feet and hauled the pieces from the woods to the site. The carpenters trimmed the logs to a point at one end and removed any branches that would keep the trunks from touching. Part of the crew was digging 1,030 feet of trench that was two and half feet deep. The cutting crews stood the trimmed, pointed logs upright in the trench and then the trenchers back filled the trench to support the poles. The cutters completed one to two trees each day. It was heavy, exhausting work and the men collapsed into their blankets for nineteen straight days.

Captain Smith did locate the boy who had the arrows and took them into his custody. He sorted them by the way the feathers were tied, the type of wood, and the type of arrowhead. Since each tribe had their own way of making arrows, the groupings suggested there were nine tribes involved in the attack. Smith shared this information with a few men he thought would understand the implications, Archer and Newport among them. With that many different groups against them and with their feelings being strong enough to unite in an attack, the urgency to build a proper fort was even grater than they had at first thought.

Captain Kendall recovered quickly. He had a bad headache and the leg wound did keep him on a crutch for several days, but he had experience in constructing palisades, so he took charge of laying out the plans the Council proposed.

They began the triangular structure at a point right in front of the old barricade. They built two walls out from that point to guard against an attack from the forest. They would build the third wall along the river last since the ships defended that approach.

To build a wall, laborers used shovels and a special tool called a scupper to dig a trench about twelve inches wide and two feet deep. With the top of each log being ten feet in the air and cut to a point, there would be no way for a person to grab the top of the wall to climb over. Musket ports would be cut after the fact at intervals along the walls so that the defenders could shoot in any direction.

Josiah was working next to John Asbie. They were digging the palisade trench on the east side. John was talkative.

"I came here to seek me fortune. Me fam-ly was just farmers up in the north county. Rocks, the land grew rocks more than crops. No one, no one in me fam-ly e're had any hard coin, but one day I was just walkin' in the street of me little village and look what I found." He reached in his weskit pocket and pulled out a silver sixpence. "Wat d'ya think of that?"

"Wonderful! I know what you mean about never having hard coin. You still have it? Nothing you wanted to buy?"

"No. I took it as a sign that me fortune was turnin'. So I said g'bye to me Mam and headed for London. That is where I met Captain Smith and he led me here. So you might say as this coin brought me to America."

He proudly started to put the coin back in his pocket when the person two down from him slipped and a shovel full of dirt flew into the air, most into John's face. John instinctively covered his eyes dropping the coin into the trench. John rushed to the river to wash out his eyes. When he returned he picked up his pick and went back to work never knowing his precious coin was not really in his pocket.

The walls were about 100 feet long and they left room at the conjunction to build a bulwark, a round outcrop that allowed a defender in the bulwark to shoot along either wall. Artillery from the ships would be mounted in these bulwarks. Once the muskets were unpacked from their crates and the men trained to use them, the fort would be easy to defend.

The current camp would be completely enclosed by the new walls. The church would end up in the center of the fort. Once the trenches for the walls were well underway, some of the laborers began work on a well in the center of the space. With access to the best mooring spot just outside one of the bulwarks, the settlers should be safe for an extended stay.

The muskets were unpacked and those who had some experience in shooting were given a gun, powder and ammunition so that there were be some immediate protection. By the end of that first day, about twenty feet of wall was built in each direction that proved valuable on the very next day when the Indians returned.

The Indians stayed out of musket range and shot only about forty arrows. Everyone stayed behind the palisade and no one was hit. Sadly, one of Gosnold's mastiffs ran out from behind the new wall to challenge the interlopers. The leader of the pack was hit several times and fell motionless to the earth. The other three dogs gathered around their fallen brother whining and nudging him with their snouts wanting him to get up. The Indians fired no more arrows and left the dogs to mourn in peace.

The teams continued working Friday and all of Saturday. Sunday would normally have been a day of worship and rest, but considering the danger, there was only a short service right after breakfast and then the team went to work. They did stop at dinnertime to allow each man a few hours to himself. Several gentlemen went to the little stream near the camp to wash a bit and perhaps do some fishing or crabbing.

On the way back, Eustace Cloville, the church builder, hung back to use the privy. He could still hear his friends' voices when a different sound cut the air, the sound of an arrow in flight. Pain exploded throughout his upper body when he was hit through his arm. He ran as fast as he could toward the fort, but there must have been several braves in the party for he was hit five more times before he stumbled past the new wall yelling, "To arms, to arms!"

"Get him under shelter," commanded Gosnold, "and find Surgeon Wotton to tend to him."

Edward Browne and Matthew Fitch, two men who had known Colville since they came together from Essex, carried him by his arms and legs to the President's tent. Archer, another Essex man, spied Wotton across the growing compound and signaled for him to follow the men. Archer and Gosnold took a careful look around the edge of the palisade. The grass and woods were still.

This hit and run tactic continued every few days. On Monday, June 1, twenty arrows were collected after a short attack. No one was hurt that day. The next two days, having several men armed and trained in the use of muskets, a party dared to go back to the woods to cut more clapboard. Another group along with two sentries went west of the fort into another grassy area to plow and plant corn.

On Thursday, June 4, William Faldoe, a prominent member of the powerful Fishmonger's Guild in London, fell prey to snipers who were hiding in the grass next to the fort walls as he was on his way to the privy. The first arrow went through his pantaloons. He immediately turned back to the fort, but another arrow cut through the sleeve of his shirt and a third arrow hit his head leaving a long open gash along the entire right side just above his ear. There was so much blood, Wotton and all who saw Faldoe thought he was killed, but Wotton pressed cloths to the head wound until the blood slowed. Then with five men holding Fladoe as still as possible, Wotton put five stitches in his scalp.

Wotton had become the de facto doctor for the company. Some people regarded surgeons as little better than butchers. Medication was a distant afterthought usually handled by a university-trained physician. Stitching a wound was part of a surgeon's expertise. The herbs, medicines and nursing were usually left to a locally trained person. However Wotton's mother had been the herb-woman for her village. In fact, she had a reputation for being the best in the county. She had been training her oldest daughter, Priscilla, to follow in her footsteps and Thomas, who was only a year younger than Pris, tagged along. It was an odd combination of knowledge and skill, but very useful to the settlement.

He took on the nursing role and kept bandages around William's head for two weeks, treating the wound with boneset and comfrey. Faldoe made a full recovery. The hair never grew back over the ugly white scar and ever after he wore a scarf, like a pirate, to hide the sight.

That was the last time the Indians came right up to the walls of the fort. On Sunday, June 7, Doctor Hunt celebrated worship.

"Lord, we thank you for helping us build the walls of our fort. You have blessed our labors and we now have a safe haven in this wild and troubled place."

Of course, the bulwarks still needed work, but the Cross of St. George flew proudly from the north bulwark. Earth had to be moved to make ramps and platforms for the cannon and their carriages. The ordinance had to be brought from the ships, set up and aimed for range. Very few of the men could hit a target at fifty paces with a musket, but, as the old saying goes, "Good walls make good neighbors" and having a solid barricade between them and the savages did give a sense of peace.

The job of mounting and aiming the cannon went to Newport's favorite gunner, Robert Tindall. A short man with keen blue eyes, he was an experienced naval artilleryman. He kept the cannon on their naval carriages, short stocky boxes on small wheels suitable for use on the smooth deck of a ship, but hard to move on solid ground. The carriage limited the range of the guns as well. That type of mounting was designed for guns when they were to shooting straight ahead into the side of another ship, using a only a fraction of the gun's full range. Eventually, the cooper and blacksmith would contrive an infantry carriage, one with larger wheels and a lighter mounting to make the guns more mobile on land and give them a greater aiming range, up and down, but for now, this was the best that could be done.

Hunt's prayers turned from thanksgiving to sadness on Monday, June 8, when Colville died. The service for Colville was the first requiem service held in the odd little church he had built. One of the prayers Hunt used had been written by Reverend William Crashaw in England, a man who somehow had a good idea of the situation in a land he had never seen. He prayed,

> "We know, O Lord, we have the Devil and all the gates
> of Hell against us, but if Thou, O lord, be on our side, we
> care not who be against us. And, seeing by Thy motion
> and work in our hearts, we have left our warm nests at
> home and put our lives into Thy hands, principally to
> honor Thy name and advance the Kingdom of Thy Son,
> Lord, give us leave to commit our lives into Thy hands."

The prayer was so well received that it was used at each change of watch for some time to come.

Another burial party was formed and a second grave was added to the little cemetery now west of the fort. On the way back from the burial service for Colville, Ratcliff was talking with Smith when he noticed two savages standing just at the edge of the woods. They were armed, but showed no signs of aggression. The company filed back into the fort except for Wingfield, Gosnold, Ratcliff, Smith and two sentries Smith had called to him. The two groups watched each other across a gap of two hundred feet. Neither made a move for several minutes. Then a shot rang out and the Indians disappeared into the woods.

"Who shot? Where did that shot come from?" demanded Wingfield. Men in the bulwarks, men at the gate and the five men outside the fort all looked around in vain. Finally, Josiah who had been watching from the eastern bulwark saw movement in the woods along the creek.

"There, sir, near the creek," he said pointing.

Edward Brinto, a mason who had evidently been out looking for pipe and brick clay again, walked from the woods, brandishing his musket. When he got closer, the men could hear what he was shouting.

"Did I get them? Did I get them?"

He walked quickly up to Wingfield and proudly said, "Miserable savages. I ran this bunch off. Saw them as I neared the clearing."

"Mr. Brinto," Ratcliff began formally, "we appreciate your enthusiasm, but those naturals showed no signs of attacking. It is possible they came on a friendly errand."

"Indeed," interjected Wingfield reclaiming his position, "you were hasty Mr. Brinto."

"Well, how was I to know." Dejected, Brinto turned and went toward the fort gate. "None of them worth anything…not going to let myself get ambushed like the others...shoot first I say..."

"Come gentlemen, this is a good time for me to address the company." And Wingfield threw up his head and led the five men back to the fort. Wingfield walked directly to the nearest bulwark shooing those collected there down onto the ground level as he stepped to the center of the raised area.

"Gentlemen, in light of recent events, I feel it is imperative that I remind you of the position of the Virginia Company. It is the view of our founding company that the naturals here in America should be used to provide us with the provisions we need, especially the corn which will be our primary source of food when the ship's stores run out, as they will do very soon. Therefore, it is imperative that we keep as many Indians as possible friendly to us and our cause. They will learn to respect and honor their new father, our great King James the First of England. But until that time comes, we must make the effort to keep them on friendly terms. To this end, I forbid anyone in the future to fire on friendly natives. I hope I have made myself, and the position of our founding and benevolent Virginia Company, clear. Thank you."

Wingfield nodded at the crowd, marched down the bulwark ramp and directly to his tent.

Josiah happened to be standing next to Smith, "What was that all about, Captain?"

"I am not sure, Josiah. Do you think you could tell a friendly Indian from one about to kill you?"

"Yes, sir, I do. Any Indian I see must be friendly because if they meant to kill me, I would never see them."

Smith stared at Josiah's back as he walked away amazed at how wise the young man had become in so short a time.

There was little talk of Wingfield's address. Apparently it had made little impression. Everyone went back to his duties. The next day, they felled yet another oak to make clapboard. Sentries went with each group who left the fort. Life went on.

Those who had been building the fort now turned to building living quarters. There was some discussion as to whether to build structures similar to those some had seen in the Indian villages or whether to build houses more like those they had left in England. Nostalgia won out over practicality. The frames were built of heavy twig or small limbs. A few timbers were fixed against these frames and the rest of the wall filled with daub and wattle, twigs and a mud mixture. Grasses were cut from areas away from the fort to be used as thatch for the roofs. The grasses did not dry waterproof, so reeds were cut from the swamps. Still it did not work as well as the thatch in England, but it looked well and kept the inside reasonably dry. There was one door and sometimes a window covered with a cloth, a deerskin or nothing.

Now that the little church was in the middle of the fort, Doctor Hunt felt it should be improved. His first step was to acquire an assistant. He approached one of Smith's favorites, the carpenter from Lincolnshire, William Laxon. Laxon has been singled out from the company to be the ensign or flag-bearer. He was well known and respected by the common men as well as being accepted as a skilled craftsman by most of the gentry.

He looked the part of a cleric. He had a long oval head dominated by a furrowed brow and a thatch of dense, dark brown hair. A bulbous nose held up bone-rimmed round glasses. The deep creases beside his mouth and a tendency to lick his lip over-often made one think of a loyal, but thirsty, hound.

"William, what do you think of our little church?"

Not knowing whether the Doctor wanted praise or a change, William tried to walk a centerline.

"It has served us well so far."

"Very diplomatic, William, but I think we could, and should, do better."

Knowing the direction the Doctor wanted to take, William proceeded more confidently.

"Are you asking for my advice, Doctor?

"Yes, your advice, and your help."

"How can I help you, Doctor?"

"I think we need more attention to be paid to the church. Perhaps by having additional clergy the company would be more aware of our role."

"Additional clergy? Were you thinking of anyone in particular?"

"You, William. I was thinking of you."

"I appreciate it, Doctor, but I have not taken Holy Orders nor even studied theology."

"The position of vicar does not require Holy Orders or advanced education. It requires a willingness to serve the church and to live a respectable life. Do you think that fits you?"

Pleased, Laxton pulled himself up to his full height, adjusted his shoulders a bit and said, "Doctor, I think that is a very good fit. How do we start?"

"Typically a vicar takes care of the church building and property. Do you think you could gather some interest in improving our space here?"

"Let me talk to some of my friends and see what we can manage."

William found two of the gentry who had been particularly nice to him, Thomas Hope and Anthony Gosnold. They were both gentlemen and Anthony was the brother of Captain Gosnold.

"Mr. Hope, Mr. Gosnold, good to see you!"

"Good to see you, William. Looks like you have something on your mind."

William explained the situation with the church. He asked them to look for small items that would enhance the space, the still needed table, candlesticks, linens, and so on. Mostly they decided to look for people who would be willing to volunteer their free time to build a better structure.

Within three days, the unofficial church committee had assembled a group of thirty men, gentle and common, who were willing to help. Anthony had told his brother about the project and Captain Gosnold mentioned it at one of the daily Council gatherings.

Wingfield saw an opportunity to appear to be a leader, "Bartholomew, this should be a company project, not an independent effort. Put together a crew and get started immediately."

No other instructions were given. No other duties were suspended to make time for the church, so nothing was done.

"Anthony, I wish you had never told your brother of our plans."

"I know, Laxon, but it was not Bart's doing. President Wingfield put his foot in it. Now if he had given some supplies or time or assigned workers, that would be different. If we go ahead without any order, I expect Wingfield will be down on us like a bird on a June bug."

"If Smith had said, build a church, we would be half done. With Wingfield, all your get is ideas, no action."

"Let me talk to Bart and see what I can do."

Anthony found his brother on the east bulwark watching the river.

"What do you see, brother?" asked Anthony.

"Hmmm… oh… a highway, little brother, a highway to anywhere we want to go. Rivers are marvels. I have often wished to be a bird, to be able to soar above the trees and see the land as a whole. but no more than I do right now."

He turned on Anthony with a great earnestness.

"Do you realize that if a man could go up high enough, the land itself would be a map. I could see where the rivers go and know the course to the South Sea. I could … You are staring. Do you think your big brother has gone mad?"

"Never, Bart, not you. You are, in every sense, a man of vision. I envy you your … sight."

"Not everyone agrees with you, Tony. But you did not come up here to have me prattle on. What is on your mind?"

"Odd that you were talking of having clear vision because that is what I cam to talk to you about, or really the lack of vision, of our President."

"Careful, little brother, mutinous talk can be dangerous."

"Not mutinous, just truthful. Wingfield has said there should be an official group to rebuild the church, yet he does nothing to make it happen. Those of us who would volunteer are afraid to do anything without his consent. So nothing gets done. We were just saying that if John Smith had said, "Build a Church," it would already be half done. If Smith had his rightful place on the Council, he could lead the rebuilding. Is there nothing you can do?"

Bartholomew happened to be looking across the compound at that moment and spied Doctor Hunt. He waved to him and motioned for him to join them in the private space.

"Robert, your church goes wanting."

"Yes, sad to say, we were ready to start and this edict of Wingfield's has stopped everything."

"My brother, here, seems to think that if Smith were on the Council properly, he could pick up the task officially and you would have your church."

"I had not considered that aspect, but I do think it is unreasonable to keep Smith from his appointed seat. He has surely proven his worth to the colony time and time again, no matter what Newport's personal opinion may be."

"Well said. Perhaps you and I could put a word in Maritn's ear and Kendall's. But we will have to convince Ratcliff as well in case it comes to a vote."

"Let me work on him," said Hunt. "Then we can both go to Newport."

"Tony, Robert, you may have your church yet."

The political discussions held everyone's attention for several days until June 13, a Saturday. On that day, the attention turned to fish.

Early in the morning, the sailors on *Discovery* were doing their usual fishing when they snagged something very heavy.

"Not sure what he got on this line, but he is a heavy one."

"Grab a long hook, boyo, and see if you can get it in him."

It took every sailor on the ship. Some used grappling hooks and one man threw a rope around its tail. After an hour's struggle, they hauled in a seven-foot sturgeon. This was an old fish, probably a legend among the Indians. The true fishermen on the ship took a moment to give reverence to the massive fish on behalf of all the men who had tried to catch it. A seven-foot fish could feed the entire camp for some time.

It was a happy day and the danger was temporarily forgotten.

But that same day, the savages became very bold and approached very close to the fort through the tall grass. Likely someone had figured out that the guns from the ships had been the source of the great explosions that had ended the attack of May 26th. Now these guns were being brought into the fort. The goal of this attack was to stop transferring the guns. They shot at two sailors, Master Ihon Catson and Master Matthew Fitch.

A sentry counted eight savages. Smith stationed a musketeer at each bulwark. Two of them fired down on the savages, but they fired several more arrows as they retreated and one arrow caught Fitch in the side. The arrow lodged between his ribs. Surgeon Wotton withdrew the shaft, but he could not remove the arrowhead.

The next day a party of braves from the Apamatica arrived by river. Newport recognized these men and welcomed them warmly. With Archer and Smith to help with translation, the conversation could cover new topics. The first thing the braves noticed was the skeleton of the great sturgeon. Indeed it was a legend, a legend named Powkoum, a tribute to Powhatan meaning chief fish. These coat-wearers had caught the Powkoum. Clearly they had powerful spirits.

When Newport told them the story of the eight Indians coming through the grass, the Indians suggested they cut the grass low enough that no one could hide. Why this simple solution had not occurred to any of the English baffled the Indians and the English. This was a basic tactic whenever a fort or castle was built in England or Europe. Any cover within bowshot was removed. Almost a month after landing and after at least two attacks through the grass, the cover was finally cut back as far as the woods.

The braves were very distressed about the attack on May 26th because so many tribes were involved. They could tell from the arrows, which Smith had kept, that these tribes were those downstream from the island that the English now referred to as Jamestown. Since they were going that way, they offered to broker peace with those tribes. For some time, there were no further large-scale attacks. Whether the efforts of the Apamatica stopped the attacks or not would never be clear.

The campaign to secure Smith his seat on the Council continued. Gosnold was in favor and after much persuasion from preacher Robert Hunt and the "church committee," Newport finally relented. He talked to Wingfield and the two of them officially swore Smith in as a member of the Council.

The settlement seemed to be prospering. The dissention within the Council had waned, the catching of the great sturgeon heralded good fishing to come and on June 15 Sir George Percy wrote in his journal, "We had built and finished out fort which was triangle-wise, having three bulwarks at every corner like a half moon, and four or five pieces of artillery mounted in them; we had made ourselves sufficiently strong for these savages."

Newport had completed his trip up the river. He had made positive contact with Parahunt, who proved to be a son of Powhatan. There was now a secure fort to protect the planters. With the help of the Apamatica, they could expect a time of peace. The stores on hand were sufficient to sustain the company for several months, especially if supplemented by corn from the Indians. It was time for Newport to go back to England.

Newport wanted to make sure everything was as stable as possible before he left. He conferred with the new Councilman, Captain John Smith, about the military situation and the security of the company. He talked with John Martin about minerals and to John Capper, Thomas Emery, William Laxon, Robert Small and Edward Pising about the available types of lumber. He was already expert in the waterways and in fishing possibilities. He was ready to make a full report to the Virginia Company.

He had one more concern, the political situation on the Council.

There was little respect for Wingfield. Martin was a caustic man and his remarks often started an argument. As the son of a three-term Lord Mayor of London and having been with Drake on his voyage around the world, Martin felt he was an authority on most things and his opinion should be taken as valid. Ratcliff and Kendall were decisive leaders but not good at developing a following among the men. Gosnold was a good man, well thought of by most in the company and a peacemaker among the Council. Newport had not completely accepted Smith, but to give the devil his due, he did see him as competent in his area. All in all, Newport saw the threat to Wingfield as Ratcliff and Gosnold. He decided the best way to neutralize the problem was to tell those men and ask for their cooperation. He sought out the two men a few days before he was scheduled to leave.

"Gentlemen, I want to speak to you about the Council. I have concerns about President Wingfield's ability to lead this settlement."

"I agree with you," said Ratcliff, and he seemed to want to continue. But Newport interrupted.

"I do not think you understand my intent. I am concerned that you are not seen as supporting our elected President. Like it or not, he is our President until next May. He is not commanding the respect he needs to do his job. You need to help him have that respect. I believe he is even afraid one of you may try to overthrow him. We cannot have that type of dissent at this early point in the plantation. I appeal to you to do your part."

The two men were taken aback. They expected Newport to suggest a change in leadership, a suggestion that he would take back to the Virginian Company for confirmation. This appeal to support Wingfield was a surprise and a disappointment. But what else could they do. Gosnold spoke for them both.

"We understand you, Captain, and we will do all we can."

"Thank you. That is all I can ask."

The night of June 21st was a picture perfect Virginia summer night. There was a soft breeze from the south carrying the scent of the tulip poplar flowers. The day birds were still active and the night birds just beginning their serenade. Dusk lasted for hours and the settlement felt suspended between earth and sky.

Newport had dinner with the Council and senior gentry outside in this fairytale atmosphere. They toasted the success of their venture so far and raised their glasses to a safe voyage for Newport home. Packets of letters were entrusted to Newport from most everyone who could write for himself or get a friend to write for him. Not everyone used Newport, the official conduit for mail. A few had need to get their information to England without Newport's knowledge or interference. A bit of coin passed hands and Francis Magnel became a mail carrier as well.

The morning of June 22nd, Newport wrote in his log that he departed from Jamestown leaving several houses built and all in good health. A bit of a stretch, perhaps, but he had no reason to believe things would not move forward as planned. Newport appointed his favorite artilleryman, Robert Tindall, as master of the *Godspeed* for the voyage home. The *Discovery* and two trained sailors, Giles and Tarman, stayed with the settlers.

Tindall showed promise as a ship's captain. First of all, he was literate, unusual for a sailor. He had faithfully written letters from January until now indicating the ability to keep a ship's log. He even drew a good map showing deep water in the Prince Henry river. This return voyage would be a final test to see if Newport would recommend him to captain a Virginia Company vessel in the future.

The company had become used to the absence of the *Susan Constant* for the week she was gone upstream, but now the harbor seemed so empty with both the *Susan Constant* and the *Godspeed* gone. Little *Discovery* did not look like much protection and certainly, there was now no way back to England until a supply fleet came to re-provision the settlement. The next few days, the men seemed deflated. Some rallied, but others continued to feel a sense of abandonment. The departure of the two big ships had redefined this trip from a short adventure to a long commitment.

The sense of being alone in a new world became even stronger on June 25th when an emissary from the great chief Powhatan arrived at Jamestown. The emissary came in full regalia, red paint, many beads and bits of metal. He had tattoos over much of his body and feathers tied in his hair. A large retinue of highly decorated men accompanied him. These men were clearly the courtiers of a great king. It was like having thirty or more of King James' nobles arrive at a little French village to summon the inhabitant to an audience with the King. The men of the Virginia Company felt for the first time the full weight of being a small group of outsiders on the land of a powerful king.

The emissary presented gifts of early squash, dried corn and beans, and hides of many types. Having learned his lesson, Wingfield gave gifts of knives, beads and bells in return. The emissary indicated that he expected to be given a gun for Powhatan, but, with some help from Archer as translator, Wingfield managed to decline gracefully. The new comers were invited to visit Powhatan's main village at any time and one of the lesser men of the party provided a map on deerskin.

Powhatan had also sent him to say that all the peoples of Powhatan would provide corn for the settlers, as it was needed, once this year's crop came in which should be within a few days. The emissary declined to stay the night and left in mid-afternoon after sharing a midday meal.

By July, Virginia summer was fully underway. The days were hot and humid and nights were too. There was little rain but at times the air would become charged with static electricity so strong the hair on a man's arm would stand up. Any standing water became green with algae and foul to drink. Mosquitoes hatched by the thousands in the swamps. The midges attacked the men's eyes almost more than the mosquitoes attacked any open skin. Existing in Jamestown became miserable.

The stores that were brought from England were growing sparse. The instructions from the Virginia Company had been to build a storehouse first to protect the provisions and arms. They had been here two months, and a storehouse had not even been begun. What provisions there were stood on bare ground covered haphazardly by old sailcloth. When there was rain, the barrels and boxes got wet from the top and the bottom. When each new barrel of flour or meal was opened, at least some had rotted from the wet.

There was some dried beef left. Very little would cause that substance to spoil, but even it was running low and the gentlemen who were accustomed to hunting in a park, a woodland kept stocked with game for that purpose, found hunting in the wild mostly unsuccessful. Cook pots often contained foul water, a bit of squirrel or possum and a few handfuls of the Indians dried corn or beans. This pitiful soup was becoming boring at best and poisonous at worst. Charges of mismanagement and graft increased as the supplies dwindled. The promised food from the peoples of Powhatan did not materialize. The settlers did not know that a drought that had begun in the previous year had continued and that the corn crop was barely enough to sustain the tribes themselves.

Not only did Powhatan's people not provide food, some of them renewed their attacks on the newcomers. There were no new attacks on the fort, but if a man ventured out alone, he was taking a great risk. Early in August, William Bruster, a gentleman from Suffolk, was out at the river's edge looking for shellfish. Hungry for anything fresh to eat, he wandered farther east than he had intended. An arrow came from out of the bushes along the swamp and stuck through his thigh. He toppled into the river and, wisely, lay there until he was fairly sure the attacker had left. He stumbled and mostly crawled back to the fort.

"Captain Kendall, Mr. Bruster's been shot," the sentry cried out to the officer of the day.

"Ailcock, get two men and go out for him. Sentry, ready your musket and give them cover."

The three men pulled Bruster in and took him to the President's tent. Wingfield had made plans for the finest house in the fort for himself. He would not deign to live in any lesser place so he kept to his tent until his "state house" could be built.

Wotton was summoned, as usual.

"William, man. You are soaked!"

'I fell into the river when I was hit and thought it better to pretend to be dead than to really be so."

Wotton marveled at the man's sense of humor in his condition. Some of these second and third sons of aristocracy had some steel in them no matter what the common sort might say.

"Son, I have to pull out the arrow. I will break off the feathers and pull it through as it went in. That should cause the least damage. If you get through tomorrow without a fever, you will likely be fine. But I have to say that getting that foul river water into this open wound does not bode well."

Doctor Hunt was standing at the flap of the tent. He spoke for all, "The best we can do is pray, my boy."

Within another few days, the situation was becoming critical. On August 6 John Asbie ceased to mourn for his lost silver coin when he died of bloody flux. Three days later, George Flowre died of a strange swelling in his throat. On Aug 10th, William Bruster succumbed to the infection that had indeed come on him from his wound.

Each of them was duly buried ceremoniously in the ever-growing cemetery against the west wall of the fort. Supporters of Smith became increasingly vocal about the poor condition of the fort and the men under Wingfield's leadership. A third group supported George Percy since he was the highest ranking person in the company and men were more comfortable with the idea of being commanded by a Lord rather than a businessman or soldier.

Minor fights broke out daily. They were mostly short lived since no one had the energy to waste on fighting. The anger was fed by hunger and fear. The fighting was fed by ale and rum, which seemed to be in greater supply than any other provision. The random Indian attacks increased and since Bruster was shot, no one would go farther from the fort than where they could be seen by the sentries.

One night, electricity was in the air again. Six of the men who wanted Percy to take over leadership were gathered in one of the houses drinking ale and talking treason. They were not thinking in terms of Council votes, only of followers. They thought they would have an influence as to who would be the next President if Wingfield were deposed. The arrogant commoner Smith had a strong following. They needed some way to weaken him. The right man was a born leader, a member of the aristocracy. The rhetoric circled round and round and the evening wore on until one of the company thought of leaving.

Dru Pickayes felt the storm coming. He had always had a good sense for changing weather. It had saved him a soaking now and again. He decided he would avoid the rain tonight too so he said farewell to his drinking companions and headed off to his usual sleeping spot in a house.

As he crossed the open ground inside the fort, lightning flashed and drew Pickayes's attention to the man walking guard duty on the stockade. He was unremarkable in height or form with the usual small mustache, but Pickayes was sure it was Alicock. Alicock was Smith's man, one of the few gentlemen who were loyal to Smith. One less of those would make it easier to have Percy take over. And Dru still held a grudge against Alicock for humiliating him on the ship because he believed in sea monsters. "Circle Dru, my ass, he muttered." Two good reasons for Alicock to die.

The plan came to him in one thought. Get his gun, wait for the storm to come closer, time his shot to be hidden by a clap of thunder and no one would be the wiser.

It took several minutes to go the short way to his room and get his pistol. He went slowly checking constantly that no one was about to see him. He took the piece outside to load it so the increasing wind would blow away any trace of the fresh smell of powder near his barracks. He wanted a clear shot before the rain started so there would be no chance of a misfire from damp powder or a quenched spark.

He retraced his steps and stopped in a deep shadow beside a half-built house just across from where his friends were still having a rowdy time. This spot would not do. It was not far, but guns were notoriously inaccurate. And if someone happened to leave the party, he could see either the flash of the shot or see Alicock fall. He wanted to be closer, but there was no other cover closer except the building where his friends were all awake.

As he thought, another great flash of lightning broke. He counted until he heard the thunder. It was only about the count of three now, the storm was about to break, likely in torrents of rain. In the flash he noticed that there was deep shadow caused by a slight overhang of the wooden floor over the dirt ramp along the bulwark where Ailcock stood guard. He counted the time Alicock had his back to that spot as he paced back and forth. Alicock seemed to stop at the end of each pass to rub his face. Pickayes thought he must have an abscessed tooth as did so many others. Each pass was at least the count of ten and Pickayes would not need even half of that to move from his current position to that deep shadow.

On Alicock's next circuit, Pickayes sprinted across the open ground. He was luckily downwind of Alicock then because his footfalls were not completely silent. He was tightly curled into the dark shadow by the time Alicock turned. The space between lightning and thunder was only a little more than the count of one now. All Pickayes needed was one good flash while Alicock's back was turned.

It came almost too soon. Alicock's boot had just landed above Pickayes's head as the light came. Pickayes had only the count of one to uncurl and fire. Alicock had taken only one step away when Pickayes stood up, aimed the gun and shot all in one movement. It was not a great shot. It caught Alicock in the side of the leg and he crumpled. The thunder rolled long enough to cover Alicock's scream. The fall onto the raised platform must have knocked the wind out of him because he did not cry out again.

Pickayes knelt on one knee so his eye was level with Alicock's. Pickayes expected to see hate in that eye, but all the next flash showed him was confusion. It was very unsatisfying. Pickayes thought of bashing Alicock in the head but then it would be obvious that someone had murdered him. Instead, Pickayes waited for the next thunderclap and discharged Alicock's gun. Then he put the matchlock on the ground hoping the others would think Alicock had dropped the gun and it had gone off, shooting him.

Huge raindrops started to pelt the compound. Pickayes knew all traces of his presence would be washed away in minutes. He backed away a few steps then turned and walked normally to his room.

Alicock was no longer breathless but no amount of shouting would cut through the sound of the torrential rain. He expected he would bleed to death before the watch changed. The rain was cold and even held some hailstones. Alicock was miserable for a short time and then he felt nothing.

After the rainstorm passed, the drinking companions started to their barracks. Someone noticed that no one was on watch and when they approached the stockade, they found Alicock. He was unconscious but breathing. They carried him to the President's tent where Wotton and Hunt took charge of the dying man.

One of Pickayes' drinking companions also shared his house. When that man came in saying that Ailcock had been shot but was still alive, Pickayes was terrified. What if Ailcock should name him as the one who shot him? He would be hung. He had always been terrified of hanging as a way to die. He had seen a man hanged in his village when he was a young boy. It took forever for the man to die and he looked barely human in the end. No, he could not hang.

There was nothing he could do now. Wotton would stay with Ailcock as long as he lived. He considered running away. There was nowhere to run to except to the Indians and who knew what they would do to him. He worried his way into a fitful sleep.

Morning brought word that Ailcock had not regained consciousness. Hunt and Wotton kept vigil by his cot.

"Doctor, this man should be dead. He should have bled to death in the time he lay there. It must have been that cold rain that slowed his blood. I cannot think of any other reason he is still alive."

"God works in mysterious way, my friend. Will he recover, do you think?

"I just do not know. He seems almost blue around the edges, his eyelids and fingertips, the tops of his ears and his lips. I have never seen a man who looked like that live out the day."

Again, a man who was that blue around the edges did not live out the day. Before noon word went around the camp that Ailcock had died. No one used the word murder. Pickayes began to believe that his scheme of planting the musket as if it had been droppcd had worked.

His tent being used as a hospital, Wingfield was in his second favorite place, a rough table with six rough chairs covered by sailcloth held up by bark-covered tent poles. He called it the Council Chamber. He did keep a fair log of the proceedings of the company and noted the death on July 14th of "Jeremy Ailcock, standard bearer, of wounds."

Wingfield's sad entries continued without let up. One of Smith's squad, George Cassen, died as did several men classed as laborers, however, Wingfield only noted the gentlemen and those of rank. In the next two weeks, seven more names were added.

Corporal Edward Morris, died suddenly
Edward Browne, gentleman of Essex
Stephen Calthrop, gentleman, aged 21
Thomas Gower, gentleman of London
Thomas Mounslie, gentleman
Robert Pennington, gentleman of Lancashire, aged 19

John Martin, gentleman, son of Councilman John Martin, aged 18

Soon all the meat and all the Indian food was gone. Rations were reduced to a small can of barley soaked in water for five men per day. The well had not been finished and their only source of drinking water was cold water from the river. There was no good time to get water from the river. It was salty at high tide and filthy at low tide. With everyone's constitution so low, anything would kill a man.

Some died from talking in too much salt from the river, though no one knew that was the cause. Some contracted a parasite or a disease from the foul river water. Some simply starved. Any injury could become infected and cause death. Any stomach disorder, injury or fever kept a man in bed. Any night might result in three or four men dying. The few who stayed healthy lived on sturgeon and sea crabs. On any day, there might be no more than five able bodied men available to guard the fort.

Either the Indians did not know how dire their condition was or else they had ceased to care about the fate of the newcomers being much more concerned about keeping their own people alive with little food and less rain.

Occasionally, someone would talk of fishing for sturgeon in the main river or making a few hooks to go fishing for smaller catch in the steams. No one thought to go off the peninsula to look for fresh water or at least boiling the water they took from the river. Or maybe the lethargy that is caused by drinking too much salt water kept them from doing the things they thought of. Whatever the reason, the company continued to be reduced day by day.

Late in August, the company lost a valuable and respected man when Captain Gosnold died. The carpenters made a particularly grand coffin with a gable lid. There was considerable discussion about where he should be buried.

Wingfield was for following the company orders. "We are not to show our dead to the natives. Gosnold was a worthy and religious man and what success we have had so far is much due to him, but he would be the first to say we must follow orders." Martin sided with him at first.

Archer thought the traditional proprieties should be observed. Archer put the case, "Captain Gosnold deserves all the proper ceremony due is status and office. In England, a leader of his stature would be interred in a church or, in time of battle, outside his fortification in clear view of his enemies. We should carry out all the rituals, show our strength, fire a full ordinance salute!" Smith added, "Captain Bartholomew Gosnold was the prime mover of this plantation. He understood what a formal show of force could do to demoralize the enemy. Let us do him proud!"

Emotion triumphed over orders and so everyone, in full military dress or what passed for their Sunday best, gathered around a well-dug grave and with many prayers and songs they buried the one man everyone respected. His captain's leading staff, a combat half pike, was buried with him. He had been a mariner, a privateer, an explorer of northern America, a soldier and the godfather of the Virginia Company and in all these roles he had ever been a practical man who would be represented, not by a fancy decorated ceremonial pike, but by a practical combat pike. Dozens of Indians stood just inside the tree line to watch this ceremony. When every ordinance in the settlement simultaneously fired a salute, the Indians evaporated.

Gosnold had been ill for three weeks, since just before the shooting of Ailcock. The absence of his calming voice signaled the beginning of political upheaval.

Men continued to die. By the end of summer, there were twenty-eight graves lying parallel or perpendicular to the west wall and the company consisted of fifty-four men. In six weeks they had lost twenty-five gentlemen, one surgeon and two others. Twice, two men had died on the same day and were buried together.

Either in spite of crisis or because of it, the political sides were lining up. Percy had his group; Smith had his. Wingfield had very few supporters left. Kendall was an unknown. With Gosnold dead and Newport gone, there were only five members of the Council left to vote. Since Wingfield, as President, had two votes, those who wanted him out of office had to be sure to out vote him. If Kendall voted with Wingfield, the vote would be three to three. With Kendall out of the way, the vote would be three to two.

On August 28th, captain George Kendall was accused of sowing discord between the President and Council and, having no jail or secure area within the fort, he was confined aboard the *Discovery*. No further action was taken. There was no trial.

On September 10th, the three remaining Council members, Smith, the grieving Martin and Ratcliff, signed a warrant deposing Wingfield. The charges in the warrant were trivial, concealing communion wine and misappropriating a tin whistle, and most seriously not owning a Bible. The charges may have been trivial and contrived, but they were sufficient to the purpose, which was to replace Wingfield with one of their own. Smith judged that for him to take over could be viewed badly, so they named Ratcliff to be President. At the same time, they created the post of Recorder of Virginia and gave it to one of their supporters, Gabriel Archer, thereby making him chief magistrate at Wingfield's trial. Wingfield joined Kendall on the *Discovery*. They had only a day together, however, because Kendall was released without explanation the following afternoon.

The small group of leaders now consisted of President John Ratcliff, Councilmen John Smith, John Martin and George Kendall, and Chief magistrate Gabriel Archer. The thirteen planned leaders had become seven by the hand of the Virginia Company and the seven had become four by absence, death and a legalized mutiny

CHAPTER 5
Plots and Counterplots

Newport and Tindall had a quick and easy five-week crossing. The *Susan Constant* and *Godspeed* arrived in England on July 29th with a hold filled with sassafras, clapboard and "gold." Newport immediately wrote to Robert Cecil, Lord Salisbury, Lord High Treasurer, Secretary of State, chief advisor to King James I and sponsor of the venture, that Virginia was a "country very rich in gold and copper."

All the digging the men had done around the camp and further afield had netted a great deal of sparkling dirt. Councilman John Martin was qualified as a goldsmith, at least his father had been in that trade in England. He had blessed this shiny dirt as bearing gold or at least copper. What they had found was a mineral not widely known in England called mica. Within ten days, the official assayers had determined that the ore was not gold. Some suggested it was iron pyrite or "fool's gold," but that was a familiar mineral to Martin at least and he would not have been fooled.

Lord Salisbury did not respond to Newport's letter. He felt it was better to simply keep his distance from the whole affair.

The investors in the Virginia Company did respond to Newport. They requested that he come to a meeting with the board of directors and explain himself. The old pirate in Newport came up with the less than believable story that he had brought the wrong sample.

The current head of the board was a man whose ears occupied the sides of his head leaving little room for anything but a fuzz of graying hair on top. His lipless mouth sat to one side of his face with his bottom teeth even further to that side. His neck was so thin his skin drew upwards behind his chin and two long wattles formed his neck. His voice was thin, reedy, more air than sound.

"The wrong sample, you say, sir?"

"Yes, we collected several samples and put those that were alike into piles near the ships for easy loading. It seemed preferable to moving the dirt and rocks twice. Councilman Martin (he hoped this appeal to authority granted by this board would give his story credence) evaluated the samples and notified me that there was an excellent sample to represent the quality of the ore in the area. There must have been some confusion with those loading the ore as to which pile was to be loaded. As I left this operation to Martin and his assistants, I was not personally aware of which sample was to be loaded. Trust me, gentlemen, that valuable sample sits safely on the shore of King James' river. I need only go back and retrieve it."

"Well, sir, you shall have that opportunity. Please, return here in a fortnight and we shall have your orders."

Newport knew his story was all fabrication. He was betting that the mineral hunters would either have found something worth shipping home on their own or that he could find out from Powhatan where the gold and copper he had seen on the chiefs came from. He needed to get back to Virginia to clear his name.

In the meantime, he had more personal matters to deal with. Much of the hold of the *Susan Constant* had been filled with sassafras roots. Once it was first found, many of the sailors spent their free time harvesting the valuable root as their personal treasure from the new world. The people of England were not enamored of using this sad little root in their food. They believed that sassafras was a cure for the French disease, syphilis, and so were willing to pay a premium price for the homely root. The sailors could not ship the root back without Newport's knowledge and permission, so they made a deal that Newport would get a split of the profits for each man. Newport needed to find out how the sale was going and collect his portion.

He had left his trusted right-hand man, Josiah Bales, to handle his interests. He went to Mr. Bales' favorite tavern. Sooner or later Mr. Bales would be there.

Newport waited just over an hour and the grizzled face of Bales appeared across the table.

"Afternoon, Cap'n"

"Bales. How did we do?"

"So far, quite well. The brokers are saying there is so much root coming on the market all at once, that the price cannot stay as high as it started."

"We might have done better to sell it off in small lots, then. I had not considered that. Can we hold any back now? Is there anyone we can trust to sell the rest later?"

"Unless I am watching them, I trust no one, and then only sometimes."

Newport smiled.

"Well, we will not be here long, so I suppose we had best take what we can get and be happy. When we get back in four to six months, maybe the market will be ready for more and then we will be more careful."

"When we get back, sir? I gather that means we are headed back to Virginy."

"Yes, Mr. Bales, the Board in its wisdom is sending me back. You've heard that the mineral samples were not gold, or even copper?"

Bales nodded.

"I thought that news would have made the rounds by now. Well I told them we had loaded the wrong sample, so we are to go back and bring the right one."

Bales grinned, the closest he ever got to a smile. He knew Newport well and knew Newport had most likely invented that story on the spot.

"I suppose you would like to know when we are leaving? So would I. I am to visit them again on the 17th to get my orders. So what do we do for two weeks? Any ideas?"

"I intend to finish with the sale of the sassafras, then take my portion and find my Maggie and stay drunk and warm 'til I hear from you, Cap'n."

Newport laughed a hearty, appreciative laugh. "A good plan, Mr. Bales. I will see if I can do as well."

Newport met once more with Bales to get his cut of the money. He invested some with key contacts in London and surrounding ports to buy information on the Spanish and on certain individuals in the government and in the Virginia Company. He also purchased some special gifts and trade goods he would keep for his own use with the Indians. When, not if, he met Powhatan, he wanted the chief to be personally indebted to him.

On August 17th, Newport went before the Board.

"Captain, we have decided to restock the company as agreed. You will Captain the *John and Francis*. Your consort on this voyage will be the nimble pinnacle, *Phoenix*. They will be loaded with food, additional arms, and cloth for the planters and for trading along with other trade goods. We have taken your information about the seasoning of settlers into consideration. We agree that moving directly into the hard season of summer may not be the best timing, so we are sending you out in November to arrive in late December or at the latest in January. There will be sufficient food for your crew and the 120 settlers we expect to be sending with you."

"One hundred and twenty settlers in two ships? That is more than I took on the first trip, and we were crowded in three ships."

"We have calculated the space, sir, and we feel it is sufficient. There will be no disassembled boat and little need to take food for these people to eat after they land since the first group will have laid in supplies, some they have grown and, of course, those provided by the naturals."

"Please let me remind you that the naturals had provided no food to the company in the two months I was there except for a token brought as a gift."

"We have competent men there, Captain. We are certain things are going according to plan by now. Please to be ready to load no later than November 15th."

"I can be ready sooner."

"Be that as it may. We have planned for mid-November. That will be all, Captain."

Newport was not sure what made him push to go sooner. Something in his gut said that the settlement might not be doing as well as had been. There had not been any food from the Indians. The settlers were not stocking up their stores on their own. The cornfields were planted but, from the little he knew of farming, those fields did not look big enough to support a hundred people for a year much less another 120 besides. He had learned to trust his instincts and his instincts said the Company plan was not going to work.

John Ratcliff was the opposite of Wingfield, who continued to sit cold and hungry, but safe, on the *Discovery*. Ratcliff was everywhere, making decisions and giving orders. He sometimes took the physical condition of a man into consideration, but since everyone was in poor shape, he felt he had to demand work from people he would usually send to sick call.

However, he was not by nature a patient man. He was particularly incensed by insubordination. He used physical punishment liberally, not the punitive kind so popular in England like the stocks or ear nailing. Ratcliff would personally slap or punch a man who he felt needed discipline. Most men respected this type of man-to-man behavior. Some, not all.

John Read, a huge man whose teeth were as off center as his nose, was the only blacksmith who had come on the first voyage. Blacksmiths had, for generations, been regarded as a special member of any community. So much of the prosperity of a village depended on the blacksmith, he was seen as an unofficial official of the village. The blacksmith made all the metal tools, he made metal rims for work wagons, he was the *de facto* gunsmith in most places, and he made all the weapons, spears, halberds and swords. Some wondered if the respect shown a blacksmith might also have to do with how strong they were. Whatever the background, blacksmiths had simply come to expect a say in the activities of their town and an extra measure of respect.

So when John Read talked back to John Ratcliff and Ratcliff struck him, Read hit him back. Ratcliff ordered him hanged.

The sentence was to be carried out immediately. Ratcliff ordered the men who had taken on the role of soldier to bind his hands, put a ladder up next to the wall by the gate and to throw a rope with a noose over the cross bar of the gate. Read was hustled up three rungs of the ladder putting his feet only three feet above the ground. With his weight and the stretch in the rope, it was doubtful the hanging would be more than a jump to the ground.

Ratcliff was not experienced in hanging men. He knew it was a death for common men, humiliating, painful and slow. He had no idea how much the drop had to be to be effective.

Standing on the ladder with hands tied, Read bargained for his life.

"Ratcliff, you might want to think twice about killing your only blacksmith. You may well need your weapons in good condition soon, for there is plot in your ranks."

Read now had everyone's attention.

"Plot, what plot,' demanded Ratcliff.

"One of your Councilmen is communicating with England on his own. In fact, right now, the *Discovery* is not heading for a fishing expedition north, she is set to head for England."

"Nonsense!" shouted Ratcliff. My Council is loyal. We all agreed to my election."

"Not all," said Read much more calmly than his position would warrant.

Smith and Martin immediately realized who Read meant. The light dawned on Ratcliff a heartbeat more slowly. Kendall had not voted for Ratcliff. Kendall was sending word to England outside of normal channels. Kendall had the power to send the *Discovery* to England instead of to the northern fishing grounds to save the settlement.

As soon as Read mentioned a plot, Kendall had started moving gently toward the gate. All eyes found him now and froze him in his tracks. He was at a spot where he could signal to the *Discovery* to leave and possibly make a break to get on the ship. Smith took the initiative and gave the general order, "Take Kendall in hand!"

The men who were in attendance had understood quickly that for the *Discovery* to go to England instead of to go fishing for food would surely mean death for them all. They were most willing to lay hands upon Kendall who they now saw as their mutual enemy.

Smith, still ahead of the situation, shouted orders to one of the bulwarks that could bear on the river, "Prepare to fire on the *Discovery*." He then marched to the bulwark and addressed the men on the *Discovery*.

"Ahoy! *Discovery*! In the name of the Council I order you to stay where you are or sink."

The sails of the *Discovery*, which were partly unfurled, started to come down. Kendall was bound and taken to the President's tent under tight guard.

Now all eyes went to Ratcliff. In their eyes, Read had just saved the colony. They had not really supported the hanging in the first place and now Ratcliff could sense that the group could easily turn on him if he continued with the sentence.

"Mr. Read, the Council is grateful for your information. Because of your service to the company, and with the agreement of my Council, I commute your sentence to house arrest for a period of a fortnight."

No one had ever been put under house arrest before, so no one was too sure what it meant. Since Read had no intention of leaving the fort in the next two weeks, it really amounted to no penalty.

The soldiers untied Read's hands and helped him off the ladder. The crowd made a path for him and many slapped his back or shook his hand in thanks and congratulations. Read's reputation, already very good, went up even higher.

Kendall, on the other hand, was tried by the Council immediately for fomenting "a dangerous conspiracy." Kendall's defense was unique.

"President Ratcliff, you have no right to preside at the trial or to vote on my guilt or innocence because you are not really John Ratcliff, the duly elected President of this company. You, sir, are John Sicklemore and why you left your real name in England I will leave to you to explain."

Everyone was momentarily shocked. The President was an imposter. What could this mean? Smith and Martin put their heads together to discuss the accusation. Others who were witnessing the trial muttered among themselves and passed the bombshell news on to those outside the "Council Chamber." Ratcliff let the clamor go on for a few minutes and then called for silence. He looked at his two Councilmen.

Smith spoke for the two, "Mr. President, we believe it would distract this court from the issue at hand to pursue the question of your identity. To avoid any appearance of impropriety, we suggest that Councilman Martin take over the trial."

Ratcliff uncharacteristically agreed meekly.

John Martin pronounced Kendall guilty as charged and condemned him to be shot. The sentence was to be carried out one hour after dawn the next day.

Executing a man by firing squad was also new to the settlers. Smith had at least seen it done when deserters were shot in the Irish campaign, so he again took charge. Three men who were good shots with muskets were named to the squad. The prisoner would be placed against a wall, secured there if he was not willing to stand calmly, with honor. The idea was that all three would aim for the heart and shoot at the same time so no one would ever know who had actually killed the condemned man.

On the morning of October 5th, 1607, the first government sanctioned execution took place in Virginia. The marksmen were not as good as Smith hoped. There were no shots near Kendall's heart but one man had hit him squarely in the head.

With Ratcliff's loss of prestige over the Read affair and the question of his background brought to light by Kendall, the men increasingly looked to Smith for direction.

Powhatan presided over the harvest celebration in his main village. It had not been a good year, but there was enough extra that he decided to trade with the "coat-wearers." His scouts had watched the fort continuously. The scout reported that other Indians were also watching the fort and whenever a man came out to hunt, he was attacked. The scout reported that the food that had come on the ships was almost gone and the men were dying. Powhatan thought that the newcomers would be desperate and willing to trade valuable items, like copper pots, swords or even a gun.

He sent a large group laden with corn, squash, berries, and game birds. The English offered their usual trade goods, beads, bells, hatchets, and bits of copper. No swords were offered, and no guns. Smith had given orders that no Indian be allowed to even touch a gun. The Indians accepted the goods, took note of the condition of the fort and the men, and most left. Two braves were instructed to stay and help the settlers as guides. Actually, they were scouts, or spies, depending on how you looked at it. They would send reports to Powhatan through other scouts who came near the fort where they could meet. They reported to Powhatan that the fort was unfinished, the men were hungry and sick, and there was really nothing to fear from them except the power of the guns.

Rejuvenated by the food from Powhatan, most of the men rallied. Some had declined too far and a few continued to die, but now there were some men strong enough to go out of the fort to seek food and to continue their job to explore this new world.

Smith was anxious to get out of the fort. He was a natural traveler and wanderer. He took a party of nine men out in early December. As always, he made maps and assigned English names to places and features of the land. The party, including one of the Indian scouts, had followed the river upstream. Smith noticed a significant creek and he and the scout moved inland to map it. After they left the river, a hunting party of Pamunkey Indians came upon the men by the river and attacked them. After two of the men were killed with arrows to the heart, the other five got in their canoe and rowed out of range.

Checking out the area, the Indians noticed the tracks of Smith and the scout going further upsteam and followed them. Finding that Smith had stopped to draw his pistol, the Pamunkey spread out to surround them. Suddenly the air was filled with arrows. Smith grabbed the Indian scout and used him as a shield. He brandished his pistol, though without time to cock it, it could not fire. The scout yelled to the Indians that he was a chief. Even between tribes, there was a protocol about not killing a chief.

As the standoff continued, Smith backed up in the direction of the river hoping to find help. He got off the trail and backed onto soft land and lost his footing. The Indian scout broke away and the hunting party detained him with respect. Smith's feet were caught so securely in the swamp that he could not move without assistance. His choice was to stay stuck in the mud or give up and trust that being with a chief would give him status as a valued captive. He put down his pistol and the Indians pulled him out.

The hunting party took both men to the closest Pamunkey village. That village chief sent Smith's scout back to Powhatan as a sign of respect for the chief of the nation. He also saw the political advantage in being the chief who sent Smith to Powhatan, but he also wanted the other villages to know he was the chief who captured Smith. So Smith was sent on a native version of the Roman triumph. He was paraded through village after village by braves from this chief's village and the story was told and retold of how this Pamunkey chief was responsible for the capture of this leader of the invaders.

At each village, Smith was asked the same questions the very first Indians he met had asked, where was he from, why was he here, and when would he leave. To that list they now added a new question, when would the great one-armed chief return? Clearly all these people knew of Newport, knew he had left and considered him to be the main chief of the English. Smith marveled at the communications network.

After several weeks of these short trips, the march finally reached Weowocomoco, the main village of Powhatan. Two hundred warriors had drawn up in a gauntlet-style double line. Smith was led through this line. He kept his stride steady and his head high. Indians valued courage and this bearded, little man showed much courage.

He was led into Powhatan's meeting chamber and given to Powhatan by the Pamunkey braves. Powhatan was sitting on his "throne" of twelve mats, each mat representing one of the tribes who recognized Powhatan as their leader. Protocol was very strict in this Algonquin culture. Before speaking with the chief, a man was to clean his hands to show he had no hidden weapons and that he would speak the truth. In his many adventures fighting all over Europe, being captured, enslaved, and escaping, Smith had developed a cosmopolitan air, capable of reading a new situation and adapting to it with grace. Smith mimicked his escort and performed the ceremony of washing his hands and drying them on feathers as if it were familiar to him.

Then Powhatan questioned him. Even braves who had known the chief all their lives tended to quail under questioning, but this man Smith met Powhatan with a direct stare and a calm voice. Smith had also developed a fair ear for languages and was able to answer Powhatan's questions with some sophistication.

"Why did the coat-wearers come?

"Great Chief, it was a mistake. We intended to fight our enemies the Spanish." (Powhatan had no love of the Spanish. Their diseases had killed hundreds of native people and especially the tribes south and west of him over that last two generations.) "Our ships were blown off course and pushed into the great mouth of Powhatan's River."

"Why do you not leave?"

"Captain Newport had to take a trip and we cannot leave until he returns with the large ships."

Powhatan thought for only a moment and then ordered, "Take him."

This exchange had felt like a formulaic ceremony to Smith. Many people, male and female, young and old were witnessing this audience. Old men he thought were priests had lit a fire and were chanting. When it turned physical he was confused. Perhaps he had misread the situation. Perhaps he was to be sacrificially killed.

Sacrifice seemed the choice when he was dragged to two large stones inside the chamber and his head was forced down. Two braves in unusual ornaments held large clubs over their heads. Smith closed his eyes and started saying his prayers.

Then there was a small body draped over his head. She, indeed it was a young girl, was speaking, no, more reciting a few formal phrases which he understood as something like, "Good father, I claim this man as my brother and ask you to spare him from (some word he could not translate at all)."

The clubs were lowered, the girl stood up, and Powhatan, in turn, recited a formula, "This man is brother to my daughter, Pocahontas, and son to me."

The two ornamented braves took his arms and helped him stand. They bowed their heads to Powhatan and Smith followed their example. Then, continuing to follow their lead, the three turned and left the chamber.

Smith was taken to a small hut where a woman brought him real washing water, food, a sweet drink, and a new blanket. The woman was handsome rather than pretty, due perhaps to an almost regal air about her. It was hard to understand her, but he made out enough to know he could wash, eat or sleep as he liked and someone would come for him.

He ate and drank a bit and did curl up on the blanket to relax, but he thought better of sleeping. After what he thought was more than an hour, it was the young girl, Pocahontas, who came for him. She had two men with her, a sort of bodyguard he thought.

"My brother, we will visit with our father."

This time, they did not go to the large ceremonial building. They went to a house just slightly larger than the rest. Powhatan was seated with several young men and women by the family fire. The older women were serving them. Pocahontas indicated he should take an open place not far from Powhatan and then she took a place directly on his left. Clearly she was a highly favored daughter.

It took more than one try for Smith to understand the nuance of his status. Finally, he realized all these men were sons or sons-in-law of Powhatan and all were chiefs. He was now a son and a chief.

The next request was perfectly clear, a chief was expected to give valuable gifts to Powhatan and what Powhatan wanted was thunder weapons, cannons, and a millstone. Smith was quick. If Powhatan had asked for muskets, he would be in a difficult position. But having asked for cannon and a millstone, Smith could agree.

"Yes, my father. Your new son and chief will give you these gifts. Send men with me to my village and they can bring them to you."

Powhatan smiled. He was very pleased with his new son.

Pocahontas smiled too.

Twelve high ranking braves escorted Smith back to Jamestown treating him as they would a chief. Of the fifty-four men who had been in the company when Smith left, two had been killed at the river and twelve more had died of illness. Only thirty-eight men remained and only ten of them were capable of work on the day Smith returned. When the one sentry saw Smith and twelve strong braves emerge from the trail into the woods, he notified Captain Gabriel Archer who had been given Smith's place on the Council. Archer evaluated the situation. He had ten able-bodied men, but they were not strong. They would be facing twelve healthy braves and Smith did not seem to be a captive. On the contrary, he seemed to be leading the group.

"Men, ready your muskets, but take no action without my orders. We will see what Captain Smith has to say."

Smith motioned for the braves to wait outside, waved at the sentry and entered the gate of the fort. All ten able-bodied men were waiting for him with Archer at their head.

"Captain Archer. It is good to be back. I have brought twelve men from the camp of Powhatan. May I bring them inside?"

"As you wish, Captain Smith."

Smith walked the few steps outside.

Ratcliff was standing next to Archer. "What are you thinking, Gabe!"

"Let him play out his hand, John. I think he will hang himself."

Smith returned and the twelve braves moved out into a semicircle behind Smith.

"Gentlemen, Powhatan has accepted me into his tribe. We will now be given provisions regularly as part of his people. In return for this, he has requested three gifts. I have agreed to give him two cannon and a millstone. These men are here to take the gifts to Powhatan."

Smith winked. Archer, Ratcliff and Martin thought he had lost his mind.

Smith turned and said, "Brothers, you see the millstone there on the ground in the center of this fort. Take it to my father."

The braves walked around the right of the small crowd to the millstone. The stone was lying on its side in the dirt. The settlers had not harvested enough corn to require its use, so weeds had grown around it and through the center hole. Two braves worked their hands under one edge of the stone and pulled up. The stone did not move. They signaled for two more to join them and four tried. It lifted an inch, but they could not hold it. A puff of dust blew up as it dropped back into place. All twelve looked at Smith. Some showed confusion. Some showed anger.

"My brothers, you must lift the stone to take it to our father. If you cannot, his gift must stay here with me until he comes for it. Let us go to the thunder weapons."

He led them to one of the bulwarks. There was a rope tied to a loop at the back of the carriage holding the cannon. Four of the Indians grabbed the rope and pulled on the gun. It moved along the boards on which it sat, but when the wheels got on the dirt, they stuck. The four continued to pull and the others pushed from the sides or front. It moved a bit further but it also sunk deeper into the dirt.

"My brothers, the thunder weapons are usually on a big ship. Perhaps we will have to wait for a big ship to take this gift to our father."

Smith had not said that Powhatan could not have the gifts, so he had not given insult. The braves talked among themselves. Neither Smith nor Archer could catch what they were saying since they spoke so fast. One of the braves spoke for the group.

"My brother, we are sad that we cannot bring your gifts to our father. We will return and tell him what we have found. Be well, my brother."

The twelve walked directly down the bulwark ramp, out the gate and into the woods.

Smith took a moment to bask in his victory, then followed the braves down the ramp and walked up to the Councilmen.

"Gentlemen, as I said, it is good to be back."

"Smith, I give you marks for cleverness," said Martin, "offering gifts that could not be moved, very good, very good indeed."

"Thank you. I wish I could take the credit, but it is what Powhatan asked for. I simply saw the advantage in being able to grant his request yet provide nothing."

The other seven men who were not on the council truly appreciated Smith's ingenuity. They had heard Smith's promise of regular provisions. in their opinion, fresh food for gifts that could not be delivered was a great trade.

Archer took charge of the conversation.

"Well, Smith, now that that charade is over. We have other business with you."

"We have much to discuss, but I have not been here for six weeks and I very much want to know how things fare. Have we lost any more men?"

"Interesting you should ask that," said Ratcliff, "we have lost twelve men to illness here in the fort while you have been playing with your new friends, but it is of the two you killed we need to speak first."

"Killed? I killed no one."

"You were in charge of the exploration up the river. Two men were killed during that expedition. You were in charge, so you are responsible for their deaths. The Council has charged you with the murder of Thomas Emery and Kenelme Throckmorton."

"Why that is absurd! And you know it! Why in the world...."

"Mr. Hope, Mr. Keale, take Captain Smith into custody."

The two men sheepishly took his arms and marched him to the Storehouse. This structure had finally been begun just before Smith's expedition had left. Ratcliff had the sense to see that Powhatan's gifts of food would need to be protected both from the elements and from two score of starving men. They built this building more on the plan of the Indian huts with twig framing and woven mats for walls and a roof. The inside had been divided into one large central room and four small "rooms" with twig walls and doors that could be chained. The mats for the roof were in place, but only the west end had mats in place for walls. It was to one of the rooms at the west end that Smith was taken. The room held two small barrels of rum and the door was chained and locked. Keale produced the key to the lock. He watched Smith as Hope moved the two barrels into the center room. Then Keale motioned for Smith to enter the room. Keale replaced the chain and lock and said,

"Sorry, sir," and they both left.

There was no real trial. Archer, Ratcliff and Martin came to the Storehouse about two hours later. One man stayed on the bulwark as sentry, but the six other able-bodied men and not a few sickly ones gathered outside the unfinished walls to hear the Council pronounce Smith as guilty and to condemn him to be shot in the morning.

The Council left immediately. Most of the others wandered off in twos and threes talking quietly. At least a dozen men came up to Smith's cell and expressed their regrets. The one who stayed was Josiah Tucker.

Josiah had been on a ladder working on this very storehouse when a man who was on the roof dropped a wooden mallet that hit Josiah's head. He fell and landed badly on his left shoulder dislocating it. Wotton was able to reposition the joint, but ordered that Tucker not use the arm for at least ten days. That was twelve days ago, but no one seemed to be counting and Josiah did not see that there was anything to do but go into rotation for guard duty, so he was keeping to his sleeping space. However, he could not let his friend Smith be alone on this terrible night to come.

"Captain, sir. I am so sorry. I do not understand this at all. I wish there was something I could do."

"Not to fret, lad. This is no doing of yours. Archer wants my place and this is his scheme. Save Divine intervention, I do not see anything to be done."

Brightening Smith continued, "Except I am hungry ... and thirsty. Can you manage some food and drink and maybe a blanket for the night? I have been used to walking and, sitting here out of the sun, I am feeling this January cold."

Josiah picked up Smith's positive attitude. "I will go see what I can do, sir. I will be back shortly."

Night came early this soon after winter solstice. Dusk was well along when Smith heard some commotion and Josiah running toward the storehouse. He burst through the door opening with a huge smile on his face, "Captain, you may have that Divine "in-vention" you asked for. Captain Newport is dropping anchor!"

It may have been the faltering light or it may have been the fancy of the desperate men, but the sails of the two ships looked like a choir of angels come to save them. Smith trusted Newport's integrity more than these other Councilmen so he too had renewed hope.

From the deck of the *John and Francis*, Newport could see that the fort had not progressed as planned. The river and marshes were filled with swans, geese, ducks, and cranes, yet only twenty or thirty skeletal men were standing between the fort wall and the river to greet him. That was not even a third of the men he had left here.

The eighty new settlers (forty of the settlers were on the smaller ship, *Phoenix*, which had become separated from the *John and Francis* during a storm) crowded to the rails and waved and shouted to the men on shore. The seasoned settlers waved back at first. Then, one by one, it dawned on them that this throng of people would be sharing their little fort and maybe their little food. The waving slowed and here and there it stopped. Then someone on the ship said, "We have food!" and the waving began again in earnest.

Men who had not left their bunks in days gathered their strength to unload the precious provision yet that night. The new, strong settlers did most of the work. Cheese, salted pork and beef, butter, hearty vegetables from home, and beer, ale and rum were all passed up by a "bucket brigade" to the storehouse. Once Newport was comfortable that the unloading was going well, he followed the line to the storehouse to direct proper storage of the goods.

When he walked into the storehouse, he saw Smith. Newport had counted only about a dozen able-bodied men from the original group in the yard and here sat what appeared to be a perfectly healthy man behind bars. Indignation struck him before any other emotion.

"Smith, why are you just sitting there? Why are you not helping?"

Smith merely pointed to the chain and lock.

"What on earth!" bellowed Newport, "What foolishness is this?"

Smith began but did not get far before the Council appeared. "Captain, it seems Captain Archer has usurped my place while I was out exploring and meeting Powhatan, so when I …"

"Captain Newport," Ratcliff interrupted, "you need not concern yourself with this. Smith has been duly tried and found guilty of murder. The execution is set for tomorrow."

"Murder? Who did he murder?"

"Two of his men, two of the men who were on an expedition with him."

"Why should he murder his own men?'

"Well, well, it is a matter of responsibility," chimed in Archer. "He was responsible for the safety of all the men on that expedition and he allowed two of them to be killed."

Newport stared at Archer.

"… yes, killed, by the savages. He was responsible."

"Gentlemen, the English do not hold officers responsible for the death of their men in warfare. On rare occasion I have heard of a man being accused of cowardice if he sacrifices his men for his own safety. You would not charge Mr. Wingfield for the deaths that happen under his command … or me."

Newport stopped and thought, "Speaking of Wingfield, where is he?"

Martin fielded this question, "He is not well, sir." He wisely left out all mention of the overthrow of the elected President and of his being held aboard the *Discovery*.

"Oh, I am sorry to hear that. But back to Smith. Get him out of there! We do not want all these new people to see discord among the leaders on their first day here. Out, I say, now!"

Archer slowly produced his key and opened the lock. Smith had to unwind the chain himself and open the door.

"Your liquor cellar, gentlemen," Smith said with a deep bow toward the now empty locker.

Then he and Newport led the Council out of the storehouse and to the Council Chamber where they rehashed the whole affair until dinner was served. The three Councilmen had to admit to the way they had deposed Wingfield and that he was still being held on the *Discovery*. Newport had seen enough of Wingfield's leadership that he agreed with the change, but he ordered that Wingfield be brought to the fort and allowed to stay so long as he worked like the other gentlemen.

In the end, Newport deposed Archer and reinstated Smith to his seat on the Council. Newport gave the newcomers three days to settle in. Some had brought letters from family for the original group. Some of those letters simply went into Newport's pouch since the addressee was no longer alive.

Housing was a great problem. The houses were planned to hold the original one hundred men. As they died, fewer houses were actually built. Now dwellings that might comfortably hold sixty men had to accommodate one hundred and twenty. It was far too cold to be sleeping outdoors, so men laid wall to wall rolled in their blankets. They were crowded but warm. And for the first time in months, their stomachs were full.

On the fourth day, Newport, who had assigned specific roles to the Councilmen, organized all of the new men and the healthy ones of the original surviving thirty-eight into work units. Shelter was item number one on the list of essential chores. Work crews were sent to cut more framing sticks. Others went to the swamps and cut reeds for mats or thatched roofing. The sailors were set to fishing. One crew was made up of carpenters, both land and ship's carpenters, with a few men for digging footings. Their assignment was to build new houses as fast as they could.

The men who were not yet ready for heavy labor were assigned to inventory everything in the storehouse. For the first time, the large barrels of cloth were opened and measured. The length matched the manifest. The quality of the cloth was another matter. From the lead seals on the bolts, Thomas Hope, a tailor, could tell that the cloth was made in 1603. Based on the date, the cloth was most likely purchased for an uncompleted voyage of the East India Company and had sat in a warehouse in these barrels since. It was moth-eaten and some fell into holes along the folded edges.

The barrels that held the other trade goods had similar markings leading Newport to believe all of these good were leftovers and sent to Jamestown because there would be no cost.

Once the material for the houses was collected, the cutting crews were set to felling larger trees for making masts for ships and the ever-present clapboard. Smith had seen another type of native house in his long trek through many villages and recommended that some of these houses be built too. The house was basically a pit dug six or seven feet into the earth with very short walls of logs above ground and pitched roofs of mat of thatch. So some crews dug pits for houses and, of course, some dug for gold.

January in coastal Virginia had variable weather. Some days the temperature would stay in the thirties and other times it could be in the sixties. So long as the men were active, they were warm. Once the sun set around five in the afternoon, the air would cool into the thirties or forties.

On the fifth day for the new settlers, dinner had been served about half past four, just before dusk. This was the second day these new people had done this type of physical labor and almost everyone had sore muscles and wanted nothing more than to go to bed.

One person from each house lit a candle or an oil lamp from the cook fire to take to the house for light. The next day, Newport guessed that someone had taken their light and fallen asleep without putting it out. Anyone could have knocked it over. However it happened, the night was a horror.

"Fire! Fire!" The panicked cry came from the sentry.

The wind had picked up after sundown and the breeze was pushing the flames from one reed roof to the next. By the time the men woke and got a bucket brigade organized from the partly frozen river, almost every building on the east end of the fort was ablaze.

The noise of the men shouting was drowned out by the roar of the flames. The older houses went up like the dry tinder they were. The materials for the newer ones were still green and moist so they burned slower and some of them could be partly saved. Three small storage building were upwind of the origin of the fire and survived with no more than some blackening from the smoke. The improved church and all of Doctor Hunt's books were lost. The Council Chamber was gone. Pieces of the few tents that were still in use were saved once the men threw water on them. Everyone lost some or all of their personal belongings.

The greatest loss was the storehouse. Most of the food and drink and many of the trade goods were destroyed. A few metal objects were salvaged after the ruins cooled. In one twist of fate, the colony was reduced from hope to imminent starvation.

The palisade was charred and breached in two places, but that at least was mostly still in place. The settlement now consisted of one hundred fifty-eight men, a few building, two and a half walls and some bits of metal.

Powhatan knew of the fire within a day. He honored his relationship with his adopted son and immediately sent food. This time he continued to send supplies every four or five days. On some of these trips to Jamestown, Smith's adopted sister, Pocahontas, came as a special emissary from their father.

The thirty-eight veterans were no longer surprised to see Indians, friendly or not. The men who had just arrived were still impressed.

William Johnson and Richard Belfield were metal refiners. The Virginia Company had sent them to assay minerals before they were shipped back to England. They went on gold digging crews to choose where the best place to dig would be, but mostly they stayed in the fort setting up an office and workshop where they could identify and classify the findings. They were using one of the unburned buildings as their workshop and happened to look out the small window just as the first mission of Indians arrived.

"Indians! Indians! Captain ..." Belfield was pointing madly.

Newport was walking slowly toward the party.

"Calm yourself, Mr. Belfield. They will not beat you with a squash. Here, come with me, you too, Mr. Johnson. It is time you met our neighbors."

Smith was coming from another direction and met Newport just as they reached the party. Newport was about to speak when two large braves stepped aside a bit and a girl stepped forward to say to Smith, "My Brother, I have come to your village to bring gifts from our father."

Newport closed his mouth and looked at Smith. Smith looked at the girl, and then glanced at Newport. Looking back at the girl he spoke to Newport.

"Captain Christopher Newport, may I present the favored daughter of Powhatan and my adopted sister, Pocahontas."

"My sister, this is the famous Captain Newport."

Newport extended his right leg and bowed as he would to English royalty.

"Daughter of the great chief, I welcome you to the town of our good King James."

She smiled and tipped her head slightly.

"Captain Newport, we know you. My father has heard of the fire and he sends gifts of food to his chief-son and his people. Where to put the food?"

She looked inquiringly at Smith, not Newport. He looked at Newport to silently ask permission to take over. Newport nodded.

"Come with me, my brothers. My sister, will you come with me or stay to speak with Captain Newport?"

"I will come to see the gifts delivered."

Smith led the group to one of the unburned buildings and Newport had nothing to do but go along. Everyone in the fort was watching the party by now, either to get their first look at the naturals or to look at the food.

One of the braves said to Smith, "My brother, we would not enter your house. Some of your people should store the gifts."

Smith was not sure if this was protocol or if the braves feared a trap inside the building. The reason did not matter, Smith simply signaled to some of the onlookers to come and put the food inside the building. As the transfer continued, Pocahontas, Smith and Newport continued to talk. Smith started to escort her away from the storage building and to the temporary Council area they had assembled earlier as a meeting spot. As they walked past Josiah, Smith told him, "Find something to offer our guests to eat and drink." Then, more quietly, "If we have nothing, go to the little building and get some of the new food. Be quick."

Smith seated Pocahontas in the best seat. Newport took the seat beside her and Smith stood close by her, as a protective brother should. They spoke of the weather, the fire and food. She asked to tour the ships. She was the picture of a king's daughter come to visit his subjects. Her poise for a girl of eleven or twelve amazed each man who heard her.

Pocahontas did not come with every food mission, but she came often enough that she became a welcome and familiar sight at the fort. The place she had first sat became known as the Princess Seat. Sometimes other women came with the mission and offered to show the men how to prepare the food in the Indian style. For the first time in a year, the James Fort community included women.

With the materials at hand, a house could be built rather quickly. Whether at ground level or in a partial dugout space, the men started by digging postholes and placing limbs of four or five inches in diameter into the holes. There was a post at each corner, on either side of a doorway and at strategic points along a longer wall. At the same time, a crew would be digging out a cellar. The earth was set aside. Lighter studs lined the walls between the larger posts. The set aside earth was turned into mud and spread over this frame to make the walls solid. A light wood frame of flexible saplings was built on the ground and lifted over the structure with long poles and set on forked poles to hold it. The roof was hipped, having the shorter ends also sloped for strength. When mud walls were dry, thatch was added to the roof frame. This style of house was called "wattle and daub", wattle for the sticks and daub for the mud.

As soon as the housing crisis was addressed, the builders turned to replacing the church. This time, it would be a proper church, sixty feet long and twenty-four feet wide with the long side placed in parallel with the gate or river side of the fort. These corner posts were ten inches in diameter with eight feet above the ground level. The church would have a true chancel and a special place for the stone baptismal font that had been sent from Richard Haykutt in England. There would be windows in each ten-foot section of the walls and finally, there would be a proper cross at the apex of the roof.

With the continuing gifts of food, everyone stayed healthy and even the twenty-eight who had been ill got well. Within two weeks of the disaster, all evidence of the fire except the char marks on the palisades was gone and there were as many houses as there had been when this First Supply had arrived.

Newport could now turn his attention to other matters.

CHAPTER 6
Sparkling Dirt

Newport was determined to meet Powhatan. He was also jealous of Smith having achieved a meeting before him, but he realized Smith was the one man who could arrange for him to meet the great chief. On one cold and wet day, he sought out Smith. Smith was in his tent writing in his journal. He tried to keep it every day, but when there was so much to be done, some nights the best he could do was a quick prayer for his family before he fell asleep. On a day when so little could be done outside, he took the opportunity to catch up.

Newport started with a few pleasantries and then got to the point. "You are the only one of us who has met Powhatan. Tell me about him."

"Gladly. He is an impressive man. What is it you wish to know?"

"I need … er … we need for him to not only refrain from attacking, but to actively assist us with food and to exercise his authority over the other tribes to do likewise. The Company thinks this is best accomplished by buying his friendship with gifts. I need to know what kind of gifts will impress him."

Captain Newport, I am not sure you … I mean … the Company understands the mind of the Indian. They exchange gifts to stay on equal footing. To give a gift without a balanced return is to show weakness. Strength, that's what needed here, We must …."

"Smith, take care," Newport snapped to his feet in warning. "You have overstepped your bounds before. Do not do so again!" He paused and then resumed his seat on a rough bench. "Now tell me what type of gift will impress this savage."

Recalling his time in irons aboard the *Susan Constant*, Smith ceased his advice. Neither would he offer an answer that was bound to result in a worst situation with Powhatan. How to find a middle path? Smith played for time to think. He knew Newport meant a gift from England, but Smith started recounting items made in America.

"When I was with the savages for those weeks, I saw a number of local goods offered in exchange. Powhatan seemed most interested in anything that was unique. I particularly remember a bow made of unusual wood and a pipe made of shiny, reddish clay carved in a most fanciful style."

"Fine, fine," interrupted Newport, "he can get those things here. What would he want that only we could give him – something we have brought from England? He may have seen many of our trade goods already. What has he not seen?"

"Sir, it has been some time since I was with him and our goods may well have passed through the nearer tribes to his home camp. The one thing he wants is something we certainly cannot give him and that is our weapons."

Newport opened his mouth to berate Smith again for overstepping. Then it dawned on him that Smith was right in one sense, but that he had also presented Newport with the answer he needed. Yes, there would be danger in giving Powhatan their superior weapons, but if Newport could think of a way to give him a weapon that could not work, there would be no danger. If he offered a musket, but no shot or powder, Powhatan would have the prestige of a unique gift with no risk. And Newport could hold out the promise of shot and powder in future negotiations. It was a clever plan.

"I see your point, Smith. Thank you," and with no further word, Newport wandered back toward the Council area.

Those who were taken in by the Company line that said the Indians would naturally want to support the new, superior and benevolent colonists took Powhatan's continued generosity as their due. The more cynical, or maybe wise, colonists could not understand why Powhatan would send food to keep them alive when, by withholding provisions, the colonist would surely die out or leave. Why would Powhatan want the colonists to stay and thrive? It was a very good questions but one that was easily overridden by the contentment of a full belly.

Braves with food came every few days. On the days the women came, some of the men paid particular attention. Men, especially men who had not been around women for many, many months, always noticed women, but the Powhatan women drew exceptional stares since they wore very little clothing. It being winter, they usually had a cloak of deer hide or a blanket for warmth, but under the cloak they wore only an apron-like girdle and moccasins. Glances ranging from appreciative to lustful were common.

Women were not sent to the fort, they chose to come. At first they were merely curious. Those who liked what they saw came back. Pocahontas was one of these women. At first the visits were short, but overtime, they stretched out. Minor friendships started between some of the broader-minded men and braves.

Several women set up a business with some of the men. They fashioned beads from the shell of a mussel that lived in the waters around Jamestown but not in the water of Chesapeake Bay. These beads would be good for trading with tribes who lived near the bay or up the Potomac River. These women created a little factory area in the fort where they would chip off flakes from inside these shells, cut them into little disks, use a sharp bit of quartz to drill a hole and then spin the disk around and file the edge down until the tiny object took the shape of a bead. These women traded the beads to the men who, in turn, would use these unique beads to trade outside the Jamestown area.

Certain men showed special attention to individual women. They gave small gifts and, in exchange, the women started to bring special dishes of food. In a few cases, this odd courtship resulted in a man and an Indian woman making some arrangement. One woman might simply provide food while another would move in like a housekeeper for a group of men. Most of the women went home to their village each night, but a few set up more permanent arrangements, sometimes with just one man.

For example, Edward Pising had joined Smith in some of his explorations. In his time with Smith, he adopted Smith's attitude toward the Indians. Indians were people worthy of knowing but not worthy of trust. Their culture was to be admired and there was much to learn from them. So Edward felt nothing strange in noticing the small woman with sweet face just as he would have noticed a pretty young girl on the streets of his town in Kent. Edward was a carpenter by trade but Smith liked having him as part of his extended "squad," the small group of trained fighting men that had grown from the original company of Smith's Lincolnshire boys, the Cassen brothers and Josiah Tucker. So Smith would have eyes and ears on the fort, he assigned at least one of them to guard duty at all times. The only exception was when Smith had them all out with him on an expedition. Then he relied on Doctor Hunt to tell him anything of interest that happened.

Smith's squad tended to live close by each other and one of the houses that was rebuilt was designed specifically for these men. It was situated along the riverside palisade near the East bulwark, close to hand in case they were needed to defend the fort from that point. There were three rooms and several men lived in each room.

A room was seventeen feet deep and was at least seventeen feet wide. Sometimes blankets or other partitions divided the space. The inside walls showed the main support of the house. Other boards could be nailed to these supports to form shelves or to support a row of pegs on which personal belongings were stored. There were some cots but many men still slept on their blankets on the ground, often with reeds below the blanket for comfort. This house had better tables and stools than most because of Edward's woodworking skills. One stool even had a back and had some notoriety as Edward's chair, the only chair owned by a commoner in the whole colony.

Edward lived in the room at the west end of the building. He had two bunkmates, but since one was usually on guard duty, most often only two were there at a time. One day, both roommates were out and about and the sweet-faced Indian girl was visiting. Edward had carved a comb from a fallen beech limb. He was a good craftsman with wood and the piece was delicate and precise. The wood was pale and had a tight, smooth grain, so that, even with no decoration, it was a lovely thing.

Edward walked to where the sweet-face girl was putting down her bundles.

"Hello," he said simply.

She straightened up, turned to stand squarely in front of him, and smiled just a bit.

"I made this for you," he said extending his hand slowly and unfolding his fingers to reveal the golden comb.

Her intake of breath was short and audible. Her hands instinctively came to her chest and she stared at the beautiful gift. Her head came up and she looked Edward in the eye.

"For me?" she said in her language, but the meaning was clear.

"Yes, for you," and he ever so slowly reached for her right hand with his left, pulled it down and placed the comb in it. He did not want to let go of her hand. He had not touched a woman in over a year and a half and the sensation was delicious.

Pocahontas had come with this party. She was in her Princess seat, as usual, talking with Smith. Some wondered about this odd friendship between a girl and a twenty-five year old man. But those who knew something of young women understood this common rite of passage, a girl's first crush on her hero. The hero might be an older brother, a teacher, a neighbor, or, as in this case, someone who has done a special service for her family. She feels a strong connection with this hero and what could be a stronger connector than having saved his life. That feeling of connection will, as a part of the girl becoming a woman, mature into various feelings, respect, admiration, and love. Pocahontas was a year or two from becoming a woman. For now, she was inexplicably drawn to this man who was unique in her experience.

Even those who could accept or ignore Pocahontas' choice still were suspicious of Smith's motives. An uncontrolled young man or an unscrupulous older man might take advantage of a girl's adoration. Most men had heard of at least one situation where a groom, an uncle, a cousin or family friend had ruined a young girl's marriage prospects by succumbing to this type of hero worship. Being aware of these suspicions, Smith took every opportunity to point out that by keeping the favored daughter of Powhatan happy, he was solidifying his friendship with the chief himself and that his personal friendship was to the benefit of the whole colony.

Pocahontas and Smith were basking in the winter sun, laughing at some small pleasantry when Josiah walked by. Smith called to him, "Josiah, fetch us a bite and some of that small beer they brought."

Josiah said, "Right away, sir," and walked quickly to one of the temporary storehouses. He put the requested refreshments on a large piece of flat bark covered with a bit of almost clean sailcloth, all proper serving vessels either having been destroyed in the fire, in the possession of a gentleman or on a ship.

When he returned, Smith said, "Keep her company a bit, lad. I do not like how those goods are being stored," and he was off across the compound. Josiah had a natural ease with girls and he wasted no time in getting to know Pocahontas. After a brief introduction of himself and checking that the food was to her liking, the conversation wandered until it landed on the subject of games.

Pocahontas explained the rudiments of a ball game played only with the feet. When it was his turn to explain a game, he realized he had not played any organized games on the farm and only darts in London, which did not seem suitable for a young woman. However, he was very limber and thought the tumbling he had taught himself would qualify as a game.

He stood up and said, "Can you do this?" and performed a perfect cartwheel.

Pocahontas was entranced. Running and jumping were regular pursuits of all Indian children, but this was magical. "Again," she demanded.

Josiah obliged, only this time he did three in a row. Pocahontas would have nothing but to learn this wonderful new thing and so Josiah showed her how to place her hand on the ground, how to push off, and how to land. When her legs did not go straight up, he guided her until she did one perfectly. His bunkmates and other young men gathered around, envious of the opportunity to touch the skin of an essentially naked girl. Pocahontas squealed with delight with her first success and proceeded to do two more somersaults in rapid succession.

"Together?" she proposed.

"On three," he said and counted "One, two, three." Off he went and Pocahontas just stood there.

"Oh, sorry." This time he explained by holding up one, two and then three fingers so she would understand the words. Actually, she had understood the concept as soon as he started after saying the word he had indicated, but she bore the explanation as the princess she was.

"On three," he said again, and then silently went through the one, two three fingers again. "One, two, three." They executed three cartwheels in a row in perfect unison. By now they had drawn a crowd including a much bemused John Smith.

Smith moved to meet them at the end of their path. "I asked you to keep her company, not make a spectacle of yourself."

Pocahontas spoke up before Josiah could, "No, John Smith, this is good!"

"More, Jo-si-ah?" she asked.

He stammered a bit not knowing who to please, Pocahontas or his mentor, Smith. Smith made the decision for him.

"Go ahead. If it pleases my sister, it pleases me."

The two set off again playing follow the leader and soon other youngsters joined in. A few older men appealed to Smith that the boys should be working, but Smith told them that pleasing Pocahontas, and indirectly her father Powhatan, was more important than any work right now.

The children, for during this interlude, they were again children, whirled until they were exhausted.

The food deliveries continued. The type of food varied with the seasons. In the deep winter, immediately after the fire, it was dried food from the previous harvest. The only fresh food was occasional venison. As the spring came on, the venison stopped. The Indians understood the circle of life and respected the fact that spring was breeding time for deer. Fish became the main food. By late March, winter squash was beginning to come in. From then on, fresh vegetables became a main part of the provisions. Once breeding season was done, stags could be shot, but the does were to be protected until the fawns were weaned. Fowl was in season as soon as the young had hatched. Then came this year's corn. The Indians ate well.

The boys in camp were entranced with the maidens who came with the provisioning parties. Some were so young they had not been ready to appreciate girls before they left England, so this was their very first attempt at courtship. For those that were a bit older, they were still in their hungry years and the presence of an attractive, or even an unattractive girl was intoxicating. It was these older boys, including Josiah, who stumbled on the "love me" game.

It was fun to teach the girls English words and phrases. The general subjects quickly moved to teasing about kissing and love. The boys thought it very clever to tease the girls by saying, "Do you love me?" or "Do you not love me?" Sometimes, once the wildflowers bloomed, they would pick the petals as young people had done for generations saying, "You love me, you love me not." The girls would giggle, delighted.

The girls went back to their village and explained the game to their friends, but not understanding the language, they confused the words a bit and the common phrase became, "Love you not me?" It all became a great joke among the young men and Indian maidens, so much so that it became a common greeting. Their elders did not understand the game.

The sailors picked up on this game too. They were extremely bored having very little to do. They were sharing the Indian's largess and the longer they stayed the more food they ate and beer they drank. Due to their many travels, the sailors had an unusual collection of trinkets to trade to the Indians. They were not trading to get a good exchange, they were trading to amuse themselves, and so they were willing to give even the coveted copper for just a small amount of corn. The Indians were just as amused by the English sailors and their inability to strike a good trade. Indians thought a man who could not fight to be a coward and a man who could not trade to be a fool. But the sailors would leave soon, so their reputation with the Indians was not the critical matter. It was that this uneven trading hurt the rate of exchange for the settlers. Whereas Smith traded a few bits of copper for many bushels of corn in 1607, now the same amount of copper would fetch only a bushel or two. The metallurgists who had come to America had brought tens of thousands of strips of copper with them in hopes of finding zinc locally and blending it with the copper to make brass to export to England. No zinc had yet been found and many of these copper strips found their way into the hands of settlers as trade goods. What should have been worth a fortune to the Indians was now nearly worthless.

The sailors were taken in because the Indians seemed to enjoy this trading game so much. Even Newport was taken in by this overly friendly time with the Indians.

Newport had fought the French, the Spanish, the Dutch and the Irish. European enemies were just that, enemies. They were not friends one week and foes the next. The European mind dealt only in black and white, ally or enemy. The Indian mind worked differently. There were no nations or states with century-old borders and injuries to be fought over. There were no standing armies to keep busy. A raid on a neighbor, not of your tribe, had a purpose. It may be to get food or to capture women to get new blood for your tribe. It was not to possess the land on which they lived. No man possessed the land. When the raid was over, the two tribes could again live side by side peacefully until the next raid. The Indians could regard a person as a friend one minute and a foe the next and find no confusion in the switch, or in switching back. Captured enemies might be killed or adopted into the tribe as Smith had been. The European mind could not conceive of this dual thinking.

Since the Indians were being so helpful, Newport thought this surely was the perfect time to meet Powhatan. At the end of February, Newport insisted that Smith escort him to Werowocomoco. Smith, who was never completely taken in by the friendly front of the Indians, took thirty or forty armed men to act as bodyguards.

Werowocomoco was only 12 miles across land but Newport wanted to make a show so they went down the James and up the Prince Henry (York) River. They took *Discovery* and a barge. Smith took the barge with twenty men in quilted armor. This soft armor, called jacks was usually used on a ship. They all wore swords and carried muskets, though still very few could shoot with any accuracy. If he could have done so, Newport would have outfitted each man in plate armor to impress Powhatan, but the armor was in the storehouse and, though the armor itself survived, the leather straps burned in fire. Tailors did not work with leather as a rule and there was very little spare leather anyway, but two men who had hunted a lot in England and tried their hand at tanning, were working with the tailors to see what could be done to replace the straps.

Powhatan's village was huge. There were over 300 huts and longhouses and a center "town square" bigger than all of James Fort. Few towns in England had 500 working age men, but there were 500 braves surrounding Powhatan's hut for this formal visit of the infamous Smith. Smith and his twenty men had come up from the river leaving Newport and the Discovery at anchor. Newport was not sure of this strategy. Smith was really more interested in the safety of the party, however he was smart enough to put it to Newport as a matter of prestige.

"The chief does not go first, Captain, a herald goes before him to ensure that all is correct for him to attend. I will be your herald."

Newport accepted the idea. Though everything seemed peaceful, he would rather Smith ran into an ambush than himself.

As Smith entered the town, he saw that Powhatan had set out a symbol of peace and in such measure that it also emphasized his wealth. There were forty or fifty piles of fresh bread laid on platters outside of Powhatan's hut. The 500 warriors gave two shouts of greeting for Smith. They formed into a ceremonial aisle for Smith to walk down, reminiscent of the gauntlet he had first walked down. He mused over how small a step it can be from captive to honored guest.

Powhatan was seated in his hut on the same twelve mats. Forty of his wives, painted and bejeweled in their finest, stood around him. Powhatan shifted his position in an obvious move to make a place for John to sit beside him.

Opposunoquonuske, queen of Appomattox, was the regal woman who had brought Smith water to wash on his first visit, though he did not know her name until now. She again brought him water as he settled down in Powhatan's hut. In this less strained situation, he revised his opinion of her and thought her a "comely young women."

They chatted for a short time while women brought refreshments. Smith showed him the gifts sent to Powhatan by his friends of the Virginia Company. The gifts were useless, but pretty and unique and therefore of value to Powhatan. There was a suit of red woolen cloth, a high "sugarloaf" hat like the one King James wore and a white greyhound.

The greyhound interested him most. Any white animal was to be revered. Besides the color, this dog had a sleek shape and fine head that he held high. It was a dog for a king.

Powhatan and Smith went through an exchange that both knew would follow a prescribed flow. Powhatan asked, "Where are the cannons that you agreed to give me?"

Smith answered, "Rawhunt refused them."

Powhatan knew the truth, that the cannon were too heavy to move, and he respected Smith for knowing how to play the game.

Smith's twenty-man bodyguard came in two by two. So many guns were very impressive to everyone who saw them and particularly to Powhatan. Powhatan said they should put the guns on the ground to respect him. Smith replied that only enemies would ask them to do that. Again Smith had shown he knew how to play the game. The conversation continued and by the time Smith and his men got back to the river, the tide had gone out and the barge was stuck in the mud. Powhatan invited them to stay over. Smith feared an ambush, but the night was quiet and all was well.

The next morning, Newport and his men came ashore. Schrivener, Gosnold's personal recruit and a friend of Smith, was with Newport. Powhatan asked Newport the same questions that he had asked of Smith. "You bring your men to guard you. We are friends, send your men away."

Newport sent the entire bodyguard back to the river. Powhatan kept his own counsel, but Smith understood that Newport had lost face by being so weak.

Smith and Powhatan had arranged a ceremony to cement the friendship between Powhatan and Newport. Newport stood up and motioned to a teenaged boy named Thomas Savage. Savage was a bright boy always up for an adventure. Smith and Newport had asked around to see if anyone would be interested in staying with the chief for a time to learn about the language and the culture and thereby become more valuable to the colony. Savage took the challenge, thinking he would stay a short while and come back when he liked.

"Great Powhatan, I give you my son Thomas Savage to stay with you as a sign of my trust and friendship."

Savage turned quickly to stare at Newport. Visiting was one thing. Being given to Powhatan was quite another. Newport waved his hand at the boy to quiet any protest. Savage took the hint and said nothing, for now.

Powhatan then played his part.

"Chief Newport, I give you my son, Namontack to stay with you as a sign of my trust and friendship." Namontack was really Powhatan's servant. He was no more Powhatan's son than Savage was Newport's son, but the proprieties had been observed and each side had a hostage to hold against misbehavior on the other side. Both hostages had a special facility with languages. They were good choices to spend time in the other culture, as they would be able to understand more quickly than most.

The exchange of gifts continued. Newport offered twelve copper pots for corn. Powhatan offered thirty bushels of corn. This was one tenth of the amount Smith would have commanded, but Newport accepted. Again he had lost face with Powhatan for poor trading.

Powhatan was in awe of some things these English could do. He knew Smith could communicate through bits of paper. He knew the power of the thundersticks. But individual English, especially this Newport, did not impress him at all.

Smith was furious with Newport for ruining the rate of exchange. He knew he had to do something to get the upper hand with Powhatan before this trading ended. Smith brought out a handful of blue beads, the color of sky. He told Powhatan that only princes wear that color in England. He acted very reluctant to part with the beads. The longer Smith delayed, the more corn Powhatan offered. In the end, Powhatan gave 300 bushel of corn for two handfuls of cheap blue glass beads. The balance of payment had been restored.

The Company did not want another fiasco about false gold so they sent the two refiners, William Dawson and Abraham Ransack, with Newport on this trip. Dawson and Ransack had evaluated each of the piles of rocks that had been left on the shore from the last trip. They found nothing of interest. Then they started their own exploration. Since the colony was on peaceful terms with the Indians at this time, the two could wander far afield to look for minerals. They had no success until they looked in the mud when the tide was out. There they found rocks that were promising. If there were ore-bearing rocks in the tidal north shore, it would suggest that the ore had washed downstream from upriver. The possibility that there was gold enough that it would simply wash downstream would make the Virginia Company very happy.

At John Martin's insistence, they did load some of the rocks that had been collected by him in the first year. The refiners had made some preliminary tests on the rocks they had found in the mud and were able to extract a mineral that could be gold. They loaded as much of that ore as they could. After fourteen weeks, the *John and Francis* was ready to sail.

Smith cared very little about the fate of the ore, however he was thrilled about the people who were leaving with Newport. The ineffectual Wingfield and the irritating Gabriel Archer were headed to England. Archer was officially going to "seek someplace of better employment." Unofficially, he was in disgrace.

Newport knew King James was delighted with curiosities. He already had quite a menagerie, so Newport took two tortoises to add to the party. He also took two particularly perfect ears of corn, a crop uncommon in England.

As a parting gift, Powhatan sent twelve turkeys to Newport. He sent word that he wanted twelve swords in return. Newport sent the swords. Besides Smith's personal warning, there was a specific directive in the Virginia Company orders not to put any English weapon, especially guns, in the hands of the natives. Smith had refused Powhatan's requests for weapons time after time. Now, when he was on his way home and in no personal danger, Newport broke the long-standing order. Smith was livid.

Newport had loaded the best food onto the ship to provide for them on the trip to England. And there was another stash of valuables on the ship. The sailors had sold their rations of corn to the settlers for their few valuables, rings, china, candlesticks and such. Then they had sold these things to the Indians for furs. The furs trapped in the winter season had exceptionally lush pelts and the sailors could sell them in London at very high prices. The furs were stored in hold in bundles packed to be as water proof as possible.

On April 10th, 1608, less than a year since landing at Jamestown, ore, food, furs and infamous Councilors were on their way to England.

Ten days later, the alarm sounded to indicate a ship had been sighted. It was the lost *Phoenix* under Captain Francis Nelson. After the storm, he had returned to the West Indies and stayed to re-provision. The forty settlers on the Phoenix were in good condition. They were, sadly, unused to manual labor, but they did manage to clear an additional four acres of ground and plant corn. They also helped to build a few houses for themselves.

In the growing season, life in the settlement was the best it had been. The Indians still came to the fort and friendships grew along with the crops and new buildings.

Edward Pising's body filled the doorway casting everything into darkness. He moved slowly to the bench against the far wall and slumped down. Bess left the hearth, took two steps to him and took his weapons. He liked this type of attention. He never spoke of it but privately he knew it made him feel like he was a gentleman with his own house and servants.
Edward and the small, sweet-faced Indian girl had meet twice more after the day he gave her the comb. On the second visit, he showed her his living quarters. On the third visit, she had brought a few things of her own, a cooking pot, some herbs, and a dish of corn bread made especially for him. After that, the visits became more regular and more similar. She would bring special food she had made or cook for him in his room. After only a few weeks, Edward had come to expect the woman Becomanuck, whom he called Bess, to be there for him.

Bess deposited his dagger, musket and shot pouch in the corner near the hearth and returned to check on dinner. She had brought a fresh turtle yesterday when she returned from her village. She would have made stew with only the turtle but the Tassantassas, white man, Edward insisted on this pig meat, so she would combine them. She had roasted the pig meat on a skewer rather than put it in the pot, otherwise the strong pig flavor would overpower the more delicate turtle. She would have to put it in soon so it would soften enough for Edward to eat it with his bad teeth. Bess always put greens in her stew and her teeth were at least sounder than those of any Tassantassas who seemed only to want meat and corn.

Edward usually burst into the room in full bluster wanting drink and food. Today he was quiet and stared at his boots. Perhaps he had learned some manners and was waiting for a formal greeting, as he should. She would try, in English.

"Good day, Edward." Bess said with a slight bow of her head.

"Not bloody good in any way!" Edward growled.

"Do you know what that bloody council wants now? They want the soldiers to help move the burned poles of the palisades. It is not enough that we protect these lazy fools, now we have to do the dirty work too.

Bess tried to be sympathetic.

"Bess is sorry Edward is not pleased."

"Pleased! God's blood! I am not pleased! I have to go back right now. I just came in to drop off the musket. They said to put on our oldest clothes, HA! These are my only clothes! Now they are going to be covered in soot from those burned poles. Why use the old ones? Let the gents cut new ones! What will they think of next?"

Edward sat forward on the bench putting his large hands on his knees. He stretched his back saying, " Smells good. I will be back."

He stood and the room darkened again as his wide shoulders passed through the doorway.

That had been the longest spoken exchange Bess had had with Edward since she had come to the fort. Maybe she would stay here, at least for a few days, instead of going to the village each night. Other village women had found a good life with a Tassantassas. Maybe she would too. She certainly liked cooking inside on bad days, but this mud house was too hot. Maybe she would go home tonight after all.

Edward joined his fellow soldiers and a band of laborers. They went to the portion of the palisade that had been charred. The posts looked upright and stable, but when two of the laborers started to pull on one it fell toward the group of soldiers with no notice.

"Move!" one shouted. The indirect instruction only caused confusion. People ran in every direction. Edward ran into another soldier who was going the other way. He fell backwards and the teetering log fell on him. The entire crew started back to help Edward when someone saw the neighboring logs start to rock. "Stay Back!" The next two logs also fell, one outside the fort and the other onto Edward.

Again they tried to reach him. They rolled the two blackened logs off. Edward's skull was fractured and his chest was crushed. There was no way to tell which had killed him, but it was certain that he was dead.

The stew was nearly cold. She had taken the pot from the coals long ago, yet she was still waiting for Edward to return. The room was dark now except for the glow of the cooking embers and a small rush light, so she did not notice when the soldier came to the doorway until he spoke.

"Edward is gone," he said simply.

Bess was not certain of the English word "gone". She thought it had to do with leaving a place, so she moved her arm in an arc opening her hand in a universal gesture of going.

"No, not going," the man imitated her motion, "dead", and he moved his two hands outward palms down. That was not a sign Bess knew for sure but when the solider mumbled "Sorry" and left, she understood.

Then he was back.

"Almost forgot. I was sent to fetch his musket."

The soldier looked around briefly, moved to the corner slowly to keep as far from Bess as the space allowed, grabbed the musket and quickly left.

Bess noticed he had not taken the shot bag Edward carried with the musket or Edward's dagger. She thought about calling after the soldier and then she considered taking these things for her village, but they belonged with Edward. If he had passed to the Great Spirit, he might need them and she was sure his people would send them with him. He was not a bad Tassantassas, not a bad man.

Bess picked up her baskets and her few other belongings, more than she remembered bringing here. She thought about taking the stew but it would be difficult to carry and Edward might need that for his after journey too. Her arms full of things, she stooped to get one last pouch of herbs. A bead pulled off the pouch, but she did not want to put everything down to pick it up. She was going home.

CHAPTER 7
Reducing the Fort

Each time Pocahontas came with the food mission, she made a point of seeing John Smith and Josiah Tucker, Smith because he was her brother-hero and Josiah because they were of an age and had become, simply, friends.

Shortly after Newport sailed, Powhatan sent the same gift of twelve turkeys to Smith with the same request for twelve swords in return. Smith flatly refused. Powhatan respected the strength and courage of Smith, however he had decided that he needed to have the same weapons as the English and that he would get them one way or the other.

He gave orders that his people, any of his people, were to get swords by any means including capturing them or stealing them. This command launched a series of small attacks and skirmishes. Perhaps because of the prestige it would bring, the early attempts were made against Smith himself.

In May, Smith was out checking on the progress of the corn crop west of the fort. Two dozen braves came across the neck of the island and worked their way around in the woods that still surrounded this field on three sides. Smith heard a blue jay screech much louder than usual and before he could sort out why, the braves came at him in a rush. Smith was armed with his standard military sword, but while he was soldiering in the Ottoman Empire, he had developed the habit of also carrying a scimitar-like blade called a falchion in his belt.

Seeing four braves coming at him through the man-high corn, he drew his long sword in his right hand and his personal blade in his left. This two-handed style had saved him many times before and served him well now. The falchion had a heavy hilt, which he used to good effect in smashing noses, ears and heads while swinging the longer sword in a large arc to keep the braves on his right at a distance. As soon as the first three on his left fell out to nurse their injuries, he used the opening to run for the fort.

Not all the Indians pursued him. Ten stayed with the injured. The one he had hit in the ear took up the chase along with nine of the others. Smith ran only as far as a small hillock where a tuft of scrub brush had been left. It was not tall enough to provide cover for an attack but it was deep enough to make it difficult for anyone to reach him from behind. Having taken up this defensive position, he picked his targets, slashing the cheek of the first brave with a backhand and catching the second with the return swing. At the same time, he thrust at a brave coming from the left and caught him in the side. He fell. The man with the sore ear also came from the left and received the hilt squarely in his face for his trouble. He dropped unconscious. The other five, who had delayed a bit to check on the condition of relatives hurt in the first attack, now slowed and checked with each other to consider a new plan of attack. Three of the four who were newly injured circled back a short way to join their companions. A few words were exchanged. Head shaking told Smith that not all were committed to have more of their blood shed.

Three refused to continue and started back toward the first group. Five, including two who were already bloodied formed a semicircle about fifteen feet from Smith. They approached slowly and in unison. Smith waited until they were about ten feet away and then dashed behind the brush hill. This unexpected maneuver confused the Indians and they broke their formation. One ran at him from the right and two from the left. Two chose to come straight through the brush. The brush had been left there because it had grown around a rotted tree stump. As the braves charged into the brush, their feet landed on the rotting timber which collapsed giving them both injured legs and leaving them on the ground tangled in the crumbling wood.

Smith spun toward the one coming alone and surprisingly ran toward him, tripping him as he ran by. Of the two now coming from behind him, one stumbled over this falling comrade and the other managed a slight blow to Smith's right shoulder before Smith spun again hitting the Indian's temple with the hilt of the falchion. This brave, like the other, fell unconscious.

At all this destruction from one man, the thirteen who had been watching from a safe distance fled the field. Seven braves were on the ground within a few feet of the brush hill. Smith thrust his long sword into its scabbard, went to one brave who was just extricating himself from the rotting log, grabbed him by the hair and held the falchion to his neck. Smith knew enough of the language to say, "Up, all up, come with me or he dies."

The Indians who had held back had melted into the trees. Those close by understood enough of Smith's command that they supported the two unconscious men and all hobbled toward the fort. The sentries had not observed this fight because the trees near the river had interrupted their line of sight. As soon as the first Indians came out from behind these trees, the sentry cried an alarm. Then, seeing that Smith was herding the party, he yelled for reinforcements.

In only a few minutes, all seven braves were sitting on the ground near the Council area being guarded by eight soldiers and watched by almost everyone in camp.

Albertson, the perfumer who had become Wooton's right-hand man, looked at the injuries of the Indians. He called Wotton to do what he could to straighten the broken nose of one Indian. He declared the others to be sore but fine without treatment.

Smith was confused as to why so many Indians would band together just to attack him, yet come at him hand-to-hand rather then shoot him from cover. He needed some answers.

He asked the group, "Why did you attack me?' No answer. "What did you want from me?" No answer. "Who told you to come for me?" Nothing.

Smith thought for a few minutes. Then he ordered that the braves be separated.

Sweeping his arm in a circle toward the guards he ordered, "Each of you take one of these men to a place where they cannot see this spot. Be sure they can hear clearly." Each guard pulled a brave up by his arm and marched him toward a building. One went to the storehouse, one to each of the small storage buildings, and two had to be taken into private houses. Smith waited five minutes and then ordered the eighth guard to fire a musket shot.

Smith walked to the nearest storage hut and entered.

"I have shot the brave with the broken nose. Tell me what I want to know or I will kill you next."

This man shouted at Smith and tried to jump at him, but the guard hit him in the stomach with the butt of the musket and he doubled over and sat down hard.

"Tie his hands and stand guard over him until I send orders."

Smith then went to the next building and repeated the threat. This man was one who had injured his leg in the rotten log. He was sweating and likely in a great deal of pain. Perhaps it was only fear or perhaps it was fear and pain combined. Whatever the reason, the threat worked. He told Smith that Powhatan had ordered all his people to find ways to steal swords or other weapons. It had been "broken nose's" idea to take Smith's own sword as a sign of valor.

Smith gave orders that all seven men should be collected in the half finished *corp de guard*, a small building in the center of the compound that would be used as a type of guardhouse. When finished, they would store the weapons there and the soldiers and sentries could use it as a gathering place. The building had its stick walls but no roof. He ordered two guards to stand at the door and one to patrol around the building. He did not want these men to escape.

Smith went to the sailcloth lean-to he had called home since the fire. Personally, he had lost very little in the fire. In the first place, as a soldier, he was accustomed to traveling and so had few clothes. He took a leather haversack with him on campaigns in which he carried most of his belongings. Having instinctively grabbed the haversack along with his weapons on the night of the fire, he still had his few key valuables. Smith was an avid journalist and he now took out his journal, pen and ink block.

He recorded the events of the day and considered the implications of Powhatan's new policy. Smith never completely trusted the natives of any place he visited. These naturals had shown themselves to be both savage and civilized. The recent good will shown by providing food after the fire had lulled the colonists into a sense that all was well. Smith chastised himself for lowering his own guard. Still, he felt a sense of betrayal. He had played well and fairly with Powhatan. The chief had no new reason to reverse his position and harm the English. Yet, in the end, it was to the advantage of the English to be on good terms with Powhatan. Smith's instinct was to use strength to restore Powhatan's respect, and even fear, of the English. Where in all these thoughts was the key to what his next step should be?

To help sort out his thoughts, Smith began a letter to his distant cousin William Smith back in Lincolnshire. Using his journal to jog his memory, he gave a short history of the colony from the day they had landed. To help his cousin understand the geography, he drew a small map of the area and included a sketch of the triangle fort with three bulwarks. Smith told his cousin, who was a farmer, about the high ground they had cleared and cultivated. He told about the process of planting the new crop maize in two ridges. He proudly told him the corn had grown to be man-high by July. To show his cousin where this field was located, he drew a large square to the north of the fort. After six pages, Smith's hand was cramping and his path forward with Powhatan was still unclear, so he put the pages away and went out to check on the prisoners.

He was walking around the guardhouse checking for weaknesses in the construction when he heard the sentry shout, "Indians!"

All the leaders from the fort converged on the north bulwark. Ratcliff was standing behind Smith shouting at the sentry.

"What now?"

"I cannot say, sir, three braves at the edge of the path from the woods. They seem to be waiting. I see no weapons."

Ratcliff took the opportunity to exercise authority over Smith.

"Captain, go up there and give me your opinion."

Smith climbed to the rampart. As soon as Smith appeared, the center of the three Indians waved an arm slowly above his head. He continued to wave as the three started to walk toward the fort.

"I believe they have come to talk, President Ratcliff. Shall I go out to them?"

"Take two musketeers and go make sure of their intent. If they wish to talk, bring them to me."

Smith picked his two most trusted men, Josiah and William Cassen. They armed themselves and went out the gate and around to the north side of the fort to meet the emissaries. Indeed they had come to talk. Powhatan had heard that seven of his men were being held in the fort and that some may be injured. He wanted the men returned. Smith said he would escort them into the fort so long as they carried no weapons. The leader and one man gave their knives to the third man who was told to wait outside. The leader also told him to move to the near woods to wait and, if he and the other man were not back when the sun touched the trees, to go back to Powhatan and tell him what had happened. Smith did not catch all of that exchange.

As the Indians conferred, Smith apprised his men of his thoughts.

"Powhatan's main camp is too far for even swift runners to have brought the news of the capture to him by now, much les for these men to have come from Powhatan. Perhaps they have a way to send messages we have yet to discover."

Josiah suggested, "Maybe Powhatan is not at home. Maybe he is visiting a closer camp."

"Possibly," said Smith, "or these men may be using his name without his knowledge. Keep alert, fellows. Something is not right here."

After repeating the request attributed to Powhatan to Ratcliff and the rest of the Council (translated by Smith), the emissaries were dismissed and taken under guard to see their comrades.

With little discussion, the Council decided not to return the men, at least not until they could negotiate some trade in the favor of the English. Smith approved and volunteered to tell them the decision.

For several days the captives languished in the little stockade while life at the fort returned to normal. The men continued to collect cedar wood and put it aboard the *Phoenix*. The building program continued. The thatched roof for the guardhouse was even put in place right over the captives' heads. As no food was coming from Powhatan, Smith went to the Council to get permission to organize hunting and fishing parties. Captain Nelson spent most of his time with the Council and spoke up as if he were a Councilor himself.

Nelson said, "Why do you not dispatch these heathens? Have we not learned in Ireland and Holland, not to mention the Indies, that to leave a native soldier alive is to commit to fighting him again? We should show strength! Kill them in sight of their fellows!"

John Martin, who had never recovered his full health since his first illness in 1607, had a different view.

"We have found bits of gold bearing ore here, Captain Nelson, but we have yet to find its source. I believe we will need the Indians to show us that source. It is not wise to break relations with them altogether."

Ratcliff ventured no opinion of his own, but looked to Smith.

Smith obliged, "Captain, I agree that a show of strength is most necessary. However, I also agree with Captain Martin that we need to keep a level of cordial relations with Powhatan and his people, for the gold, to be sure, but more for food. Since they have stopped supplying us, our stockpile of provisions has been dropping at an alarming rate. I do not see how we can survive this winter without their help. What we need is a middle course, strength without an irreparable break."

They talked more, with each man repeating his position in a variety of ways. But it was Powhatan who offered the out they needed when he finally sent a party led by two known emissaries, Rawhunt and Pocahontas.

They also brought a deer. One deer was not a lot for all the colonists, but it was a show of good faith and the English took it as such. Pocahontas entered the fort and went to the spot of her Princess seat. The seat itself had been destroyed in the fire, but Josiah noticed the need and quickly brought up a rough bench he had constructed just that week. She tilted her head to Josiah in thanks and sat regally and silently.

Rawhunt was sent to do the talking. He indicated the many people, mostly women and children, who had come with them. He said these were the relatives of the captive men and that their families needed them in order to hunt for them.

"No harm was meant to you personally, Captain Smith. The Great Chief Powhatan thought that Captain Newport had made a bargain, twelve turkeys for twelve swords and that when you, esteemed Captain, refused the same offer that you were declaring a game. It was only a game. Please, return our men so they can provide for their families."

Smith knew the story of the game was a lie, but it was a convenient out. Powhatan could play the trade game very well.

Ratcliff, aware of the rank involved, turned to Pocahontas and asked, "Do you wish the men to be returned?"

She had been ordered by her father not to beg, but to maintain the status of a Princess. She was learning the game too.

"It would be the act of a friend."

Ratcliff and Martin both looked at Smith. Nelson noticed the silent exchange and decided the other men deferred to Smith in matters about these naturals. Smith gave a slight nod, and then quickly lifted his hand just a bit. "Princess, we will confer," announced Ratcliff and the three councilors walked away a little.

Smith began, "It is a good way to settle the matter, but we can do even more. Let us say we are not doing this for the families but only for the sake of Pocahontas. She will be indebted to us, personally indebted, a debt of honor. You understand that, do you not, gentlemen?"

They looked at each other and said nothing.

"Oh, and to make a greater show of dominance, let us require that they pray to our God. And let us attend the service in all the armor and weaponry we can muster. There are a great many people here who will be most impressed and take word back through unofficial channels that the English are too powerful to conquer."

"Very good, Smith," said Martin, "very good. As we go back, I shall move in the direction of Doctor Hunt and tell him he needs to make arrangements."

And so it was. The prisoners were reunited with their waiting families. All were told to meet at the unfinished church in a quarter hour. The men went in shifts to put on all the armor they had and to gather swords, pikes, and muskets. The sight of almost a hundred men in metal suits awed the Indians, young and old. When these metal men knelt to pray to their God, the Indians thought that God must be powerful indeed.

After the service, the men lined up in two rows, like a gauntlet. Smith returned the Indian's bows, arrows and clubs. All the Indians had to pass down the gauntlet of metal men knowing that the brave would note how puny their weapons looked in comparison. Smith had found a way to use this occasion as a propaganda coup.

Pocahontas and Rawhunt were the last to go. Pocahontas walked up to Smith and said, "Most interesting, Smeeth. I will tell our father."

Rawhunt walked down the gauntlet of men, but before Pocahontas reached the line, Smith ordered them to step back two paces, making a much wider and more inviting aisle. He made his best formal bow to Pocahontas waving his hat in the direction of the gate. She smiled just a little, understanding the deference he was showing her. She held her head high and walked slowly as a Princess should.

Hunt came up to Smith, "That was well done, John. She is our friend in spite of what her father does."

"I agree with you, Doctor, but remember Powhatan is my father too. Though there are times I wonder what that means to him. Still I value our connection."

"He does blow hot and cold," observed Hunt.

"Unlike you, Doctor," John said, wrapping his arm around Hunt's shoulder, "you are as consistent and true as the North Star." The men laughed together and went in search of refreshment.

That was the last conversation Smith had with Doctor Hunt. The next morning, Hunt was found collapsed in the back of his new church. Wotton guessed it was his heart. The beloved Doctor was buried in front of the altar of the unfinished church, the first person to be buried in a church in the new world.

The next day dawned as perfect as a May day in tidewater Virginia can be. The winter had been dry and cold. Spring had come late and there was so little rain that corn had broken the ground two weeks later than expected. In the last two weeks, the weather had changed and showers came through at least every other day, late in the afternoon. The rain had painted the world green. Every growing thing was bright and lush and calling to every man with any love of the outdoors.

Ratcliff loved to hunt. He really did not care if he put food on the table, actually did not even enjoy the act of killing, but he did love the pageantry. Since the Indians had brought a deer, he figured the birthing season must be done, so he proposed a group go deer hunting.

A group of five gentlemen joined Ratcliff. They brought muskets and enough powder and shot for each man to have five tries. Gentlemen understood how to hunt deer in England. In the deer parks of England, deer were bred. There were, therefore, many more deer per acre than there would be in the wild. The park deer were fed by a gamekeeper if fodder became scarce, so they were somewhat familiar with man and therefore more easily found. The deer parks were also fenced. It was a very large area, but the deer could not leave the park. Each hunter had at least one groom to support them by having a loaded gun ready for a second shot if the first should miss. Under those circumstances, five shots in a day for a hunter would be generous but reasonable. In the open woods of Virginia where the deer had never heard a gun, the first shot would scare the deer away for a radius of a mile or more. Having never tried this sport in Virginia, no one in the party understood this.

Two men had personal servants who they brought along as grooms. Everyone carried a gun that was loaded and primed for there would be no time to do either once an animal was spotted.

A black powder gun is a touchy thing. The powder must be put into the barrel and tamped down with a small wad of cloth or paper. Then the lead shot is put into the barrel and it is tamped again. There is a small hole in the back of the barrel, which is filled with a bit of raw powder. A gun in this condition is called loaded and primed. When it is time to fire, a spark is touched to the bit of powder in the hole. It takes the spark down to the large amount of powder in the barrel, which burns, creating a quick expansion of gas and pushes the lead shot out of the barrel at a high rate of speed. If you move a gun a great deal once it is loaded and primed, the shot can move, the powder can become loose, the powder in the small hole can fall out or some part of the powder or wadding can become damp. If any of these things happen, the gun is likely to misfire in some way. It can fail to spark or it can fire but the shot get stuck in the barrel. The first is frustrating; the second can be fatal.

The eight men walked for two hours without seeing any wildlife bigger than a squirrel. Finally they entered an old growth forest where there was little brush and the ground was covered with decade's worth of spongy fallen oak leaves. Their steps were silenced by the soft footing and within ten minutes they came upon an entire herd of deer. Once a deer was sighted, these experienced hunters knew what to do and what not to do. They were luckily downwind. Everyone froze and slowly aimed their muskets. Tradition said the ranking member of the party had the honor of the first shot. Everyone held his fire waiting for Ratcliff who, being President, was the ranking member.

Muskets are very inaccurate past 100 yards. The deer were about 150 yards away across a clearing. Ratcliff knew the chance of dropping an animal with one musket shot was small, but he needed to make as good as shot as possible to uphold his reputation. He was carrying a flintlock, a mechanism that made the necessary spark by a flint scraping steel near that small priming hole. The flint moved when the trigger was pulled. Ratcliff, in good form, slowly pulled the trigger.

There was a bright flash between Ratcliff's hands and a much louder noise than there should have been. The deer disappeared as quickly as the flash. No one else tried a shot. Then Ratcliff screamed. It had taken a heartbeat for him to register the pain in his right hand.

The wadding had shifted and blocked the shot in the barrel. When the powder exploded, there was nowhere for the pressure to go, so the metal of the barrel to split at its weakest point which happened to be on the right side near the stock. Ratcliff's trigger hand was in the path of that explosion and his palm, thumb and inner arm were cut by the splinters of metal and severely burned by the powder flash.

Each man put his weapon on the ground carefully as if it was a live snake. One of the young servants, not needing to watch the deer, had already noticed a lovely rock-bedded stream at the far edge of the clearing. When one of the gentlemen yelled, "Water," the servant pointed out the stream. Four men picked up Ratcliff who was now near to passing out. They took him to the stream and put his entire right arm into the cool water. With that shock, Ratcliff lost consciousness entirely.

One man demanded his servant surrender his shirt as a bandage. They were going to wrap the arm in the wet shirt in hopes of keeping it moist for the two-hour walk home. On a day that was going to be over 70 degrees, this was unlikely. The shirtless servant suggested they collect moss from the rocks in the stream and pack it in the folds of the shirt since the moss would keep moist better than the linen of the shirt. Taking advice from a young servant felt uncomfortable, but the gentlemen saw the wisdom of the suggestion and told the servant to wade into the stream and collect the moss.

After trying a number of combinations to carry the unconscious man, one hunter, who had been a solider, suggested that each man take his turn carrying Ratcliff on his back rather than trying to share the weight through the narrow paths. The servant rigged a sling of musket straps and the shirt of the other servant. Passing Ratcliff from man to man and using the sling to support his weight, the party managed to get back to the fort in just over three hours.

John Fleischer, a man trained at university with a specialty in plants and herbs, commended the men on thinking to pack the arm in moss as moss both kept the wound moist and provided a soothing substance for burns. The gentlemen of the party accepted the compliment giving no credit to the boy who had actually suggested the treatment.

Fleischer took out the medicines that had been sent from England for the use of the colony. The salves and mixtures were shipped in colorful cylindrical earthenware jars decorated with bands of geometric shapes in blue and yellow. Some were as small as a drinking cup and some could hold three or more gallons of prepared syrup. Fleischer had looked for some of the more rare plants that were used to make these medications and for sources of new treatments. The Company had sent more empty containers in this set to be used to ship these new products home. He had found none.

As the party left Fleischer's house, Thomas Hope, a tailor turned soldier, who had suggested the sling, took the two servants aside.

"You fellows did well out there. I am sorry no one thanked you for your part. Let me thank you."

The two boys looked at each other. They were not accustomed to this type of acknowledgement. They were a bit embarrassed by having a man of higher rank address them so.

The boy who suggested the moss finally said, "Thank you, sir. The man needed what help we could give."

"I will see what I can do about reclaiming your shirts or having them repaired. Come see me day after tomorrow," and he turned and walked toward the other gentlemen.

On June 2, 1608, the *Phoenix* prepared to depart with her hold filled with cedar wood. Smith's letter to his cousin finally ran to forty pages. Smith personally gave it to Captain Nelson.

"Captain, I have addressed this letter to my cousin William in Lincolnshire. I have asked him to find a way to get a large Union [1] flag or cause one to be made. I have taken the liberty of offering your name as a person to contact to arrange for the flag to be sent here as soon as he obtains it. Will that do for you?"

"Glad to help any way I can. Perhaps I can even put him by a source I know in London. I agree this place needs a visible flag to announce it as a part of England. I will see your letter safe to your cousin."

[[1] Once James became king of both Scotland and England, a new flag was created combining the cross of St. Andrew for Scotland and the cross of St. George for England. The new flag was known as the Union flag.]

Smith was leaving Jamestown at the same time, but not for England. Smith was off on yet another exploration with his picked squad of men. "My pinnacle is loaded. I believe the men are on board. I will join them now and we will be ready to go down river with you as far as the mouth of the James. I will be glad of your company."

"We will make a strange sight, Captain Smith, but I suppose everything we do seems strange to the savages."

"I think we are still a novelty. Is Captain Martin on board?"

"Not yet, I expect him at any moment. The tide will turn within the hour."

"If I see him on my way, I will try to hurry him along. I thank you, sir, and pleasant voyage."

John Martin's health continued to fail. He had decided to return to England with Nelson. Just after Smith entered the gate of the fort, he was nearly run down by Anas Todkill, Martin's personal servant.

"Anas, slow down, son."

"Beg pardon, Captain, Master Martin sent me to deliver one or two last items before he leaves."

"How is he feeling? Will he take the voyage well?"

"Ah, sir, it is not my place to say, but as I shall never see him again, I will tell you the truth. Master Martin has told me that he so wishes to be in London when his gold is confirmed that he would sail half-dead through hell to be there."

Smith laughed. "Well, Anas, I sincerely hope your master will be neither half dead nor will the trip be like hell. Your master has done good service to our little colony and I wish him all the praise he deserves."

"You are too good, Captain. Until his gold is proven, I think he may be called 'unservicable' to James Fort, but we will hope for the best."

"Please hurry your master along. Captain Nelson says the tide will turn soon."

The original Council of seven was almost gone. Kendall had been executed as a spy; Gosnold had died in the first autumn; Wingfield had gone back to England; and the beloved Reverend Hunt succumbed in the spring. Newport was somewhere between Jamestown and London. With Martin now leaving and Ratcliff badly hurt, Smith was effectually in sole charge.

At this critical time, Smith made the incredible decision to leave the fort for a long expedition. His plan was to go down the James and then journey up the Chesapeake Bay to the northern most river that flowed from the northwest. He was going to evaluate what products this vast land had to offer to the merchants of England. As always, he was also looking for the promised passage to the South Sea and China. It was planned as a 3000-mile trip that would take several months. He was taking only fourteen men. Ratcliff would still be in charge at Jamestown, though his health and even his survival was still in question. Knowing the colonists would respect the leadership of a university educated man, Smith had chosen Doctor Walter Russell, a new arrival, as his agent and explained his plans and his view of the current situation with the Indians. Smith had made the choice that finding sources of provisions and valuable products was more important to the survival of the fort than his being present to deal with the Indians or internal colony issues. Or maybe he just wanted an adventure.

For whatever reason, Smith, and his best and favored soldiers were leaving. Smith also included Richard Keale, a London fishmonger, to evaluate the potential of the Chesapeake area as a source of fish as a commercial product.

Russell nearly cried when the two ships lifted anchor. At his best, Ratcliff was an erratic leader. Russell was competent to deal with problems between two students, but he had no experience managing a settlement or dealing with Indians. He understood Smith's logic, but he did not agree with his priorities. Why did he not send a party of trusted men on this expedition and stay with the fledgling colony? Russell thought it a completely irresponsible decision. He was angry; he was hurt; he was scared.

His fears were realized before dinner. Ratcliff rose from his sick bed and made the rounds of the fort. He was obviously fevered and often swayed when he stood still. He gave odd, silly, and unreasonable orders.

He approached the Council area and found the usual gentry gathered there.

"Gentlemen, I see you are preparing for dinner. I think we should have the table set correctly from now on. We need linen and proper silver. As we will no doubt drink Madeira past dark, we need a candelabra. Please see to it."

Seeing a laborer moving bushels of corn, "Young man, it is surely time to harvest the corn. I want to see a full storehouse by morning."

And to the fort as a whole, "I would like the palisade to be higher."
Russell went to the gentlemen and to the young laborer and simply told them to wait to do anything until they got further orders. Then he went to find Ratcliff. He found him at the railing like that of a corral, but there were no horses in Jamestown.

"John, what brings you here?"

"I miss my horses, Walter, I miss my home." He sniffled a little and tears appeared in his eyes.

"Yes, John, we all miss home. Here now, come with me and we will talk of home." Russell put his arm around Ratcliff's shoulder and walked him back to his house.

Ratcliff's house had been among the first to be rebuilt. He had a proper bed with a grass and reed stuffed mattress. As President, he lived alone. There was, however a larger than normal table which served as the Council chamber when necessary. Usually Council business was conducted around another similar table with benches outside under the one large tree that still stood inside the fort.

Russell sent a boy to fetch some small beer and to find some hot soup or stew. When the boy brought the food, Russell stayed with Ratcliff to see that he ate and then talked with him until Ratcliff fell asleep. As soon as he was sure Ratcliff was well asleep, he left the boy to keep watch and went to find Albertson to see if he knew of anything more to do to break the fever and clear Ratcliff's mind.

Albertson and Wotton did what they could. Wotton tried bleeding to balance the humours. Albertson concocted various potions he thought would help. As the weeks passed, Ratcliff had good days of clarity and bad days of confusion. It became the usual practice to ignore any of his orders unless Russell reinforced them.

The result was that there was no one in charge of the fort. No one organized hunting and fishing. The building projects slowed. And most critically, no one managed the distribution of the provisions that had been stockpiled. Each man worked and ate as he saw fit. There was more eating than working.

In early July, Ratcliff had recovered enough that he really took charge. He was more organized, but his decisions were still questionable. He commandeered the servant of another man. This servant had a reputation as a good cook, so Ratcliff ordered him to go to the storehouse and pick the best of the provisions and bring them to Ratcliff's residence. The men were not pleased at this, but they were so used to the aristocracy taking what they wanted, this did not seem too out of line.

Ratcliff's next idea did cross the line. The homesickness that manifested itself in the early days of his fevers had become an obsession. He took a company of six gentlemen to a place a half-mile into the woods. There he asked their advice on the best design of a hunting lodge.

"I personally favor a classic fortified house. I would like brick but we can start with a sound daub and wattle and brick it over later. Do you think it should be one story or two?"

The buildings in the fort were not complete. A real church had been begun but not finished. A foundation of cobble, large stones, and two rows of bricks was put down to make the floor level and to keep the timbers off of the wet ground. Then large logs were squared and laid down for the four sides. The rest had been built like an English house with half-timber and mud filling, but the front was to be covered in classic clapboard and the pew benches were to be of sawed boards. The men had dug a sawpit for this purpose and to increase the amount of dressed lumber they could produce for export. It was a closed structure now, but the church still needed some work.

There was not enough food for the rest of the summer much less any for winter. Nothing had been heard from Powhatan in weeks. And Ratcliff wanted all the men pulled off of whatever they were doing to build his hunting lodge in the grand English country style. The man had to be mad.

The laborers were sent to the site the next day and they began clearing the spot. There was already a clearing within site of the designated spot, but Ratcliff would have none of it. His seat would be where he wanted it, not 100 yards away. After two weeks of this foolish effort, the ground was cleared, a cellar had been dug and the anchor poles had been cut.

At the mouth of the James, Nelson gave one pistol shot of farewell and headed east out to sea. Smith returned the salute and tacked north up Chesapeake Bay. Each time they stopped they looked for promising ore samples and clay suitable for pipes. On one occasion, they found something sparkling in a streambed and scooped out what they thought was silver.

The flora and fauna changed as they moved north. The trees actually became more familiar. The animals they saw when they moved even ten miles inland had beautiful fur, a product that would definitely be welcomed in England. In the never-ending quest to claim all of America, Smith continued to give key features English names.

The weather got hotter. The insects became more active. The men became more miserable. England never had weather this bad, at least the fond memories of home would not admit to it.

There were fish everywhere. In the bay, the fish were not as easy to see, but when they were spotted, they were very large. In the rivers and streams there were so many fish you could nearly walk across the water on them. No one had thought to bring a net to catch fish as food. One day, someone thought to try scooping the plentiful fish into a long-handled skillet. If the pan would have had holes in the bottom so the water could run out, the system might have worked, but the water kept the fish afloat enough for each one to wriggle out.

When they got into another small stream when the fish were very dense, Smith simply speared them with a pike and then his sword. One that he got with his sword was a very odd fish with wide flat wings and a barbed tail. One of the party who had encountered this animal before in the Caribbean called it a stingray. While pulling it from the water, the stingray flipped its tail in defense and caught Smith in the arm.

Smith yelped with the pain, but he still managed to get the beast into the boat. He pulled out his sword and stabbed it again in the head. Within a few minutes, his arm was swelling alarmingly. They got to shore as quickly as possible and got him on land where they could build a fire. At Smith's orders, one of his men opened the wound to drain the poison and then he applied a substance carried in the medical kit. This "precious oil" had a good effect and by evening, Smith was mending. In his bravado style, Smith ordered that the stingray be cooked and he had it for dinner.

This place, which Smith named Stingray Point, was the end of their journey out. Though he was out of eminent danger, he was still quite ill and he called off the rest of the trip. The made the best time they could back to James Fort and arrived on July 21st.

Smith dropped anchor and came ashore looking for Russell and some help to unload his ship. No sentry announced his arrival. He did not see a single laborer and it took him some time to track down Russell doing inventory in the storehouse.

"Walter, what on earth is going on? There is no sentry. And where are all the men?"

"John, oh, John, thank God you are back! The men are in the woods with Ratcliff. He has them building a house for him out past the neck."

"WHAT!"

"Oh that is the most foolish of his actions, but not the worst. I am here counting what we have left to eat because he has taken much of the best for himself and no one has been regulating what the men take from here. You can see that there is still much to do on the fort buildings. And he left no one to tend the corn. We have had no rain here and it is all dried up. He has swung from sanity to madness day by day. I am so glad you are back!"

Smith's action was immediate and severe. He marched to his ship and gathered his trusted company of soldiers. Then he and his troop marched toward the neck.

When they reached the site, Smith halted his men and walked up to Ratcliff.

"President Ratcliff, you are not well. Sir, I formally relieve you of duty."

Ratcliff's unconscious reaction was to salute as he would in his old regiment, but then he came to himself and said, "You have no right."

"Indeed I do, sir. By our charter, if a leader becomes incapacitated, he can be relieved of office and another appointed. Or sir, I can arrest you for misuse of company goods and put you in irons."

At this, a cheer went up from the assembled workers. Smith flashed them an ugly look and the sound stopped.

"Josiah, take President Ratcliff back to his house."

As Josiah led him by his arm, in a disquieting reference to Kendall's trial the year before, Ratcliff shouted, "I am not President Ratcliff. I am President Sicklemore. You have no case against Sicklemore. No case!"

Josiah and Smith's troop surrounded Ratcliff and marched him back to the fort where Russell met them and stayed with Ratcliff until Smith returned.

Smith then addressed the workmen. "Men this farce is over. Return to the fort and resume your duties. If you are not sure of your duties, meet me in the center of the compound in half an hour and I will assign you a task. Gather all the tools; leave nothing of use. If you have cut logs, bring them or let me know and we will come back later for them."

Smith met with a dozen men in half an hour and assigned them purposeful work. Even those who liked to avoid work as a rule appreciated doing something for the good of themselves and the colony rather than being made fools by building a palace in the woods.

Smith conferred with Russell through the evening. Just before dusk, which was very late, it being just weeks past summer solstice, Matthew Schivner, the personal recruit of Bartholomew Gosnold, was invited into the discussion. The next morning, Smith sent out word that all the men should gather together in the compound. Russell stayed with Ratcliff. The short Smith stood on the council table under the tree.

"Men, President Ratcliff is not well. He will no longer be President. I am assuming that office effective immediately."

His men cheered, a few others joined, many were silent, no one objected.

"I am appointing Matthew Scrivener to be my deputy. His is well known to the directors of the Virginia Company and I believe they will confirm my choice at their first opportunity. There will be greater discipline in this colony in the future. Rations will be carefully monitored and given out only by the storekeeper whom I will appoint shortly. In the meantime, Doctor Russell will fill that office. Work assignments will be tracked and if someone is not pulling his weight, measures will be taken. "

The men went to work and the next two days were very productive. On the 24th of July, Smith was off again. The soldier Smith expected his orders to followed whether he was present or not and provisions were sorely needed. This was a scaled down version of the great Chesapeake expedition. He took his favorites but did not take the fish expert. He took Surgeon Anthony Bagnall leaving Doctor Russell again as his personal agent at Jamestown. His return date was uncertain.

Ratcliff had been kept on house arrest since the "palace" incident. After Smith left, Ratcliff refused to keep to his house. Scrivener posted guards, but they were not sure who was really in charge.

Ratcliff began giving orders and countermanding Scrivener's orders.

"Mister Scrivener, you have no standing. Smith had no right to remove me as President and no right to appoint you to any station. I am President not Smith and certainly not you!"

"Captain Ratcliif, I must insist you return to your house."

"Or what? What would you dare do? Watch yourself, or you will be arrested."

It was a stalemate. Neither man had any real backing and Smith's reliable soldiers were with him. The tie was broken when the sickness started.

Scrivener was one of the first to fall victim to the flux. It was probably bad food that a group ate because not everyone contracted the illness. But then a second different aliment started to spread. Doctor Russell had no name for the disease. People could not hold down food or water and those who died succumbed to dehydration.

Ratcliff was as indecisive and useless as ever. There was little he could do about the sickness, but he had discontinued Smith's regular examination of each building to ensure it remained sound. Therefore no one noticed when part of the roof of the storehouse leaked and much of the stored corn got wet and rotted. He did not send out hunting or fishing parties. The fort and its people degenerated quickly.

Fleischer did what he could with his medicines. The perfumers set up their fuming pots and burned herbs to drive out the sicknesses. The surgeons were at a loss for anything they could do. Each of the medical men became sick in turn. Some recovered but Fleischer died.

After almost a month, Scrivener recovered his strength. He and Russell gathered four other men and they rearrested Ratcliff. This time he was kept in his house by guards. Scrivener assembled several crews who would work in shifts to harvest the corn that Ratcliff was allowing to rot in the fields. The degeneration was stopped but after a terrible price.

Smith, unaware that the future of his beloved colony was at great risk, continued his best effort to keep the settlers alive and safe. He made maps of the best fishing and of trails that led to rich hunting grounds. He noted oyster beds and places crabs were plentiful.

He met Indians who were obviously from a different nation. The Susquehonnock Indians were all unusually tall, literally standing head and shoulders above the short Smith. These people had European hatchets, knives and other tools they had acquired through indirect trade with Canada. Smith learned there was an extensive trading network that covered the area from lower Canada to Spanish Florida. He was sure that by integrating with this network, he would finally learn of the route to China.

166

On the way back, a storm blew Smith's ship across the estuary to Nansemond Creek. Since fate had sent him here, he decided to explore this little river. Several miles up he met Indians who greeted him and told him of other tribes further up the river who would want to trade with the English. Smith continued but the creek narrowed quickly and as soon as the craft could no longer maneuver easily, the Indians ambushed the boat.

Smith fought back delaying the attack long enough for the men to back up and turn the boat. Furious at this trickery, Smith retaliated on the way back. He stopped wherever he saw signs of a camp, burned the cornfields and smashed the precious canoes. The village leaders came to him and asked what it would take for him to leave. He demanded 400 bushel of corn, a chain of pearls, one of the canoes and many bows and arrows. Smith had seen how effective this weapon was in this type of territory and he decided his men should learn to use it. Word of Smith's actions spread quickly through the tribes and they did their best to conceal their camps from being seen from the river.

Seeing no more camps to raid, Smith headed home. He arrived on September 7th, almost too late.

When Newport had arrived in January, there were only 38 men of the original 104 left alive. Newport and Nelson had brought 80 and 40 additional settlers for a total of 158. A few had gone back to England and this last round of sickness had taken 40 more. There were now about 120 men to fit in fort built for less than 100. A new cemetery next to the cornfield west of the fort had to be consecrated. The west cemetery and the small burial ground inside the fort held almost as many settlers as were still alive.

The only provisions in the storehouse were the bushels of corn the men had just harvested. The structures were desperately in need of repair. It seemed that each time Smith left the fort, it collapsed. Russell and Scrivener, being the only people with any official standing, spoke to all of the men. They agreed that Smith was the one who should be in charge and so they confirmed Smith's Presidency on September 10th.

He launched into a concentrated building program. He repaired the church yet again and the roof of the storehouse. To make more room, Smith reduced or redesigned the fort. The new walls were made taller, up to fifteen feet high, and more cannon were added until there were twenty-four guns on the bulwarks. He began to add three walls out from the northeast wall creating a 5-square or 5-sided form. A short wall began at the base of the east bulwark. A slightly longer wall began at the north bulwark and slanted eastward. A long wall that was not quite parallel to the original wall joined these two shorter walls. This quadrangle was devoted to gardens for now. Smith hoped to grow a quick crop of squash or peas yet this season. The space could be used for additional housing when needed. To have a place the Indians could come to trade without entering the fort, he built a structure for a barracks and storehouse at the corner of the short south wall and long east wall of the new section. Remembering how often they had needed a place of confinement, Smith had the men dig a cellar at the west end and put a wall of saplings near the foot of the stairs. The resulting room could be used as a jail when necessary.

Smith also instituted a program of regular military exercises each Saturday. The soldiers would use the area just outside the west bulwark of the fort. Quickly the place was given the name "Smithfield" because of Smith and to remind the colonists of the site in London of that name. Each week the file of soldiers would fire at least one volley into a designated tree. Many of the settlers would watch from the fort and dozens of Indians would watch in amazement and horror, as the volley would destroy a tree.

All along, Doctor Russell had encouraged Smith to be very tough on cursing.

Smith recalled him saying, "John, there have been days when every sentence I heard contained a curse. We are a settlement dedicated to the Lord, we must respect his Commandments."

Smith had been known to curse in extreme situations, but as a rule, he objected to the practice as much as Doctor Russell had. So the next Sunday, at the end of the morning service, Smith addressed the men.

"The swearing will stop now. It is out of control. Henceforth, anyone who swears or takes the Lord's name in vain will have river water poured down his sleeve. That may not sound like much of a punishment, but try working in soaking wet sleeves and smelling like the river and you may change your mind."

CHAPTER 8
Crowning Powhatan

Smith had officially been President for almost three weeks when the ship from the Second Supply arrived at the improved five-square fort. Captain Newport had returned. This time he had a ship named the *Mary and Margaret* with a crew of fifteen and 70 new settlers. Five were of particular note. Two new men had been appointed to the Council, Captain Peter Winne and Captain Richard Waldo. One new man was Thomas West, the brother of Lord De La Warr, a member of the Virginia Company board. Of greater interest to the 120 men in the fort was the arrival of two women.

Thomas Forrest had brought his wife and her servant, thirteen year-old Anne Burris. Mistress Forrest had married Thomas 6 years before. They had inherited her father's property, she being an only child, and they had lived reasonably well with tenants farming most of the land. They had started and lost nine babies in those six years, none having survived the first trimester. She was depressed and her health had suffered with so many pregnancies. The farm seemed to follow her in decline. Thomas had suggested a change of scene and the idea of a new world and a new start seemed just the thing to revive his beloved wife. So they had sold up, took only her body servant Anne, and booked passage to Virginia.

The trip, though not a bad one by sailors' standards, was difficult for all three landlubbers. Thomas did better than the women and Anne did better than her Mistress.

As the little group crawled out of the skiff on to shore, the word had gone around to the men and every one of them was gathered on the strip of land between the fort and the river. They stood in silent awe. The Indian women had reminded them that they were men. These two women reminded them of home.

The men were happy to provide the best accommodations they could for the weary women. They offered arms of support. They carried anything the women would let loose of. They would have carried the women themselves. They were ready to shuffle Ratcliff right out of the best house in the fort, but Newport took charge of the situation.

"Mr. Forrest, Mistress Forrest. Welcome to Jamestown and Virginia. Bales!" he called for his old mate, "escort our new family to an available house. You two," waving at two nearby men, "take their belongings." Then turning to Doctor Russell, "Doctor, where is President Ratcliff?"

"Captain, if we might speak together alone. There are many things to tell you. Much has happened since you left."

"Yes, well. Let us first get our new friends established and then we can talk."

He addressed the group still standing outside the fort, "Gentlemen of Jamestown, we have newly-come friends. You who have spare places in your house, introduce yourselves to these gentlemen and invite them to share your space."

Then to the fourteen new tradesmen, "We have a cooper, a pipe maker, three blacksmiths, several carpenters, a surgeon, and apothecary, a perfumer, and three tailors. I suspect you can identify them by their tools and shops. I suggest you pair up with one of them and share their work space." Newport had expected all the tradesmen to have their shops set up and be hard at work. Because of the lack of leadership, no one but the blacksmith had a permanent space.

"Does anyone here speak German?"

Peter Keffer, a gunner who had come with Newport on the last ship spoke up. "I speak some Dutch from my time there in the wars."

"That will do." Newport walked over to a huddle of oddly dressed men and spoke to the crowd, "These fine fellows are from Germany and Poland. They have skills in making glass. We will be building a glass factory if their trials prove that the sand here is suitable. Keffer, see to finding them lodging."

Having sorted out the new settlers, Newport went over to Russell who had been watching the proceedings. "Alright, Walter, what have you to tell me?"

170

As they walked back into the fort and on to the newly repaired church, Russell told Newport of Ratcliff's erratic behavior, Smith's election as President and his appointment of Scrivner as his deputy. He also told him of the spoiled grain, Smith's narrow escape and his success in calming Powhatan's people and bringing back new corn and maps of where to get fish. The explanation was decidedly in Smith's favor.

Newport's reply startled, Russell. "Thank you for your report. Now we need to put things back to rights. I would like to see those three men here as soon as possible."

Russell went to Smith and Scrivener who were directing the unloading of the ship and storage of its contents.

"Newport would like to see you two as soon as possible. He also wants Ratcliff."

"Does he now," said Smith. "I doubt the guards will let him wander off without my permission, so I had best go get him. I will meet you two. Where, Doctor, at the Council area?"

"No, I left him at the church."

Smith went by Ratcliff's house and ordered the two guards to escort Ratcliff to the church. The others were already there, just sitting and waiting.

Newport addressed Ratcliff first. "President Ratcliff, are you well?"

"Not Ratcliff, Sicklemore. I am John Sicklemore."

Before he could say any more, Smith spoke up. "He is no longer President. He was removed for misuse of public goods and is now charged with mutiny for countermanding the orders of the rightful Deputy President and, as you can see, is held under house arrest. By lawful vote, I have been elected President."

"Interesting, Smith, but whatever has happened in my absence is now nullified. We have new orders from the Company. After they heard my report, they included specific orders that you are no longer to be a member of the council, much less its President. You will return to your duties as

171

military advisor. President Ratcliff will no longer be under house arrest. I require his advice. Mr. Scrivener can resume whatever duties he had previously. Since I have been informed of the orders personally, I will take charge of their execution.

Smith, you have overstepped your authority – again. Watch yourself or you will return to England as you came here, in irons! That will be all."

After sixteen months of struggling to keep the colony alive, overcoming famine, sickness, Indians, three brushes with death, and foolish Councilors, Smith was back where he was the day they had arrived. He was stunned. Short of murdering Newport on the spot, there was not much he could do. He looked at Russell for some answer, some word of explanation or comfort. Russell hung his head and would not even meet his eyes. Smith performed a flawless military about-face and marched away. Scrivener and the two guards melted off into the bustle of the compound leaving Ratcliff on his own for the first time in weeks.

Smith kept as far away from Newport as possible. His favored soldiers stayed near him whenever they could, including Josiah. They got word of the new orders from the Virginia Company through the grapevine. Considering the overcrowding of the fort, one order made sense, to spread out the settlers. Another was to go above the falls. If it had been to find better farming lands, it would have been a sound idea, but the order was to go there to look for gold. And the third order made sense only to those who had no understanding of the native people of this new world. The order was to crown Powhatan as king of his own people.

Worse yet, the orders were to impress upon Powhatan, that since King James had crowned him, he owed allegiance to King James. The Indians understood the concept of one wereoance having some control over others. Powhatan was the leading wereoance of many villages and tribes over an area as large as old Mercia. To expect him to meekly become an "under-king" when he was the chief wereoance, much like an emperor, was like expecting the King of France to accept King James of England as his overlord. England was new to overseas empire building. They had a lot to learn about how to treat the royalty, and the people, native to a country they wanted to rule.

Partly to reinforce the fact that Newport was giving the orders and partly because he knew who would be the best man for the thankless job of informing Powhattan of this plan, Newport directed that John Smith would go to Powhatan to make the arrangement for the coronation. The basic plan was for Powhatan to come to James Fort where he would be crowned and given fine gifts, a red coat, a ewer selected personally by King James, several finger rings and a huge Elizabethan style bed. Even Ratcliff wondered, "Why a bed?" There was no further explanation in the orders.

Smith was so secure of his reception that he took only three men and Namontack, the brave who had gone to England with Newport and returned with him.

Namontack had been a fine observer while in England. Powhatan asked him to count the number of men of fighting age. Namontack started counting when he first stepped on to the dock in London. By the time he had reached the inn two blocks up from the wharf, he had run out of numbers. His language had no reason to have numbers larger than our hundreds. More than that was just "many" or "very many" and in two blocks he had seen "very many" men who would be warriors in his tribe.

The Indians knew of wheels. But in London, Namontack had seen wheels ever everywhere. He had seen all sort of people, even women and children, riding in open and closed chariots pulled by huge horses crowding the streets. The houses were stacked, one on top of the other with flat wooden boards to climb up to get to the upper ones. There were some of these flat wooden boards inside the inn where they stayed and he climbed up and down them several times a day to get to the room he stayed in. The people called the upper house "upstairs."

There were several very long bridges across the river that ran through London. They were made of stone and so big that people had built houses on them. People spent their days in other buildings besides houses. They were called shops or stores and people made things in them and "sold" them. This "selling" was a kind of trading. A man would give another man food, but all the man would give in return was a little disc of metal, maybe two. It was all amazing, but what impressed him the most were the public buildings. He was taken to a church, and a cathedral, a huge fort they called a castle, and a palace, each one bigger and full of more wonders than the one before it.

Powhatan listened to all these wonders and thought the coat-wearers to be even more foolish than before. They could build all these amazing things, but they could not feed themselves.

Powhatan's "capital" or home village, was on the north bank of a river the English had named the Prince Henry River, then started calling it the Charles and finally the York. The Indians had always called it the Pamunkey River.

The banks here were low with many places to land a canoe on the bay the English named Puritan. Powhatan's scouts constantly watched the bay. Anyone approaching the chief's stronghold from the water could be seen for over a mile. Besides, the village was some distance inland from the river, so there was time to warn the village while any intruder covered a quarter of a mile on a narrow track.

When they reached Werowocomoco, Powhatan was not there. He was not far, they were told and would return the next day. Someone must have gone to tell Pocahontas of Smith's arrival. He saw her in the distance, running between houses, but she slowed her pace when she got nearer and appeared from around the side of Powhatan's ceremonial house smoothing her skirt and adjusting her hair.

She offered to entertain Smith and his men.

"You showed us how your god wants you to pray to him, in formal clothes, on your knees, and very quietly. I want to show you how our gods want us to pray to them with much happiness and joy. Sit and we will show you."

A special stack of wood was kept dry at all times to be used on a fire that was never allowed to go completely out. She had this fire built up while she and many other young women dressed as warriors and put antlers on their heads. They came running from woods, yelling and brandishing war clubs. Smith reacted as if he was being attacked. He jumped up, drew his sword and made ready to defend himself and his companions.

Pocahontas signaled for the women to all stop where they were. She walked slowly up to her hero-brother and put her arms on his.

174

"My brother, we will do you no harm. This is how we show our gods that we rejoice in the gifts they have given us. Sit. Let us finish. I promise you all be well."

With this personal assurance, Smith resumed his seat and the "antics" as he called the dancing in his journal that day, continued. Once he got used to the pantomime, he actually enjoyed seeing the young women move and play at being warriors.

Powhatan returned the next day. Smith put forth he proposal that Powhatan come to the James Fort to be crowned. Powhatan grasped the politics of the situation immediately. He said, "I am king here, I do not come to Newport, he comes to me. And I am here only eight more days before I leave this camp. I will not wait."

Smith was delighted with Powhatan's reply. He disagreed with the whole concept. To give Powhatan impressive gifts without expected equal in return was to look stupid in the eyes of the Indians and he felt a right fool just having to suggest it. If Newport gave Powhatan all these things for nothing, Powhatan would just want more. It would cause nothing but trouble for the settlers in future dealing with the Indians.

Smith took great private pleasure in telling Newport the outcome of his visit. Newport, complacent as ever, made no counter offer. He simply made arrangements to haul everything for the coronation to Werowocomoco.

Sir George Percy was the only member of the colony who had ever witnessed a coronation. All the peers of England had been invited to Westminster Abbey for the coronation of James I. Of course most people had heard tales of the crowning of kings, in fairy tales or ballads. Certain elements were usually present; a throne, a robe, and a crown. They would have to rely on Powhatan having some type of throne. The red coat would stand in for the robe. And they did have a crown, a copper affair, not gold or bejeweled, but sufficient for a savage king.

Percy sketched out a ceremony consisting of the presentation of gifts, having Powhatan don the red coat, having him kneel as Newport placed the crown on his head signifying that his power now came from the greater king James, followed by a salute from the cannons on the ships that would carry the English to Powhatan's village. This last took the most coordination because the village was not in sight of the river. Percy organized a sort of relay team who would run the news of the crowning back to signal the ship to fire.

Newport asked, "Lord, Percy, you say Westminster was full for the coronation? Then we should take a considerable force with us to impress the chief of our numbers and to add dignity to the ceremony."

"I quite agree, Captain. A well-turned out force."

The well-turned out force turned out to be 120 of the 200 men in the colony, leaving only 80, and those the less-able bodied, and two women to see to the crops and maintain the fort. Everyone of social rank, and nearly all the trained fighting men, would be on this trip.

They could not carry the huge bed overland for twelve miles, so they loaded it on three barges along with seventy of the men and Captain Smith. The other fifty walked the twelve miles with Newport. Smith, having traveled by both means, set the departure times so that the two groups would rendezvous just as the ship reached the anchoring point on the Prince Henry River. The timing was good, however, since the group on foot still had to cross the river, it took some time for the first seventy to debark so one of the barges could come to the south side of the river and pick up the fifty on foot to ferry them over. Once they finally assembled, they managed to port the bed and all to Powhatan's village.

People called him Wahunsenacawh, not Powhatan. They were really quite superstitious about names. No matter what he was called, now in his seventies, he was still a formidable man. He had been in power for almost twenty years and had united the local tribes more tightly than anyone in memory.

He presented an imposing appearance for a man in his seventies. He was still tall and broad shouldered. He had a round face with gray hair braided down onto his shoulders. His whole being told of an active, ambitious, and successful life. Though he rarely used it now, his ability to strike terror and awe into his own people and be harsh and even cruel to his enemies had left its mark on his face. He was now secure and took great pleasure in the luxuries of living in abundance and peace. He liked being king.

Smith greeted Powhatan and then gave the floor to Newport who spoke briefly about the great king over the ocean who sent the great Powhatan his warmest regards. He explained about the elaborate basin and ewer that the king had chosen with his own hand. He presented the finger rings as if they were the privy seal. He spoke (perhaps a bit longingly) of the comfort of the huge bed that the men had duly assembled, along with its heavy hangings and linens, in Powhatan's longhouse where the ceremony was to take place.

Powhatan accepted all these gifts patiently and graciously. They were not as interesting as the white greyhound, but still unique. Then Newport called for the red coat. Powhatan balked. To be wrapped in an English coat, to be one like the coat-wearer, this could be very evil magic. Newport and Percy did not understand the delay or why Powhatan would no longer cooperate. They appealed to Namontack who spoke quietly to Powhatan assuring him there was no evil. Reluctantly, the chief put on the coat, but he was not happy about it and looked for the first opportunity to shed it.

Then it was time for the actual crowning. Had there been a "throne" of some kind where Powhatan could sit to be crowned, this might not have been as difficult as it proved to be. Confusing crowning a king with dubbing a knight, Percy had told Newport that Powhatan should kneel before him. Powhatan would have no part of that. He had been told that the English knelt to their god and he would not treat Newport or this King James as a god. To kneel was to surrender to someone who had beaten you. It was a posture for captives and supplicants, not kings.

Finally, Percy got into a position where he could push Powhatan's shoulders from behind causing him to bend a bit to keep his balance. As soon as his head dipped, the one-armed Newport stuck the cheap copper crown on his head. Percy nodded to the first of the relay team and in about two minutes, just as the furor over a stranger pushing the chief had begun to die down, the cannons blasted. The shots put the camp into an uproar. Most had never heard the cannon nor seen the smoke that billowed into the sky. They were terrified. Those who had experienced gunfire before thought it might be an ambush and went into a defensive action to protect the village and the king. It took the better part of an hour for the village to settle down and return their attention to the ceremony.

Powhatan knew that, having been given these special gifts, he was expected to offer gifts in return. He did not consider anything the English had brought to be of any great value to him. He had long been a king and he did not need Newport or this King James to make him a king. He thought the whole thing was foolish. So he offered a gift to show his true feelings. He picked up a deerskin mantle painted with figures of a hunter and deer and an old pair of his moccasins and gave them grandly to Newport. Newport accepted these paltry gifts as if they were of great value and ordered one of the men to wrap them well and see to it they were put in his cabin aboard his ship so he could take them to England and present them to those who had sent him.

As a vassal to his new liege lord, King James, Newport now demanded that Powhatan provide guides and men to support Newport's expedition above the falls to the land of Powhatan's enemies, the Monacans. Powhatan understood none of the talk of vassal and liege lords, but he understood Newport wanted a guide, so he sent only Namontack. He also gave the English eight bushels of corn, a proper gift for a family, not an entire colony.

The English stayed in the village the rest of the day. Some bought corn directly from individual Indians. Some traded for other things. Josiah, who had come with Smith as usual, traded for nothing, but he did renew some old friendships with braves who had brought food to the fort earlier in the year. He also had a chance to say hello to Pocahontas who was naturally present for the ceremony.

While in England, Newport had received a request from a founder of Virginia. Though he was still kept in the Tower of London for treason, Sir Walter Raleigh continued to influence his Virginia Company. He had asked that Newport and the settlers make inquiries about the fate of the Roanoke colonists whenever they could.

During the pipe smoking and eating that followed the ceremony, Newport asked if Powhatan knew what became of the colonists. Powhatan said he had been present at the slaughter of the Roanoke colony some 19 years before. There was no fight, he said. The Indians just went to the settlement to wipe it out. Perhaps it was true, or perhaps Powhatan was sending Newport a message, "we can just walk in and wipe you out any time we want." Newport tried to hide his shock, but to think he was sharing food with a man who had murdered 90 of his countrymen, 17 women and 11 children, turned his stomach. He recovered enough to ask, "Did any of them live?"

Powhatan said he did not remember for certain, but that he thought he recalled that some were taken as captives and may have later been exchanged down the trade road into Catawba country or they may have been adopted into one tribe or the other. Mostly, they were dead.

Newport's resolve to befriend these Indians was shaken quite a bit that day.

The seventy sailed back down the Prince Henry and up the James while Smith and his fifty walked home. Namontack went with Smith. When they got to Jamestown, Newport resupplied all 120 and got ready to go up the James. The new orders had said to go above the falls and look for gold. To be more certain of what he was finding, Newport brought along a certified refiner of gold, one William Callicut.

For this purpose, the Company had sent a barge broken up into five pieces, any one of which was heavier than the huge bed. The plan was to ship the barge in pieces to the falls, have men portage the pieces around to the head of the falls and assemble it there so they could continue upstream. No one thought this was a very good idea. Perhaps Smith said it best in his journal where he wrote, "The barge could only be carried if it was burned to ashes and carried in a bag."

John Laydon shared Smith's opinion. John was a carpenter and Newport had ordered him to determine if the barge had survived the crossing and was in "ship shape", so to speak. Assembly required some connecting parts and Laydon was to determine if those were all present as there would be little way to concoct new parts after they had reached the falls.

Laydon pronounced the assembly in good order, but warned Newport, "Sir, these connecting pins were done on a lathe. If they are lost or broken, I cannot guarantee a less professional replacement will hold her together. Also, I do not see any handholds. The men who carry these pieces will have no solid way to grab hold and so the chances of dropping a piece are very high."

Having managed with only one arm for many years, Newport was acutely aware of the difficulty of lifting a thing with no solid point to grab. He told Laydon, "Show me the best place to take hold."

Laydon motioned to another carpenter to help and the two of them found the best places they could and lifted the section. They held it for less than two minutes before it began to slip. They set it down and Laydon started to explain the problem. Newport waved at him to be silent and then walked to the section and lifted one end himself. He set it back down, look at Laydon and said, "Store this somewhere. We will not be taking it with us." Thus ended the saga of the barge.

Anne Burris, the thirteen-year-old maid to Mrs. Forrest, was headed back to her Mistress's house when she noticed the men talking about the barge. Truthfully, it was John Laydon she noticed. As happens more often than one might think, she had picked John out of the two hundred men who had met her ship at the dock. From that first day, she was drawn to him. The attraction was mutual. They had found only a few times to chat briefly and now they both created situations so they could meet.

She watched as John lifted the heavy section of the barge. She loved to watch him move. He had removed his jerkin and worn his leather apron over a thin linen shirt with the sleeves rolled up above his elbows. When he lifted the barge piece, his muscles swelled and pulled the linen tight over his back and shoulders. It nearly took her breath away. He was clearly an important man too, for here he was conferring with the Captain of her ship and the leader of the fort. Sadly, her Mistress was waiting for her, so she reluctantly tore herself away from the scene.

It was late October and the colors of autumn graced the turning leaves while the evergreens provided a rich backdrop to the party. The expedition beyond the falls would feel more like a sightseeing trip if the weather would hold. On Monday morning, Newport and 120 men boarded the *Mary and Margaret* and the old reliable *Discovery* and headed up the James.

Smith was left with a laundry list of dull chores and 80 mostly half-fit men to do the work of a hundred able-bodied men. A few hale fellows were still in the fort. John Laydon stayed behind to help build or repair the containers for the pitch, tar, potash, vegetables, and gold to be shipped back to England.

The Germans and the Poles stayed too. They were to set up a glass making facility. Glass would seem to be a risky thing to put on a ship to cross an ocean, but the need for glass in England was large and the means to make it there almost exhausted. The key thing needed to make glass is sand and enough hardwood that burns hot enough to make a fire that can melt it. Surrey had been the center of glass making in England. It had been a very lucrative business and the owners did not want to give it up. Robert Mansell was one of the key players in the glass making trade. He was also a member of the Virginia Company Board. When he heard Newport's report of the mighty virgin forests of Virginia, he convinced the council that they should try making glass. He personally had found the Germans who, having seen their work, directed him to the Poles.

Because of the heat and the risk of fire, they needed a place at some distance from the fort. Smith, never one to waste effort, suggested they look at the site of the Ratcliff's "palace in the woods" to see if it would do for their purpose. At least the clearing of the trees and the digging of the cellar might be put to some good use. It was nearly a mile away, but the artisans went to see it. They liked the site of the "palace", but instead chose a place on the mainland at the north end of the causeway. The sand from the river and the less salty water of the Back River were both nearby. And there was plenty of hardwood close by that would burn at a very high temperature.

They and few helpers began to construct a house and a furnace for making glass. Though they had been working in England for some time and had been on the ships with the English for two months, they were still not completely comfortable with English ways. Having a place apart personally suited them very much. The site immediately gained the name of Glass Point.

Setting up small industries did not inspire Smith, but he dutifully supported the men in taking time to work on these projects. There were also reasons to create some of these products to use at the settlement. Two byproducts, resin and tar, were both needed for the fort.

Earlier in the year, when Powhatan was being generous with food, some men took time to look for pine trees that had resin oozing out of wounds in the bark. The collected resin was put in barrels and stored in one of the smaller buildings. One of the men who had come this time with Newport had some expertise in making tar and pitch. Smith assigned him a team of six men and they started boiling down the sap into the thick, useful but noxious substances.

Since insects and other debris were embedded in the sticky mass, it needed to be purified before it was of use. The knots were melted in a shallow iron or copper pot. As the foreign material was released someone had to pick it out with a stick. The melted clear resin was known as pitch and was sometimes transferred to a barrel as a product to be sold in England. It was the basis of many types of glue. The resin could also be changed into tar, which was used to seal the space between the boards of a ship, to coat ropes and to weather proof almost anything.

The transformation of pitch into tar required two additional ingredients, charcoal and a binding agent. Charcoal is incompletely burned wood. The grade of charcoal needed for tar could be found in any fire pit. The commonly used binding agent was fibrous plant material. It had to be ground into fine particles to make the best glue. This could be difficult and time-consuming work, so people learned to use a natural source of ground plant fiber, the scat of herbivores. Deer droppings were common.

Even after the digestive process, the material needed to be ground further and the charcoal also had to be ground into a fine powder. The settlers adopted the Indian tools of using a flat rock as a base and a rounded rock as a pestle to grind the charcoal and plant material. The finer the better so it was worth expending a little extra time and effort in the process.

Melting pitch is exceedingly flammable. If flames get near melted pitch even the fumes can catch fire. It was usually wiser to wait until the fire was reduced to a bed of hot coals to minimize the potential for a conflagration in the pitch glue cooking pot. Still, the operation was set up right in the middle of the most open spot in the fort to further reduce the possibility of starting a fire.

The common recipe was one part charcoal to one part binder to five parts pitch. The pitch would become a thick, black, sticky, tar-like substance. The glue mixture stiffened very quickly upon removal from the heat source but could be made soft again by reheating. Once it was cool and solid, it could be stored in barrels and transported to England.

Part of the pitch and tar were set aside to use locally.

Another useful product was potash. It was used in making soap. It was a product of burning wood. Since the ash was only about 10% of the original hardwood, it took a great deal of wood to create potash. Wood was something of which England now had a shortage. It was also labor and time intensive and, because of the caustic nature of the ash, the utensils could not be used for any other purpose. The Dutch had developed a method to make what they called *potaschen*. This was done by leaching water through the wood ashes and then evaporating the resulting solution in large iron pots, leaving a white residue called, in the straightforward Germanic manner, "pot ash".

John Lewes had been sent as a general cooper and to make the special barrels needed for this task. He was also familiar with making potash and lye water, so he would supervise the process. The cooper made three small waterproof barrels that had a lot of holes drilled in the bottom. He made support stands and more waterproof containers to catch the water. He gave a lecture to the men who had been selected to make the lye water.

"Put a layer of gravel in the bottom of the barrel over the holes, then put a layer of straw over the gravel. Fill the rest of the barrel with hardwood ash leaving a couple of inches at the top clear. Now it has to be hardwood. If you put in any pine or poplar the sap will ruin the mixture and stop up the holes.

"Pour rainwater into the barrel. It must be rainwater, pure. Brackish water will contaminate the ash with salt. Swampy water will leave sediment. After a long time the water in the barrel will start to drip into the container. Leave it alone until it stops. You do not want to lose any water nor do you want it to drip onto the ground, so, when you remove one container, you put an empty container in place in case of odd drips."

Boiling the dripped water in an iron pot until the water evaporated leaving a residue that could be collected and easily shipped completed the process of making potash. However, the only way to know if the potash was of the proper quality was to complete the process of making lye water. The team needed to experiment to see if their wood and process were correct. Lewes continued the lecture.

"Transfer the water to an iron pot. Boil the water until it is so concentrated that a fresh egg in the shell floats on top. You must destroy the egg for it is now poisoned. Remember to take all precautions not the let the liquid lye touch your skin or clothing.

"If you can get salt, there is a better way to measure the strength of the lye but when salt is scarce, the egg test is good. When you have done this many times, you will be able to tell you are close just by how the liquid stirs.

"Oak is a good wood for making lye. For really white soap, use apple wood, but I suppose there are no apples here yet. Whatever wood is used, it should be burned in a very hot fire to make very white ashes. When cold, the ashes can be stored in a covered wooden barrel, or a clay pot that has been fired in a pottery-making kiln. If you use one that has just dried in the sun, the water can leak through."

Clearly this process took precision and patience, not characteristics common to young gentlemen or boys. The laborers had so many other tasks and were so often out of the fort that they were not chosen. That left the tradesmen. Some of them had no reason to practice their trades yet. The pipe maker, Robert Cotton, had not found any suitable clay. Daniel Stalings, the jeweler, had no fine metals, no jewels, and no wealthy patrons. Because they were familiar with architecture, John Herd and William Garett, bricklayers, participated in laying out the buildings, but that did not occupy much of their time. There was no need of brick as yet. So these four men became the heart of the potash team. They were joined by some of the tailors, Thomas Hope, William Beckwith, William Yonge, Laurence Towtales, and William Ward, when more men were needed to take shifts to tend the dripping barrels.

The first batch went well. The potash proved to be of good quality. From then on, they stopped the process at the potash stage.

Since the very first voyage, the Virginia Company had required the colonists to make clapboard. To make clapboard, first you need to cut down oak or ash trees. Then you cut the logs into four-foot lengths. Using a maul and froe and moving in a radial pattern, you split the log into quarters, then eighths and so on until you have pieces that are 3/8" to ½" thick. Later each surface would be smoothed with a drawknife.

Since it followed the tree's natural structure, the grain ran parallel to its length and tangent across its edge. This straight grain, which runs vertically to the board, resists warping and twisting. Clapboard siding on a house had been known to last for generations.

During the three days Smith was at the fort back in July, he had met with Doctor Russell and they had devised a way to get the gentlemen of the colony to participate in this hard labor. Russell and Smith goaded thirty gentlemen into cutting clapboard by convincing them it was healthy exercise. They set up a contest between teams. Betting was allowed. Within a week, these gentlemen, who had mostly been talking, drinking, playing at bowls in the streets or all three, had become expert clapboard makers, blisters notwithstanding. The clapboard had been left at the cutting site in the summer and it now had to be brought to the fort.

Smith put all these plans in motion and then he got ready to leave. The colony would be desperate for food and Smith would not depend on Newport to bring back enough food. So he prepared a party to go to the Chickamoninies to get corn.

Newport had taken most of the able-bodied men, but two of Smith's favorites, Josiah Tucker and Richard Savage, had been under the weather when he left, so they were still in the fort and, naturally, accompanied Smith. He did not need a large force and, in any case, he had few useful men to choose from. In the end, he took only twelve.

When he got to the camp of the Chickamoninies, at first he said he wanted to trade for the corn. They seemed reluctant, in fact they insulted him, so Smith changed his tactics. He reminded them of their role in his capture the previous year and told them his honor forced him to pay them back. Knowing that he had been made a weroance and "son" of Powhatan, they gave in and gave him fish, fowl and 279 bushels of corn.

Newport and his army of 120 men had marched 40 miles and found 2 Monacan villages. He abandoned his usual policy of placating the natives. Instead he put shackles on their weroance and forced him to guide them through the new country. Word of the treatment of the weroance spread quickly so that Newport did not find another inhabited village for the rest of his trip.

The gold refiner who had gone with Newport, William Callecut, said he did find some silver. It was in the mud of the river and was a very small amount. They looked for several days, but did not find the source of the mineral. The promised wealth of the new world still eluded the English.

Not being needed on a river excursion, some of the crew of the *Mary and Margaret* stayed on at James Port. While the few remaining colonists subsisted on a bit of corn and some stored vegetables, the sailors, who had kept rations from the ship, were eating very well. Thinking they would bargain for some of the sailors' food, some settlers robbed the storehouse of axes, pickaxes, hoes, chisels, pike heads, and even gunpowder. They offered these to the sailors for butter, cheese, beef, pork, biscuits, oatmeal, oil, beer and alcohol. The ship's kitchen had indeed been well stocked. The sailors then traded the tools and gunpowder to the Indians for furs. They had learned from sailors on the last ship to return to England that these furs would be very valuable back home. They were to be somewhat disappointed, because this bunch of furs was gathered during the summer when animals shed their coats to be cooler. The last ship had carried furs from the winterkill and they were much more luxuriant and sold for exceptional prices.

In the time Smith and Newport were both out of the fort, about seven weeks, the stock of two- to three- hundred tools was down to 20. This was a disaster for the colony because those tools could not be replaced until Newport went back to England (two months) and a new supply could be outfitted and sent (three months or more). That would put them virtually unarmed throughout the winter and well into the planting season without axes or hoes.

There was a "cape merchant" or storehouse keeper, but he neither stopped the thievery or reported it. In fact, once he discovered what the settlers were doing, he joined in.

Smith was first to return. He was furious!

Once again, he had left the fort in search of provisions and those left behind had done irreparable damage. He immediately made a policy of no contact between the settlers and the sailors. He took inventory of what remained in the storehouse, including what he had managed to collect on his expedition. The count was frightening. He hoped that Newport had found good hunting.

Newport had not. He returned with 120 hungry mouths, a bit of possible silver and no food to add to the storehouse. He had left behind a large number of angry, insulted Indians. Winter for the colonists looked bleak.

Smith asked Newport to meet him in the Council house.

"Captain Newport, with very little food, few armaments and no farming tools, I simply do not see how we will survive this winter. We do not have enough space on your ship and the Discovery to transport 200 people back to England. I am somewhat at a loss as to what the Virginia Company expects us to do."

"The Company board must have foreseen this eventuality, Smith, for one of their orders was to disperse the colonists. I must be leaving or we will hit the winter storms. I leave it to you to carryout the Company orders."

Newport denied Smith any title or official role in the colony, yet when it came time to actually get something done, he expected Smith to do the impossible. Smith nearly pulled his pistol on Newport. It was a close thing. From some blessed corner of his mind, Smith had the thought that Newport would soon be gone, maybe forever, and Smith could take charge as he had for the previous year. Smith took a deep breath, stared at Newport one beat longer and then pointedly said, "Yes, sir."

Before he left, Newport sought out Ratcliff. He had a bit of news to share. There had been no rush to tell Ratcliff and no need to tell anyone else.

"John, walk with me."

They strolled across the compound speaking of nothing in particular. When they got out of the gate, they walked slowly side by side as if they were inspecting the palisade.

"What is it, Christopher? You have gone to great pains to have privacy."

"Do you recall one of the sailors who was with me on the *Susan Constant*, a man named Francis Magnel?"

"No, is there a reason I should? Should this man mean something to me?

"Magnel was working with the Irish, the ones who ran to Spain. We caught a ship that was coming from Spain to Ireland and when the judges questioned some of those captured, they told a wild tale of a man called Magnel. Seems he was a spy, sent to Jamestown to collect intelligence for Spanish. He gave them our exact location and explained our defenses. He also told them of our good and bad relations with the naturals.

More to the point, he told them that he had been in contact with one of our leaders who was a hiding Catholic and wanted to come to Spain to reveal everything about our colony and the plans of the Virginia Company."

"Surely, he did not name me as that man?!"

"No, John, not you, Kendall."

"Then he truly was a spy!"

"Perhaps. The curious thing is that another of the captives said that he had talked with Magnel personally and Magnel had claimed to be in the service of Lord Salisbury…as had another of our Captains, a John Sickelmore."

Ratcliff stopped. He seemed like he would protest. Then he relaxed, and simply nodded.

"It is true that I am John Sickelmore. I have said as much here, in the fort. I wished to preside in my true name, not that which I had assumed."

"Smith happened to mention that you had sent a personal letter addressed to Lord Salisbury with Captain Nelson. John, tell me, in the name of what we have been through together, are you working for Salisbury?"

"I do not understand, Christopher. The Virginia Company is sanctioned by the crown. Reports go to Salisbury regularly from the board of the Company. Why would he need to have anyone in his employ?"

"You know what we put in the reports. We put the best face we could on the situation. It is possible he wanted, shall we say, a second opinion."

"So are you saying that Kendall was sending letters directly to Salisbury or to Spain? I find this very confusing."

"As do I, John. I do not know if Kendall sent reports to the Secretary of State or the King of Spain. What I need to know now is why did you write to Salisbury. What did you say about our condition?

"I certainly have never corresponded with anyone in Spain."

"John, you are being evasive."

"Christopher, I swear to you, I have never written to Salisbury anything more than a friendly note."

"John, people may be watching. We should keep moving."

They resumed their walk.

"I believe you, John. I would like to say that I believe you just for yourself. But there is information circulating in London that did not come from our reports. It had to come from somewhere. It must have been Kendall. If the two of you were both working for Salisbury, you would never have condemned him. I think it best that you return with me. You no longer have … er … your illness has compromised your authority here. If you persist in being John Sickelmore, I cannot account for your safety here."

He slapped John jovially on his back.

"Come with me, John, lest the company cut your throat some night."

"Yes, Christopher, I think it is time I went home."

———————————————————————————————————

The courtship of Anne Burris by John Laydon had progressed over the two months they were among the few left in the fort. The day before Newport sailed, the colony marked a momentous first. John and Anne were married, the first marriage in Jamestown.

Her mistress, Mrs. Forrest had not adapted well to the new climate and diet. She had arrived in Virginia weak from the crossing and had really never regained her strength. Six weeks after she arrived, she contracted a stomach ailment. It was not something that spread among the settlers. She was the only victim. She could keep neither food or drink down and, in a matter of five days, she died. Thomas Forrest was devastated. Anne tried to cook for him and keep up his house, but the arrangement became the talk of the fort. It was not seemly for an unmarried woman to stay in the same house as a recently widowed man. John Laydon was sympathetic to her situation. So long as she was a lady's maid, she must remain single. Now that she had no mistress and she could not reasonably stay with Mr. Forrest, John proposed.

For three days, Anne moved her belongings into one of the small storage buildings. On the fourth day, she married John Laydon.

When Newport left, Schrivener and Winne followed him to the mouth of the James. Why they would bother to take a barge thirty miles down river just to turn around and come back mystified Smith. However, the writing was on the wall, Scrivener was no longer Smith's man, he had allied himself with Newport and the Company representatives. Smith was alone, alone except for the 200 men and one woman still at Jamestown who depended on him for their very lives.

CHAPTER 9
The End of Smith

Having done so well with the Chickamoninies with a combination of good will and threats, Smith next took on the Nanesmond. They had no particular reason to trade or feel threatened. Sensing that he had no real bargaining position, Smith simply resorted to force and took 100 bushels of their corn. News spread fast in the woodland network. Other tribes that lived along Smiths path simply hid their corn in the woods and disappeared until he was gone. Raiding as a source of food had dried up.

With only a few weeks of food in the storehouse, Smith was very concerned about provisions. So, in January, when Powhatan sent a messenger to entice Smith to visit by promising a boatload of corn, Smith buried his misgivings and went. He asked for volunteers but only 38 of the two hundred stepped up. These recent immigrants seemed to expect someone else to provide for them. The 38 who did volunteer were Smith's troop of soldiers and a lot of people the colony could not afford to lose, Percy, Frances West (brother of Lord De La Warr), William Phettiplace (Captain of the pinnacle), Robert Ford (clerk of Council), several other gentlemen, and surgeon Antony Bagnall.

Powhatan's messengers told Smith what he wanted for his boatload of corn. He demanded an English house to put his bed in, a grindstone, copper and beads, 50 swords, a hen and rooster, and guns. Smith considered, that if Powhatan had all that extra corn to give for these things, then the corn could be taken if necessary. But he decided to try giving Powhatan some of what he asked to see if he would send the corn.

He sent four Dutchmen ahead to build the house and also two English, Richard Savage, the boy who had been left as Newport's "son," and Edward Brinton, both of whom now knew some of the native's language.

Smith put Schrivener in charge as deputy and told Waldo to stand ready to rush to the rescue if Smith sent word. Smith's party took a shallow draft barge and a deeper draft pinnacle, with twelve in the barge and 26 men with three sailors in the pinnacle. The winter of 1608, like that of 1607, was extremely cold, among the coldest in memory not just in Virginia but also in the entire northern hemisphere. The Prince Henry River was partly frozen, a very unusual occurrence.

The first night out, they stopped on the south side of the river at King Tackonekintaco's village at Warraskoyack. The king entertained Smith and his men. When they were leaving the next morning, the king said a most peculiar thing.

"Friend Smith, Powhatan is dangerous to you. Protect your weapons for he has sent for you only to cut your throats."

Part way up the river, a terrible blizzard swept in. It was December 21st, winter solstice, and the solstice curse had hit again. They stopped at Kecoughton for Christmas week. The Indians also celebrated at this time of year, not for the reasons Christians do, but for the more basic reason that the length of the day began to grow again. People since the beginning of time had celebrated the return of the sun. Christians set the date of birth of the Savior to capitalize on this ancient tradition recognizing the rebirth of the sun.

Back in the fort, Christmas was observed by bringing fresh evergreen branches into each house. Such as they could, they made traditional dishes. They had everything for hasty pudding except quality butter. They used goat's milk and when they boiled the Back River water it improved the taste quite a lot. Cornmeal had become a staple. They tried honey instead of butter. It became a favorite.

The colonists sorely wanted a roast pig or two for Christmas dinner. Scrivener took it upon himself to ignore Smith's orders and to leave the fort and go to Hogs Island for pigs to please the newcomers.

Smith's party reached the landing for Werowocomoco on January 12th. At that point, the river was frozen up to a half mile from shore. Smith used the barge as an icebreaker, but that got it stranded in the mud and they had to wade in icy mud to shore. They were still far from Werowocomoco, so Powhatan sent turkey, venison and bread and had his braves show them where to shelter in abandoned Indian huts. This level of courtesy ended once they sat down to discuss the corn.

Powhatan claimed he had not sent for Smith but only for the house builders. While they dickered for days, the Dutchmen built the house. But they had decided that life with the Indians was better than being hungry with the English. Having no loyalty to the English crown or to their European comrades in the fort and to ingratiate themselves with Powhatan, they told him the quickest way to get rid of all the settlers was to kill John Smith.

Powhatan took the advice to heart and sent men to attack Smith and the sixteen men camping with him not far from the village. Pocahontas, knowing of her father's plan, came herself, in the darkness of night to warn Smith.

"My brother, John Smeeth, our father wishes to do you harm. Leave now or guard yourself closely. Any food brought to you may be poisoned."

"Thank you, my sister. I plan on leaving in the morning to visit your uncle Opechancanough. Tonight I will post extra guards and keep alert. I wish to give you a present in exchange for the aid you have given."

Smith, wanting to impress Pocahontas, as well as the men listening, with how much of the Indian language he had learned, extended his offer to say "kekatan pokahontas patiaquagh ningh tanks manotyens neer mowhick rawrenock audowgh," a sentence he had prepared in his diary. He hoped it meant, "Bid Pocahontas to bring hither two little baskets and I will give her white beads to make her a chain." White beads being the sign that a girl was recognized as having become a woman, offering many white beads was a remarkable way to honor her.

His translation must have been fairly accurate for she replied, "I must return quickly and I cannot return with anything new or my father would know I had been here. Be safe, my brother," and she was off.

A short time later, a group of Indians did come with food. With the warning of Pocahontas added to the warning from Tackonekintaco, Smith had to believe that Powhatan meant to kill him and his men. He would not eat any of the food until the Indians had tasted every dish. The Indians had not planned to poison Smith but to wait in the nearby woods, all night if necessary, in hopes they would find an opportunity to kill Smith. The plan was thwarted since he stayed alert and with the extra guards, the braves had no chance.

In fact, there were several attempts on his life in the next few days. When Smith returned to Powhatan's village to take his leave, Powhatan had directed that Smith should be escorted into a hut where he and Powhatan's extended family were waiting for him. After a short while, Powhatan and his family snuck out the back. The women kept Smith fed to distract him but he became suspicious. He surreptitiously pulled and cocked his pistol. Perhaps it was a sound too close to the side of the lodge, perhaps it was one of the women looking up at the doorway, but some instinct told John to switch positions and aim at the door.

At that moment, several braves, led by a tall, muscular man, came in through the front while dozens more surrounded the hut. Smith shot into the crowd by the door. The tall man was not hit, but the roar of the pistol shot at such close range stunned him into stillness. He recovered in a heartbeat and began to back out of the door mashing into the rest of the group. Between the noise, the smoke and the retreating leader, the rest turned and ran in panic. Smith swung around to see if the women were attacking him from the rear, but they had disappeared.

Smith looked for the back entrance to the lodge and found it easily. Expecting it to be guarded, he bent low and edged his head out the doorway. He sensed no presence of others and so moved out farther. He saw a few Indians gathered on the edge of the woods across from the main entrance to the lodge. By staying in the shadows and keeping the building between him and the Indians, John managed to move to the protection of the far woods.

Smith arrived safely at his camp. The next day, Powhatan sent a pearl bracelet and a chain as an apology for his absence just as if nothing had happened.

The next morning Smith went to search for corn. He went to the village of Powhatan's half-brother Openchancarough. Seven hundred warriors tried to lure him outside to ambush. Smith encouraged his men, " Fight like men, fellows! Do not die like sheep!" Fearing the overwhelming odds, Smith grabbed the chief by the bird's crest in his hair and held his pistol to his chest.

The Indians backed off. They reasoned that any man who would so insult a chief must not fear death. The myths about Smith were growing.

A day later, Smith was napping, having had little sleep for two nights. The Indians tried to get close to him but he woke and got to his sword to fend them off. Another time they did try poison. He drank the poisoned cider and he threw up. The Indians decided he had magic and could not be killed.

Powhatan tried a second plan to get weapons. He sent two Dutchmen (Adam and Francis) back to the fort. They told the settlers all was well, but that they needed more tools. They took clothing and almost all of the weapons that remained from the last shipment, 300 hatchets, 50 swords, 8 muskets, and 8 pikes. The Dutchmen told some of the newcomers about how pleasant it was to live with the Indians. They spoke of ample food, dry huts, and friendly neighbors. Some colonists agreed with the Dutchmen and resolved to defect to the Indians as soon as possible. As a show of friendship, they helped to steal the weapons and tools the Dutchmen had come for, making Adam and Francis promise to tell Powhatan of their help.

Three English were left in Powhatan's camp, Thomas Savage, Samuel Collier, Smith's page who was to learn the language, and Edward Brinton who was to learn the native way to fish. When they saw the Dutchmen with the tools and weapons, Savage and Brinton left to tell the fort officials about the theft. Powhatan wanted to protect his new German friends so he sent braves after Savage and Brinton to bring them back.

Scrivener's trip to Hogs Island would have been simple in good weather, but with the ice in the river and the same blizzard that had stopped Smith hitting Jamestown, the trip should never have been attempted. Scrivener ordered Waldo to go with him to Hogs Island to get the pigs for Christmas. Other prominent people wanted the adventure and some of the good will this would bring from the new settlers. The party now included Anthony Gosnold and 8 other gentlemen. The river was icy and the wind was rising with the coming storm. The boat was already low in the water with just the men. How would it also hold two squirming hogs?

By nightfall, the pig party had not returned. The next day Indians found the bodies washing up in the river or no one would have known what happened.

Apparently the boat capsized and all were killed. Christmas in the fort became a wake.

Captain Peter Winne, the only appointed Council member in the fort, needed to tell Smith about the accident. Winne could not gather a party who was willing to go to Powhatan's village. Richard Wiffin, sixth ranking gentleman from the First Supply, finally volunteered to go alone. When he got there, Pocahontas sought him out. She was afraid the stolen tools incident would put Wiffin in danger, so she hid him and then helped him get to Openchancarough's camp to find Smith.

Smith was proud of Wiffin, grateful to Pocahontas again, and furious with Powhatan. Smith went back by way of Werowocomoco to try to get at the traitorous Dutchmen but Powhatan had evacuated the camp.

Wiffin joined Smith's party. On the way back, Wiffin was walking in the lead. He had gotten a hundred yards ahead of the rest and was walking quietly on long pine needles. As he rounded a rock that was overhanging the trail, he literally ran into one of four men from the fort.

"Oh, sorry, Perkins," Wiffin instinctively apologized.

He looked beyond this Perkins and saw Perkins' brother and the two Salvage brothers all lately arrived.

"What brings all of you out this far?"

The two sets of brothers had been among those who had taken tools from the storehouse and they were actually on their way to join the Indians. Each carried a small haversack containing their clothes, a bit of food, and some trade goods they intended to use to ingratiate themselves to the natives. They each also carried a musket and a more than average supply of powder and shot. By the time this brief exchange had taken place, Smith and the rest of the company had joined them.

Smith took over the inquiry, "Men, are you looking for us?"

Perkins was about to take the offered excuse, but the older Salvage thought faster and realized there was no reason for them to be looking for Smith, so he interrupted, "We … we were hunting and we got lost. Glad we ran into you."

Smith was either distracted or tired because his usual instincts for lying and treachery did not detect the absurdity of this excuse when the men were clearly carrying all they possessed and then some.

"Yes, good fortune indeed," said Smith and left it at that. The Perkins and Salvages joined the company hanging to the rear to avoid more questions.

 When they returned to Jamestown, Smith and Winne were the only surviving members of the Council. Winne deferred in all things to Smith.

The party had brought back 279 bushels of corn and some deer suet. With great care, it might be enough to last until early harvest. To get the new settlers moving, he instituted a "work to eat" policy. Colonists did not like Smith's demanding ways but they did work and did eat. In fact, it being the depth of winter, the work helped to keep them warm. Most of the duties involved either manual labor or, for all of the products England demanded, working near a fire.

The nascent industries had produced a significant amount to be sent to England. They had samples of pitch, tar, potash and a trial of glass. The carpenters led teams to build twenty houses. The church had not been maintained for months and was in a terrible state, nearly falling down. Doctor Russell, who was filing the role of spiritual leader of the colony, was thrilled to have people repair the structure and become more faithful and devout in their attendance.

Spring in Virginia is a magical time. What yesterday was nothing but a muddy bank today is a carpet of crocuses. The twigs of the trees fuzz out in tints of pink, green and grey. And by Easter, the iris line every wet spot with color and heavenly scent, the dogwoods fill the forest with lace, the redbuds are streaks of magenta and the native azaleas dot the world with splashes of impossible color. The air itself ripens into warm afternoons and cool nights. And everywhere there are a hundred shades of green announcing new life. Almost all of the 200 colonists, thanks to Smith, had survived the winter.

With the coming of spring, Smith built a blockhouse on the neck of the island. He garrisoned it with a troop of twenty who stayed there for two weeks at a time. No one was to pass without the President's explicit orders. This shut off most direct access to the mainland. Indians could not come to the peninsula and the settlers could not go to the Indians.

Smith had another blockhouse built on Hogs Island, where the three sows had multiplied to more than sixty. The blockhouse was not to guard the pigs but as a second watch on the river. There was little to do at this outpost, so Smith set these men to cutting the clapboard pieces.

In March, the colonists cleared and planted forty more acres. Two Indians had been brought back to the fort from one of Smith's corn raids. They wore fetters so they could not run away, but over time, they had come to enjoy being with the English. It was common in the Indian culture to adopt prisoners. Kemps and Tassore considered themselves adopted English and so when Smith told the two braves to show the settlers how the Indian women planted corn and other vegetables together, they took it as a sign of acceptance and trust. Among the rows of corn they planted squash. The large leaves of the vines gave cover to the ground and the vines would climb up the stacks as the corn grew. Pumpkins would be planted a bit later.

Since the day when the sailors had caught the giant sturgeon in 1607, fishing had continued whenever there was someone available and it was safe to be outside the fort. All sturgeon are large fish. The settlers had learned to use every part of the fish. They ate the flesh and fed it to their dogs. They even found a way to dry some of the fish and grind it into a kind of flour suitable to make bread.

Once things were running smoothly, Smith left Winne in charge and left to build another fort across the estuary on Grey's. This was a simple earthen fort and it quickly took on the name of "Smith's Fort."

While he was building this earthen fort, Winne sent word that disaster had stuck again. Rats, hiding on the ships from England, had multiplied by the thousands and eaten the corn in the storehouse. There had been no rats in America before. This might have been an excuse if Indians had been inundated with rats, but the English were very familiar with the vermin and should have known to take precautions. How no one noticed thousands of rats in the camp was a mystery. They sorted out what was still even marginally edible. The corn that remained would be gone by the end of April, at least three months before the new crop began to come in.

With few options, Smith decided to do as the new orders had demanded and disperse the colonists. The orders presumed the Indians would be supplying the needs of the colonists and the dispersal would be merely the beginning of a larger colony. The truth was that the colonist would now have to learn to live off the land like the Indians. Sixty-five were sent downriver to live off the oyster beds. Another twenty went back down to Point Comfort under the command of George Percy to find fish. Some went to stay nearby with friendly Indians.

Those who stayed at the fort finally finished the first well. The well was twelve feet deep. It was lined with wood and had sun dried bricks above ground as a coping. After two years, the fort finally had a source of fresh water.

"A toast," Doctor Russell called out to the assembled settlers, "a toast in thanksgiving for a clear cool drink!"

"Huzzah!" answered the throng.

Russell continued, "President Smith, this may be your greatest achievement."

"Thank you Doctor, but I would feel much better if there had been anyone here who had built a well like this before. I mean, a well so close to sea level and so near brackish water. I think we have created a sound structure, but I cannot promise how long the water will stay fresh."

"Then we will add that to our prayers," Russell bowed his head, "that the water remain pure."

By spring equinox, the remaining Dutchmen and the Poles had created a comfortable place at Glass Point. They had a tidy house, shaped more like the longhouses of the Indians than the fort houses. It was built of sturdy timbers, not sticks and mud. As they cut trees for their glassmaking, they had first taken out rough boards to build the house and glass works and then burned the rest. The glass works were a distance apart from the house in case of sparks or an explosion.

The furnace was working well. The first experiments were simply to create glass ingots, essentially short rods of glass. This was to test the viability of the sand and the furnace.

The glass works, being accessible on the neck without going through the blockhouse, had secretly become a meeting place for the traitorous Dutch, the Indians and disgruntled settlers. On March 25, a report reached Smith that two of the renegade Dutchmen were at Glass House and so were Wowinchopunck and forty Paspaghas. Smith went with 20 men to capture the Dutchmen. The Dutchmen and the Indians retreated into the woods. The twenty men went after them and Smith, oddly, went back to the fort alone.

When Smith was about half way between the blockhouse on the neck and the fort, the chief of the Paspaghas stepped out from behind bushes with his bow drawn. Smith had only his personal short sword or falchion. Smith knocked the bow aside and grabbed the king. The king held Smith, Smith held king, and, as they struggled, both went into the river. They tried to drown each other. Smith got the upper hand and held the king's head under. He was going to cut the chief's throat but thought better of it and took him prisoner instead. He hauled him back to the fort and housed him in chains. Before he could make a trade for the chief, perhaps with help from a disaffected settler, the chief managed to escape. Nothing was really gained by the effort, but the incident of Smith capturing the chief grew rapidly in the retelling.

The colonists at the fort did well that spring. With fresh water, some corn, and a bit of hunting and fishing, they did not flourish, but they did maintain themselves. The oyster-eaters did well too. They stayed in their place throughout 1609 and into 1610.

The twenty who went to Point Comfort did not do so well. George Percy was their leader. This was his first chance to show his abilities. Sadly, he was burned in a flash of gunpowder and could not perform as he would have wished. At least that was what he said when he showed up at the fort after six weeks. He said his infirmity (he did sport a hugely bandaged hand) had kept him from being able to command the sixty-five men to do their duty. In fact, he said, that in the six weeks he was with them, they did not throw a single net to fish. Presumably, they were living on something else, because he did not report any deaths and only had Percy returned.

With hunting, fishing and some early crops, the colonists were making do. Indians were again getting permission to visit the fort, sometimes bringing corn to trade. Two young brothers came often and became friendly with a number of the settlers. These brothers sometimes brought a friend along. He was not as well known and when a pistol went missing, a settler complained to the two brothers that their absent friend had stolen it.

David ap Hugh was a Welshman. The Welsh had a long tradition of paying compensation for injuries, accidental deaths and missing property. When he explained his accusation to Smith, he simply either wanted his property returned or he wanted compensation for it.

"My pistol, one I brought with me, my own property, was right there on the table in my house, Sir, President Smith, Sir. I had been cleaning it, it being somewhat old, having belonged to my father. That boy who comes with these two had been standing at my door watching me. As I needed to, well answer nature's call, if you get my meaning, I left to do my business. When I got back, there was no Indian and no pistol."

"Calm yourself, David, we will have your pistol back. Seize these two boys!"

Smith's personal troop did so. One man grabbed each arm so that the boys were sandwiched between two armed men.

"You," Smith pointed to the taller one, "go to your village. Find the thief and find the gun. Return here with that pistol by sundown tomorrow or I hang your brother."

Both boys were terrified. They looked at each other and strained to touch each other. Then the taller one looked at Robert Savage who had been his friend in the Indian camp and since his return. Robert translated what Smith had said and the boys became even more frightened. The taller one chattered on. His face alone told the story that he did not know anything about the pistol and that he had no idea if he could find the gun or the thief. Savage translated as fast as he could.

"I do not believe you," pronounced Smith. "Go or your brother will die."

Savage translated and added, "I will watch over your brother. Do your best. Come back quickly."

The two soldiers marched the boy to the gate of the fort and shoved him out. The other two soldiers took the shorter brother to the "dungeon."

The dungeon was below the southern most room in a three-bay house, a mud and stud longhouse at the end of the 50-foot palisade extending the fort to the east of the southeast bulwark. The building was the biggest so far, seventy-two feet long but the standard seventeen feet wide. The dungeon was in a partially wood-lined cellar. When the building was begun, a cellar was dug under the one room, but a bit later, they dug out a small additional area making the space an L-shape.

A short flight of entrance steps descended from the west and fanned toward the south. The natural subsoil was exposed in the "L" addition but sandy soil had filled in the original north half. In the original section they had sunk two barrels up to the top in the sandy fill to be a sump pump in this repeatedly wet space. A line of "bars", saplings buried in the soil and laced with twigs tied with reeds, formed a light wall that contained a door made in the same fashion. The door was secured by a chain and lock, the same one as had been used before in the locked area of the old storehouse. This small, damp, windowless area set apart by this light wall had been named the "dungeon."

The two soldiers, Josiah and Nathaniel Pecock, led the boy to the top of the stairs. One grabbed the neck of his shirt and marched him down the stairs and through the door.

"You will stay here until your brother returns with the pistol," Josiah said. "I will check on you later."

Tom wrapped the chain tight and turned the key in the lock. He gave the key to Josiah saying, "If you are tending this lad, you will need this."

Savage was waiting outside the longhouse for Josiah to say, "I told this boy's brother I would watch out for him. I want to keep my word."

Josiah was sympathetic. He actually thought his hero, Smith, had gone too far in this affair. "Let me take care of it," he told Savage and went in search of Smith.

"Cap'n, (only his favored troop of soldiers still had his permission to call Smith Captain), that boy will need food and drink and a blanket later."

"Take care of it, son. I mean him no harm, he is only a hostage until the pistol is returned."

"Thank you, sir." Josiah's faith in Smith was partially restored.

There was always at least one common pot of food on a fire near the old Council area. It was never good food. Usually it was corn gruel perhaps with a few chunks of meat hiding in it. A small stack of wooden bowls and spoons sat on the end of the Council table. There was also a pitcher of water and two or three wooden cups on the table. Josiah filled a cup with water and a bowl with corn soup. He took these to the longhouse. One room of the longhouse served as a sort of trading post. Many of the trade items were kept there and the Indians could come to this building without entering the main fort. From the trade goods, Josiah took a blanket. It was not a good blanket but folded in half, the wool would keep most of the damp from the boy's clothing. Josiah threw the blanket over his shoulder, picked up the bowl and cup and went to the dungeon.

"Here," said Josiah, "a bit of food and some water and a blanket for the night."

"Thank you," said the boy. It is very cold here. I would like to make a fire."

"Hmm, well, I will ask the Captain."

Josiah did not ask Smith after all. The Captain had told him to take care of the boy and so he would. He gathered six small logs and some kindling. He carried them to the dungeon and placed them next to the bars.

"Here is a bit of wood for a fire for later. When I bring supper, I will bring fire to light it. Give me the bowl and cup, I will bring more later."

Just at dusk, Josiah returned with food, drink and fire. The Indian boy had put two logs and some kindling on the hard soil by the west wall. He lit the kindling and added one log to rest on the other two. It would not be a big fire but it would alleviate the chill of the damp ground.

The next morning, Josiah brought a fresh bowl of soup and cup of water. When he reached the bars he called out, "Wake up sleepy head, it is morning!" The boy did not move. Josiah called again, but there was still no answer. He put down the bowl and cup on the shelf where the musketeers could stand to shoot through ground level openings. He unlocked the door and shook the boy by the shoulder. He appeared to be dead. Josiah ran out shouting, "Captain Smith, help, Captain!"

Everyone in earshot gathered round. Smith came too and brought the boy's brother who had returned at first light.

"Stay back, everyone. Josiah, lead us to him."

Josiah, Smith and the boy's brother managed to fit into the space behind the bars. Smith noticed the charcoal beside the wall and the baked red clay under it. The place smelled of a cold fire.

"Josiah, did you let this boy have a fire here last night?'

"Yes, sir. He was cold. I was trying to take care of him. Did I do wrong?"

"Not exactly. There is no ventilation in this space. He breathed in too much smoke. Go, quickly, bring me some rum."

Josiah was back in minutes with a large cup of rum. Smith rolled the boy over and pressed the cup to his lips. A little dribbled into his mouth. In a moment he swallowed. Smith forced more rum. The boy coughed, curled up in a ball, and coughed more until he threw up. Then he gagged and took in large gulps of air. As soon as he was breathing normally again, he spotted his brother and smiled. His brother's mouth was hanging open. It seemed as if Smith had raised the boy from the dead.

First he defied death and now he had conquered it. Smith's reputation with the Indians had reached nearly supernatural status.

Across the ocean, Captain Newport was mounting a new supply. This would be a large fleet of seven ships and up to 600 settlers. They started out in mid-May, stopped at Plymouth on May 20th to pick up passengers, and then had to stay at Falmouth through the month of June.

This large venture and the appointment of a new governor, Sir Thomas Gates, was the idea of Thomas West, Lord De La Warr, who had been on the board of the Virginia Company from the first. Not only would Smith's detractor Newport return to Jamestown, but so would the rest of the old Council members who hated Smith. What no one knew was that De La Warr was negotiating to have himself appointed Governor General of Jamestown for life. A second charter for the Virginia Company was on the desk, so to speak, of King James I. It would be a few more days before he would sign and seal the charter, so for now, the fleet would go assuming Gates to be Governor.

Newport would be the admiral of the flagship, *Sea Venture*. This ship would also carry the new governor Gates, Captain George Somers, a new Council member and a gentleman named William Strachy. The "silly" former President, John "Sicklemore" Ratcliff, would command the *Diamond* as vice admiral of the fleet. The rear admiral of the fleet would be the *Falcon*, captained by brothers Martin and Francis Nelson. Apparently not having found better employment, Gabriel Archer would captain the *Blessing*. He was bringing the first horses to Jamestown, in fact six horses and two mares in foal. The rest of the fleet consisted of the *Unity*, the *Lion*, the *Swallow*, two smaller vessels, a two-masted ketch and the famous pinnacle *Virginia*, the first ship to be built in America. It had been built in the Popham colony, a plantation near the mouth of the Kennebec River set up by the rival Virginia Company of Plymouth in late 1607 that was abandoned in 1608. Another pair of brothers, Captains Robert and James Davies who had been part of the Popham expedition, would captain the *Virginia*.

Word of this new expedition reached Jamestown long before the fleet. In July of 1609, the *Mary and John*, was lying outside the breakers holding a funeral for one of their men who had died. He was the oldest man on the ship. He had been at sea since the age of nine when his uncle, who had sailed for Good King Henry, had signed him on as a cabin boy. He had sailed with Drake in the attack on Cadiz and during the destruction of the Spanish Armada. He was one of the men Drake had taken along to receive the thanks of the magnificent Queen Elizabeth I. Two days ago, he was climbing in the rigging as he had done for over forty years. Then yesterday, he had gone to his hammock, fallen asleep and died. He was a legend among his fellow sailors, so they took the day to commit his remains to his beloved ocean and to honor him with tall tales of his many exploits.

As the sun set, the orange rays lit up the sails of a ship on the eastern horizon. The sentry in the crow's nest called down that it was a Spanish galleon. Wanting to avoid an encounter, the captain hoisted the anchor, put on all sail and ran into the dark of the bay. He stayed near the southern shore hiding behind the point. He moved well into the night and finally dropped anchor once the sentry could no longer identify the mouth of the bay.

The ship was on the move just after first light on the 25th. They wanted to be in the safety of the river, so they went ahead, knowing they were fighting the tide. The *Mary and John* continued up the James and late in the day the fort sentry cry went up for spotting a vessel in the river.

The *Mary and John* was a commercial fishing vessel. They were looking for sturgeon. This was the first vessel to come to use James Fort as an English port in the new world. James Fort was now James Port, on its way to being the equal of Kingstown, Jamaica.

This alone would have been sufficient reason for great celebration, but besides being the first "customer" of James Port, the Captain of the ship was Captain Samuel Argall, cousin by marriage to Thomas Smythe, new treasurer of Virginia Company and related to the wife of Lord De La Warr. It was probably no accident that this particular Captain chose to dock at Jamestown. He carried some startling news.

Smith and Winne were the only Council members present to greet their first customer.

Smith took the lead, "Captain Argall, how was your crossing?"

"Exceptionally smooth, President Smith, except for the loss of a beloved comrade. We buried him at sea just outside the Bay. A Spanish ship may have spotted us while we were at anchor, but I believe we eluded them. The river here is a pleasure to navigate. I am happy to have found you so easily."

"We had a three-mile notice of your coming. I believe we have chosen a good place for a port."

"I would have hoped to find more of the Council present. "

"Alas, Captain, most have returned to England. Captain Gosnold succumbed here after only three months and we lost both Scrivener and Waldo in a boating accident just before Christmas last."

"Sad tidings indeed. Then I shall deliver my news to you. The Virginia Company has written a new Charter and decided to change the government. They have appointed a Governor, Sir Thomas Gates. He is close behind me with a fleet of seven ships and 600 colonists. I came by the short route through the Azores, but they are traveling the usual route through the Caribbean. The fleet should arrive in two or three weeks."

Smith was at a loss. He was shocked and angry. The silence was going on too long. He fell back on a weak civility, "I am sure Sir Thomas will bring good ideas for the settlement."

No President, no Council, an aristocrat in charge. It felt like Jamestown would become the estate of one man. What would happen to the promise of shared profits? To the freedom they had to select their own leader?

Captain Argall decided some time on land would be a good for himself and his crew so they settled in for an extended stay.

The same day the Spanish spotted the *Mary and John* outside Chesapeake Bay, the fleet, which had left over a month later than planned, sailed directly into a hurricane or rather the hurricane sailed into the fleet. The storm moved along slowly westward carrying the ships with it but pushing them apart. It lasted from Monday July 24 to until Friday July 28. The Sea Venture lost the ketch it was trailing and ended up just off the Bermuda coast where the winds pushed them toward the reefs.

The *Sea Venture* drove bow first into the fork of a coral and stuck there. All 150 passengers and crew got off safely. They moved what they could of the hull ¾ mile to Westerly where they began to assemble two ships from the wreckage, adding cedar wood from the island. This had been done before when other ships wrecked but there was no one to help and it took the passengers and crew months to rebuild and refit.

While the rebuilding was going on, the other remaining ships were straggling into Chesapeake Bay. The Blessing arrived first. On August 3, the *Lion* caught up with *Blessing*, then the *Falcon* came and then the *Unity*. They gathered near Point Comfort to take stock of their conditions. Two had a few casualties. The *Falcon* was said to have plague, so no one went to the ship or was allowed off of it. The *Unity* was in sorry shape with only ten of her seventy settlers fit and only the master, his servant and one sailor well enough to do their duties. The *Blessing* and *Lion* loaned a few crewmembers to the *Unity* and took on some of the ailing passengers for better care. Then the four vessels moved together into the James River on August 11 and arrived at Jamestown that evening.

The river sentry called out, "Four ships, two miles out!"

Smith came to the gate of the fort. As he watched the people come off the ship, he worried about where they would stay, what they would eat, what they would do and how cooperative they would be. Each time a new supply came, so many of the newcomers sickened and died in the first few months, he wondered how many of these people would be alive by Christmas.

As he was lost in thought, the Captain of the *Blessing* came to the rail. He caught Smith's eye. It was Archer. Smith had thought he was rid of him forever. Now here he was back with new orders and in the company of the new Governor. Smith was contemplating how fast he could mount a party to go somewhere away from the fort when he noticed another old face on the bridge of the *Falcon* – John Martin. Smith's spirits fell further. He turned and went back to his tent to contemplate his next move.

Smith had been content to keep using the small marquee tent that had been used by Wingfield and Ratcliff. This tent was used as the meeting place for all official gatherings and as the hospital tent as needed. There was a cot in the back at one end and another near the front on the other side. A table and four small rough benches completed the furniture. With three seated on each cot, the space could hold ten men seated and a few more standing. A lantern brought from the *Discovery* provided light and a small writing desk left by Wingfield also sat on the table. Smith's personal belongings were hung in packs on pegs set in the two main tent poles.

It was not long before Archer presented himself at Smith's door. With exaggeration on his new title and thick sarcasm in his voice, Archer greeted Smith.

"President...Smith. It is good to see you again."

In the brief time he had to think about this new development, Smith had decided to keep a low profile until he could find out exactly what he was up against.

"Captain Archer, thank you. How was your voyage?"

"Until two weeks ago, very pleasant. Just as we came into the Caribbean, the fleet was hit by a hurricane. All of the ships are damaged and we have not seen the *Sea Venture*, the *Diamond*, the *Virginia* or the *Swallow* since. My ship, the *Blessing*, the *Unity* and the *Lion* are here as well as the *Falcon*. She is captained by an old friend of yours, John Martin."

Archer had hoped to shock Smith, but having seen Martin, Smith frustrated Archer by keeping a calm face.

"Yes, I saw John on his ship. Why is he not with you?"

"There were rumors of plague on his ship. He called down to me that he would hold everyone aboard until we, ... er..., you determined what should be done."

This was a whole new dimension to the coming of all these new settlers. If they brought plague, the colony could be wiped out. To leave them isolated on the ship might condemn all aboard.

"Does he have sufficient medical help, do you know?"

"He does not. He asked if you have a physician here now."

"Wotton is still with us. And we have a new surgeon, Post Gittnat. I will ask if either of them is willing to go aboard. Wait a moment while I send for them."

Smith went outside and waved down one of his squad, John Herd.

"John, go find Doctor Wotton and Post Gittnat. Ask them to come here as quickly as suits."

Archer and Smith spoke more of the voyage for a few minutes and then both medical men arrived. Smith apprised them of the situation. Wotton was reluctant to go, having never encountered plague before. Gittnat, however, had traveled extensively and assured Smith that he had seen many sicknesses called the plague, none of which had turn out to be that. He would go and check those ill and either report or send word back to Smith.

Archer used this lull to drop what he hoped was more bad news on Smith. "I did not mention who the other Captains are, did I? Ratcliff captains the *Diamond* and Newport is the Admiral of the fleet on the *Sea Venture*. You may also have heard of the brothers Robert and James Davies, the men who helped build the *Virginia* at Popham, they Captain her."

They discussed the Popham colony a bit especially the rumors that the politics of the Virginia Company had caused its failure. This conversation was interrupted by the arrival of John Martin with Martin's man Anas Todkill carrying their gear. Todkill held back the tent flap with one arm, Martin's eyes met Smith's and he smiled.

"Your surgeon has given us a bill of good health. I am his messenger. He is arranging for those who are ill to be brought into camp. How are you, John?"

Martin had sided with those who were against Smith but he had never been the cause of any grief. Smith smiled back.

"I am well, John. Good to hear we do not have plague to deal with on top of everything else. We have not had time or manpower to build lodging for your people. I hope your people are prepared to do for themselves."

Archer responded, "We have women and children with us this time. But, on the good side, we have a number of men who have recently ended service in the Netherlands and are experienced as soldiers and builders. They will need a day or two to get their land legs, but should be able to go directly to work.

What you need to know, Smith, is that we have new orders from the Virginia Company."

Archer thought he would lay a bombshell on Smith. But since Captain Nelson had already delivered the news about the Governor, Archers bomb fizzled. Archer stated the situation in as hurtful terms as he could.

"The Company has abolished the office of President. You no longer have any authority. A Governor, Sir Thomas Gates, has been appointed and he brings a new charter."

Smith had had some time to consider the new arrangement and had decided to accept it, but with Archer goading him, and with no Governor in evidence, he chose to look for a loophole.

"Where is the Governor?"

"He was on the *Sea Venture*."

"Where is this new charter?"

"It is on the flagship with him."

"And does he have a second in command?"

"Yes, Admiral George Somers."

"And he is …?"

"On the *Sea Venture*."

Archer's hope of a coup had faded with each question.

"Then, Captains, I believe the proper course is to continue under the existing charter until such time as the new charter or the new Governor arrive. Do you agree?"

Martin nodded immediately. Archer hemmed and hawed a bit, but could find no sound argument against Smith's position. He grabbed at one last straw.

"Yes, I agree we should continue with the existing charter, but I think we should reconsider who is in charge."

"Let us leave things as they are until we are more certain of the fate of the missing ships. Since I am familiar with the current situation here, I believe I am in the best position to help get everyone settled. Let us take up the matter of leadership at a later date."

Martin asserted himself, "I agree. Let us get settled, Gabriel, and return to this topic later."

Archer had no support so he agreed.

Two days later, Smith's woes increased with the arrival of John Ratcliff and the *Diamond*. Both main masts had been snapped in the storm and many passengers and crew were extremely ill. A few days later, the *Swallow* landed in much the same shape. The American-made *Virginia* returned home a few days after the *Swallow*. She was a smaller and slower ship and, though she was in good condition, it had taken her Captains longer to come from the Caribbean and, since they had not been there before, to find the Chesapeake and Jamestown.

600 had left England. Thirty-two were dead on the *Diamond* and *Swallow*. 150 were missing with the *Sea Venture*. Still there were nearly 400 new colonists to accommodate. The soldiers Archer mentioned amounted to about 50 of the newcomers, 50 were women and a few children, and the rest were divided into useful tradesmen and laborers and, what Smith called, "unruly gallants."

On Sunday, August 23, after a thanksgiving church service, Smith assembled the remaining councilman, Winne, and the fleet Captains to discuss governing the colony. He asked Ratcliff to review what he knew of the new charter. Then he put forth his argument for continuing to govern by the original charter until the new one arrived. No one disagreed with staying with the original charter, but Archer again brought up the question of who should be in charge. Having had almost two weeks to think on it, Smith had a plan. In response to Archer's request, Smith offered to surrender the Presidency to John Martin. He considered Martin to be much the lesser of evils among the three returning men. Since Martin had been one of the original Councilmen and one who had never been deposed, as had Ratcliff, there was no good argument against Martin. Winne and the Davies brothers, not being aware of the undercurrents between Archer and Smith, readily agreed to this appointment.

Smith suggested that Martin dismiss the meeting and left the President's tent promising to return later for his personal belongings. Martin could command a ship, but he had no experience in managing an entire city. He started making lists of what he needed to do. After three hours, he went out looking for Smith. He found him in the west bulwark watching the river, smoking a pipe. Smith greeted him warmly,

"Hello, John, how is it going?"

"I do not know how you do this. It is beyond my abilities." He stood at attention and declared, "President Smith, I return the office to you."

"Now John, Archer and Ratcliff are not going to take kindly to my being in charge. You know that."

Martin relaxed, "I do. I do. I will take them aside and explain that this is no longer a small adventure. You have been here to grow into this role. None of us are qualified to deal with all the people, the industries, the building, it is just more than any of us can do. I really do not know how you do it."

"Thank you, John. You are correct. I have grown into it. We have been through a lot here. But even I am at a loss as to how to house 500 people in a fort meant for a hundred. I have been thinking that the new order to disperse into several locations is our only option. Let's go back to the tent and consider where we might locate some new settlements."

Smith reclaimed the President's tent having never moved his personal belongings. Since he had won over Martin, Smith wisely kept him close as an advisor. However, Smith still relied on only Doctor Russell and "Smith's Squad" for real decision-making and leadership.

Having horses was a great benefit, but it presented new challenges. Smith ordered that a rough corral be thrown up along the middle of the east palisade. He sent a small party to the west end of the island to cut long grass for feed. With a little room to exercise and some fresh food, the horses started to recover quickly. But clearly it would be a continuing chore to bring in fodder daily, so Smith decided the horses should be led or ridden to a spot where they could forage for themselves. This too consumed a man or two, but it seemed better for the animals and Smith appreciated horses.

He was daydreaming about riding a good horse across the meadows of Lincolnshire on the day that a party of eight approached him led by Archer.

"We will be taking the horses out for a good ride today," he said while pulling on a new pair of expensive riding gloves. Ratcliff, Martin, and Percy, his old nemeses, were in the group along with newcomers Captain Francis Nelson and Captain Francis West. The company was clearly meant to be the cream of Jamestown society. Curiously Dru Pickayes was the seventh gentleman in the group. They had commandeered young Josiah Tucker apparently to act as groom.

Smith would generally have told this group a flat "no," but he had just spent a pleasant quarter hour at the corral and knew the animals needed a good outing. But he could not resist poking at them a bit and so made a point of speaking to none of them, but to Josiah.

"Riding, Josiah, oh yes, you must have some experience with horses from the farm."

Josiah hung his head a bit, thinking he was betraying his mentor to be in the company of these enemies.

"Very well, gentlemen. Did you have a destination in mind?" he asked cordially.

"We will be following the Company orders to seek a new location for the capital of Virginia." Archer turned, bowed slightly in the direction of the whole group and smiled.

"Today?" Smith exclaimed. How far do you think you can go in a day and be back to the protection of the fort by dark?"

"Mr. Smith," West said, intentionally not using Smith's title, "a good horseman can cover forty mile in a day's riding. Right gentlemen?" It was not a question, he was merely asking for agreement from the gentle folk in the company. "Let us be off!"

As soon as Smith had agreed to the outing, Josiah had scurried off to saddle the horses. By the time the rest of the group arrived, he had five of the eight ready.

"Come along, youngster, we have not got all day to wait for you," prodded West who had taken the lead in this adventure.

After a bit of commotion over who would take which animal, Josiah had finished his task and they all mounted and rode out sounding like a happy party going on a fox hunt. Nelson even hooted to sound rather like a hunting horn.

As soon as thy cleared the gate, each one took off at the fastest gait they could manage. All but Josiah had reached a good canter as they entered the main path to the neck of the peninsula. West was in the lead. The path had been used enough in the last year that the first two hundred feet were wide open. All seven gentlemen had entered the woods within the short time it took West to reach the point where the trail closed in quickly.

Until today, every being that had passed along the path had been no more than seven feet tall including muskets held on shoulders and tall hats. A mounted rider reaches eight, nine or ten feet depending on the size of the horse and length of the back of the rider. The branches up to seven feet had all been broken away over time but no higher. West looked back over his shoulder to shout at his fellows just as he rode headlong beyond the wide part of the path an into a bunch of branches eight and nine feet above the ground.

A rather sturdy pine bough slapped him hard up the side of his head knocking his sugarloaf hat into the bushes. He instinctively tugged hard on the reins, too hard, and his unfamiliar mount reared and twisted to free itself of the painful bit. This threw West into more low hanging branches that swatted at him from all sides. Finally the horse gave a mighty twist in the opposite direction and West went flying. He landed hard on his rump.

The others had been thrown into great disarray by the flailing horse but all had managed to keep their seats. As one, they dismounted and ran to their fallen leader like a covey of protective quail.

While they all clucked at West and sought his hat in the brambles, Percy salvaged the day, "Captain West, it was a wretched racoon! I saw it dash under your mount's legs. I do not doubt we will find those sharp claws scored the stallion. No man could have overcome such an attack."

West completely understood the prevarication and he accepted the excuse gladly and gratefully.

"Was that what it was? I have not seen such a creature before. Native to this area, I gather? Quite a creature, quite a monster!" And they all obediently laughed with him. All except Josiah, who had come along at a more reasonable pace yet witnessed the entire event. He did not feel so disloyal to Smith now. Smith would hear every detail just as soon as they got back to the fort.

Hat and dignity recovered, the gentlemen remounted and continued up the trail at a walk.

All of this tidewater geography was similar. It was only a few feet above sea level and land near water was inundated twice daily with the tide. This made for lush grass and reed beds that were passable at low tide and wet at high tide surrounded by first growth forest that was mainly pines with some oak and birch. The Indians had cleared some spots as corn, squash or bean fields. Once abandoned, those might still be grassy or have gone to second growth forest of smaller trees, again some varieties of pine and poplar as well as even smaller flora like magnolia and rhododendron interspersed with scrub brush. In the grassy areas and first growth forests with little ground cover, the riders could trot and canter, but nowhere was there continuous space enough to gallop.

Soon the gallants were frustrated, hungry and bored. They were also lost.

"Percy, have you been here before?" asked West.

"No, I have not traveled inland much. I did accompany Newport to Powhatan's home village but that was in the other direction… I think."

The gents talked among themselves for a while and when the conversation quieted, Josiah spoke, "I believe I know where we are."

All heads snapped toward him.

Percy took the lead, "Then why did you not say so, boy! Get us back to a familiar road and be quick about it."

Josiah had considered whether he should speak up or not. He had seen this before. A gentleman would always make a workingman responsible but never give him the credit. However he wanted to go home too and could not see how he could go without taking them along.

"This way, gentlemen." He did not go back the way they had most recently come. West and Percy had, in fact, been leading the troop in circles for some time. Josiah struck out down a narrow trail that ran due south. In twenty minutes, they crossed a much wider trail that ran in sight of the river from time to time. This trail led to the neck of the island. They were on the known trail for almost an hour before anyone recognized it.

Percy said, "The way is clear to me now, Captain West, see that clump of trees up ahead, that is a marker. We will be at the fort within the hour."

In another thirty minutes, just as the sun set, they were in sight of the fort.

West, again feeling confident, challenged the others, "Well done, Percy. Race you to the fort!" and they were off. Josiah sighed. He was used to such treatment but it never failed to hurt.

There was a critical need to move most of the new settlers to new locations. George Martin and George Percy went downstream with 60 men and

Michael Sicklemore (no relation to Ratcliff/Sicklemore) as lieutenant. They force marched south. The rest of men went by boat to the west bank of the Nansemond River to Dumpling Island.

Percy sent messengers to buy the land from the local tribe. The Indians really had no sense of "owning" the land. When the messengers came into the village with a basket of copper, the Indians did not know what to make of them. The men continued to move toward the largest hut in the village. Warriors tried to stop them. The messengers would not stop. The Indians had received Powhatan's announcement about harassing the English and this insult to their weroance was enough to trigger them into action. They seized the messengers and killed them.

Even before they knew the messengers were dead, Percy and Martin had led the men in beating the native inhabitants off the island. They burned their houses, ransacked their temples, took down the corpses of their dead kings from their elevated tombs, and carried away pearls, copper and bracelets for the burials.

The son of the local king was on the island visiting the village. As the representative of his father, the young man and his companion, stood up to the English when they attacked the village. He was immediately overwhelmed. Martin captured the king's son and one other Indian and took them to their camp. There a boy from the latest supply, wanting to show his manhood, shot the king's son. In the commotion, both Indians broke away. The wound was not serious and the king's son and his friend swam to the mainland and spread the word of his treatment. The story of the king's son was known in all parts of Powhatan's world in a matter of days.

Percy returned to Jamestown to report their success in inhabiting the island. Before he left he had told Martin he felt that he was a marked man and that if he stayed on the island, he would be targeted by the king and his people. Martin understood the feeling. He would have gladly returned to Jamestown as well, but since Percy had been made the ranking commander, Percy returned and Martin stayed.

The Virginia Company board wanted a significant exploration of the upper James River above the falls. Captain Francis West used his influence as the brother of Lord De La Warr to claim leadership of this adventure. He assembled a large party of 130 men. He took thirty of them to the storehouse where the supplies that had come on the *Mary and Margaret* were stored. He ordered them to collect food, tools and trade goods, enough to supply the party for six months. He also took an excessive amount of powder and shot and an extra musket for every other man. They loaded all but a week's food supply onto a barge and a pinnacle. A small crew would bring the supplies up to the falls and leave the barge as a means of quick return or to hold the ore they were to find. The pinnacle would bring all the crewmen back.

Smith had made this trip in three days. His groups were small and knew how to travel light and fast. A group of over a hundred people, unused to rough terrain, took a great deal longer. Smith had provided an excellent map. They were going by the shortest route, but there were not many locations suitable for 130 men to camp, so when one was located within ninety minutes of sundown, they stopped. The gentlemen were used to eating at the beginning of the day, again at one with a food break at four and a supper at seven. The soldiers were not, they had learned to eat many meals on the march, but the gentlemen complained about having to limit themselves to two meals a day.

On the second day, a group of about fifteen young gentlemen rebelled and stopped at a stream just after noon. They had hung to the back in the line of march and slowly fell further behind as the sun reached its zenith. Each had gathered some extra food at breakfast and they all sat on logs or rocks near the stream to picnic.

Once settled, the ringleader laughed loudly and announced, "I knew they were being overcautious. There is no reason why a proper gentleman should have to miss his midday meal."

The others laughed as well and fell to munching and chatting in twos and threes. Someone started circulating a rude joke and as the laughter grew three arrows shot through the group and landed in the water. It took a couple of heartbeats for the gents to realize what had happened. Then they reacted as one. They dropped the food in their hands, grabbed the belongings they had put down while jumping to their feet. They took off down the trail toward the rest of the party as fast as their legs could carry them. Three more arrows shot past them, one knocking the hat off the last man.

They were running so fast that they could not stop when they came upon the end of the column and they ran into the soldiers who were the rear guard.

Holding the young men up as they nearly fell from the impact, the oldest soldier said, "Hang on there, young gentlemen. What has you on the run?"

The ringleader was still too scared to speak. His sideman spoke for the group, "Needed the privy." He gasped for breath. "Did not want to loose you."

The soldiers chuckled, "Alright, you have found us. Here, get in front of us and let us know if you feel the need to leave again."

The inconsistent attitude of Powhatan had swung to the negative again when he was told of the arrival of women. He had wanted to believe these men would leave once they found what they were looking for, but women meant permanence. He had given permission for his braves to harass the coat-wearers whenever they could. This was the only outright attack on the traveling group, but they were unknowingly shadowed by Indians almost the entire time.

On the fifth day, West was studying Smith's map. It looked like they were just past half way to the falls. He asked his lieutenants to evaluate the food supply and was told that the supplies they were carrying were running low if they still had five days to go. A few men were already borrowing from others and many more had one or two days of food left. West gave orders to go on half rations, news that was met with much grumbling from mouths and stomachs. The soldiers were used to better planning from their officers and the gentlemen were used to having food just for the asking.

The eighth day, they heard the falls and an hour before sundown they found a suitable camping place. West was now sending scouts out to look an hour ahead and they reported that the company could round the falls in just over an hour. West decided to continue the march and arrive at their destination before stopping. West and the front of the column did well. They rounded the falls and picked a good camping spot just as the sun went behind the horizon. However, the second half of column was trying to round the falls in the deepening dusk, the very end in full darkness. Even the soldiers objected to being asked to traverse treacherous ground in the pitch dark.

The first half had time to make a rough camp, but the second half reached the open meadow of the camp and simply fell where they could and slept.

The next morning, West gave no direction to the men. He and his staff explored the meadow and determined where they would establish themselves. Left on their own, over a hundred men roamed the area. The soldiers in the group went in search of the barge and pinnacle to retrieve the other supplies. The young gents went out looking for whatever they could find. One group found an Indian camp, a fortified camp with fenced gardens and harvested crops. Seeing easy pickings, most kept watch while two of their number crept to the fencing and stole two ducks and several squash, all hung along the fence. This was only the beginning of raiding this well-established village.

The soldiers did find the barge tied to two trees on the south bank of the river about half a mile below the falls. The pinnacle was nowhere in sight. Apparently, the crews had tired of waiting for the land party, anchored the barge and headed home. They pulled enough supplies out for themselves and their friends and headed back to the meadow.

Late in the day, West sounded a bugle call to gather the company. He pointed out the location he had chosen to build a fortification. He assigned work crews for the next day. Then he assigned a scouting party to look for the barge.

"Shall we tell him we found it?" asked one soldier.

His friend answered, "I have been with some ineffective officers in my time, but a man who looks for a fort site before he looks for food is about the worst. No, let him waste his time, we have food."

The soldier nodded slowly and sadly.

Percy was very happy to have Archer, Ratcliff, and Martin back. He was hoping Newport and the new Governor would arrive soon. The commoner Smith had been in charge far too long. Percy was ready to give the upper class the upper hand again. He had long been irritated that he had not been appointed to the Council. When the silly Ratcliff had been deposed, he, Percy, should have been the logical choice, not Smith.

Percy noted that number of deaths in 1609 was much lower than it had been in the two years before. Those few who had survived the summer and fall of 1607 had become accustomed to the climate, the food, the water, and the need to watch for danger. Those who had come in the second supply and were still alive were acquiring this naturalization. Death for these groups was now limited to the usual hazards of personal illness and accident. The newcomers were a different story and how soon they would adapt was still to be seen.

There was still some danger from the Indians for everyone, but the fort was safe. So were those settlers who had gone to neighboring friendly Indian villages. About 200 settlers were in the fort or in these friendly villages. Forty were still at Point Comfort living off the seafood. 130 were with West at the falls. Thirty men were at the glass house and the blockhouse at the neck. There were eight crews in port with their ships, including the commercial fishing ship, the *John and Mary*. Things seemed to be at a stable point. If only the Governor would arrive now, Percy could easily discount Smith's role in their progress and claim his own rightful place in the government.

Smith was aware that Percy was disgruntled, but he had no time to worry about such petty matters. He was completely involved in keeping the industries moving along and keeping the colony safe and fed. He sent Ratcliff up the Pamunkey River with a small group to bargain with Powhatan for more corn. There had been no serious attacks recently and the trip seemed relatively safe. Unfortunately, this village was still hostile and when Ratcliff's men came on shore, they were killed and Ratcliff himself was taken prisoner. He was handed over to the women of the village who knew how to give a man a long and painful death.

Knowing nothing of the fate of Ratcliff's party, Smith continued hopeful of turning out a significant set of product for shipment to England. Every product seemed have run into some difficulty. For example, the making of clapboard had slowed to a crawl because it had become difficult to find a trees fit to be a source. The scouts had found a stand of trees five miles from the fort. The trees could not be dragged that far so the logs would need to be sectioned into lengths suitable for transport by cart or by floating them down the small rivers to nearer the island.

Smith concentrated on how to get soft-handed, lazy young gentlemen to perform such hard labor. He revived the plan of advertising the cutting as a form of healthy exercise and gamesmanship. He took a party of thirty gentlemen on a five-mile hike carrying axes and froes. When they reached the site of the oak trees, they divided the group into three teams and made felling the trees a competition. It took all afternoon for each team to bring down its first tree. They all had blisters but felt like they had conquered the world. They bound up their blisters and created their own competition for the next day. Within a week they were actually good at the process and enjoyed hearing the trees thunder to the ground. Sectioning the logs was less fun, but the competition made the work worth it.

The summer had been the best of the three years at Jamestown. They were moving into the fall with great hopes.

Above the falls, West had chosen a natural depression in the meadow through which a small brook constantly ran. He considered having this source of fresh water a brilliant stroke.

He had 130 shovels, but only fifty men could fit in the trenches, so digging progress was slower than he had hoped. They piled the dirt in a mound outside the trench and, contrary to usual practice, the saplings were staked into the top of the dirt pile to form a wall about ten feet high. The saplings were only about five feet high so that the settlers could shoot over them easily while any attacking Indian would have to climb up five feet of loose dirt into the mouths of the muskets. There was only one entrance blocked by a gate of interlaced saplings. It was awkward to move and so was typically left partly open.

The supplies were carried up to the new fort and stored in the center covered again by the oiled sailcloth that the crew had put on the barge. Having them piled together this way made it inconvenient to find what was needed. This combined with a growing fever for finding gold led to more raiding of the Indian village to steal food.

The raiding became so hurtful that the village set up regular patrols. In only a few days, the little fort had become a prison. Anyone who left the fort returned hurt or did not return at all. West could not put up with this situation. He set up a watch to find out where the Indians set up their ambush. He put together a team and surrounded the spot. When the Indian patrol changed shifts, West and his team closed in and took three Indians hostage.

When the Indians discovered that the patrol had been captured, the attacks turned into warnings. Anyone who left the fort was shot at, but the Indians always missed. They wanted the settlers to know they were there and watching. West did not take the hint. He sent out groups to look for gold.

One day, when he was out with one of these gold parties, twelve Indians rushed from the trees and attacked some stragglers as they reentered the fort. They pushed them through the gate, smashing the weak, stick-built gate. The savages yelled and brandished their war clubs. The three hostages were not in any building but only tied together against the far wall of the fort. The attackers cut them free and rushed out of the gate and back into the forest before the settlers mounted any kind of defense.

One of Smith's first tasks after West left James Fort was to take inventory of the remaining supplies. When he realized how many supplies West had taken, he resolved to go upriver and bring back the overage. It had taken him several days to get the newcomers settled. The *Sea Venture* had still not arrived and Smith made it known that he intended to keep his post as President until September 10 when his term would end. He wanted to get to the falls and back with the supplies before the September 10 deadline.

Smith took his canoe. He had traded for it on one of his trips. He wanted to be able to travel the rivers as quickly and easily as the Indians. He wanted to take his usual squad with him for this trip, but he was nervous about leaving Ratcliff, Archer and Percy at the fort without someone there to carry out his orders. He talked to John Dixon, the only member of Smith's squad who held the rank of gentleman.

"Our men are very competent," said Dixon, "but they are young and not experienced in command."

"I agree with you. Josiah is the best. Someday he will take his place as a leader, but he is very young and I fear the Captains would not respect him."

"True, John. So what can we do?"

"Dixon, I would like to name you as my deputy and you can use my squad to be sure your orders are enforced."

"Me ... me be in command? Oh, John, I do not know about that. I think at least some might respect my rank and, as you say, the men could be my eyes and ears, but I am no leader, John. ... How long will you be gone?"

"It should be four days at the most."

"Alright, John, I will do my best."

Having talked himself into the idea, Dixon took up his responsibility with fervor. He was off with Josiah and three more of Smith's squad to inspect the glass house and blockhouse, both near the neck of the island.

Smith asked for volunteers to go with him to the falls. The canoe only held twelve and he wanted room for supplies, so he asked for six men. Common men who had come in the last supply volunteered. Riding the tide up river in the light canoe, Smith camped just below the falls on the first night out. The next morning, he and the six men walked into West's fort.

Smith looked at the terrain. The brook looked inviting in the late summer drought but the marks on the banks clearly showed that the entire depression would be flooded in any heavy rain and in the spring flood time. He expressed his opinion to those in the fort. West was not there. He was out on the gold hunting expedition and the hostages had been retaken just the day before. The settlers were arguing with Smith. They explained about the Indians and the raids on their gardens and houses. As the argument went on, West returned. He took great exception to Smith's remarks. They nearly came to blows.

Smith put an end to the argument by leaving to visit the Indian village. It turned out the village belonged Smith's friend Parahunt. They talked for a time and Parahunt had secretly decided it was autumn and time to move to winter quarters, so when Smith offered to buy the fortified town that held up to 200 for some copper and an English boy, Parahunt accepted quickly. The boy was Henry Spelman. Smith was not certain why Parahunt wanted an English boy, perhaps to learn some of the language, but the boy did not seem terribly reluctant to go.

Smith admired the place. It had 300 plantable acres protected by a fence of poles and bark. The huts were in good shape. The village had a small stream for fresh water, one that showed no signs of flooding. Smith declared there was no such place as this delightful village and so he named it Nonsuch. Parahunt moved his people out in one day. Smith went back to West's fort and forced the settlers to relocate to the now empty village.

Smith stayed one more night, but he did not sleep well. There was no one in the entire fort he trusted, so he stayed awake most of the night. He left the next morning. As soon as he was out of sight, West instructed the settlers to move back to the original site.

On the way back, Smith laid down in the canoe for nap. After the accident, no one could say how it happened. A stray spark must have fallen on the powder bag hanging from his belt. There was a flash explosion. Smith woke, screamed and jumped into the river all in one move. The men in the canoe hauled him back in. They quickly assessed that he had been burned on his side. They pulled his clothes away from the area. Smith screamed with the pain. The burn turned out to be the size of a man palm and very deep. The made a poultice of mud and grass to keep the area damp and cool. Then they rushed down river as fast as they could.

Back in Jamestown, there was still no flagship. September 10th had passed and Smith was now badly injured. The leaders gathered. They had to assume the *Sea Venture* had been sunk. They decided to name an interim President and to send back to England for further instructions. Percy, much to his delight, was named President. Archer and Ratcliff took prominent places in the self-styled government and they gave Smith no role at all.

Percy had established his own residence and stayed there. Smith remained in the President's tent or hospital. Wotton tended the wound. It was slow to respond. Josiah visited often, sometimes sitting on one of the benches sleeping with his head on the table all night.

"Cap'n, seems like we have been in this position before. It is not much different than our time on the ship coming here."

"True, Josiah. We have been through so much. We have had the colony moving in the right direction time and again only to have some foolish set back. But you, Josiah, you are different. Two years ago you were a puppy, a loyal puppy. Today, you are a man. I would trust you with my life before almost anyone in this country. Not everyone recognizes this yet, mind you, but you should know … you should know I am proud of you, proud to call you my friend."

Josiah hung his head. His hero had addressed him as an equal. He had no experience in this, so he simply looked at the little man, weak with pain and fever, and smiled.

This night, Josiah stayed over. Instead of sitting in his usual place, he stretched out on the other cot. In the wee hours of the moonless night, he woke to the sound of the tent flap opening. It was odd for Wotton to come by in the night. Josiah came fully awake worried that Smith had taken a turn for the worse. But the figure in the doorway did not advance. He stood in the darkness breathing heavily. Josiah bunched his muscles in case he needed to leap at the man and quietly asked, "What is you business?" He felt more than saw the man look his way. Then the man turned and dashed outside. Josiah was up and out a split second later. He could not identify the man, but he did see the firelight flicker on a metal gun barrel as the man ran past the common pot. An assassin. It could not be anything else. Josiah did not sleep again that night.

The next morning, after helping Smith with his breakfast, Josiah told him of the night visitor.

"One of them fears me so much they would kill me now rather than wait to see if I die of this wound. Now I wonder if the spark in the canoe was an accident. Josiah, I do not see how I can have any meaningful place here with all these vultures in charge. When the Governor comes, he will listen to the gentlemen, not to me. Josiah, I think it is time for me to go back to England. Would you want to come with me? I have no position there. I can promise you nothing, but I would be glad of your company."

"Are you sure, Cap'n? You may be right. You may not be safe here. I will think on going with you."

Later that day, Smith asked to see John Martin and told him he would like to return to England for proper medical treatment.

Martin told the others. Like sharks sensing blood in the water, Smith's real enemies went in for the kill. Not satisfied with ruining Smith's future in the New World, they conspired to ruin is reputation in England as well. Ratcliff sent a letter to Lord Salisbury detailing many misdemeanors on which Smith should be questioned. The boy Spelman who had been payment for Parahunt's village was sent home when West abandoned the place. He was angry enough with Smith to accept the suggestions of Archer and Ratcliff to accuse Smith of conspiring with the Indians to attack West and his settlement. His reward would be to go home to England with Captain Argall.

Through Josiah, Smith made arrangements with the Davies brothers to sail with them. The letters of accusation were sent on the *John and Mary* with Captain Argall. They thought the information would go directly to the Virginia Company and Lord De La Warr because of Argall's family ties.

Josiah came to visit the day before Smith was to leave.

"Cap'n, I appreciate your offer to go with you, but I have nothing in England. I may not have much more here, but, as you said, I have found a place here, so here I will stay."

"I understand that feeling, son. I wish you all the best. Let me hear from you if you can." And with that, the foster father and son parted.

In October of 1609, four ships left James Port or James Fort or Jamestown, as it was becoming known. John Smith, who had kept the Jamestown colony alive time and again, left his dream.

Powhatan's scouts sent word that Smith had not been seen in the fort for many days. Powhatan sent a messenger to ask what had happened to his adopted son and weroance. Archer took a perverse pleasure in sending word that Smith was dead.

When the messenger returned and gave Powhatan this news, Pocahontas was present.

"My father, I know you have not been happy with my brother, but his death saddens me."

"Do not be too sad, my daughter. He may be dead, he may not be. One thing I have learned about these English, these coat-wearers. They lie."

CHAPTER 10
Surviving

Josiah and the other men of Smith's squad were at a loss. Their Cap'n had kept them busy. They were happiest when they were out adventuring, but it was also good to be scouting or checking on matters as Smith required. With no direction from Smith, they sat outside their long house and talked, mostly about the trips they had taken. This was amusing for about two days and then they got restless.

Herd said, "We could go to the new President and ask for work. Maybe they would let me make brick for some of the building going on."

Fenton shook his head, "I have no skill 'cept what the Cap'n taught me. Unless I can fight or explore, I would just be doin' common labor. Not interested in that, me bucko."

"I could go back to work as a carpenter, but I would rather not," said Laxton.

Josiah, who also had no other skills, had another idea, "What if we stuck together as a squad and ask for work in hunting, guarding, exploring, … the things we know?"

Jimmy Brumfield, whose eleventh birthday had just passed, chipped in, "But we would need a leader, like Josiah."

Out of the mouths of babes came a great idea. Even Dixon, who was the only gentleman in the squad and a few years older than Josiah, supported the idea of Josiah leading the group. "Captain Smith treated you as his lieutenant, Josiah. I trust his judgment."

The question was who would be most likely to accept the idea of an independent military unit. Percy had no love of Smith and would not be likely to want to keep Smith's squad together. The new man, West, hated Smith too. Archer and Ratcliff were poor choices. The only leader who liked Smith at all was Martin. Martin was still at Dumpling Island. Maybe they should just go there and volunteer to help.

Dixon continued, "I think our story would be more easily accepted if we suggested we go hunting and just happen to end up at Dumpling Island."

Thomas Cassen, speaking for both brothers as usual, said, "We agree."

So Dods, young Peacock, Fenton, Herd, young Brumfeld, Laxton, Dixon, Tucker, and the two Cassens made a pact. They would stick together, they would honor Smith's teaching, and they would be soldiers. They went to Doctor Russell and told him they would go hunting. Russell understood more than they said and gladly took responsibility for sending them out of the fort.

There would be no reason to take the young boys hunting, so they had to get them out of the fort without being seen. They gathered their few belongings, hoisted Brumfeld and Peacock on to the roof of the longhouse and handed their packs up to them. The boys threw the packs over the palisade. Fenton being the tallest, climbed on the roof, lay on his stomach and handed down each of the boys as far as he could reach. They had to drop from there. They were young but plucky and they dropped without a cry.

The rest collected their guns and ammunition and walked casually out the gate. No one even spoke to them much less tried to stop them. They walked slowly around the east wall of the five-sided fort. When they were at the north end of the longhouse, they met the boys and picked up their packs. They held the packs in front of themselves as they walked west to the neck. Once they were across the neck and past the glass house they gathered in a clearing. In later years, no one could recall who started it. The first said, "Woo," and the second responded, "woo," the third and so forth until the whole group was shouting, "Woo, woo, woo." This became the life-long greeting and recognition sign for the squad.

They took their time. They hunted for themselves, fished when they found a stream, and looked around as they liked. It took ten days for the squad to reach Dumpling Island. They went directly to Martin. Dixon and Josiah did the talking. They had decided that Martin would be more agreeable if the gentleman of the group started the conversation.

"Captain Martin, we have come to volunteer our services to you. Since you are so removed from the fort, we thought you would appreciate having some professional protection. We can also hunt for the plantation and allow your men to stay and work on the industries. It would increase your output considerably."

Martin was not sure what to make of these men, but he knew he felt threatened because of the damage they had done to the king's son and he knew Percy had abandoned him here. If fate sent him nine solid men and a couple of boys to protect him and to make his work more profitable in the bargain, who was he to turn them down.

"I accept your service and gladly. We have only tents at the moment and they are all full. Can you provide your own shelter?" asked Martin.

Dixon kept quiet and nodded slightly to Josiah, "We will do for ourselves, sir." Martin was a bit taken aback when this common boy spoke as a leader, but Dixon and he had agreed ahead of time that Josiah would speak as soon as Dixon nodded and start right off letting Martin know who led these men.

"Then report to Lieutenant Sicklemore, he will direct you where to camp."

Sicklemore was nowhere to be found, so Josiah evaluated the possible attack points and decided they would make their spot at the place most likely to need defense.

The settlers had torn down the Indian huts but they had been lazy about clearing away the debris preferring to use the material as firewood. Josiah picked a dry, high knoll near a shallow crossing to the mainland and directed the men and boys to collect the poles and mats needed to reconstruct an Indian hut. By nightfall, they had a roof over their heads and space big enough to house all of them together. Because of its strategic position and because everyone in the settlement soon regarded them as their personal militia, their hut became known as "the guardhouse." Smith's squad, through individual initiative and a bit of bending the rules had made a place for themselves in the Virginia colony.

Back at the fort, President Percy was doing his best to fill Smith's shoes. Richard Potts, a young and ambitious council clerk and an unapologetic supporter of Smith had presented Percy with an inventory that was, in essence, an inventory of Smith's accomplishments. He listed:

4 ships sailed
3 remained and 7 boats
Harvest was in
Provisions in storehouse for 10 weeks
6 mares and 1 horse
500 to 600 hogs
500 to 600 chickens and hens
Goats and sheep in numbers
490 people
24 cannon
300 muskets, snaphaunces, firelocks,
Helmets, body armor, swords and pikes, more than men to wear them
50 to 60 houses
5 to 6 other forts and plantations
1 carpenter and 3 apprentices
2 blacksmiths
2 sailors

It was now Percy's job to keep all this in tact and to start turning a profit for the Virginia Company. He did not have an easy road. His support among the elite members of the colony had been weak since the early months of the settlement when he alone had opposed deposing Wingfield in 1607. Archer, Ratcliff, Martin and Smith had generally ignored his voice since then. He had coveted the position of President for two years and now, with or without support, he had it. Sometimes you should be careful what you wish for.

Percy would not have been thought handsome in any age. His brow was high and his black, straight hair was receding even though he was only twenty-eight. His nose was long and narrow and overshadowed his small, petulant mouth and tiny chin. He had been a sickly child, a condition that left him chronically weak as an adult and he coughed constantly. He was fit to be a maudlin poet rather than a military President. In fact, he was often a mere figurehead with Archer, Ratcliff and Martin making the decisions and engaging with the colonists to make sure progress was being made.

Percy was the eighth son of the earl of Northumberland. With seven older brothers and a strong father, George had never had any power in his family. This was his first taste of authority and he intended to use it. He decided to send a leader to build a fort across the river from Martin's Dumpling Island.

Ratcliff walked up to Percy one day asking, "What are we to do about these pesky natives? They are here underfoot and, as far as I can tell, their brothers are out in the woods trying to kill anyone of us that strays far from the fort."

Percy knew which way the wind was blowing, so he took the offensive, "I believe Captain Archer took charge of the relations with the natives."

"Archer," Ratcliff grumped, "he has no more rapport with these savages than, …than Martin. And he cannot stand the sight of them. Something must be done, President Percy, something very firm and very soon."

Percy did not like having the old President in the fort with him. He feared it might encourage divided loyalty and he saw Ratcliff's complaints as an opportunity to be rid of him. He sent Ratcliff down the river with sixty men to build a fortification and to live off the crabs and other shellfish that were so common in those waters. He ordered that the fort be named Algernon after the son of his brother the earl of Northumberland.

This fort would be on the north side of river where Martin was on the south shore at the entrance to the James. On a map, it looked like the two forts would be very close, but Martin's island was really nine miles up the river so the idea of quick communications was not a reality.

Matters with the Indians had fallen apart rather badly since Smith left, at least that was how Percy thought of it. Had Smith been present to speak with Powhatan, the settlers might have understood that it was not Smith's departure that set off this new spree of attacks, but the arrival of women. Twenty women, including Tomasine Cawsey, Elizabeth Joones, Amtyte Waine, and Temperance Flowerdew had arrived on August 11th on the *Blessing*. The proximity of Smith's departure and new attacks was purely coincidental.

Powhatan was told that women had come to the fort and he knew that meant the settlement was here to stay. He had been making half-hearted attempts to run the foreigners off his land and back across the sea. As long as they were there to trade and maybe help him against his traditional enemies, he could tolerate them. The braves of his tribe would sometimes venture into lands occupied by other tribes and even camp for a season. But when he took women and children with him, he was making a permanent village. The English could not be so very different. If there were women, these men were here to occupy the Powhatan lands. This he would not tolerate. He sent word to all his weroances that they should send men to besiege the fort and starve out the coat-wearers. They must leave or die.

The corn in the fort was disappearing rapidly. Percy rationed what was left to make it last as long as possible. Portions were down to half a can of meal per man per day. This continued for 3 months from late November until February. In desperation, Percy sent a deputation to Powhatan who had moved from Werowocomoco to an older campsite at Orapakes farther west between Chickhominie and Pamunkey rivers. But the Indians were running out of food for themselves because the harvest had been bad two years in a row. By this time, Powhatan wanted his people to stay away from the colonists.

To cut off all friendly contact with the English, Powhatan commanded that no Indian would enter the fort or meet with a coat-wearer without his permission. To reinforce his message, he sent along stories of the damage that had been done by Indians mixing with these foreigners.

One of the stories was about a group of five Indians who were visiting the fort. A soldier was showing them his gun and the black powder that made the thunder. The powder was damp and the soldier said it would not work unless it was dry, so he told the Indians to get one of the pieces of metal the soldiers wore and to spread the powder on the metal and then hold it over the fire to dry. The soldier told the others to watch closely and then he left. In a short time the powder made the thunder without the gun. Three of the Indians were killed and the other two were burned badly and received no help until they ran all the way back to their village.

Truthfully, the foolish Indian had thought of drying the powder over the fire himself and the doctor at the fort offered to put his medicine on the burned men, but the story was much more effective told this way.

The Indians watched the fort constantly and anyone who moved beyond the wall was met with arrows. All through the fall of 1609 and the winter and early spring of 1610, James Fort again became a prison. Two hundred and fifteen people had very limited food. They could not go outside the fort to hunt or fish. All the waste stayed in the fort or was thrown over the walls.

As the disease, poor nutrition and occasional killing continued, they could not leave to bury the dead. The southwest corner of the fort became the cemetery as it had been in 1607.

In England, a new supply was forming up. Thomas West, Lord De La Warr was preparing to take his place as Governor of the Virginia colony. This convoy would bring women and children as well as an entire year's worth of supplies. The news that had arrived with the returning ships had spread throughout London and even into the countryside. The fleet had planned for another 1000 colonist to accompany the Governor, but the bad news had caused many of those who were considering the trip to back out. Now there were only two ships loading for the voyage and about 150 passengers signed on.

Bridget, the girl who helped Josiah evade the theft charge three years before, was in church on February 21, the Sunday before the fleet sailed. The Reverend William Crashaw, who was friends with several owners of the Virginia Company and had been asked to counter the accusations against the company, was railing against the colonists in Jamestown.

"Sloth is one of the seven cardinal sins! And these men, who have taken advantage of the generosity of the gentlemen of the Virginia Company, have committed this sin time and again. You have heard that conditions in his majesty's colony are less than we had hoped. It is these loose, lewd, licentious, riotous and disordered men, these lazy, slothful men who have done such harm to that blessed land. They are the very excrement of a full and swelling state. Such fellows as these are the scum and scouring of the streets and though raked up out of the kennels they are sent to be the founders of a worthy state. Yet they work little. They refuse to provide food for themselves and demand provisions be carried thousands of miles rather than call off their bowling games. We must provide better men for our new world!"

She remembered Josiah, in fact she had thought about him quite a lot. She did not think he was lazy and doubted he even knew how to play at bowls. It had been three years since she had seen him and then only once, yet she felt very defensive on his behalf. She suddenly had a strong desire to prove the preacher wrong.

Bridget had continued to work for the same household since the time she had met Josiah. But the lady of the house had recently died having her third child and the man of the house was beginning to pay far too much attention to Bridget for her liking. She had thought about looking for a new position. She had never thought about going to the new world. She had never even thought about going to the country. But Josiah was there and, in that new land, she was sure he would be a hard-working man, not a slothful sinner. Maybe she should go and see for herself.

Her path home took her near the docks so she decided to take a look at these ships that were bound for Josiah. As she approached the docks, she heard a couple nearing the point of argument.

A well-dressed young woman was near tears, "It is bad enough that you are uprooting your family and taking us half way around the world, but now I find that you expect me to be housekeeper, cook, farm wife and nanny. John, I just cannot handle all that. We have had servants all our lives, how can we even consider ..."

"Now, Hannah. I am sorry that your maid refused to go with us. You knew we could not bring any of the other servants. Others have managed and we will too."

Now she was nearly hysterical, "John, oh no, John, I just cannot, I will die, I know I will!"

Bridget never knew what possessed her, but she walked up to the couple and said, "Pardon me, sir, madam. Did I hear you are looking for a maid?"

John, who was becoming desperate for a way to calm his wife, was first appalled at this girl's effrontery and then amazed as his good luck. "Er, yes, yes we may be in the market for a maid. Is that your profession?" Then recovering his dignity, "Do you have references?"

Hannah was sniffling, trying to get herself under control. "John, please." Hannah gave John the look that had melted his heart in the first place.

He gave in with out another thought, "Er, well, are you available to leave tomorrow? Do you have your things nearby? ... And do you have references?"

Hannah beamed.

The small settlement at Dumpling Island was harassed by the local tribes. Martin was not a strong leader and Sicklemore was young and inexperienced. Neither commanded any respect from the men. Gradually, many turned to Dixon and Tucker for direction.

"You need to stay on the island as much as possible and keep this neck and ford guarded at all times," Tucker had said. "My men will do the hunting. Fish on the riverside where you can see if anyone is coming by water. Under no circumstances should you let the Indians lure you off the island."

Tucker reminded the men of his advice just before he and Smith's old squad waded off to the mainland to go hunting. Within the hour, what appeared to be only a few braves came out of the woods toward the ford and stood at the edge of the water taunting the remaining men. George Forrest, who had more courage than sense, took the bait.

"There are only six of them. We can take them before they can reach the trees. Load up men! Take a shot, reload and then keep where you can get a clear shot as we chase them across the beach."

A dozen undisciplined men cheered the idea and loaded their muskets. They stood in a line behind Tucker's barrier and shot at the six braves. None were hit, though one did have sand blown into his eyes when the shot hit the beach. The six turned and fled slowly toward the woods. Forrest and his band reloaded and followed them.

The men each took their shot as the Indians crossed the beach. Again they reloaded and headed into the trees. A few more shots were heard and then silence. After two minutes of tense waiting, the men on the island saw Forrest running and stumbling out of the woods and across the beach. He reached the ford and fell face first into the water. Three men dared to go out to get him. He had been shot by seventeen arrows. One had gone straight through his side. He had just enough energy to mutter, "All dead," before he fainted.

The men who were left did what they could to make Forrest comfortable. They were able to work out all but two of the arrows and arrowheads. They put some moss from the water on the wounds and used pieces of his shirt to hold what they could in place. There was no medical help on the island and in two days, Forrest died.

The men on Dumpling Island were discontent. They were afraid and they had very little purpose. Martin was particularly afraid and used his position as current leader to follow in Percy's footsteps and go to Jamestown. Young Sicklemore was left in charge. If it had not been for Josiah and the squad, the men would have gone hungry in the midst of plenty. After many weeks of this, seventeen men mutinied. They took a boat and crossed the James to the town of Kecoughtan in hope of trading for food. Sicklemore was indecisive. Should he go to get the missing men or leave them to their fate? After several days, Sicklemore and a few loyal others took their one boat and went after them. Half way to Kecoughtan, they found all of them dead with their mouths full of bread. As they examined the site, a single arrow came from out of the woods and pierced Sicklemore through the heart. The men picked up Sicklemore's body and ran for their longboat. Two men took word to Percy in Jamestown and he ordered the island abandoned. The same two men returned and the few remaining colonists left. They gave no thought to the fate of the squad who had been out hunting again. When Josiah returned, the island was deserted. There was no note, no indication of what had happened except two fresh graves.

The squad gathered on the riverside.

"Well, men. What shall we do?" began Tucker.

"I suppose we could go back to the fort," offered James Brumfield, the youngest.

"Percy is still in charge, as far as we know," added Dixon, "and I, for one, am not interested in reporting to him."

All heads nodded.

"If the Indians are raiding like this here, are they doing the same at the fort? There are women there now," suggested John Dods who had mentioned Elizabeth Joones many times since leaving the fort.

A few knowing looks passed over his head and Tucker decided, "Then for the sake of the women, we should go that way and see how things stand. Mind you, I am not saying we will even go into the fort much less put ourselves under Percy, but there is nothing to keep us here and someone should be told of the fate of these men."

With no more than that, the band stood and gathered what looked to be salvageable from the settlement. They checked each house. They added the few claimed items to the packs of meat and roots they had brought back from hunting and headed back across the ford.

In every age, there seem to be a small number of people who can move freely through warring armies and local anarchy. Smith's, now Tucker's squad were such men. Whether the Indians respected their abilities or whether they were just such good woodsmen, something kept them alive through these adventures.

At the camp at the falls, West had lost eleven men. The natives had also stolen one of the boats. While there was still a boat left to take them back to Jamestown, West withdrew. No one returned from Point Comfort, but the other settlers who had been staying with friendly tribes nearby had been sent away and so returned to Jamestown. With them came the news of the death of the Germans who had stayed with the Indians. There was no explanation. Powhatan's braves had simply turned on them one day and killed them.

Percy appointed James Davies to replace Ratcliff in command at Fort Algernon. He also sent Francis West and thirty-two others to Chesapeake Bay to trade with the Patanwoeke on Potomac Creek. The Patanwoeke were happy to trade and West loaded his pinnacle with enough grain to maintain the colony for a while.

West got to Point Comfort where he met Davies. West's men wandered around the fort and a few were outside the tent and overheard West and Davies talking. They were calculating how long this corn would last. Davies joked that it was about enough to get a boatload of men back to England, but he was not sure how long it would last at the fort. When West's ship left in the morning, they got out of sight of the fort and the crew, led by those who had overheard the conversation, attacked West and took over the ship. They turned toward the ocean and they, and the saving grain, headed back to England.

All the horses had been killed and eaten. The goats went next. The Indians killed all the pigs on Hogs Island, but the colonists would not have survived the Indian attacks to get them anyway. There were few options, so Percy sent Ratcliff and a company of about thirty men to Powhatan to bargain for food. They arrived at Powhatan's village and the hungry, undisciplined men scattered and helped themselves to whatever they found. Whether it was the stealing or whether it was Powhatan's plan all along, the hospitality turned to mayhem and the men were set upon. They fought back but they were far outnumbered and only one named Jeffrey Shortridge made his way out. Most of the men were killed outright, but Ratcliff was handed over to the women who knew ways to kill a man slowly and horribly.

Disease took many people at the fort while the weather was still cool. Not knowing if the disease was contagious, these people were buried with touching them as little as possible. They did not even remove their clothes, a valuable commodity at the best of times, but essential with winter coming on. When the hard frost hit, so most of the disease stopped. Now the killers were simple malnutrition and starvation.

On a Wednesday, Hugh Pryse ran out into the "marketplace" screaming, "if there were a God, he would not suffer his creatures whom he had made and framed to endure these miseries." Before anyone realized what they were doing, Pryse and a still-fat butcher ran out the gate and toward the woods. The people who watched from the bulwark saw them shot by Indian snipers. They were left where they fell. Overnight, animals tore Pryse's bony corpse to shreds while twenty feet away they did not touch the fat butcher. To the colonists, Pryse had received the justice of the gods.

It came to a choice of starving or eating pets, vermin, or people. Some lived on the blood of their fallen neighbors. Some of the "poorest sort" dug up a slain and buried Indian and ate him. Some went the other route and once the dogs and the cats were eaten, then people had only vermin who came into the fort, rats, mice and snakes as food.

Every few days, when they met for prayers in the church, one or two people would be missing, having either died in the night or run off in hopes of joining the Indians. Those who stayed ate what they could find. Food became frozen roots, boiled leather, and worse. President Percy sacrificed the starch he had ordered from London in July of the previous year, at the cost of four pounds 6 shillings, to make a porridge.

One morning, someone noticed that Henry Collings was not as emaciated as the others. The crowd transformed into a mob and surrounded him.

"You must have food," said one. "Where is your stash?" asked another.

Percy, for once, took charge and called for quiet.

"Henry, it is obvious you have a source of food. Tell us where it is or we will tear your house apart to find it."

The crowd needed no more invitation. They invaded Collings' room and opened or upended everything. One unlucky soul pulled the cover off of a barrel and was greeted with a floating eye. He screeched and fainted still holding the cover.

The nearest person looked in the barrel and gasped, then turn to face Henry Collings, "That is your wife, you devil!"

"You said she wandered off weeks ago," recalled another.

Henry was firmly in the grasp of two men by this time and Percy approached him with a face that said Henry smelled worse than anything imaginable.

"Take this man, this cannibal, to the dungeon. No wait! Let us not spoil the jail with such filth. Tie him hand and foot in the center of the commons."

Percy assembled what council there was and in minutes, with anyone who was able to stand gathered around, declared Henry Collings a murderer and determined that he should be burned alive for his heinous crime. Fewer appeared for his execution than had been present at his trial.

No one was willing to deal with the meager remains of Mrs.Collings, so Percy had to order two men to seal the lid and side roll the barrel to a newly dug shallow gravesite. As the night came on about five in the afternoon, the men tipped the contents of the barrel into the grave and quickly shoveled the dirt back in. They each claimed they had kept their faces averted and seen nothing.

With the loads they carried and the need to be cautious, it took Josiah and his friends two weeks to make their way to the neck of the island. The glass works were empty. They assumed all the Germans and Poles had either gone to the fort or the Indians. They worked their way along the back river to a point where they could see the fort by climbing trees. They all took a long look. Nothing moved outside the fort. They saw a bit of smoke rising from three chimneys and one place in the commons. They were upwind of the fort, so they smelled and heard nothing.

They waited for three days. There was no change. On the third night, the lookout woke them each silently and pointed toward the neck. They moved quietly through the trees and brush and met the two men who had run from the fort just as they came onto the mainland.

Tucker stepped out saying, "Stop." The two men yelped and fell to the ground in surrender. Then it must have occurred to them that the word had been English for their attitude changed entirely. They stood up, brushed at their clothes and challenged Tucker, "What do you mean by stopping us. We have a perfect right to go where we want."

"You most certainly do. But we have need to know how things fare inside the fort."

It was a moonless night and threatened snow. These men had come on the last ships and even if they could see his face, they had never met Josiah Tucker before.

"Who the devil are you?" demanded one.

The rest of the squad stepped into the path surrounding the two men. Again their attitude changed abruptly.

"Sorry, no offense intended. But how do you come to be here, outside the fort?"

Tucker obliged them with an answer of sorts.

"We were at one of the other settlements. Tell us what is happening here."

The two men took turns to exclaim the horrid conditions in the fort. They did not need to exaggerate. They explained that they were going to take their chances with the Indians.

Tucker took a silent poll of his men and feeling, more than seeing, no objection, he made to let the two pass on their way.

As they started to move away, John Dods asked one more question, "The women, are the women still alive? Particularly Miss Elizabeth Joones?"

The two men looked at each other. One said to the other, "Did you know Miss Joones, Harry?"

Harry answered, "Not by name. Sorry lad, but I think I do know the names of all the women still alive and she is not among them."

John turned toward the trees. William Laxon, who had an unofficial standing as the group's religious leader, put his arm around John's shoulder and spoke to him in whispers.

After Harry and his friend had gone and John and Will had rejoined the group, Tucker asked, "What do you want to do now?"

Logical Dick Dixon spoke up, "If we let anyone in the fort know we are here, we will be locked inside with them, starving. No point in that. But maybe we could hunt for them and leave the food where they could find it."

John Herd reminded them, "If we are caught, Percy will skin us alive and eat us." Everyone laughed a little and then stopped.

Tucker again declared the decision, "Herd is right. We must be very careful. There may be lookouts even though Harry and his partner said they always fall asleep. We can get to the river under cover of the trees just upstream. If we rig a raft or small canoe, we can put food on it and let it drift to within sight. They will know someone is giving them food, but they will never see us."

One soft giggle let Josiah know at least one of the team thought his idea silly, but no one openly objected. They headed back to their roost to figure out how to make a float, how to get enough line to guide it to the fort, and how to avoid the Indians who, apparently, were all around the fort.

They were stymied at every turn. The grape vines that would have served well in summer for making a rope had gone brittle with the frost and broke but would not bend. Young Nathaniel Peacock, who liked Bible stories, suggested making baskets of reeds like for Moses as a baby, but the reeds were dead and brittle with winter as well. Robert Fenton who had made a study of Indian ways thought a small dugout canoe would be best, but the noise of hammering and the smoke from the fire needed to burn out the middle would bring the Indians down on them. Finally, they decided on two small bark canoes bound at the ends by rawhide they could take from the deer carcasses. More rawhide would have to do for the line supplemented with the bit of rope they always carried.

Having made the preparations, they waited until the early nightfall and made their way along the back river, on to the neck and began to enter the stand of trees still left along the west and south shores of the island. Dixon, the man watching the back trail, had gone about twenty feet into the trees when the woods erupted with motion.

Indians appeared on every side of the group. The undergrowth moved as arrows began to speed among the squad. As they had learned from experience, they dropped their packs together in a line to make a small point of cover but with Indians on all sides, it was no use here. Each man called his target so as not to waste shot by two men aiming at one Indian. They marched with their muskets primed so all they needed to do was touch the match to fire. All this transpired within five short seconds, but by then John Dods and Nathaniel had already been hit by arrows.

Small as he was, Nathaniel was in a bad way. The arrow had gone all the way through from front to back just below his bottom rib. Dods had three arrows in his pack before he dropped it and one in his thigh, but it had ricocheted off the pack and so was not deeply set.

Dixon spotted a cluster of trees a few feet to the right of the group and herded them that direction carrying Peacock by himself. The trees protected almost half of the perimeter for the group. There they formed an outward facing ring, making use of the trees as best they could. Herd took an arrow in the upper left arm as they moved to cover. He could no longer balance his musket to shoot. Only three had been able to reload. Tucker looked at Dixon. In a glance they agreed on the hopelessness of their situation.

"Retreat! Grab what you can! Move!" shouted Tucker.

Dixon threw the unconscious Peacock over his shoulder. Fenton helped Dods. Laxon got the two smallest packs as he ran past the pile. Young Brumfield snatched two brace of birds and the musket mount they were tied to. Tucker slung one pack on his shoulder quickly, but he kept his gun ready and acted as rear guard.

Oddly, the Indians shot no more and they did not pursue the men after they left the shelter of the woods. They had not really tried to kill the men of the squad, only to run them off from helping the fort. They crossed the neck and gathered at the glass house to take stock. The bark canoes were gone as well as the rawhide and rope. Most of the food had been left behind. Three of the seven were wounded. It took little conversation to decide that the rescue attempt was a failure. They patched up the three as best they could and moved off into the forest to a place they had used before, a place off the Indian tracks and difficult to find. They called it their hideout.

The colonists were desperate. As the weather eased, a few managed to get to the river and catch or spear a fish or two. Three times these fishing expeditions ended with a gunshot. The Indians had gotten guns and ammunition from the outer settlements and they had become very accurate at close range. Each man was shot in the head.

To keep warm and boil water, the men first tore down the houses of those who had died and then started on the fort itself. At one point, someone had the idea to use the gates as rafts and pole down the river to get away. A group worked at it most of one day. When it was finally down, they were too exhausted to go anywhere. The gate stayed where it had fallen.

With the spring growth came a small ray of hope. Parties went out of the fort in search of new roots and young plants. They found a few small animals. Since there were so few left, the little bit of food did keep the sixty survivors alive but barely. It was still dangerous to go outside the fort, so the hunting, fishing and gathering was kept to a minimum.

Percy had not heard from the settlers at Point Comfort since fall. He had been sick himself in the winter. He had thought of the men in Fort Algernon at Point Comfort from time to time and had presumed they were in the same poor shape as the people at James Fort or, worse yet, all dead. Once spring came, he delayed checking on those men again. Finally, in May, he decided to find out if the men were still alive and, if the shellfish were still there, to collect all the food he could to bring back to his starving settlement.

He took a canoe and two men to row. The tide took them swiftly and as they approached they saw smoke from fires and people on the beach. They looked fine, not at all thin or ill. They beached the canoe and Percy strode angrily to the tent of Captain Davies.

"So, Captain, I find you and all your men in good health! Have you no idea the suffering of your fellow settlers? They are starving, dying, while you sit here stuffing your selves, and your hogs, with all the food you can eat. Were you deliberately concealing supplies so you few could take ship to England once the rest of us were dead? Are you not ashamed?!"

"President Percy, I had no idea, no idea at all! You say there is hunger and death? We will send supplies immediately. But why have you not sent to us before? We have never lacked for food."

Percy had no answer for that, so he defensively changed the subject.

"Yes, do get together all the food you can. It is too late to start back tonight, but first thing tomorrow, you must send a relief party. For now, I require quarters for the night. See to it."

Davies took the dismissal with good grace and left without further comment. While he was moving about arranging for Percy's quarters and for a shipment to James Fort, a sentry posted on a high spot on the point yelled, "Ships!" Forty defenders stood through the night waiting to be invaded by the Spanish. In the morning, they fired a warning shot just as the ships moved close enough to identify them as English.

CHAPTER 11
Strachey Comes to James Towne

The two ships that were approaching Point Comfort had arrived after a strange and amazing journey. It began when the *Sea Venture* left England as one of seven ships in a supply fleet. The flagship carried the deputy governor, Sir Thomas Gates and the fleet's admiral, George Somers. Also aboard were the two Indians sent by Powhatan, Namontack, on his second trip back, and Machumps.

William Strachey, who was thirty-seven in 1610, had been friendly with the theatrical and literary lights of London for many years. He was very pleased to have been selected to come on *Sea Venture* with Newport, Somers, and Gates. It was a perfect situation for him to be able to communicate with the Indians and learn their language.

The *Sea Venture* had 153 aboard, 35 mariners, 118 gentlemen, gentlewomen and children, servants, artisans, and peasants including a few family members. One of the servants was Elizabeth Persons. She was employed by a Mistress Horton. One of the gentlemen was John Rolfe, a twenty-four year old who was traveling with his wife who was, unknowingly, expecting a baby. Another gentleman was the Reverend Richard Buck, a twenty-seven year-old graduate from Cambridge and an ordained Anglican minister. Stephen Hopkins, an unusually literate commoner, was chosen to be Buck's clerk. He was a loudmouth shopkeeper who was prone to quoting the Bible.

William Pierce was traveling on the *Sea Venture* while his wife Joan and child Joan had been booked on the *Blessing*. They had all been on the *Blessing*, but when a spot on the *Sea Venture* came open at the last minute, Joan had encouraged her husband to sail on that ship where he would be likely to have personal contact with the powerful men of the colony. At the time, it seemed like a smart political move, but once they were on board, they realized they would have no contact for two or three months except hailing each other when the two ships were close enough. They already regretted their decision, but there was no going back now.

Sending a hundred and fifty-three people thousands of miles over water in the seventeenth century was a logistical nightmare. To have any fresh food on the trip, it had to be carried on the hoof. Animals that would be needed at the end of the journey also had to be transported. Live animals, including oxen, ponies, stallions, fourteen or fifteen mares, hogs, bulls, cows, bucks and nanny goats, heath sheep, chickens, dogs and mastiffs and cats were either tethered to belaying pins on deck, secured in slings below decks, or, where useful to the ship like dogs and cats, allowed to roam free.

There was no way to convert seawater to potable water, so all drinking liquids had to be taken along in casks or kegs. Preserved food like dried beef was also stored in casks. One commodity that was deemed a necessity had to be made on board frequently and that was bread. An entire room below decks was devoted to this task. The flour and other ingredients required were stored in the room or nearby. Personal belongings were to be kept to a minimum for most passengers, though some gentlemen took amazing objects along like beds and, on one later voyage, a printing press.

Then there were the supplies needed for the ship like additional canvass for sails, tar, pitch, and the longboats for getting close to shore. To use all of the available storage space, the area at the bottom of the ship, the bilge, where the walls and floor were curved, had to be specially prepared. To provide a level ground, the hull was loaded with scrap iron and large stones to put great weight below the waterline for stability. These were covered with gravel to make a bed for casks, crates, and barrels. The heaviest items were usually put in the bilge to add to the bottom weight of the vessel.

Where the sailors and passengers stayed was different depending on the type and size of ship. The sailors typically slept either in bunks or in hammocks on the first level below the deck. The higher status passengers also stayed on the top level while those of lesser status stayed on lower decks. Most simply made a pallet of some kind on the boards. A few had some small cot or bunk. Individuals strung blankets as partitions to offer some privacy.

It was crowded, progressively filthy, airless, damp, and often too cold or too hot. It was noisy and smelly and seemed endless. Many passengers had no idea what the conditions would be like. Had they known, they may well never have embarked on such a voyage. Once away from England, they had no further choice.

The durable Captain Christopher Newport, who had already made nearly a half-score runs across the Atlantic, commanded the *Sea Venture*. Newport was born in 1559 and at 26 he went with Drake to the Caribbean and South America to raid the Spanish. That fleet had stopped to visit the location of the ill-fated Roanoke colony. There he met his first natives and had his first taste of life in the American wilderness. Along the way, he lost his left hand and part of his arm, but still he had fought at Cadiz and was knighted in 1596. He went to the Dutch wars in1604 and in 1608 he was granted leave to go to Jamestown the first time. This was his third voyage to Jamestown.

For seven weeks, the fleet sailed uneventfully in convoy. The little ship, *Virginia*, could not keep up and, so, returned to England early on. They followed the usual route down the west coast of Africa, across the Atlantic, dipping down through the Caribbean before heading north for the Virginia coast.

On a Monday night in late July, with a week to go to Jamestown, a hurricane came up from behind and as they turned north toward Jamestown, it hit. They first experienced northeast winds. Within an hour, the fleet was scattered. On Tuesday, the ketch, under Michael Philes with 30 people, had to be cut loose or it could ram the flagship. After signaling between the ships, line was cut. It was never seen again.

No passenger had ever seen a hurricane in Europe. The few sailors who had been through one before said this storm was stronger than any they had seen. Certain death was the prevailing, mostly unspoken, opinion. The pilot was the fleet admiral, George Somers. He chose to turn the ship bow-first into the wind. This let them ride each wave as it approached. The sturdy galleon preformed well until the oakum between the planks of the hull crumbled and the ship started taking on water. The extra weight of the water in the bilges could cause the ship to roll over or even sink, so the sailors searched for leaks in the hull in the dim and dark below decks with candles. When they identified a possible weakness, they would wedge the candlestick in boards above the spot and plug the gaps with animal fat and ashes or oatmeal bags or raw beef. Dried beef proved to be to the best repair because it would expand with water and truly close the breach. One hundred crew and passengers bailed constantly in shifts. They moved 1200 buckets per hour and still made no headway against the rising water. Three pumps, with the men pushing more than 15 times per minute, could not overcome the biggest leak that must have been under the water level in the hull and, therefore, was never found. No matter how hard they pumped, the ship kept taking on water.

Very little food and drink was accessible, so the men worked without eating or drinking. Reaching the point of last resort, they removed weight, first by sending the starboard side guns overboard and then by breaking open any kegs or barrels of liquid, beer, ale, vinegar, cider, wine, and oil, that they could reach. The shortage of drinkables was now even worse.

At dusk on Tuesday, the sky lightened as they moved into the eye of the hurricane. They had been fighting the storm for twenty-four hours. The calmer winds of the eye gave them a short rest in spite of the choppy seas. It was only a few hours and then they were back into the storm. Somers gave instructions to the helmsmen to work in shifts but he piloted without a break or sleep. After two days, of pitching and yawing, a wall of water hit from directly behind. The *Sea Venture* passed through the wave instead of over it. The pressure of the water tore the rutter lever from the hand of the helmsman. He tried several times to grab it, but failed. Luckily, another helmsman who was on the deck waiting to change shifts was able to hang on or the ship would have rolled.

The passengers sensed the difference in the motion and the roar of the wind stopped. The entire ship was underwater and the sense of drowning inside the ship was universal. Even knowing they would surely die outside, dozens of men, women and children climbed the ladders and tried to go up on deck. Through the skill of Somers, the luck of the helmsman, and a small miracle, the ship remained afloat. When the ship emerged from the monster wave, the noise of the wind returned. The people realized they had another chance, and they went back down the ladders and resumed bailing.

Wednesday and Thursday were a blur of water and buckets and creaking wood. There was still no food or drink to speak of. In the small hours of Friday morning, Somers called out to his crew to come and see a wonder. In the midst of all the horror, the static electricity of the storm had created the blue lightning called St. Elmo's fire. Sailors often saw it for a moment or two, but this time, it danced in the rigging all night. The passengers and crew hailed it as either as a sign of good fortune or, more likely, a sign that they would be called to heaven by morning.

By dawn on Friday, the men were so tired they had given up. As they ended their shifts, they passed around the last of the alcohol and took leave of each other. They were sure that night would be their last. Then Captain Somers, in a raspy but sure voice, called, "Land."

The land was Bermuda, which had been discovered by the Spanish in 1505 and had appeared on most maps since 1511. Sailors had spread the word that it was a dangerous place. The odd weather and extensive coral reefs certainly did make the area treacherous for sailing vessels. Rumors that it was an enchanted island were more common but less well founded. For the exhausted people on the *Sea Venture*, reefs or not, it was a blessed place. As if to prove the blessing, as they came into lee of island, the wind slacked. They were about a mile from shore and the sailors knew they would run aground. The question was whether they would tip over and die crushed against the coral by the breakers. Whether by luck or the protection of angels, they ran straight in between two points of a coral reef, wedging the bow and keeping the ship upright.

No time was allowed for rest or even thanksgiving. No one knew how long the ship would stay secure between the reefs, so the sailors who had pumped for four straight days now lowered the long boats and began rowing back and forth to shore. They landed the first load of passengers in a bay they named Gates Bay.

As they approached the shore, Edward Samuel, one of the sailors mumbled, "Damned place must be full a' fairies and pixies, who e're heard of pink sand?"

"You may be right, Ed, "replied his mate, "pink sand and rocks as black as pitch. May be fairies or pixies or the devil himself. I do not like the looks of this place."

"I agrees wid' ya, mate, I have a real bad feeling 'bout 'dis, but it is better than the storm."

The long boat glided onto the fine sand and fourteen passengers disembarked. First they built a signal fire on the beach to guide the rowboats back. They left one person to tend the fire and the rest went a half-mile into the palm forest to make a camp and a second fire. There was plenty of driftwood and fallen dry leaves from the palm trees. In a short while, these few passengers were dry for the first time in days.

The teams of sailors rowed seven miles through the reefs each way. They made at least five trips that first day. As maritime tradition demands, Newport and Somers were the last off ship. When they arrived at the camp in the trees, they took stock and determined that, miraculously, no one had died or even suffered a serious injury during the entire five days.

There is a point at which the human body is pushed beyond its limits. You find you have done something with no recollection of doing it. You find yourself in a place without any idea of how you got there. You do a task with no thought of what comes next relying solely on instinct and habit. If you live past that time, you stop and cannot help but fall asleep. With a little rest, you graduate from operating in your sleep to mere exhaustion. With one full night's rest, you become simply tired. After a good night's sleep, those on the *Sea Venture* who were in good physical shape, the sailors and the working folk, were ready to resume normal duties. For the gentlefolk it took one or two more days of rest to regain any real stamina. That first rough camp served the group until most of them recovered their strength.

No one lived on Bermuda. There was no evidence that anyone had ever lived there permanently, though there were marks of human visitation. The Spanish had made the island a sort of storehouse by leaving hogs there as a food source for their ships on route between Spain and their many possessions in the new world. The hogs had multiplied and had little fear of man, so finding fresh meat would be relatively easy.

Gates organized teams the next morning to look for food and water. Sailors continued to make trips to the ship until virtually everything of use was on land. The colonists dug a hole and sunk a barrel in it to collect fresh water. One of the teams found a pond of fresh water not far inland. The live hogs brought from England and the few undamaged containers of food and drink were the first things brought from the ship. Refreshed with a decent meal, the colonists were anxious to improve their situation. The sailors brought fishing equipment that allowed the colonists to catch as many fish as they wanted. The women arranged to hang some of the spare canvass to make shade and have a dry place during the frequent afternoon rain showers. With all the things the sailors brought from the ships, the camp became a little English village in the tropics.

The purebred mastiffs were not interested in hunting, but the ship's mongrel dog helped to track the wild boar. The hunters noticed that the hogs ate the berries of a certain type of palm tree, so the settlers tried the fruit and found it very tasty. The base of the leaves was edible too. A typical base weighed twenty pounds. It could be eaten raw or boiled or grilled. The agreement was it tasted like fried melons with the texture of cabbage.

Another new food was the edible pear of a cactus that became known as a prickly pear. The center was filled with maroon juice that looked and tasted like a mulberries. A type of bay grape was native to these islands and it was found to be efficacious for the flux. Olives and pawpaws were native and recognizable as edible items. Salt was made by boiling the brine carried onboard ship and, later, by boiling salt water. Between keeping the signal fire and the cooking fires burning and boiling sea water for salt, cutting the abundant wood was a constant occupation. Bermuda was shaping up to be a very easy place to live.

There were many islands in the Bermuda archipelago. The landing spot was on the northeastern-most island. The officers wanted to explore more of the islands, but eating was the priority. They tried planting, but everything stopped at the sprouting stage. By digging up the failed plants they determined that grubs had eaten the roots. With no way to combat the grubs, they abandoned the effort.

Besides being hurt by the grubs, the mosquitoes, flies, and caca-roaches were also troublesome. The settlers were familiar with mosquitoes and flies, but this type of roach was new. It was their dung that ruined anything they got into, hence the name.

The attitude of Edward Samuel, one of the doubting sailors, had improved with time. He had little work to do, a warm, stationary place to sleep, and food was easy to come by. However, even in this land of comfort and plenty, ownership of food could be a matter for dispute, especially when fueled by "bibby." "Bibby" was the name given to a drink made from the watered and fermented sap of the palmetto tree. On one fateful day, Samuel accused Robert Waters of helping himself to the "bibby" Samuels had made.

"Rob, ya know for sure and certain that was my stock of "bibbi." Ya gots no right to be takin' my beer."

"Now Ed," soothed Waters, "how can you be knowin' it was your "bibbi". We all make "bibbi."

"It was in my own cup, you rock-headed idiot."

"Idiot!, is it?"

And with that, the fight was on. The tension of the storm coupled with the idleness on the island combined to make what should have been a short wrestling match into a bare-knuckles fight. Once blood was drawn, the adrenaline took over and the reason for the fight was forgotten. All that mattered was winning.

Samuel took a cheap shot at Waters below the waist. Waters dodged the blow and as he swung around, he grabbed a shovel leaning on a nearby barrel. Unarmed, Samuel picked up a double handful of the fine sand and threw it in Water's face. Half blind, Waters stuck out with the shovel and connected squarely with Samuel's head. Edward dropped to his knees and slowly toppled forward. His premonition about Bermuda had been right. He was dead.

The sailors who had seen the fight considered it a fair one with sad consequences. According to their code of the sea, the matter was settled and all that was left to do was to bury Samuel. So they were taken aback when Captain Gates arrived on the scene and declared that Waters be taken into custody to await trial. Two of Gates' men grabbed Waters roughly by the arms and manhandled him as they took him off toward Gates' campsite.

Waters was tied to a tree overnight and given only a little palmetto "cabbage" and water to eat. The next day, the same two men brought Waters to stand before a table where Gates sat as judge. The evening before, Captain George Somers had appealed to Gates to be lenient explaining that fights like that were not uncommon among sailors and that he did not believe Waters had intended to kill Samuel. He considered the blow from the shovel to be an unlucky accident. Gates conducted a fairly formal trial asking for the accounts of witnesses and allowing for some testimony as to Waters normally fine character. After about three-quarters of an hour, Gates rendered his verdict. Waters had undoubtedly killed Samuel, but it was unintentional manslaughter, not murder. He pardoned Waters dependent upon a promise of future good behavior, which Waters gave readily.

Reactions to the verdict and sentence were varied. The sailors were glad that their mate was free, but resentful of Gates and the landlubbers for appropriating jurisdiction over what was strictly a maritime issue in their eyes. The non-sailor community, both the soldiers with Gates and the passengers, expected sterner justice for a man who had killed another and saw the pardon and Gates as soft.

The incident of the fight emphasized that the sailors needed a purpose. These survivors needed a way off the island and after some inspection, it was clear the *Sea Venture* could not be repaired. The answer to both challenges was to build a new boat. There was some discussion about whether they should try to build another galleon, but Somers insisted the men should try something simpler first. So, in August, they began building a flat-bottomed boat, similar to a Venetian gondola, to explore the islands. When no one was exploring, the boat was used to fish beyond the shallows and to collect shellfish.

Even before the sailors began working on their boat, the two Indians had made two canoes of cedar. They fished and the catch was plenty for them with a great deal left over to share with the others. This was the only regular contact between the Indians and the English, but Strachey visited their fire often. He had no honest respect for the natives and their culture, however he was excited by the intellectual challenge of learning the language and he thought being able to translate would make him more valuable to the colony leaders.

When the gondola was finished, the building crew moved on to fit their longboat with mast, deck, sails and cabin.

"Mister Forbisher," Somers asked, "how certain are you that this converted longboat can make it to Jamestown?"

Forbisher, who was a carpenter and ship builder by trade, answered with great confidence, "We will do the best we can, Captain. What choice do we have?"

"If a small group can cross 500 miles, they can get aid and likely a larger ship for the return trip. There should be a ship in harbor there, maybe one from our fleet. You are right, what choice do we have."

The building crew was made up of a few sailors who had some experience in repairing ships in the middle of a voyage but all the other workers were amateurs. Luckily, there were three other carpenters on the *Sea Venture* besides Richard Forbisher, who led building. Somer himself was responsible for the design of each vessel.

Henry Ravens would pilot the refitted longboat. He tried to leave on August 28th, with six sailors and cape-merchant, Thomas Whittingham. Two days later they were back, not having found a way out of the reefs. They rested two days, restocked, and departed farther to the east. This time they made it past the reefs. The little boat would go slower than the big galleon, so they estimated it would take at least three weeks before a ship could return.

It was unlikely that there would be a large ship in port at Jamestown. The ships in their fleet, if they had arrived safely, may have already left to return to England. They would probably need to provide their own transportation, at least part of it. The key structural elements of the *Sea Venture* had not been damaged. Somers calculated how large a ship could be made from the salvageable pieces and how much new wood would be required. He sent crews to fell cedar trees and make the new planks. He sent sailors and two carpenters to the wreck to pull out the large timbers they needed. Within a few days, they laid the keel of new pinnacle.

The comfortable life on Bermuda was seductive. Some of the passengers decided they would rather stay on Bermuda and wait for a passing ship to take them to England. As a bonus, or maybe as an excuse, they would lay claim to Bermuda for the crown. This plan was betrayed to Gates on September 1st and six men were arrested and tried for mutiny. This time, Gates did punish the miscreants, more out of a need to stop the spread of their heresy than to penalize the mutineers. They were set on a small island in the archipelago and fed regularly but kept away from the rest of the party. The duration of the sentence was to be until the castaways were ready to leave for Virginia.

Muchamps and Namontack hunted or fished together every few days. No one paid much attention to what they did as long as the food they provided came regularly. Usually Namontack brought the food to the colonists, but sometime in September, it was Muchamps who took over that task. After two weeks of this new behavior, Gates asked about Namontack. Muchamps said they had gone out hunting together. They separated which they often did. Namontack did not return. Gates tried several ways to find out when Namontack had disappeared, but except for days, the English and the Indians did not measure time in the same increments. There was no reason to think that Muchamps would kill the only other Indian on the island and Muchamps continued to keep to himself, so Gates did not press any charges. After two trips to England and having been a trusted member of Powhatan's council, disappearing without a trace was an ignoble end for the adventurous Namontack.

The shipbuilding continued. The island still provided for the castaways. The speculation about fairies and pixies had subsided until one night in November.

As the first stars appeared, cries of "ca-how" came from the deep forest. The darker the night, the more the cries. The seventeenth century was a time of great superstition and many of the colonists jumped to the conclusion that spirits had invaded the island. The more enlightened members of the group resolved to look for a natural cause in the morning. This resolve was put to the test overnight as the number of "ca-hows" increased a hundredfold. By midnight, it was if the very land itself was screaming "ca-how." No one slept until just before dawn when the sound decreased even more abruptly than it had begun.

At first light, the scientists of the party ventured into the forest. As soon as they looked at the ground under the trees, they mystery was solved. Thousands of birds were roosting. They were mostly asleep now and quiet. One of the passengers was a student of ornithology and he declared them night birds probably of the family of petrels. Assuming this species had not been identified before, they named it the cahow to match the sound it made. Apparently cahows came on migration in November. Once they had nested, the cries were not as strident, but for weeks, the night was filled with the eerie cries. When they visited other islands, they found that the birds mostly nested on a place they, naturally, called Bird Island. Since they were not afraid of men, they could be hunted by the hundreds with only a stick. The noisy birds proved to be a good source of food.

George Somers' cook, a Welshman named Thomas Powell, appreciated the birds. He was truly a chef and even over an open fire, he could make some delicious dishes with the addition of fresh fowl. Thomas was in the camp most of the time as were the women and children. He and Elizabeth Persons grew fond of each other during the fall. The fondness grew to love and love led to marriage. On Sunday November 26th, the women gathered late blooming flowers and dressed Elizabeth in the dress another of the women had worn at her wedding just before she had left England. Captain Gates, who was more of the same size as Thomas than was Captain Somers, provided a fine wardrobe of a chocolate brown velvet suit and fresh linen for the groom. Thomas spent Friday and Saturday preparing a feast. With as much old world tradition as could be mustered in this new world, the Reverend Buck officiated at the first, and only, English marriage on Bermuda.

Everyone enjoyed the wedding, but the next day returned to normal. The ill feeling between the sailors and soldiers that had begun with the trial of Waters had grown over the months. It did not make much sense. The sailors and soldiers had worked side by side with the passengers to keep the *Sea Venture* afloat. They were still working side by side to build the ship that could take them off the island. There was no logic in the division, but there is no accounting for emotion and the sailors did feel aggrieved and shut out by the settlers.

For some time, they had kept a separate campfire. Eventually, Somers asked if they could build their own boat. Since it had been well over four weeks and Raven and the converted longboat had not returned, Gates and Somers concluded that they would need to make a second ship to accommodate all of the survivors, so Somers' offer made good sense for all concerned. Somers and the sailors moved to the main island of the group and communications between the two camps passed through the two knights.

Christmas was also marked with as much English tradition as could be emulated in this topical paradise. This world was always green, so bringing greens into the tents and campsites had no great meaning, but they did it anyway. The feast consisted of the same basic foods they had been eating all along with one addition. As if part of the Christmas miracle, the cahows started laying their eggs right on Christmas Day. Even though the settlers had hunted the birds extensively, there were thousands of them and so there were plenty of eggs. Sadly, the settlers did not know that a cahow lays only one egg at each nesting time, so in taking that egg, they effectively ended that bird's reproduction for the year. But they did not know this and treated the birds as if they were chickens and would be laying eggs every day. The eggs gave a new dimension to their diet and allowed for a variation of Christmas puddings on the twelve days of Christmas.

In early 1610, Stephen Hopkins, the bible-quoter, revived the idea of staying on Bermuda and claiming it for England instead of going on the Jamestown. Gates was a man of great loyalty. He had signed on with the Virginia Company to go to Jamestown and he could not conceive of doing anything else. He considered deviating from this plan as mutiny, so when Hopkins and his friends were reported to Gates, they were arrested. There was another trial. In preparation of his defense, Hopkins spoke with Strachey and Newport. These two gentlemen and others accepted that he was sorry for his actions. They persuaded Gates to accept Hopkins parole. Hopkins gave his solemn word that he would not say any more about staying and he was allowed to remain a free man. Again Gates appeared to different factions as pliant or weak.

The days passed and the baby Rolfe, who had made herself known to her mother about the time they sailed into the Caribbean Sea, decided it was time to come into the world. Like every first father, Rolfe wanted to leap into action and fix his wife's suffering, but birth requires patience, not fixing.

Rolfe came bustling into the common work area. "My wife, my wife says the baby is coming. Coming now, I mean. Right now." He addressed himself in turn to every woman present.

One among them, a woman who had served as a midwife before, took charge. "Calm yourself, Master Rolfe. I have seen babes into this world dozens of times." Addressing herself to the women, she said, "We need to bring Mistress Rolfe to the small hut. Which of you are willing to help me?"

Almost all the women, except the very youngest ones, volunteered. The midwife picked four and they went with Rolfe to get his wife. Knowing the baby was on the way, the women had directed the men to build a small hut with a raised cot and a short stool. Giving birth in this place would keep the mess away from the regular living area.

In England, she might have been shut away for days leading up to the birth and the windows of her room would have been kept tightly shut for fear of the vapors in the night air. Here, there was no way to know of the time of delivery until the baby announced it, so it was not until the morning of February 11th that the expectant mother was guided to the hut where still warm tropical breezes came through the very walls keeping her cool and as comfortable as the circumstances allowed. John stayed with his friends at the common campfire pacing and smoking and waiting. Late in the day, she delivered a baby girl whom they named Bermuda.

Twice, groups of men had planned to stay on Bermuda rather than risk the perils of life in the troubled colony of Virginia and Gates considered these plans mutiny against the Virginia Company. On March 3rd, mutiny was again the charge, but this time it was not for a philosophical reason, it was plan insubordination and disobedience to a direct order. Henry Paine refused to stand his watch. He said there was no need to guard a storehouse from a Spanish attack that would never come. Colorfully, he cursed the sergeant who challenged him and expanded on his insults to the officer who was called into the argument.

Paine was tried by Gates in a purely military fashion and found guilty. He was sentenced by the prevailing military code to be shot. Without preamble, he was taken in manacles, placed in front of a tree, and shot by a firing squad. The soldiers accepted the verdict as just. The settlers were more confused than before. Why would a governor pardon murder and plots to abandon their mission and then execute a man for making a sensible argument?

More settlers defected to the sailors' camp. Gate threatened to come to the big island and round up all those who had run off, so everyone but Somers fled to the woods. Somers and Gates put their knighted heads together and worked out an amnesty. The terms did include submitting to Gates' authority, something that two men, Christopher Carter and Robert Waters, would not do. Both had been tried by Gates before. Waters was the one who had killed a fellow sailor with a shovel. Carter was one of those who had been banned to the distant island. That exile had been commuted when they were needed to help build the new boats. Carter and Waters remained at large. There was a tense armistice, but work on the ships got back to a normal pace.

In another month, the first pinnacle was ready to be moved from the beach where it had been built to a cove where masts and sails could be added and provisions could be loaded more easily. While the boat builders celebrated, the Rolfes mourned. Little Bermuda had lived only three months. The mother blamed the heavy topical air and the constant insects. There had been no spread of sickness during their stay on the island, so it was not a contagious disease. It was not uncommon for a child anywhere to die young, but it comforted Mistress Rolfe to think the tropics were the cause. That way she would be more certain of another child surviving in a more "normal" climate.

As if to balance the mandala of life, a baby boy was born that same week to Edward Eason and his wife. They called him Bermudas. Strachey had befriended both of the fathers during the voyage and was named godfather to both children.

In the nine months they were marooned in Bermuda, the collective party had built quite a navy. The Indians had built two canoes. The gondola was built to go between islands. The original team had built the *Deliverance*, a style of pinnacle half the size of the *Sea Venture*, and, from all native materials, Somers' sailors had built a smaller pinnacle, the *Patience*. The names were very apt.

Strachey had documented all of the adventures from the beginning of the storm through the building and launching of the two main ships in his personal journal. He wrote to the Excellent Lady, Countess of Bedford, patron of the famous poet, John Donne, and retold the tale based on his records. It had been a pleasant pastime and he hoped it would impress the Countess enough that she might offer to be his patron as well. All that remained was to find a way to send the letter to England.

In early May, both pinnacles sat in the cove and the camps were slowly being broken down so that the supplies, provisions and belongings that had been salvaged from the *Sea Venture* or gathered on Bermuda could be loaded. Gates made a memorial on a copper plate stating the salvation of the crew and passengers of the *Sea Venture* and their feat of creating two boats in order to continue their journey. He and a few others featured prominently in the memorial.

By May 10th, everything was ready, and nearly one hundred souls boarded the two ships. They brought along the canoes but left the gondola on the big island, not wanting to strand even the two outlaws without some transportation. It took two days to make deep water. Two children had been born in those nine months and five people had died, Jeffery Briars, Richard Lewis, William Hitchman, Bermuda Rolfe, and Edward Samuel the sailor. Namontack was not on Gates' list as his death had not been proved or, possibly, Gates was only counting Englishmen.

The route from the Caribbean to the east coast of America was well known and supported by the ocean current. Bermuda is not on this route. It lies about 500 miles due east of the Carolina coast. Prevailing winds are from the west and so the trip from Bermuda to Jamestown was uncommon in every way. On midnight of the tenth day out, Strachey caught a sweet smell from shore. He was not alone. The entire ship came alive with anticipation. Even the sails seemed to stretch a bit as if to strain toward port. An hour after daybreak, the watch spotted land. It took another day for the ships to come to Point Comfort. That day, May 21st, was stormy with squalls of thunder and lightening. Sight was limited and those on watch at Point Comfort saw only unfamiliar shapes in the mist. Newport, Gates, Somers and everyone on the two ships had their sense of victory cut short when the fort at Point Comfort fired on them.

Gates ignored the fire, but he did stand near the bow and salute the shore. From the *Deliverance*, Gates dropped one of the canoes they had made in Bermuda and came to shore. He was not happy with the situation he found. Gates chastised Percy for leaving this fort with so little defense. He berated the men for being lazy and when he heard that the settlers at James Fort were starving when these men had an abundance of provisions, he resolved to take his supplies and all that these men could load onto his ships to the colonists the next day.

The ships were loaded yet that night and they lifted anchor at dawn the next morning. There were no winds to fill the sails so only the incoming tide would move them. It took two days for Gates to get up the river.

By mid-May, the sixty men and women at James Fort were hanging on by a thread. No one did anything that was not absolutely necessary to keep alive that day. So, no one was watching when the ships from Bermuda approached from down river.

On May 23rd, they approached the island and were surprised that the fort looked abandoned, with the palisade torn down, the ports open, the gates off their hinges, and parts of empty houses that had been burned for wood. A strong storm made it difficult for the ships to get near shore. They had to wait until the storm slacked off to solve this mystery.

Gates and Somers dropped anchor at the same place the *Godspeed* and *Discovery* had three years before. Again, the passengers could simply jump into the shallow water and wade ashore. In spite of the continuing drizzle, supplies were quickly unloaded and the new settlers ministered to the people of James Fort.

Jane Pierce and her daughter Jane were at the front of the crowd that gathered as soon as word went out that those presumed dead had arrived. Her husband was standing at the bow of the *Patience* straining to seeing each face in the crowd. Jane saw him just before he spotted her. He swung over the rail and dropped into the shallows. He sloshed toward shore. Jane pulled up her skirts and waded to meet him. They embraced with such passion that they fell. They helped each other up and came laughing and soaked to envelope their daughter in a three-way hug.

"I am wet, Papa!" she complained, and they all laughed all the more.

Some food was immediately passed out to the old settlers and as soon as they had eaten, the Reverend Buck preached a service of thanksgiving. With healthy people to do the work and enough food for the first time in months, most of the colonists recovered. Three who were too weak did die, but finally, the little cemetery in the corner of the fort received its last guest and the phoenix that was the colony of Jamestown rose again from its own ashes.

Gates brought the news that there was to be a new capital for the Virginia colony. The board wanted a location far from a navigable river except by small boats. James Fort was to be only a port without so much as a storehouse. But there would be more houses to accommodate all the workers needed at a port. There was a plan for a layout of two streets. The location would formally be known as James Towne.

Percy relinquished command to Gates. Little Jim Blumfield, who was not the smallest of Josiah's squad any more having growth to five feet nine inches at twelve years old, was up in the observation tree watching the people eat, watching the Reverend hold services and watching the ceremony between Percy and a new well-dressed man.

"Well, boys," Josiah said," I think this is our chance to rejoin the others, if we want to. The newcomers will think we are part of the old settlers and the old ones probably will not recognize us and will think we came with the ships."

Dods, ever the worrier, asked, "What if someone remembers us?"

Dixon, the oldest, replied, "I am at the most danger there. All of you young men have changed considerably in the last year since we left. Only the men from Dumpling Island, if any are left, are likely to know you and they never knew we were not sent by the council."

"There may be some uncomfortable questions, but I still think this is our best chance. We will wait until just before dawn and walk in one or two at a time as if we are returning from the privy," Josiah suggested.

Nathaniel Peacock, now known as Nate, spoke for the squad when he said, "Whatever you say, Josiah. You have yet to steer us wrong." Such was the loyalty and trust that sound and successful leadership can bring.

Dixon volunteered cheerfully, "And if we do not like this fellow, we can always leave again."

The comrades laughed and Nate started a round of "Woo, woo, woo!"

Gates took stock of the fort. The food he had brought would not keep all of the settlers until harvest time. After a few days, the new colonists began to succumb to the usual problems of newcomers to James Towne. Even though they had brought cahow birds and salted fish with them, they were soon trying to survive on two fish cakes a day. The lack of fresh water and the insects took their toll. The mastiff who had survived being shot in the head, was ceremoniously dispatched to provide one more meal for the colonists. As the newcomers became sick and the lack of food became more obvious, Gates made the hard decision. He would evacuate the colony.

He arranged teams to pack out or store everything valuable. His intent was to take these people to a place where they could recuperate and resupply. He would go to Point Comfort, pick up those men and stock up on food from there and then head for Newfoundland where he was sure the fishing would offer plenty of provisions for a trip to England.

The members of the squad fit in as they could, picking up whatever work they were asked to do. Percy never laid eyes on them and no one else found their reappearance worthy of comment. Perhaps it was because nine strong and healthy young men contributed so much to the work.

One day, Josiah and Strachey were assigned to the same work team. One large team rolled the twenty-four cannons that weighed 1100 to 5500 pounds each down from the bulwarks and tipped the barrels into the ditches outside the fort where Strachey and Josiah's team covered them with the dirt that had originally been dug for the earthworks. Some armor was also buried in the ditches. Strachey had not done much physical labor in his life and the shoveling was very difficult for him. As the day got warmer, sweat poured down Strachey's face, neck, arms and legs. He was miserable.

In spite of his class snobbery, Strachey enjoyed talking with Josiah. Josiah was fascinated with his tales of the London theater and talking about something from London distracted William from his misery.

"I believe my favorite production was Edward Alleyn in Tamburlaine the Great. The playwright Marlowe himself was involved. … Or perhaps it was Faustus. … No, I think Tamburlaine. It is difficult to decide. I particularly like the poetry, not the quality of Johnson, of course, but very good. Ben Johnson, by the way, looked quite a lot like your Captain Newport. But back to what I was saying, the costumes for Tamburlaine were impressive. As Timur changed from shepherd to king, Alleyn began with only his own clothing and, by the end of the play, he had added a bit each time he left the stage until he was in full regal regalia. I am not certain whose idea the gradual change was, but it was most effective."

And so it went for hour upon hour as Strachey talked and Josiah listened. Sometimes Strachey would get so involved in his recreation of a scene that he would drop his shovel and take on a character. He would leap away from the ditch and move about as if on stage. After one of these diversions, Strachey prepared to resume shoveling by wiping his hands up and down his breeches. His signet ring slipped from his finger and into the trench. He was so involved in his story that did not notice. It was buried along with the armor and cannons.

All the ships were pulled into the shallow water, tipped on their sides and re-caulked. They had not had the proper caulking for the two ships built in Bermuda and the others had not been refreshed since they came to the new world. It would take a significant amount of tar and pitch to do the job right. The colonist had some stored but they had to make more to have enough for all four boats.

Tradesmen packed their tools. The order was not to leave anything that could be of help to the natives, so people threw all sorts of things into Smith's well or abandoned odds and ends in trash pits or wherever they were.

One of the children who had come on Gates ship took all this hiding to heart. He took his most special things, a green and white border ware candlestick and a square glass-case bottle full of pebbles to the northernmost room of a building along the eastern wall. He dug under the edge of a chimney in one of the long houses and tucked his treasures in the hole. He was as certain as any eight-year-old can be that he would be one of the adventurers who would return.

Gates proposed to get his people back on *Deliverance* and *Patience* and have the others crowd onto *Discovery* and *Virginia*, which had finally arrived on her own. Hopefully, they would be able to trade for at least one larger ship in Newfoundland before they crossed the Atlantic.

Gates listed who went on which ship and what goods and products were taken. Josiah and the squad had completely integrated into the company again and hence their names were duly entered on Gates' roll for the *Discovery*. The *Virginia* was sent ahead to give notice to Fort Algernon and to start packing up those men and provisions.

On the morning of June 7, 1610, Gates ordered his ensign to beat the drum as a call for all to board. There had been threats to burn the fort, especially by those who had suffered through part or all of the last three years, so Gates and his staff stayed on shore and boarded last to protect the fort. Once everyone was on board, he ordered a volley of small shot as a farewell. That first afternoon, they went only five miles downstream and reached Hogs Island by dark. The next day, they ran with the ebb tide to Mulberry Island. On the morning of June 9th, the plan was to pick up the men still at Point Comfort, cross Chesapeake Bay, enter the protected waters between the outer banks and the coast and head north.

CHAPTER 12
Governor for Life

Never was there a more perfect day in June in Virginia. The water was at its proper level, the land was all over luscious greens with intense points of color and the sky above was that saturated hue now called Carolina blue. The breeze was just right. Breakfast was just right. Colonists on the ships shared a feeling of salvation and the exhilaration that comes from knowing you are on your way home.

They were only thirty minutes from having lifted anchors when the lookout on the *Deliverance* spotted the long boat. The men at Point Comfort had no long boat, but the vessel was most certainly English. As soon as they were within hailing distance, Gates called out.

"Ahoy, the longboat. Who are you?"

"Ahoy, the ship. We are from the *De La Warr.*"

"Percy, do you know of a ship named for his Lordship?" Gates asked Sir George Percy. It was foolish to ask Percy since he had not been in England in three years, but he was the gentleman closest to hand and old habits die hard.

Percy replied, "No, Captain, I certainly do not."

Gates went back to the source of the confusion.

"You say you are from the ship *De La Warr*?

"The ship ... and the man ... His Lordship De La Warr is coming up the river behind us in his own ship ... with his own name."

"Well, I will be ...," exhaled Gates.

Gates had known De La Warr was to mount a supply in the year following his own departure, but to encounter him in the middle of the James River just on the day they were abandoning the settlement was too much to believe. Those on the other boats had heard the exchange and were equally dumbfounded. Pushed by the ebb tide, all the boats had floated somewhat down river during this conversation which brought them just close enough to see the foresail of the lord's ship *De La Warr* as it cleared the point called Hampton Roads.

Captain Samuel Argall, familiar to the few remaining old settlers, commanded this grand new ship that brought the Governor himself. Between the two ships in this tiny fleet there were also 150 passengers and food for four hundred people for a year. The river was placid and the ships drew near enough for Lord De La Warr to address the Captains of the departing ships.

Tall, imposing, well-bred and well-clothed, looking every bit a part of the aristocracy with his dark hair and blue eyes, Lord De la Warr stood at the bow of his ship the very picture of arrogance and competence. "Gates, What is this I see? Are you taking part of the colony to plant a settlement elsewhere?"

Gates answered, "No, my Lord, this is the entire colony. We are out of food and besieged by marauding Indians. We are … we were on our way to find a source of food so we could restock and come to you in England."

De La Warr turned nearly purple with rage. "Indeed not, sir. Turn these vessels around immediately! I have provisions a plenty and you will NOT abandon my colony! Turn about, I say!"

As quickly as each could manage, the boats reversed course and headed back up the now neutral river. The spirits of the old colonists and the Bermuda survivors also reversed course. They were returning to what had been two weeks to three years of misery and terror. Food was nice, but England was better.

One by one the ships and boats dropped anchor near that same spot that had been used since 1607. Some waded ashore while the gentry were rowed in longboats. When the Governor landed he fervently knelt and pronounced a long prayer of thanksgiving with a little condemnation of cowards thrown in for good measure. Once his staff was assembled, they marched the short distance into the fort.

He looked around to determine what was the most prestigious residence assuming that would be the house for the Governor, but the whole fort looked like a rubbish heap. He gravitated to the clear spot that was still referred to as the Council Chamber. His personal servants (among whom was the retuning interpreter, Henry Spellman) brought a chair and refreshments from the ship and made His Lordship as comfortable as possible. Once the company had disembarked, he paraded to the northern bulwark. He motioned for his staff to form a semicircle of honor behind him and, with his personal banner and the flags of England and King James as his backdrop, he again knelt. He waited until everyone in the fort followed his lead. He prayed. He indicated that each minister should offer a prayer. Then he stood and his secretary read his commission from the Virginia Company to be Governor for life of all of Virginia that now was defined as running west to the far ocean.

Sir Thomas West, Lord De La Warr, a sturdy man with the beard of a prophet, stood in great dignity, with no change of expression, while the commission was read. The secretary retired to the background and De La Warr stepped to the front edge of the bulwark as if he were an actor moving into the footlights. He stuck a stately pose and said in a clear measured voice, "I hereby accept this commission." No one moved, not knowing if this was the end of the impromptu ceremony. It was not.

He then launched into a lengthy speech, some of which seemed to be prepared but some of which was clearly extemporaneous as he listed the many defects he found in the fort and berated these tattered survivors for vanity and idleness. He said not a word of praise for the fortitude of those who had born shipwreck or starvation. In the twenty minutes he spoke, he became a most unpopular man.

While the Governor was conducting this ceremony, Bridget Malone had been moving stealthily through the crowd trying to spot Josiah. She had come on the second ship of De La Warr's little fleet. All of the Jamestown ships had held back letting those two ships anchor first, so Bridget and her shipmates were near the front of the assembled group while Josiah and the squad had stopped at the gate, half in and half out of the fort. He saw her before she saw him.

Josiah elbowed Dixon, "Rich, do you see that girl with the black curls?"

"Where?" he asked.

"Right there, to the left of the new Governor, about twenty feet in front of the bulwark," he said as he pointed.

At that moment, she moved again and Richard Dixon had clear sight of her. "Oh, yes, I see her. Got your eye on a girl already, Josiah?"

"Well, sort of, I think I know her."

"Now, Josiah, there are maybe a score of women here, two at most, and you think one of them is someone you knew in England? How likely is that?"

"Not very, I grant you, but there is something about her. Do you remember I told you the story of the girl who saved me from being arrested on the day I met Captain Smith? That is her. I am sure of it."

"And I gather, from the way you are craning your neck to see her, that you would like to remake her acquaintance?"

"A ... a ... well, yes, I would."

"Then you had best be about it, my boy, the competition is going to be fierce."

Dixon grinned. Josiah smiled the widest smile Richard had ever seen on his face. Josiah grabbed Richard's hand and shook it heartily and then melted into the throng as only a practiced woodsman can.

He stalked his prey as he would a nervous deer. When she turned to the right to check out a young, tall man, he stepped noiselessly up to her left. As he had planned, in turning back, she bumped him.

"Oh, sorry, she whispered."

"My fault, Miss Malone," he whispered in return.

She jerked her head up to meet his beaming face and let out a small squeal. He needlessly brought his finger to his lips to tell her to be quiet. Then he took her elbow and very slowly moved her toward the palisade.

At the edge of the crowd, they slipped along side a small storage building and then to the back of it ending in the old street that ran just inside the fort wall and out of sight of the man preaching on the bulwark. They stood silently for a moment. Josiah seemed to realize that he was touching Bridget and pulled his hand away awkwardly.

"Hello," she began.

"Hello," he obliged.

Two young people who had each longed for the other over lost years and long miles stood not two feet apart, speechless.

He broke the impasse, "Were you looking for me?

Regaining some of her usual spunk, "Yes, I was. I knew you had sailed for here three years ago and I wondered," here she halted, "I wondered if you were … alive."

"So I am," he teased, taking a step back and throwing his arms wide. Then the man he had become took charge. "And I am glad to see you."

She melted. Any pretense she had planned, any idea of being the coquette, vanished with that one heartfelt statement.

"And I, you. I came … to find you. I … hoped you were alright."

"I am better now," he said gallantly.

Getting down to practical matters, he asked, "How did you come? With your family?"

She shook her head and those black curls bounced in the sunlight.

"Indentured?" he asked sadly. If she were indentured to someone, he would either have to wait until her term was done or find the money to buy out her contract before they could marry. He surprised himself that he was thinking of marriage so soon.

"No," she said quickly, perhaps having gone through similar thoughts and wanting to relieve him as quickly as she could, "I am a paid servant of a couple who have one child and are expecting another."

This was excellent news. Josiah had not been paid at all in three years. Technically the Virginia Company provided for all his needs. Actually, he had been one of the main providers for the entire fort for some time. The idea of being paid in hard coin had not even occurred to him since he left England. As a paid servant, she was at liberty to leave her position to marry or possibly even keep her position as a day job if the family agreed. There it was again, thinking of marriage. This girl was having a much stronger effect on him than he had imagined, but he liked it.

Remembering that she had just defined her position, he thought he should also.

"I ... well I am not quite sure what I am here now. I was one of John Smith's hand picked soldiers. Since he left, I have led a group of hunters who provide food for this fort or one of the others we have. Since Captain Gates came last month, I have done a lot of digging, a laborer, I guess. I am not sure what this new Governor will want me to do."

"Do you have a home?"

They both blushed a bit sensing the implication that she might join him.

"I do. I bunk with some of my mates in a house on the far side of the fort. Would you like to see it?" he offered.

She wanted to see it, very much, to be in a building on land for the first time in weeks, to see how people lived in this strange place, to be away from other people for a while, and to be with Josiah. The audience was cheering now.

"Huzzah, huzzah, huzzah!"

They were free from attending the speech. But Bridget hesitated.

"I would very much like to see where you live, but I feel I should find my mistress and see to the child." This was true. Beyond her sense of duty, she somehow felt that to go directly to his rooms on their first meeting would cause him to think ill of her. Maybe her employer would hear of it and consider it unseemly. Something primal was warning her against it.

"Of course," he demurred. May I accompany you to look for them?"

She was torn. She would like to stay with him longer. She would like his protection as she went around this fort full of men who had already stared at her in most disquieting ways. She did not know how her master would take her knowing someone who was already here. But she and Hannah had become very close in last weeks and she would like her mistress to meet her friend, Josiah.

"Yes, please, come and meet the Crofts."

He took her hand, pulled it through his crooked arm, placed it on his wrist and gave it a short pat. He threw back his head. She did the same and they walked out together into their new life.

The Governor's next move was to appoint a full compliment of officers including appointing Strachey as secretary and recorder for the colony and appointing Percy as Commander of the Fort. Then he moved on to improving the defenses at Jamestown and at Point Comfort.

Gates had been appalled at the lack of fortifications at Point Comfort. Fort Algernon was really no fort at all. They had moved some sand and earth to make a small berm and had erected poles to hold up a length of sailcloth. These defenses and some tents constituted Fort Algernon. De La Warr ordered that proper walls be built. The trees on Point Comfort did not come near the fort so building a palisade like at James Fort would be a great deal more work. One of the newly appointed officers who was doing an inventory of the island found some boards left near the old sawpit and more at the site of Ratcliff's abandoned "palace." He suggested to De La Warr that these boards could be nailed to some anchor poles to construct a secure fort. They needed another fifty or sixty boards that were cut and sawed in short order. Then all the building materials were sent down river on a barge while a crew of laborers and carpenters followed on the *Patience*. It took only three days to create a very respectable fort.

De La Warr did not wait even a day to begin reconstruction on James Fort. He demanded secondary gates be built at each bulwark to offer more exits than the main gate on the river. The palisades were reinforced and six-foot wide musketeer platforms were added along the south wall. All public buildings were put to rights. New houses were built, some inside and some outside the original fort. The old plan of a two street town was revived. Five hundred well-fed, motivated people can do a great deal in a few days.

The chapel was his next target. Services were being held in the storehouse, so his first attention was to the abandoned church. He rebuilt the church with many improvements. The chancel was constructed in cedar with the communion table carved from black walnut. The pews were of cedar and four broad windows could be left opened or covered by shutters. A new pulpit was built and two bells the Governor had brought from England were installed at the west end.

De La Warr was writing a set of laws for the settlement that included requiring attendance at church twice each day as well as Sunday morning and Thursday after dinner. The church needed work to accommodate this level of use by 500 people. The essential structure of the building was sound, but the Governor expected a proper choir stall for himself and his council. This included an ornate chair with a cover of brocade both of which were taken from his ship, but the canopy to support the cover and the raised dais to hold the chair needed to be created. One of the ministers who had come with De La Warr was a musician and choral director and he wanted a formal choir stall built so the men's choir he wanted would have a home. A harpsichord was among the Governor's personal possessions on his ship and it would be installed across from the choir when the rest of the work was complete.

Lord De La Warr loved ceremony. As Governor for life, he was essentially the king of Virginia and the ceremony appealed to his sense of royalty. Coupled with this formality was a near addiction to discipline. His concept of law was strict and absolute and his idea of a just sentence was extraordinarily harsh. Punishment in the seventeenth century was extreme with death or maiming the penalty for most crimes, even petty ones. When the colonists heard of the new laws, they wondered who would be first to feel De La Warr's wrath. But first, there was the matter of food.

One of the newly appointed officers was in charge of all inventories except weapons and armor. As Sergeant Major, George Webb tracked food, clothing, building materials, trade goods, any and everything supplied by the Virginia Company. He was a good planner and when he heard that there was a variety of foods to be had in Bermuda, he advised Lord De La Warr that a supply run to that island storehouse would do well to augment the supplies paid for by the Virginia Company. This idea was mentioned at an extended meeting of De La Warr's advisors on June 13th. Captain Somers volunteered to make the trip to Bermuda on the *Patience* to bring back fish, birds and hogs. He estimated it would take eleven days each way and several days to round up the animals. He should be back before the heavy part of the hurricane season came on. The trip seemed such a good idea that Captain Argall was assigned to go along on the *Discovery* so the haul would be doubled.

Preparations began, and they left a few days before the reopening of the church on Sunday June 24th. De La Warr had taken up residence in a long house along the western palisade that he called the statehouse. For special occasions, he envisioned a full dress procession, but it was less than one hundred feet from his house to the door of the church, and he wanted more of a show. He gathered all his officers, the minister, the choir members, and his drummer. He had them form up double-file with banners and flags flying and parade around the entire perimeter of the fort, from his house to the north bulwark, to the east bulwark, along the riverside palisade to the west bulwark, half way up the west wall and then turn so that they marched directly into the church door. The colonists were expected to fall in behind the formal parade and follow the official party into the building. Five hundred people did not fit into the sixty by twenty-four foot church, so the late joiners stood outside. De La Warr liked the parade so much, he repeated it every Sunday, rain or shine.

Somers and Argall had headed east –southeast and after five hundred miles they should have arrived at Bermuda, but it was not there. Somers led the search and they crisscrossed the areas for twenty-three days. The enchanted Bermuda archipelago seemly had disappeared. One more tale was added to the legend of the Bermuda triangle as Somers gave up and diverted the trip to Cape Cod.

After three weeks of sailing side-by-side and only twenty miles from shore, the two ships lost sight of each other in a dense fog. Somers had just signaled that they should "stand for River Sagadahoc (Kennebec)." Argall found the river easily, but Somers was not there. Argall waited six days and finally opened a mysterious box that Somers had given him along with the instruction to open it only in a dire emergency. The box contained one small paper that said simply, "Go home." But where was home? Did it mean England or Virginia? Argall was a soldier to the core and an order was an order. He puzzled over the cryptic message for an entire day and then headed toward Jamestown. Practical as well as disciplined, he stopped at the old site of the Hudson Bay colony and loaded up with cod.

Back at the fort, De La Warr set a crew to dig up the armor and cannons. Josiah was assigned to this detail and he mused over the foolishness of having to dig up what he had just buried. Sometimes, he wondered if he and the squad should just melt back into the forest, but he did enjoy the company of all these new people and especially Bridget.

With the church revived with freshly transplanted wildflowers, additional fields cleared and planted and regular forays off the island to gather local food, De La Warr now turned his mind to the Indians.

He sent a messenger to Powhatan to return everything and everyone he had stolen or captured. Powhatan replied that the coat-wearers should stay in Jamestown and send no more messengers unless they brought a carriage and three horses as gifts to show that they considered him as important as the king in England who traveled in that way. De La Warr was not amused.

He sent Gates with a large party, including Strachey, to attack the village of Koughtan. The heat of early July was smothering. Gates did not want to fight a pitched battle so he used his drummer Thomas Dowse to attract the Indians. Dowse was a tabor, one who used the drum for rhythm and then danced. The Indians were curious and a large group came to watch the performance. Once the natives were in between the two flanks of Gates' men, the settlers started shooting. At that close range, they killed fifteen braves, but some got away and warned Koughtan. The weroance moved his people quickly away and Gates' prize of the day was a few baskets of old wheat, beans, peas and tobacco. The real prize was the acres of corn the

Indians had planted which Gates staked out and ordered guarded for the English until harvest.

On July 20th, the *Blessing* sailed for England. She was being sent back to show the Virginia Company Council how much progress De la Warr had made in only two months. The *Blessing* was loaded with lumber and iron ore and a special passenger, Kainta, the son of the king of the Warraskoyacks. The Captain carried the first dispatches that Strachey had sent to the company in his official capacity. They were filled with condemnation of those who preceded De La Warr and extensive praise for everything he had done since his arrival.

Three weeks later, De La Warr sent Percy to attack the Paspahgahs and the Chickahomies. Percy had enslaved an Indian captive named Kemps. The brave's normal duties were to take care of the menial tasks for Percy's household, but on this occasion he was forced to guide the troops. As De La Warr demanded, they traveled up river in two barges and then marched on the villages in military order. The Indians had never seen anything like this formal troop of soldiers. They were completely surprised at how fast the troops switched from a formal parade to killing. Fifteen Indians were killed outright, one was wounded, and the queen and her children were made captive. They burned the village to the ground not even looking for valuable plunder. A band of soldiers pulled the wounded brave aside and held him down while their sergeant used his sword to decapitate the man. Percy did nothing to stop them.

By the time they returned to the barges, the soldiers had been whispering among themselves and a spokesman asked Percy why they were keeping any Indians alive, even just a woman and her children.

"This woman is the queen of her tribe and will be a valuable hostage."

"Well, Sir, why must we be taking these brats along. The boys will just grow up to kill us."

Percy was afraid the men would do as they wanted and it would be seen as mutiny. Thinking the men would maim the boys, he gave them their way.

"My concern is the queen. Do as you think best with the children."

In less than a minute, the soldiers had thrown the three children overboard and men from both barges were shooting at the children. All three were shot in the head and slowly sunk beneath the water. Percy expected the queen to become hysterical at this horrific sight. She screamed once, loud and long, and then she closed her eyes and sat silently in the bottom of the boat. The fire went out of the soldiers at her reaction. Their hooting and shouting ceased and they were as silent as the grieving queen.

The stillness continued for about two miles down the river until arrows shot out from the shore. All regret vanished with the first arrow and Percy ordered James Davies to take half of the men inland in pursuit. Davies would not let up. He pushed his troops fourteen miles until they found a village where they burned the crops and the village including a spacious, beautiful temple where the bodies of chiefs were placed on an elevated platform with their treasures. They returned to the boat empty handed and continued on to Jamestown giving no thought to the foolish action of destroying food they would need over the winter much less the ill-will they had caused by their sacrilege.

When they reached Jamestown, Percy and Davies took the queen, dressed as all Indian women were in summer in only a leather apron and her jewelry, to Lord De La Warr. They marched up to his house, but found Strachy instead.

"Doctor Bohun advised my Lord De La Warr that his poor health was most likely caused by the bad air here, primarily the miasma rising from the back swamp. He all but insisted that Lord De La Warr return to live on his ship in hope the river breezes would improve his health. He has been there for some days now."

"Then we shall seek him there, Master Strachey," said Percy. "Captain Davies, have the queen secured somewhere, you and I will go out to the ship alone."

When they got to the ship, Percy inexplicably told Davies to make the report.

He began, "My Lord, we found the Paspahgahs. We entered in strict military order and fell on them. They were completely awed by our appearance and none of our men were hurt. We destroyed the entire village, killing sixteen warriors and various youngsters. And we brought their queen back with us as a hostage."

De La Warr sat for a moment, sucking the marrow from the bone of a roasted fowl, and then calmly remarked, "Well done. One less village to trouble us. But why did you bother bringing this heathen queen? ... Never mind, as long as she is here, let us make an example of her. Burn her."

Both Percy and Davies turned pale at the thought of burning anyone, but Percy was bold enough to speak, "My Lord, is not such barbarism beneath us? Let us dispatch her quietly."

De La Warr sucked another bone while he said, "Oh bother, do what you like but I do not want her alive in this fort."

As they rowed back, Percy and Davies discussed what to do. Percy was more shaken by the murder of the children than he wanted to admit. He could not bear to kill the mother as well, so he pulled rank and ordered Davies to take her to the woods and dispatch her either by gun or knife. Davies never said how it came to pass and Percy never mentioned it again.

The Governor's poor health was real. Due to his poor diet he quickly developed scurvy and gout. His reaction to the swamp air was actually malaria contracted from a mosquito bite. "Modern" medicine of the time said nature was made up of four elements, earth, wind, fire and water and that in a man they were represented respectively by blood, phlegm, black bile and yellow bile. The treatment for an imbalance in any of these four humors in the body was to bleed the patient. Naturally, this did nothing more than weaken the person further. In his ever-weakening condition, eventually he developed dysentery. At times he suffered from all these ailments at once.

Doctor Bohun also recommended that Sir Ferdinando Wainman, Master of ordinance, spend his time on the ship, but Wainman felt his position demanded he be near the Corp de Guard. This was the new name for the rebuilt storehouse, where the weapons were now kept. Wainman came down with a malaria-like illness and dysentery not unlike the Governor's problems, but his proved fatal. De La Warr made one of his infrequent trips to shore to attend the funeral of this proud knight, who was buried in the chancel of the church with full honors. His claymore and breastplate were buried with him as symbols of his status since no one in the colony had the talent to carve a proper effigy on the coffin.

Crowding contributed to poor health for other settlers too, so work on the houses outside the fort became the key activity. Each day was interrupted at ten and four when the sexton rang the bell. Everyone would stop what they were doing and make their way to the church for thirty minutes of prayers. Then they would return to their duties. To not do one's duty and work for at least six hours each day was one of the actions that could bring harsh punishment, so, even more than during Smith's "work to eat" program, everyone worked.

Strachey, as secretary of the colony, did no physical labor. He was at his journal and accounts daily and wrote all the official communications to the Virginia Company. Josiah could not read. He could write his name, which in some circles classified him as literate, but he could not read. Whenever his path took him near Strachey's space in the Governor's house, Josiah would lean in the window and greet William. The uneven friendship that had been born while burying cannons continued. One day Josiah plucked up his courage and asked William, "Will you teach me to read?"

William was both shocked and pleased; shocked that he had befriended a person who could not read and pleased that the lad would think him a fit teacher.

"Read, eh? Do you want to read Master Johnson's plays yourself?" he teased.

"Oh not so much as that, sir, though the idea is exciting. I have watched you writing and the words are ... well they are beautiful, like little pictures. And I know that if I am to succeed in this world, it is better if I can read and write."

Strachey found this an extraordinary idea and wondered where in the world a farmer's son had gotten the notion of succeeding in the world beyond being a good farmer. However, he was getting bored with nothing to occupy his time but work.

"I think we could have you learn your letters. Join me outside my lodging after supper. But do not be late or we will loose the light."

That night, and every night they were both in the fort, Strachey used a piece of slate and a bit of slate pencil to show Josiah the alphabet and simple words. Every free moment, Josiah would practice using a stick in the dirt to make the letters. After several weeks, the pencil was worn to a nub, but by that time, they had graduated to reading from a book. The slate had become Josiah's teaching tool. Strachey discovered Josiah had a natural talent for drawing, so now they traded lessons.

They started drawing simple objects like leaves and trees. Strachey tried to explain the cahow bird and they drew many birds before Josiah understood the special nature of that species. Strachey was particularly proud of his rendition of a soldier in full gear.

Powhatan's ban on contact between his people and the English was fairly successful, but some braves could not resist the lure of trade goods. Penalties for ignoring the ban were equally harsh from both leaders. A warrior named Amarice went into the fort to trade for a good knife. He found a willing colonist and came home with a steel blade. Powhatan ordered one of his champions to use the knife to kill Amarice as an example to the others of the consequences of disobeying his command. Another brave who came to bring fresh meat to trade ran afoul of De La Warr. The Governor accused him of spying and had his hand cut off. After these incidents, no Indians came near the fort for some time so the news that Powhatan's favored daughter Pocahontas had been married at the mid-summer feast to a prince of tribe on the Potomac, a man named Kocoum, was not known to her friend Josiah for months.

Just because the Indians did not enter the fort did not mean they left the colonists alone. If someone left the island, they were at great risk of being hurt or killed, but so long as they stayed on their side of the neck, they went unmolested. Houses outside the fort grew along two streets. Homes had stone or brick foundations and brick fireplaces and chimneys. Each home had a small garden to supply its kitchen, and flowers were planted in front of most houses.

The last day of August, the very tardy *Discovery* finally returned with a load of cod. Salted and stored, this would be excellent food for the many days of the fall and winter when Anglicans refrained from eating meat. As the weather cooled, some of the settlers who had spent more time with the

Indians taught those who had come with Gates or De La Warr to use the fish in a stew made of boiled corn with beans. It could be made in a large pot to serve many at a time. It needed to boil steadily, so to keep the fire hot enough, someone had to stand by and keep air moving to the flames with a grass fan. The Indians had used a fish called Pausarowmena, but only the older colonists knew the cod had altered the taste of the dish.

De La Warr continued his persecution of the natives. He sent Argall to attack Warraskoyacks , the old king whose son was taken to England to be converted and returned to his people in order to convince them of the superiority of the English. When Argall reached the village, the natives had vanished. His orders said to burn crops and houses. He knew this was destroying the food the settlers needed but Argall, ever the soldier, followed orders.

Argall had not been able to explain what had become of Admiral Somers, but shortly after he returned from the raid, a ship that had recently made port in Bermuda came to Jamestown. Argall brought the report to the Governor.

"Sir, there is a ship in port that has been to Bermuda and they have brought news of the fate of Admiral Somers. Apparently he did eventually come to collect hogs to bring back to the settlement, but he ate too much of the pork and died there on November 9th."

Exhibiting his typical level of concern for others, De La Warr said, "What a strange tale. Too bad about the hogs. We need to tell his nephew."

Argall first told Gates. He was crushed. " Dead. Our savior Admiral Somers who could not be felled by a hurricane succumbed to indigestion. Life never ceases to amaze me."

 Argall and Gates went together to tell Matthew Somers.

"I would like to go to Bermuda and bury my uncle properly. Do you think the Governor will agree?"

Gates took up the cause, " I feel I owe my life to your uncle's piloting skills on the *Sea Venture*. I will go myself and plead with Governor De La Warr to grant your request. I know your uncle left instructions that he wanted to be buried here in Virginia."

De La Warr agreed with conditions, "I am reluctant to send another ship after the last fiasco but we could use the hogs. If you will bring back the provisions as well as Admiral Somers' body, you may take the *Patience*. Captain Gates is due to go to England soon. Perhaps you could travel together as far as Bermuda."

Gates was surprised by this suggestion. "Ah, Sir, I had not planned to go by way of Bermuda and I am not yet ready to depart. I am sure Matthew would like to retrieve his uncle's body as soon as possible."

"Undoubtedly, undoubtedly. Then go ahead, young Somers. I wish you well."

Matthew had no trouble getting to Bermuda, but, ignoring his uncle's written wishes and his promise to De La Warr, Matthew buried Somer's heart and entrails in Bermuda and used the colony's ship Patience to take the rest of the remains to England. He wasted no time because he knew he needed to get to England ahead of Gates and put forth his version of the story before Gates told the Company that he was supposed to be returning to Jamestown.

Matthew need not have hurried so much. Gates did not leave Jamestown for almost three weeks. When he got to England and found that Matthew had gone there instead of Jamestown. Gates did go to the Company Council, but Matthew had spun a sad tale of knowing his family would be devastated if Admiral Somers were not interred in the family vault. The *Patience*, being built from new materials in Bermuda, was not even on their ship inventory, so they had no real issue with his using a ship that could be considered as belonging to his own uncle.

Doctor Laurence Bohun changed his mind about De La Warr's residence as the winter came on. He said a solid house would be better than the ship so a row house was constructed at the northern end of the west wall. Every design element that could be managed was included. The foundation was made of the largest stones available. Some had been brought as ballast in various ships, including one unusual stone that was placed in the very front. The stone was rubble from a medieval castle and De La Warr, who recognized it, thought it gave a sense of continuity to his Governorship. The row house was not built as all the other fort buildings had been. It was a traditional timber framed house, not unlike the one Ratcliff had wanted built in the forest.

As the year moved into deep winter, the house did keep out the cold winds and the fireplaces made it cozy. De La Warr outfitted it with all the fine trappings of his stateroom on his ship. If Powhatan had seen De La Warr's rooms, he would have seen a little piece of London.

All of Jamestown was becoming a very English place. Either in the fort or along the two burgeoning streets you could find most of the essential services for a Londoner. William Beckwith, a tailor, was working on a new doublet for Sir George Percy, made from the three and a quarter yards of deep red fustian he had ordered through his brother the Earl. The Germans in Augsburg gave this fabric a proper silky finish that made this cool, inexpensive cloth of linen and cotton look almost like velvet. As he got up from his cross-legged position on the table by the sunlit window, Beckwith dropped his favorite thimble and when he leaned over to pick it up, the string of copper buttons meant for Percy's doublet slid off the table and out the window. He knew he would be in a lot of trouble with Sir George for losing those buttons.

He looked all around his shop and decided he would walk outside in hopes he would see the buttons when he came back looking with fresh eyes. He walked next door to where women were standing by wooden tubs of hot water scrubbing clothes for men of all ranks while others were sitting inside, next to the only table in the house, using a flat pressing iron or a linen smoother to take out wrinkles and a goffering iron to make the curves in the neck ruffs. Bridget was there, borrowing the goffering iron to press her master's ruff. William said good day to all the ladies and paid special attention to Bridget, but she did not return the attention.

William walked over to the building where two men had recently set up a "still" to test minerals that were found in the colony. Faldoe and Callicut had been on the first supply and had worked with John Martin as he looked for gold and silver. Rumor had it that someone had found a silver mine on one of the river journeys and Argall had mentioned the Potomac Indians speaking of silver, but no good ore had yet been located. Still, hope ran high and every sample that was brought in by a hunting or exploring party was duly tested.

Another recent addition to the tradesmen's row was Robert Cotton. Each supply brought some tobacco, but keeping the brittle clay pipes from breaking was the real problem for smokers. Cotton had finally found a deposit of clay that was suitable for making pipes and he had a tidy personal business going with the settlers as well as beginning to make some pipes for export to England. He was proud of his work and marked each item with his symbol, multiple fleurs-de-lis in a diamond shape.

Three blacksmiths were fully employed in bustling James Towne. Their usual products were tools, hinges, horseshoes and an endless number of drawn nails. With all of the military action against the natives, there was a new business in adapting armor. The rods that were used in Europe to support the heavy muskets were impractical in the forests of Virginia, so James Read, who had avoided being hung in the first year, riveted a gun support on to the breastplate of the armor.

As the weather got even hotter, one of the soldiers suggested adapting body armor by cutting the metal into small bits and having a tailor sew them onto a cloth jacket called a coat of jacks. Sailors had worn this type of protection for some time and it would make the men more mobile in the forest as well as keeping them cooler. John Smith would have applauded the idea, but De La Warr was skeptical. William Beckham was working with Read on a prototype to show the Governor the advantages, so he stopped by to see if James had finished cutting the metal bits.

"How goes the work, James?"

"It goes."

"I will have time to work on the coat of jacks after today. How many metal pieces have you cut and punched?"

"I have been doing a few at the end of each day as the fire cools. Last I counted there were two hundred or more. How many do you need?"

"I am not sure, but two hundred should be plenty to start. Shall I take them now?"

"Better for me if you come back at the end of the day."

"Then that is what I will do." Not wanting to return to his shop, he picked up a new subject. "Have you heard how it worked out with Henry Philpot?"

"No one tells me anything directly anymore, but I still have my sources. The blow to the back of his head was bad, very bad. The doctor tried everything but finally admitted poor old Henry's brain was pressing on his skull … or was it the other way 'round … in any case, there was nothing for it but to cut a hole in the poor man's head."

"Good G…. You are not serious!" William was very careful not to curse, he had been punished once for what was now considered a crime and the second offense brought a much greater penalty.

"Indeed I am. They called the surgeon and he took a special tool and drilled a hole like this," holding up his thumb and forefinger in a circle, "and he lived through it. But it did not reduce the pressure enough, so he drilled a second hole."

"My word! So, he is recuperating?"

"No, he lived through the drilling, but either the loss of blood or the shock got him because he died within the hour."

"Poor man. Not bad enough to have your head caved in by an Indian stone axe, then your doctor makes another hole …two holes, that kill you."

"For myself, William, if I am ever sick or hurt, get me to a wise woman. I want nothing to do with physicians or surgeons or whatever they call themselves."

William laughed lightly, "I will, James, if you will do the same for me."

And they both laughed.

Read had only the first part of the sad story. The doctors were so interested in what had happened inside Henry's head that they kept it when they buried his body. Later, in secret, they cut off the top of his skull and when they had learned all they could, they dumped the remains of his head in the trash pit.

The medical men, particularly Doctor Bohun, were about to influence the lives of William and James and everyone else in Virginia. Lord De La Warr was seriously ill. The doctor said he simply must get away from Jamestown before another summer, so in March of 1611, the Governor, at age 33, packed up his belongings and decamped to go to the West Indies for a rest.

He put Sir George Percy, who had been Commander of the Fort, in charge until such time as a deputy Governor could be sent or until De La Warr returned. Sir George Yeardley, a friend of Captain Gates, had arrived the previous fall and he proved to be an excellent right-hand-man for the perpetually ill Percy.

Percy, in full dress, with Yeardley at his side, saw De La Warr off. They returned to the fort. On their way in, one of the officers, a lieutenant, was taking a small number of men outside the fort.

He saluted the Governor and Percy acknowledged him, "Lieutenant, what are you about?"

"Wood detail, sir."

"Carry on," and he turned to speak to Yeardley. Just as they got to the center of the fort, they heard yelps and screams.

A few Indians who were watching the fort shot at the party as they neared the tree line and killed every one. The Indians gave a triumphant shout and cried their tribal name, Paspahegh!, Paspahegh! When the colonists heard this, fifty or more took up the challenge and, after some scrambling around to get arms and get organized, they ran out of the fort in pursuit right past the confused Governor and his aide. The Indians fled, still screaming the name of the tribe they had avenged.

Within a few days, a new Captain, Robert Adams, landed with new men and provisions and the news that Sir Thomas Dale was coming and would have the role of Marshall and, as needed, Deputy Governor. Percy was crushed. Adams stayed only a short time, being ordered by Dale to return to England as soon as possible. He left soon, carrying reports and letters to update the Virginia Company on the status of the colony.

Strachey suspected that Dale might keep him on as secretary, but William wanted to go home. Easter was early that year. The ship was ready to leave in late March, but that was Holy Week and everyone was expected to keep Holy Week and Easter. Saturday before Easter was the one open night of that week and Strachey and Josiah got together for the last time.

"I will miss our time together, Sir. I hope you have a pleasant voyage."

"I will miss it too, Josiah. I have enjoyed your art lessons." He pulled out the slate they had used. "I want you to have the slate to continue your writing lessons."

Taking the slate reverently in his hands, Josiah said, "You, and this bit of slate have changed my life. I will be always grateful."

With the difference in their ranks, they could do no more. Josiah stood, nodded toward Strachey, and took his leave. The next morning, Strachey boarded the ship. Josiah and Bridget stood by the gate and waved goodbye.

"I see you bid farewell to Master Strachey." John Rolfe had walked up behind Josiah.

"I do," said Josiah, "I will miss his company."

"Rumor has it, he was teaching you to read. I have a few books. You may come and practice when you have time."

Surprised and most pleased, Josiah bowed slightly and said, "I would be grateful, Sir. I am Josiah Tucker and this is my friend Bridget Malone, who works for the Croft family."

"I know John Croft and his wife. I believe I have seen you, Mistress Malone, when my wife and I have visited. My name is John Rolfe. I am staying in a small house along the east wall. Stop by any evening. Good day to you both." Rolfe smiled and went back into the fort.

"Josiah," Bridget asked, "how is it that yet another gentleman takes an interest in you and your reading?"

"I have no idea, but I have plans, Bridget, big plans and the support of gentlemen and being able to read may both be of help. This land has great possibilities. Until Lord De La Warr came, my men and I were making our own way. We could have gone off the island and found a bit of land. There are Indians not far from here who would have let us farm. Someday, I will have my own land and be my own master. I saw my way before. I am not sure what to do now that Sir Thomas and his rules are in place. Maybe we should not have come back to the fort."

He emerged from his reverie and looked straight into her eyes, "But then I would not have found you."

CHAPTER 13
Henrico

Sir Thomas Dale arrived. He was a narrow man of normal height but slender in body, slim in the limbs, sharp in the nose, tight of lips, and narrow in mind. He immediately found fault with everyone and everything.

At every opportunity, Dale shouted at anyone except his officers. At them, he yelled outright. He inspected the palisades, "Who engineered these walls?! These logs are uneven. The crew who cut and mounted them were lazy and uncaring. Had I been in charge, they would be of regular size and height. Put that on the repair list." George Yeardley dutifully added "even palisades" to the growing list.

The thirty some men who still survived from among the hundred who had cut those 800 pound trees, drug them from the forest and erected this palisade in record time were insulted and hurt on their own behalf and in the name of all their dead comrades. Dale's credibility was gone before the first week was over.

He condemned the housing and the public buildings, not considering that the Governor for life had approved of them only a few weeks before. He berated each and every tradesman for tawdry work and lack of ambition. His style was entirely military and, though some appreciated the order and discipline he demanded, none of the settlers had bargained for living in a military garrison.

The penalties for misbehavior in Dale's Code were even more extreme than those De La Warr had imposed. For swearing the first time, a whipping; the second time, a bodkin through the tongue; the third time, execution. For missing church services three times without good reason, a man would be given to a ship's captain for six months to serve as a galley slave. For picking flowers or grapes without permission, the person's ears would be cut off.

Perhaps the three hundred settlers who came with Dale had become accustomed to his type of discipline, but the five hundred who had been at Jamestown, especially those who had been there before De La Warr, chafed under these laws. The settlers who had survived the first deaths in 1607 and the Starving Time of 1609 and 1610 felt they had earned the right to direct their own lives. Individual initiative had let these people endure while their fellows did not. To have that initiative cut off was taken as a personal reprimand.

Very few of the items on the "repair list" were attempted. Dale did have a second well dug and also had "bridge" post sunk to support a jetty.

Dale brought the first professional troop of soldiers. He took these soldiers and other men on a raid of the Nansemonds. Francis West and John Martin were among the hundred men in the party. This was the first time the Indians had been challenged by a troop completely in armor. The outcome was a forgone conclusion.

Powhatan sent word to the fort that he would not tolerate any more incursions into his territory. He threatened to "cripple with drink" any men who ventured there. Dale took it as a joke and continued to raid. While making camp on their next excursion upriver to the falls, the men heard a strange noise

"Did you hear that, Sergeant? It sounded like someone was saying 'hup, hup' ."

Before the sergeant could answer there was a different noise, "Oho, oho." That cry was repeated as an Indian seemed to appear from nowhere and leap over the fire. He continued crying and running into the nearby cornfield.

The sergeant called out, "To arms, men!" The men reacted and grabbed their weapons, but every man grabbed the wrong end of the gun and in the confusion that ensued, knocked out several of their comrades.

The ruckus continued for fifteen minutes and then the entire troop seemed to wake having no understanding and little memory of the event. Those who heard of this odd occurrence attributed it to the men being drugged, perhaps by the Indians putting a locally known hallucinogen in their water. It seemed Powhatan had made good on his threat.

Dale not only replaced the squad with professional soldiers, he also brought more provisions, and so hunting was not as necessary as it had been. Josiah and the squad lost all their special status. They did not want to go back to what they had been before they became Smith's squad. Josiah decided to talk to the Governor about staying together as a fighting unit.

He approached the Governor's residence but was stopped by two guards who stood on either side of the door. They asked his business and when he said it was about fighting they said he must first see the Sergeant Major, Captain George Webb. He went to the Corp de Guard where Webb was known to spend most of his time. Even to see Webb he had to go through another two guards.

"Sir, I have come to ask for a proper assignment for me and my lads. We have served the fort as soldiers and hunters. Captain Smith himself trained us to operate well in these forests and around the Indian tribes. I believe we could be of help."

Webb listened patiently. Then he gave a sideways smile and said, "Trust me son, I will speak to the Governor about you. You may go."

Apparently, Webb did speak to the Governor for orders came to Josiah the next day that he and his men would be kept together in charge of tending the livestock. This included a small herd of cows, two bulls, a dozen horses, and thirty sheep. They were pleased to be together and to be out of the fort but they had worked hard to hone their skills of hunting, tracking and fighting. Looking after animals was beneath them.

The animals were fenced on the mainland, just over the neck. The sheep had to be kept apart from the others since they would eat the grass too short for the cattle. With two separate herds, it took all of them to watch the animals save one, so each had one day off each nine days. That was the only day they could return to the fort so Josiah could see Bridget only once every nine days. Sometimes she would be so busy with her work that they could not meet. Then it would be over a fortnight between visits.

Since the founding of Roanoke, the English settlements had expected to be attacked by the Spanish. There had been several false alarms in the colony, but one day, shortly after Dale arrived, the alarm was real.

A caravel, a ship with triangular sails and a high poop deck and definitely not English, appeared off Point Comfort. Captain James Davis in Fort

Algernon set up his men as an ambush and waited to see who was coming ashore. A Spaniard in full court dress and two attendants came in a longboat. As soon as they landed, the armed men surrounded them. The well-dressed man spoke some English and identified himself as Don Diego de Molina, the commander of a fort in the West Indies. His companions were Ensign Antonio Pereos and the ship's pilot who went by the name A Spanyard. Molina explained that they were off course and asked that Davis supply an English pilot to take them to safe waters. Molina offered to stay along with his pilot until the English pilot was returned.

Davis found this arrangement reasonable courtesy of the seas. He sent his pilot out in the longboat. As soon as the pilot was on the ship, the Spanish pulled up anchor and headed out to sea under full sail. Davis challenged Molina.

"Sir, what is the meaning of this!"

"Señor, I am very sorry. I had no idea my compatriots would abandon me. Have no fear. I am certain your man will be well treated."

"I do not want him well-treated, I want him here!"

"I do not know what I can do, Señor. If there was something I could do, I would."

Davis was furious and he knew he would be in huge trouble with Dale. He interrogated the three further and discovered that A Spanyard was not Spanish at all. He was Francisco Lembri, an Englishman who had defected to the Spanish. Percy was in Fort Algernon and he and Davis decided Percy would accompany the prisoners on a ship to Jamestown to report to Dale.

At the same time, Gate's fleet was arriving.

When Percy and the Spaniards arrived at Jamestown, Dale assumed the kidnapping of the pilot was a prelude to an invasion. There was a fleet coming up the James River. Gates was returning from England. But Dale did not know this, so he continued to prepare to fight the Spanish.

He ordered the trumpets and drums sounded to alert the soldiers to get into their armor, grab their weapons, and assemble at their stations. He called an emergency council meeting and asked for opinions on a plan of defense.

Yeardley spoke up first. "We should man the cannon and line the walls with muskets to show our strength." There were murmurs of agreement but no strong support. Someone, who tried to remain anonymous said, "Man the ships."

Percy, politically naïve as ever, supported the on ship approach, "If we put the men on the ships, they would be committed, I mean, they would not be able to turn tail and run."

In spite of the implied insult, Dale agreed with the logic and loaded the soldiers and provisions onto the *Star*, the *Prosperous* and the ever-present *Discovery*. Dale gave a stirring but pessimistic speech.

Shouting from the poop deck of the largest ship, he stuck a dramatic pose, "Men, our hour is upon us. We have feared an attack from the Spanish for lo these many years. It has come. Only you stand between this English homeland and disgrace. We are few and we may not prevail, but do your best, men, for England and King James!"

They had pulled anchor and made their way into he center of the river when the fleet got close enough to be recognized as English. The few who were watching Dale's face saw him turn scarlet with anger and embarrassment. He quickly pulled himself together and, as if it were the most natural thing in the world, shouted from his perch, "Men, it is our countrymen. Let us greet them in military order."

Dale used the assembled soldiers as an honor guard to greet the fleet. He was surprised to see his old friend Gates on the flagship. Gates had come as the Lieutenant Governor.

When the two men were together on shore, Gates was cheerful and magnanimous. "Governor Dale, you have done a remarkable job here. The Company sends its thanks for your good service and I personally thank you. The Company is pleased you will now be able to attend fully to your position as Marshall."

To keep face, Dale threw himself wholeheartedly into the role of Marshall. In his supply, Gates had brought a great deal of old armor from the Tower of London. The renewed possibility of a Spanish attack prompted Dale to outfit every man and to order them to keep the metal bright and in good repair so they could be called to wear it at a moment's notice. No one except the soldiers ever wore the armor. Keeping it clean became a bad joke. It also wasted half an hour a day at a useless job. Dale was a strong believer in idle hands being the devil's workshop and he found more and more time consuming tasks for the colonists.

With many more people in the fort, another sound well was needed. There had been bricklayers in the settlement since 1607 but Gates had brought bricklayers who knew how to build a well. They started by making sun baked bricks. They had just finished laying out the last of the newly molded bricks when the brick mason heard a great commotion.

"Here now! What's all that ruckus?" he asked his young helpers.

Boys, being alert to any mischief in the area, George, a witty ten-year old said, " It is the Gov'ners mastiffs, sir, they are fightin' right over there. As he pointed toward the Statehouse, the two dogs broke apart and began a chase. Their path took them directly into the drying yard and across the wet clay leaving paw prints on several of the bricks.

"Now that's gone and done it! Look at those prints! Go quickly, boys, and turn those over before any one sees. I don't want to be making a new brick on account of some dog." So the paw prints stayed in the bricks for the well.

As the laborers dug the well, they reinforced the sides with boards. When they reached the water table, they placed a ring of cypress wood, very slow to rot in the damp, and then started to build up brick walls in front of the boards. Above the ground they built a collar of bricks six deep and about waist high. Gates wanted the latest for his fort, so he had brought pumps to install in the wells. They never worked very well.

Dale commanded that new privies be dug over a quarter mile from the fort. For the health of the populace, this was a good idea. For their convenience, it was not. The older colonists would never have thought to go that far for fear of being killed by Indians, but the island was safe now and so, because the penalty for answering nature's call any closer was severe, people planned in time to take the long walk.

The Indians left the island alone but anyone who wandered outside of that protected place was at great risk. Any merciful thoughts the Indians might have had toward the colonists were erased with each raid Percy, De La Warr or Dale had launched against them.

There was a brave named Nemattamon. He wanted his people to fight boldly against the invaders and to encourage them he declared that he was invincible. He covered himself in feathers with swan wings on his shoulders and promised if the warriors would follow him into battle, they would be victorious. Time after time, the man the soldiers came to call the Jack of Feathers survived. The warrior became a legend and legends are hard to defeat.

The terrible drought of the last years, one that would later be recognized as the worst in a century, came to an end. The fields of the colonists thrived as did those of the Indians. The older colonists had learned how to plant corn in the Indian fashion and they taught the newcomers. They planted corn in rows, poking a hole, then putting several seeds in each. While the Indians had only a deer antler tied with sinew to a wooden pole as a hoe, the settlers had much more efficient metal hoe blades.

The one thing the settlers did not have on the island was a ready source of fresh water to irrigate the plants when needed. So in spite of the danger, fields were planted on the mainland where water was available close by. Many a farmer returned to James Towne midday with cloth or flesh torn by an arrow. But the colonists were multiplying much faster than the Indians, so the expansion of the area occupied by the English proceeded in spite of a few arrows.

On March 12, 1612 the Virginia Company had received its third charter from King James. This charter extended the control of Virginia from the newly claimed Bermuda to the South Sea (Pacific Ocean), effectively all across the continent. The news made its way to Jamestown later in the year vindicating the position of all those survivors who wanted to stay in Bermuda. That small paradise raised a great deal of interest in England causing supplies that might have come to Jamestown to be sent there to help develop the islands.

This new charter also reorganized the role of the company stockholders, giving the common stockholder some voting rights. There was a groundswell in England about the common man exercising his right to vote. This reorganization was one example. The rise of the Parliamentary Party was another. The rights of common men had been growing in England since Magna Carta four hundred years earlier, but this voting business was new.

Gates had brought two hundred eighty men and twenty women. The twenty women were particularly welcome. The feeling of home increased with having more women in the population and with having the livestock count increased significantly. Two hundred new head of cattle and a herd of two hundred hogs was too much for the nine men of the squad who had been tending all the animals. Gates doubled that number and the unique identity of the squad was all but lost.

Again improvements were made to the colony's defenses and the growing town. In the town, Gates constructed a true Governor's House. To serve the increasing number of ships using James Port, he built a new wharf. They finished sinking the support poles mostly at low tide, but it was still hard work. Once the poles were stuck, they built a support structure and laid planks to make an excellent dock.

Gates' wife and daughters had accompanied him on this trip. Sadly, his wife had died during the voyage. He never spoke of it, so no one knew the details. He knew he must send his daughters back on the next ship, but, in the meantime, he planted the small fruit orchard his wife had wanted and coached the girls in how to tend the young trees. Hannah Croft watched the girls and thought they really needed the influence of a woman, so she approached the Governor one day and offered to oversee the girls as long as they were in the colony. He gratefully accepted her offer.

John Rolfe was walking back from his tobacco field when he saw his wife's very proper friend, Hannah Croft, digging manure around fruit trees with the Gates girls. He opened the door of his house and, wanting to share the news about Hannah, called out to his wife.

"Sweetheart. Sweetheart! You will never guess what I saw!"

He heard no response. He walked through to the back of the house and there, in the small garden patch, he saw her face down on the ground. He called for help and several neighbors rushed over. Hannah Croft, dirt still on her hands, was one of the neighbors who answered the panicked scream. She made Mistress Rolfe comfortable and put cool towels on her forehead while another neighbor ran for the physician.

The doctor did not touch the patient, merely asked what had happened. Then he pronounced his opinion, "I believe it is her heart, Mr. Rolfe. She is responding and she may be fine, but once she has had an episode like this, she can have more."

"What can I do? I know nothing of how to care for her?"

"I would suggest you find someone to stay with her, especially when you are not at home. Is there someone?"

Hannah had waited to hear the doctor's verdict.

She spoke up, "I have a servant, Bridget. I can spare her to help, John. Let me go and fetch her so the doctor can tell her what needs to be done."

"Thank you, Hannah. Thank you."

She was better the next day. Bridget made a special broth of beef and vegetables that she fed to Mistress Rolfe every few hours. John made a pallet on the floor so he would not disturb her sleep. He thought she was getting back to normal. On the third morning, he woke and checked on her. She was not breathing. He called her name and shook her by the shoulders, but there was no response. He knelt on the floor, put his head on her stomach and cried.

When Bridget came to prepare breakfast, she found John sobbing. She helped him to his feet and sent him for the minister. The minister had no role to play until it came time for the funeral but it gave Rolfe something to do and the minister might give him some comfort. Bridget prepared the body for the wake.

After the burial, John asked Bridget to take all of his wife's things and distribute them to whoever needed them. While she was away from the Croft's house, Rolfe called on John Croft. "John, your Bridget has been very kind. She was such a comfort to my wife and me. I know it would not be seemly for one to reward your servant, but, please, keep these few coins for her, maybe as a dowry against the day she may marry."

The Crofts had come to care very much for their maid, in spite of her lack of references. Croft accepted the gift graciously, "You are a good man, John Rolfe, to be thinking of Bridget at a time like this. Certainly, I will keep this safe for her." And with that small gesture, Bridget took a large step toward her independence.

By the end of the summer, Gates decided it was time to expand the number of settlements. Part of the orders from the Virginia Company since his first time as Governor had been to make new settlements and spread out the colony. He now had enough people to do this effectively. He sent Dale and three hundred people to clear out the Powhatans who had reclaimed Parahunt's village that Smith had recommended years before. Dale and his staff went the eighty miles by boat. The rest went overland. Indians harassed the people on land, but no one was killed. At least one of the attacks was led by the Jack of Feathers who survived again.

Dale named this settlement, for his friend, Henry, the Prince of Wales. Henrico became Dale's pet project. In ten days they had a palisade around seven acres with strong watchtowers at the corners. There were five of these watchtowers that served as dwellings for the time being. Soon Gates sent a wider range of settlers to Henrico.

He sent Dale's favorite minister, the Reverend Alexander Whitaker. Some colonists volunteered to relocate while others were assigned to go to Henrico or Fort Algernon. The Crofts volunteered to move to Henrico. On one of his ninth-day visits to the fort, Bridget gave Josiah the news.

"We will be leaving within the week. Master John thinks there will be more opportunities there and less crowded living conditions. He wants to build a house for his family alone. He says I will have an entire room of my own."

"But Henrico is eighty miles away. I will never get to see you."

"I know, my dear friend. Perhaps some day…"

The next day, they found that Bridget had been prophetic. Josiah was ordered to take a quarter of the livestock and half his men and move to Henrico. Josiah called the squad together at the fence between the sheep and the cows.

"Since Captain Smith brought us together, we have not been separated for more than a day. Now we must split in two and not see each the others for months or years. I am not Dale, I will not order who is to go where; we will decide this together."

Dixon spoke first, "If someone must go away, let it be me."

'I thank you, James, but if it all the same to you, I would like to go to Henrico. Bridget is moving there."

The squad let out a long "woo, woo" and Josiah blushed.

Young Jamie Brumfield, Dods, Fenton and Herd all chose to go with Josiah. The two Cassens wanted to stay near the fort, so they would stay with Dixon. That left young Nate Peacock. He bravely said he would stay with Dixon, but he was not fooling anyone. He nearly had tears in his eyes. He had been like a brother with Jamie and Josiah had been nearly a father to him. Josiah looked at Dods, Fenton and Herd in turn. They were all willing to trade but Dods thought of a face-saving reason for Nate.

"If William Cassen is staying, then I will too. I would miss his music too much. Here, Nate, will you do me a favor and go with Josiah?"

Nate could not suppress his immediate smile, but quickly brought it under control and walked calmly to embrace Dods. "Thank you," he whispered in his ear.

The split settled, the herds were divided and the departing young men headed their charges toward the river.

The livestock and palisade sections went on the barges, the people on two ships. They left with the tide and had fair winds, so the ships reached their destination that day. The barges had to tie up and complete their journey the following day.

The soldiers who came and all of the healthy men had brought full armor. The shiny armor did have a terrifying effect on the Indians. The first time Dale's soldiers attacked in full armor and the Indians saw their arrows bounce off the men's chests, they ran. From then on they asked the god Okee to send rain to put out the burning wicks of the guns and to make the ground muddy so the metal men could not move.

The Indians had learned that they rarely killed a man wearing the metal suit, but when men were building a fort, they could not wear the metal suits. The Indians waited all day until the men were as tired as they would be. Then they attacked. Only a few died in each attack, but soon the numbers of wounded and dead counted up and Dale had to send more men to replace those who had been hurt or killed.

Though the fall and winter Henrico slowly grew as did the connection between Bridget and Josiah. The main fort was again built but this time on higher ground. It was built on the same concept as James Fort. Josiah had a small hut near the animals and the Crofts allowed him to stay in their outbuilding when he stayed in the fort.

Reverend Whitaker went to Henrico with some of the replacements. The town was laid out in three streets and, by spring, they had built a wooden church and good house for the Reverend. The foundation for a very large brick church was in place as well as a sound storehouse. Eventually, the Reverend was assigned one hundred acres to serve the parsonage. He named this estate Rock Hill.

Even though Henrico was booming, some settlers found running to the Indians more interesting. As the soldiers continued attacks or simply patrolled the area, they found some of these defectors and brought them to Jamestown. Gates had learned his lesson during the Bermuda months and he was now a more decisive leader. These defectors were considered traitors and were sentenced to die in various horrible ways. Hanging or a firing squad were the kind ways for a traitor to die. Dale, as Marshall, also used methods associated with the Inquisition, burning, being broken on the wheel, or staked out.

At Jamestown, the fort and town were in good condition. Captain Christopher Newport had come again with one of the regular supplies and Gates determined it was time for his daughters to return to England. In December, Gates and the girls said a tearful farewell and he placed them in Newport's care.

Dale continued his attacks on villages. In September, he came to the area of Henrico and attacked the Appamattuck. This was the tribe responsible for massacring one of De La Warr's parties after feasting with them. He wiped out the village and left soldiers there.

When he returned to Jamestown he outfitted a groups of colonists and sent them to yet other new settlements in Bermuda Hundred and Rochedale.

Supply fleets continued to arrive at Jamestown and depart in time. By spring of 1612, there were a total of eight hundred English in Virginia. They brought the usual provisions and they brought news. King James himself had commissioned a standard English version of the Bible to be written and printed in many copies. Some of these Bibles came on these ships either as goods to be sold or as presents to individual colonists from a family member or friend in England. Reverend Whitacker received a Bible from his bishop in England.

Another publication came on one of the ships as a gift from William Strachey to Josiah Tucker. It was a copy of a new play by William Shakespeare entitled "The Tempest." It told the story of a hurricane and shipwreck in Bermuda. Along with it came a brief note that said:

>Friend Tucker,
>It seems one of my letters to a great lady came into the hands of Master Shakespeare. The tales I told her of our misadventures in Bermuda found their way into his new play. I have seen it and the settings for the storm were magnificent. Enjoy practicing your reading.
>Your friend, Strachey

P.S. I am missing the signet ring I took to Virginia. Should you find it, please return it to me by any homebound ship's Captain.

P.P.S. If you do send the ring, enclose a few of Cotton's pipes. I brag on them to my friends.

It took another three months for the letter to reach Josiah in Henrico. When it came, Dale's messenger was told that Tucker was up in "the fields" and that the letter could be left with the Crofts, so Bridget knew of it even before Josiah. He came to the fort the next evening and they met as usual in an arbor in the side yard. Bridget came dashing from the house.

"Josiah, you have a letter!"

"A letter? Who would write to me?"

"I do not know. I cannot read the fancy writing and the seal is a shield of some kind. I have never known someone who received a letter."

"Where is it?"

"Oh my, I am just a fool, it is in the parlor on the mantle. The safest place I could think of. Come."

He grabbed her by the wrist as she darted away, "Bridget, I have never gone into the Croft's parlor." He looked scared.

She first thought him foolish and then realized he might be right. The Crofts might consider that overstepping his bounds.

"Alright, I will go and get it for you. Wait here."

He paced like a man waiting for a verdict until he saw her coming out the door. Then he walked quickly to meet her. He could not bear to tear it open. He carefully pried open the seal and haltingly read the script. He had to sound out the long words but, on the second reading, he did quite well.

That William Strachey, former secretary of the colony, would write to him was amazing enough, but that he now owned a book of his own was more than he could dream. This was the first proof he had seen that his plan to read and to associate with gentlemen would help him move to a higher place in society. He was proud of himself and Bridget was even prouder of him.

The English had kept a presence at Fort Algernon all along and now they also settled at Kecoughtan. Some of the new settlers relocated there too. The James River now had five settlements.

Percy, one of the last founding settlers at Jamestown, decided it was time to leave. He saw no hope of returning to the leadership position of the colony and the climate continued to impair his health. On April 22, he boarded a ship quietly and went home.

In five years, the original concept of a council of wealthy young gentlemen taking over land from the natives who would be happy to submit to them had changed to a single governmental unit run by one man in a closely disciplined culture. The day of the gentleman adventurer was over.

The new gentlemen were now farmers. John Rolfe had harvested his first crossbred tobacco crop in 1612. It grew much higher than the more bitter Indian tobacco so it was called "tall tobacco." Josiah heard of it when some was brought to Henrico. The smokers in Virginia now had locally grown tobacco to smoke in their locally made pipes. A few of the pipes had been exported to England. Rolfe wondered if he could grow enough tall tobacco to export that as well.

It would be a long wait between the crop of 1612 and the one of 1613. Rolfe had only his standard allotment of three acres of land on Jamestown Island. He invited his friend Thomas Dale to dinner to ask a favor.

"Thomas, I have had good success with my new tobacco this year. I would like to plant more for next year to see if there can be enough to export as a product to England. My problem is, I have no more land to plant. Do you have any ideas on how I could get more land?"

"I tasted your new crop, John. It is good, much better than we have gotten from the natives. I think you might be able to get extra land near Henrico."

"Excellent, Thom. I would like to go away from Jamestown for a while. Who would need to give permission?"

"Governor Gates would need to agree, but I think if we went to him together, there would be no problem."

"How soon could we go to the Governor? The timing of planting is crucial."

"If you are set on this idea, I could arrange something for tomorrow or the next day. But how will you tend both fields? We could establish a regular run between here and Henrico," he joked.

"That is a problem, Thom, but if I can get the land, I trust a solution will present itself."

Two days later, Rolfe had permission to plant tobacco on as much land near Henrico as he found useful. He arranged to go with the next supply barge to Henrico. When he arrived at Henrico, one of the first people he ran into was Josiah.

"Josiah, how goes the reading?"

"Mr. Rolfe, it is good to see you. I have been practicing. Master Strachey sent me a book! It is a play by Master Shakespeare. Would you like to read it?"

"I would. I will be here for a time, so perhaps I could borrow it while I am here."

"You are staying for a while? May I ask what brings you here?"

"Planting, my young friend, planting tobacco. I have been given permission to plant as much land as I can use in the area. I need reasonably flat land with good drainage. There can be a gentle slope since we build up rows for the planting. Full sun is important. Would you know of land to match that description?"

"There is a lot of land but it is not all in one place. If we could use two horses, I could show you many spots in a day."

"I think I can arrange that. Do you have a free day soon?"

"I can trade some free time with another of the herders. It may take a day or two. Would Friday be good for you?"

"Friday or Saturday. What ever you can work out. You have seen the field at Jamestown. I would rather someone who has at least seen a tobacco field would help me look for the right land."

They shook hands, as would equals, and Josiah returned to his work.

Rolfe and Josiah surveyed the available land and Rolfe planted in several fields. When he was done, he went back to see Josiah.

"Thank you for your help. Now I have an offer for you."

"An offer, sir. What can I do for you?"

"I need to go back to Jamestown and plant the field there. It will be about two weeks before the plants here break ground and I hope to be back by then, but in case I am delayed, I need for someone to know what to do for the young plants. Would you be able to watch after them if I cannot get back?"

"I know nothing about tobacco, sir, but if you will tell me what is to be done, I will do my best for you."

"I knew I could count on you, Josiah. And this is not a favor. It is only fair that you share in the profits from your work."

"Mr. Rolfe! That would be wonderful. I have been trying to find a way to ask Bridget Malone to marry me. I dare not ask until I can provide for her. To have a bit of hard money would make all the difference."

"She is a fine woman, Josiah. You would be lucky to get her. She was very helpful while my dearly departed wife was ill. I am glad our partnership might give her a good life. But I must warn you, that I cannot promise any hard money for some time. The crop will have to mature, be dried, shipped to England and sold and then the money will have to come back. That could be a year or more, but if we have good luck, I may be able to forward you a nest egg."

"Even a year is much sooner than I had hoped for. But did you say your wife has died? I am sorry to hear it."

"Yes, I try not to talk of it."

To quickly change the subject, Josiah asked, "Please, tell me, what will our plants need?"

Rolfe explained the whole process of growing, cutting and drying tobacco to Josiah. John stayed a few more days until a vessel was going to Jamestown. He planted his field there and would have returned to Henrico, but there was no boat going upriver at that time, so he decided to wait until the Jamestown field broke ground and to do the first weeding before he left.

By the time Rolfe got back to Henrico, Josiah had done the first weeding and had experimented with bringing irrigation ditches to some of the rows near a creek. John was intrigued by this innovation.

"How did you think of that, Josiah?"

"My Father and I had talked of it back on the farm in England. We did not have a creek near enough to our wheat field to try it."

"Let us see if it makes a difference."

Rolfe had planted all of the land he had seed for and he and Josiah tended the crops carefully. The growing season was favorable and, in summer of 1613, he harvested a bumper crop. A small sample of freshly cut tobacco was sent back to England in June. It would be months before it was dried and cured so it could be smoked. When Rolfe's tobacco made it into the clubs of London, there was an instant demand for all that could be produced.

News of the demand for this first successful American crop would not reach Jamestown for months. The immediate problem was still to get enough food for 800 people. The Potomac Indians were still willing to trade for food so Captain Argall took another expedition north.

CHAPTER 14
Rebecca

Some tribes had submitted to the English. Others were not precisely under the control of the English, but they were willing to accept the presence of the coat-wearers and bring them into the trading confederation. That confederation carried goods from the Great Lakes to Florida. The English had already seen European goods in Indians camps that must have come from France or even Russia and many things from the Spanish colony around St. Augustine. Captain Argall began trading with the Indians called the Potomac. He had met a man named Japizaws who was the brother of a Potomac chief. He was a particularly greedy and ambitious man. Argall sometimes found him useful.

On one of his visits with Japizaws, they had ventured far into the interior of Virginia and hunted a remarkable creature. It was larger than a cow with heavy front haunches and a huge head. The Indians prized this creature. Its coat was as warm as a bear. The hide was tougher than any other creature. The meat was excellent with a great deal of fat that could be used to cook with and to add richness to other food. Even the hooves could be boiled to produce glue.

On this trip, Argall needed Japizaws to confirm a rumor. Argall had heard that Pocahontas was living in the neighborhood. It had been four years since she had visited Jamestown. Then she had come to see John Smith. When Smith had left for England, word had been put around to the Indians that he had died. Still, at times when the English would encounter a Powhatan Indian in friendly enough circumstances to talk, they asked about John Smith. Only a few left knew what had really happened, so the story was repeated, that he was dead.

In this April of 1613, Pocahontas was now seventeen. The rumor about her also said she had married and she lived with her husband in the area. Another version of the story said she had come as an emissary of her father to trade with the Potomac who were only loosely under his rule. Argall did not care why she was near, only if it was true. He found Japizaws who checked with his brother the chief and confirmed that Pocahontas was a few miles away. Argall asked him to bring Pocahontas to his ship if he could. Japizaws and his equally greedy wife found the princess and told her about there being an English ship on the river. Japizaws's wife said she very much wanted to see the ship but that her husband would not allow her to go without a companion. After a great deal of pleading, Pocahontas agreed to go. She knew neither Powhatan or Kocoum would like it, but the woman would not be quiet.

All three toured the ship *Treasurer* and, as it was near dinner, Argall invited them to stay. After dinner, Pocahontas was shown to a place to rest before starting the journey back. As planned, Japizaws and his wife did not rest and, having been given the copper pot Argall promised as a gift, they slipped off the ship. When Pocahontas went in search of her friends, she was prevented from leaving. With the help of James Swift and Rob Sparkes as translators, Argall explained to Pocahontas that she was a hostage and that Japizaws had sent a messenger to her father to offer her in exchange for all English prisoners. She remained silent, the proper response of a captive in her culture. It took a day and a half for the messenger to return. Powhatan had said he would give Argall what he asked if her would "use his daughter well' and sail into "his river." Not wanting to miss this chance to gain Dale's gratitude, Argall ignored the offer, pulled up anchor and went toward Jamestown. He stopped many times to acquire food and explore, finally arriving at Jamestown on June 4.

Gates received the princess.

"Madam, I am told you are Pocahontas, favored daughter of the great chief Powhatan."

He expected a response. Pocahontas gave none partly because the man had stated a fact, not asked a question, and partly because she considered herself a prisoner and therefore was not obliged to speak.

After a short wait, Gates realized he had not actually asked a question, so he remedied that, "Is this so?"

Again the prisoner did not speak.

In matters of state, Gates was slow to anger. Thinking he may have breached protocol, he tried another approach.

"Argall, please present me to her Highness."

314

Argall used a standard form, "Princess Pocahontas, may I take the liberty to present His Honor, the Deputy Governor of the Colony of Virginia, Sir Thomas Gates."

Gates picked up the formula with a graceful leg forward and a measured swing of his right arm, "Your Highness, you are most welcome to Jamestown."

Pocahontas recognized this formal greeting from the days with John Smith. She knew she was no longer being treated as a prisoner, so she answered the form, "My Lord Gates, I thank you for your welcome. Why am I here?" Argall, having gone through the trouble of using a translator to communicate with Pocahontas, understood and was angered by the insult she had given him by not speaking English.

Gates was shocked by both her knowledge of English and English proprieties. He had expected a savage with pidgin English at best. This put a new light on the situation. When Argall sent word upon landing that he had brought the chief's daughter as a hostage, Gates had meant to treat her well, but now he felt duty bound to treat her as he would a royal European hostage. That meant she should be housed with a person of her rank, given the best that household had to offer, and allowed her freedom of the fort once she had given her personal bond. There could be no type of jail for this lady.

"Madam, Captain Argall has brought you to me to assist us in persuading your father to end hostilities. We also hope he will return those of our settlers who he holds as captives as well as the weapons he has … (he thought better of saying her father was a thief) … some of his wayward people have taken from us. Would you be willing to help us?"

She stood silent and proud for a few moments composing her reply.

"My Lord, peace is a good thing for all. Some of your people and weapons may be prizes of battle. These now belong to the Powhatan by our custom. Send word to my father that I am well and that you wish to talk with him when he comes to take me home. I will support you in seeking peace."

It was a speech worthy of a queen, or at least an astute politician.

Gates was baffled now. He thought of her as a hostage. She clearly did not. He needed to have her somewhere safe. Wanting to pursue one of the original aims of the Virginia Company, to Christianize the Indians, he preferred to have her in the care of someone who could see to her religious training. The Reverend Buck was not terribly interested in converting Indians, in spite of company propaganda, so he had to go farther a field to think of a suitable situation. He struck upon the Reverend Whitaker. He was at Henrico and that fort was better defended than Jamestown, at this point, having five forts surrounding it. The traffic in and out of Henrico was less, as well, and John Croft and his wife were there too. That would be a woman to help with the girl. Now that he had solved his dilemma, he wanted her there as soon as possible. He called in Marshall Dale.

"Thomas, I want you to take charge of Her Highness, Princess Pocahontas. Take her with best possible speed to Rock Hill, the home of Reverend Alexander Whitaker. There she is to be housed comfortably and educated. You may enlist Mistress Croft to aid in her care. Prepare to depart immediately."

Having given her full and proper title, he assumed Dale would follow his orders and accommodate her appropriately. Then to her he said, "Please wait here with Captain Argall until Marshall Dale is ready to depart." With that, he bowed formally and took his leave.

Dale did depart that same day, but the trip was too long to make before nightfall, so they stopped mid-river just to pass the dark of night and then proceeded to Henrico where he put her under the charge of Reverend Whitaker.

Henrico itself was situated on a peninsula on the northern bank of the James River. Perched on steep cliffs, the five blockhouses formed a circle of security. A tall fence surrounded the town and the land for two miles inland. The houses were built along three streets centered on the church. However, Pocahontas was not to stay in the town, she was to live in the household of Reverend Whitaker at Rock Hill across the river in a new expanded area arranged similarly to the town.

Young Reverend Whitaker dedicated himself to turning Pocahontas into a proper English Christian. He was also impressed with the English she had learned from her earlier visits to the fort, but he felt she could do better, so he gave her lessons that built on that foundation. Converting her to English ways was another matter. He believed the way to change a person was to take away everything from their old life. He ordered Hannah Croft, who was enlisted to act as chaperone and maid, to take away all of Pocahontas' own belongings and give her only English clothes to wear.

Pocahontas joined the Reverend at table and learned to use the fine patterned china and pewter tableware. The meat served, usually venison, was familiar, but some of the vegetables grown in the English garden, especially the onions, turnips, cabbage and cauliflower, upset her stomach.

He thought of her much as early Roman Christians considered the ancient Britons – equal in intellectual faculties and only in need of exposure to the true and right ways of their version of Christianity. He would not let her speak of her religious beliefs or pray to her god. If she mentioned Okee, he said he was a devil not a god and that her magic chants were worthless. If she raised her arms to the sun, he said the sun could not see or hear her. He lectured her twice a day in church and constantly at home. When she demonstrated that she had learned what he had tried to teach her, Whitaker openly expressed his joy and pleasure. He was a very effective teacher.

She was not asked to do any work, so she knew she was not a captive or slave, but this constant teaching was like punishment. She liked learning new things, but the intensity was beyond anything she had ever known. One day while Mistress Croft was helping her dress, she noticed how sad Pocahontas seemed.

"My dear, are you quite well? You are melancholy and that is not like you."

Pocahontas did her best to be correct in her English.

"Mistress Croft, I am told to study and practice every hour of the day. I am not ac-cus-tomed to this. I have no time for doing what I wish to do. Is this the way of all English?"

Hannah, who now had two boisterous children of her own and another on the way looked at the Princess and saw the girl. No one had mentioned her age, but Hannah guessed she was no more than sixteen. Even for a girl of the English aristocracy, sixteen was still a time when pleasure and feminine pastimes were a part of every day.

"No, my dear, not all English girls study all day. You are a very special girl and so more care is being taken in your education. But I think what you are saying is that you would like to have a little fun, a little free time. Is that it?"

"Oh, yes, please. Something that is fun not study. And are there other young women here? I would like to meet them."

"Not many, but some. You have been shut up here at Rock Hill. Henrico is a tiny place, but we do have some society. Let me talk to Reverend Whitaker. I think something might be arranged."

After serious discussion, Hannah convinced the Reverend that meeting the rest of the population of Henrico and spending time with many different people would help Pocahontas with her English. Hannah pointed out that by making her feel at home, she would be more inclined to favor the English cause with her father. He made all the arguments of a pious and protective guardian, but the lady prevailed and a community supper for the next Sunday was to be the introduction of Pocahontas to Henrico society.

After services that Sunday, trestle tables were set up in the commons and each household contributed a platter or pot of food. The common kettle was added to the fare and anyone who was not doing an essential duty that day was invited to join in. It happened to be a day off for Josiah. His first thought was that he would be able to spend the entire afternoon and evening with Bridget. His second thought was that he would get to meet Pocahontas, the friend of his youth, once again.

He had helped Bridget bring the contributions of the Croft family to the table and they were seated together at one end of a bench when the Reverend Whitaker ceremoniously escorted Pocahontas through the fort gate. Josiah did not recognize her. She was four years older and there is a great change in a girl between thirteen and seventeen. Rumor had it that she even was, or had been, married. On top of the normal change, this person was dressed in English clothes. If he had not been told that Pocahontas was with the Reverend, he would never have known her.

Having failed to recognize her, he was not surprised when she did not recognize him. She was seated on an individual chair and a sort of receiving line had formed so each person could be introduced to the Princess. He and Bridget waited in line together with her arm in his. When it was his turn, Whitaker stated his name as Mister Tucker and he was expected to say something to her.

He said, "Hello, my old friend. Love you not me?"

The reaction of everyone in earshot was pronounced. Whitaker took in an abrupt breath, Mistress Croft grabbed her throat as if she were about to faint, Bridget whirled on him with daggers in her eyes, and the collective heads of the onlookers swiveled back and forth seeking some explanation of this odd greeting. Pocahontas smiled a little at the reminder of the old teasing game and stared intensely at this young man.

Josiah carefully unwrapped Bridget's arm from his, held up his forefinger first to her and then to Pocahontas as if to say, "Hold on, just a minute." Then he ran a couple of steps and executed a perfect cartwheel.

Bridget giggled, the onlookers gasped and Pocahontas squealed with glee. She jumped out of her chair of honor, ran to where Josiah was standing in his dismount pose, and threw her arms around his neck. Then she backed off, hoisted her skirt ran three steps, and when she dropped her skirt in order to put her hands on the ground to do her own cartwheel, she tripped and fell heels over head onto the dusty ground. Josiah rushed to her aid, lifting her from behind and brushing the dirt off her shoulders and back while she tended to the front of her outfit. By this time, Mistress Croft had joined them and beat the dirt off the back of her skirt and inquired if she had hurt herself.

The community was still aghast at the whole display. It was obvious that the Reverend was building up steam for a full-fledged sermon on the sin of frivolity, so Princess Pocahontas took the floor.

"My good friend, Josiah Tucker. I am very pleased to see you again. Thank you for your gift of fond memories of our youth at James Fort. I am sorry, but I cannot follow you in these English clothes." Then she put her hand onto his as Whitaker had taught her that morning and, taking the cue, he escorted her back to her place of honor.

Whitaker was at a loss. He could not very well contradict the guest of honor. He might take that young man aside later and chastise him, but the Princess seemed to think highly of him. Perhaps that would not be in Whitaker's own best interest. He checked the temperature of the crowd, decided they had accepted the girl's explanation and were more interested in eating than lectures, and let the matter pass, for now.

Once Pocahontas was properly seated, Josiah completed his official time in line by introducing Bridget as his particular friend. Pocahontas stood and gave her a sisterly hug. The young couple was marked from that moment as people of note because they were the intimate friends of the Princess Pocahontas.

Weeks passed as the settlers feasted and trained Pocahontas, but Powhatan did nothing to rescue her. She felt abandoned. She became convinced that her father no longer valued her. Finally after three months, Powhatan offered a mere seven muskets, some of which were broken, and a few English captives in exchange for his daughter. He also offered 500 bushels of corn.

Gates turned down this meager offer. Pocahontas heard of the offer and it only served to reinforce that her father had deserted her. The rejection by her father coupled with the attention from Reverend Whitaker, Josiah and all the residents of Henrico, resulted in Pocahontas deciding to stay with English and become a Christian.

Another factor may have been one particular settler, John Rolfe. John was now a handsome, twenty-eight year old widower and chain smoker, who Reverend Whitaker enlisted to help with her English lessons. At first, John called at the parsonage strictly to teach English, but the sessions slowly became more like courting. By the spring, Pocahontas was asking to be baptized. The Reverend Whitaker officiated and Hannah and John Croft stood as godparents as the new Christian soul Rebecca was reborn.

Pocahontas was told that the Crofts and John Rolfe were to be invited to a celebration supper following the baptism and she asked that Josiah and Bridget be included in the invitation. Whitaker was opposed to the idea since Josiah was classified as a laborer now and Bridget was a paid servant, but John Rolfe was much indebted to Bridget and he liked Josiah, so he spoke to John Croft and between them, they convinced the Reverend to honor Rebecca's wishes.

This supper was the first and last time the young couple was included in a supper party with the gentry, but, though he was somewhat uncomfortable and felt like a fish out of water, he liked the food, the fine table setting and the good conversation. As the day wore on, he and the others forgot that he was a commoner among gentlemen. Bridget normally ate with the Croft children, not the parents, so she continued to feel out of place at the table with them, but so long as she talked with Rebecca, she was fine.

Nothing more had been heard from Powhatan, so on one of his visits to Henrico, Dale talked with his friend Rolfe about an idea of bringing Rebecca along for one last try at getting the guns and prisoners back from her father. Rolfe was not happy with the plan. There was some physical danger in the trip, but, more than that, he feared that either her tribe would do her harm for having come over to the English or that she might be forced to stay with her father.

"What is the value of putting her at such risk, Thomas?"

"Several things, John. We think her presence would mean safe passage for our people. Also, she has been well-treated and, seeing that, we hope her father will be encouraged to deal honorably with us."

"Can you guarantee her safety, Thom? It means a lot to me, personally. I have come to care a great deal for her."

"Really? Alexander told me you had been helping with her lessons. But I hear much more than the interest of a teacher, John."

John considered for a moment. Dale had been a friend to him and he needed to test how the leadership would react to something he had been thinking about for some time. He decided to take the chance. "She is special to me, very special. What would you think if I wanted to marry her?"

Dale paused and a smile grew on his face as he spoke. "Some of the common men in the fort have taken Indian women, but none have married them. Of course they could not, since none are Christian. Since she has been baptized, I suppose it would be possible. It feels so strange to ask, but do you love her, John?"

"How can I be sure, Thom? I thought I had married once and forever, yet here I am only two years later drawn strongly to this young woman. She has filled my loneliness and I want to take care of her. Is that love?"

"I am not the man to ask. I know little of love and less of marriage. I married a fine woman and immediately left her to come thousands of miles to this place. I have not seen her since only days after the wedding. You will have to work this out yourself, but let me say, I would have no objection to you marrying."

'Thank you, Thomas, your support means a lot. And if you think Rebecca would help our cause, then take her along."

Dale made preparations for an extensive embassy. John decided it was time to speak to Rebecca about his feelings for her. Just a few minutes into their English lesson on the next day, he took the book from her hands and began haltingly.

"Dear Rebecca, I … I want to speak to you … to tell you … that I consider you much more than … a pupil. I have very much enjoyed our time together reading … to improve your English. And you are doing marvelously! I … I have enjoyed all of our time together. I wanted to ask if … if you had enjoyed it too?"

Rebecca had a hard time sorting out this mis-structured declaration.

"I certainly have enjoyed this time, Master Rolfe. Is that what you wanted to know?"

"I am glad for that, Rebecca. I did want to know that and I also want to know if you would want to spend even more time together."

"Would it be more time in study?" She was not interested in any more studying.

"No, no. I was not thinking of study, I was thinking of perhaps making a life together, a home. Do you know what I mean?"

She was starting to get the drift. This was not the way a man asked a woman to be his wife in her culture. They played with each other and teased each other. Then the man negotiated a bride price with her father and then the father would tell the woman what arrangements had been made. There had been little play and no teasing and, of course, John had not worked out a price with her father. She thought quickly of Kocoum who she had put aside since she could not remain married to a non-Christian, according to Reverend Whitaker. Then she focused on John.

"I think I am beginning to understand. To make a life together, does that mean to live together?"

"Yes, to live together as man and wife. Rebecca, if I can get permission from the Governor, would you be my wife?"

Maybe this permission from the Governor is how they worked out the bride price, she thought. The English did many things with words that the Powhatan did with their whole being, singing, worshiping their god, and loving. The English must use words instead of playing and teasing. Well, if she was going to be an English Christian, she would have to learn this too.

"I would like to live with you as man and wife, John Rolfe."

"Oh thank you, Rebecca, thank you. You have made me very happy. I will seek permission from the Governor as soon as I can." He paused, thinking, then explained, "I did not want you to go to your father without knowing that you have a permanent and honorable place here, as my wife. You do not have to remain with the Whitakers or go back to your father. Do you understand?"

"This I do understand, John Rolfe. I can choose to stay as an English Christian. Not on anyone's charity, but as the wife of a respected member of this village. This is good. Thank you, John Rolfe."

Honor, status and respectability were not new concepts for Rebecca. They are pretty much universal ideas manifested and valued in every culture. Sometimes, they are just hard to recognize.

Dale marched with one hundred and fifty men and Pocahontas to the home village of Powhatan. On his way up the York River, Dale told the natives that if he did not get the guns back he would take their canoes, destroy their fishing nets and burn their villages. The Indians responded to this message by shooting arrows at the ship. Dale sent longboats of men to the shore and did exactly what he had promised.

At one stop, two brothers of Pocahontas came on the ship. They saw that she was treated well, as Dale had planned. Dale had hoped she would speak to her brothers about cooperating with English. No one understood everything she said, but they did understand her to say that she had waited for a year for her father to redeem her and now she would stay on and marry John Rolfe.

Dale sent Master Sparkes and Rolfe to negotiate with Powhatan. While they were gone, Ralph Hamor gave a letter to Captain Dale. Rolfe had asked Hamor, who wrote a fine hand, to scribe the formal letter asking Dale's permission for him to marry Rebecca. Rolfe had planned to speak to Governor Gates, but he felt he should first ask his friend Dale. He was uncomfortable presuming that their casual conversation should serve as permission and he felt foolish addressing his good friend in a formal interview. The letter seemed a reasonable compromise.

Pocahontas choosing to stay with the English changed the political situation dramatically from the Indians' point of view. Now that his daughter wanted to stay with the English, she was no longer a hostage. Powhatan was no longer in negotiations with the English. To cooperate now would not be seen by his people as surrender. He sent word that he was ready for peace. He returned more guns and released all captives. Dale responded to Powhatan that he accepted the offer of peace and that there would be no more raids so long as the Indians did no harm to the colonists.

Dale formally granted permission for the marriage. Rolfe formally asked Rebecca to marry him before witnesses and she accepted. Word was sent to Jamestown and to Powhatan. The women in Jamestown went into full wedding mode. They arranged every English custom they could to make the first state wedding to be held in the church a most festive occasion. Spring flowers were gathered from the gardens in front of the new two story frame houses. A feast was prepared using food from the three large new storehouses. Everyone got out their finest clothes and used the wedding as an excuse to make new ones. The women held a meeting at which each woman brought the best clothes or material they had that could be used to dress Rebecca.

Powhatan would not come into an English camp or fort even to attend the marriage of his daughter. He sent his brother and gifts of fresh water pearls. He also gave control of some land to Pocahontas, not to Rolfe. The Indians came in their best ceremonial outfits. They wore their usual aprons with a mantle of deerskin embroidered with beads from shells and even one of turkey feathers.

As was suitable for a princess, her wedding was held in the largest church in the colony in the capital, Jamestown. On April 5, 1614, with all the officials of the colony in attendance, she and John Rolfe were joined in marriage by the Reverend Buck. She wore a dress of red brocade, the richest-looking material that could be found in Jamestown, accented by her father's pearls. Even the Spanish spy, Molina, attended the ceremony and eventually reported the details of the event to his king. She was happy to be married to John Rolfe and it pleased her that she was a countryman of her father/brother John Smith.

As a widower, Rolfe had been living in a dwelling with other unmarried men. Now he and his wife would establish their own home, outside the protective fence at Henrico, where he could expand his experiments with the new tobacco. With land at Jamestown, at Henrico and, under English law, the land Powhatan had dowered to Pocohontas, Rolfe was now a very wealthy man.

With the Governor-for-life safe in England and his friend Thomas Gates scheduled to return to England soon, Dale felt quite secure in his role as deputy Governor. His *Lawes Divine, Morall and Martiall, &c.* had become the law of the colony and, though people were not wholly comfortable with their severity, they were becoming used to them.

Feeling secure, Dale took personal initiative in making a bold move. He saw that his friend Rolfe was very happy with Rebecca and he admitted that their marriage had been the key to peace with the Indians. To capitalize on this, he decided to he wanted to marry Pocahontas' sister. He worked with Ralph Hamor to make arrangements with Powhatan. Hamor and the ubiquitous Thomas Savage, as interpreter, went to Powhatan's home village.

Powhatan turned him down. He said, though she was only twelve years old, she was to marry an Indian prince, who had offered two bushels of beads for her. Hamor tripled the offer, but Powhatan still refused. As a sign of good will, Powhatan sent animal skins as a gift and asked for a shaving knife, a grindstone, two bone combs, one hundred fishhooks, a cat and a dog in return. Dale took some time to assemble this odd assortment of gifts. The most difficult part was containing a cat long enough to move it to Powhatan.

In June of 1614, Samuel Argall took *Treasurer*, a ship in which he was part owner, back to England. Ralph Hamor went along. They had the pleasure of telling the Company board about the peace with the Powhatan's. It had come to be called the Peace of Pocahontas. A treaty had also been made with the Chickahominies. That tribe had agreed that the English would be overlords so long as the eight-member tribal council would run everyday affairs. Each member of the tribe would wear a badge to indicate they were friends of the English so there would be no accidental harm done to these Indians. With the two closest tribes at peace, the company was encouraged about the prospects for the colony. They were also encouraged by a type of cargo carried by Argall, a full shipment of Rolfe's "tall tobacco."

The renewed enthusiasm of the Company was not completely reflected in the colony. True, there were now two fair rows of houses, most two stories high and built of lumber cut in the sawpits where the two Cassens had found work. The harvest of 1614 was good, still not enough to sustain all the settlements across the winter without supplements from England, but improving. The focus continued to be on creating either raw materials or products that would make a profit for the Virginia Company. They had seeded a variety of industries. The settlers had little success at growing pineapples or oranges, raising silk worms, or making wine from vines imported through England from France. With this series of failures the Company became more and more interested in Bermuda colony than in Jamestown. Jamestown, the first colony, needed a public relations boost.

The state of Jamestown was overshadowed by a singular event, the birth of the first Anglo-Indian baby. Pocahontas, again attended by many of the Jamestown ladies, gave birth to a son. John named the boy Thomas after his good friend Thomas Dale. January 30, 1615 was a cold and snowy day, but the birth of a child brightened the hearts of everyone in the settlement.

Rolfe's tobacco was still the most profitable commodity the colony had produced. It was a new strain of tobacco, much sweeter than the native *Nicotania rustica*. John Rolfe had obtained seeds of a large-leaf variety of Spanish tobacco known as *Nicotania tabacum*. This crop was grown exclusively in South America and was protected by Spanish law from being exported. Rolfe possibly obtained the seed illegally from Don Fernando de Berrio, the governor of Trinidad who, in 1612, had been fined by Spain for trading with the enemy. Judging from the quality of the tobacco, Rolfe's seeds definitely came from Trinidad likely smuggled by a Dutch or English seaman. Rolfe never told anyone how he had arranged to get those precious seeds.

When Argall returned to Virginia, he brought the news that the young men of London wanted all the sweet Virginia tobacco they could get. The leaders of the colony, especially Dale and Rolfe, talked about how to capitalize on that through 1615 and into 1616. Rolfe projected he could send over 2,000 pounds in 1615 and ten times that much the following year if all went well. Then Dale hit upon an idea. He brought it up to his friend Rolfe who was central to the plan.

"John, you and your family are the talk of London. The tall tobacco is much in demand and everyone is curious to see your wife. In my last dispatches, I asked the Company if they would finance a voyage for you and your family to visit England. How do you feel about that?"

"Taking the baby across the ocean. I am not sure that is wise, Thom. And what would Rebecca do in England? She is still uncomfortable here in Jamestown. She prefers little Henrico. Do you know there are only thirty-eight men still there and sixteen of them work directly for the Company? Tobacco grows well there, but it is too isolated for the men to want to stay. But, to get back to the subject, knowing that an Englishman has married a native is one thing, seeing them together with their child, well, I am not sure how welcome we will be."

"That is exactly the point. You will cause a sensation! And, I have it on the authority of the Company treasurer, you will not only be welcome, but received at court."

"You cannot be serious! Court! … I would think a sensation would be last thing you would want."

"No. Think about it, John. The Company is concentrating on Bermuda. The idea of an island paradise has caught the fancy of the investors. We need to do something to call attention to ourselves in a positive way so they will continue to send supplies and reinforcements to us." Dale jumped up and started pacing and waving his hands to illustrate his ideas. "We will send her as a princess, with a court of her own. Maybe her brothers and serving women, all dressed in the finest English attire. We will send interpreters with instructions to … to temper what is said. We will both be with them at all times to make sure the impression is correct."

Dale finally ran out of breath.

"I really do not know, Thom," John said shaking his head, "but if you are set on this, tell me how we would begin."

Dale, having recovered his air, continued to act out his plans. It took a great deal of discussion and several visits to Powhatan to work out the details.

While Dale was pursuing the political agenda, the others who were leaving attended to their own interests. John Martin would be returning to England too. At fifty-two, he was far from certain he would ever get back to Virginia, so he went in search of the resting place of his son who had died in the terrible, early months of 1607.

The southwest corner of the original fort had changed. Where once there had been small wooden crosses marking individual graves, now there was a large building covering at least half of that original cemetery. John's son, also John, had been buried about in the middle of the group of graves, but with so many graves added in later years and then the building built over a large portion of the area, Martin could no longer determine where the middle would be. He had placed two particular stones next to the little cross for his son. As he wandered around the area, he saw one of the stones incorporated into the foundation of the State House next door. It was filling in the uneven space below a large stone someone had once pointed out to him as having belonged in a medieval castle. The ancient stone, the same on De la Warr had noticed in the foundation of the Statehouse, had been ballast in a ship and was dumped at some point and then reused.

James Brumfield, who had returned from Henrico and apprenticed with one of the blacksmiths, noticed the old man retracing his steps. James thought he might have dropped something, so he offered his help.

"Sir, did you lose something? May I help you find it?"

"Lost something, you say. Yes, I have lost a great deal." The futile search for his son had left Martin in a philosophical frame of mind. "I lost a lot of friends, a lot of time, and I lost my son."

"Oh you were looking for the old graveyard?"

"How would you know about that? You are only a youngster. You can know nothing of those first terrible years."

"I was here for every one of them, sir. I came on Captain Newport's ship with Captain Smith. You may not remember me, I was only nine at the time."

Josiah had come to Jamestown for supplies. Whenever he came, as many of the squad who could gathered and relived the good days. He had gone looking for James and heard his voice. He now walked up to the pair as the truth was just dawning on Martin.

"You are that skinny little boy who used to tag around after Smith! Goodness, you are the size of a house. What happened to the rest of Smith's favorites?"

"Well, I am one of them, Captain Martin. Josiah Tucker," said Josiah as he approached and he stopped and nodded his head slightly in introduction. "You may remember some of the others. Richard Dixon works with me on John Rolfe's place. The two Cassen brothers work in the sawmill. John Herd, John Dods and Robert Fenton are employed here in Jamestown. And I am not sure who Nate Peacock is with now. Do you know, James?"

"Nate has apprenticed with the store master. He has a flair for business, it seems. So, with you, Captain Martin, that accounts for almost a third of us who have survived from the first voyage."

Martin sighed deeply, "I will not be here much longer. I sail with Argall."

"I am sorry to hear that, sir," said Josiah politely. He was actually pleased whenever any of Smith's old enemies left or died. "I wish you a good voyage." Then to James, "We should go find Nate, James," and they walked shoulder to shoulder away from Martin.

John turned back to the old graveyard and said quietly, "God be with you, son."

The Spanish spy, Molina, had proved himself to be worthy of his parole. He never left the fort without permission and one of his assigned keepers. He had little to pack but he did need to check with his secret messenger. Molina had been a model prisoner and a model spy. Without creating so much as a ripple of suspicion, he had set up an arrangement with a family of sailors. Several sons and cousins in this family worked on the ships that called at Jamestown regularly. Molina had paid one son to take a message to the next port in the West Indies where a Cambridge educated Spaniard received the letter and forwarded it to Spain. The son had shared word of his arrangement with his brothers and cousins and each in turn had contacted Molina on their next visit to Jamestown and let him know they would accept the same pay for this service. This system had been going on since about two months after Molina had been abandoned by his ship, or planted by his government.

It was simpler when his companion Antonio Pereos was alive. He was not watched as closely as Molina or Francisco Lenbri, the expatriated Englishman. For the last three months, Molina had made the contacts himself. The last time, he was sure they had been seen passing the message, but nothing had come of it. He was relieved to be going back to Europe. He had had quite enough of the swampy island and its humid climate.

John Rolfe's tobacco farms looked to be the salvation of the colony. With him going to England for an undetermined amount of time, the proper care of those farms was critical. He had given a great deal of thought to who he could trust to carry through with his instructions. He had considered several of the other gentlemen who had also had successful crops. Each of those men had their own acres to tend. None had extra help to assign to Rolfe's land. After much consideration, he had settled on asking Josiah. It was one of the reasons he had sent for him. Josiah thought he was only coming to Jamestown to take back supplies, so Rolfe's first question confused him.

"Josiah, can you tell me how to grow tobacco?"

"Pardon me, sir, I do not understand what you are asking me. You know more than anyone about growing tobacco."

"I want to know what you know. Tell me, from the beginning, how do you make a successful tobacco crop?"

Still somewhat confused, Josiah began at the point he had started out with Rolfe – seeds.

"You use seeds taken from the best plants of the previous year, put the tiny seeds into a bed indoors in March. The seeds spring up in May and you set the plants out in small hillocks in June.

"Where?" Rolfe interjected.

"Preferably in a field that has been recently cleared of trees and burned. A southern or southwestern exposure is best but always make sure the land slopes to allow for runoff so the plants do not sit in water.

"Good, continue."

"You wait until the plants have about twelve leaves and then top them by removing the seed head so all the growth is in the leaves. Keep trimming the suckers and lugs until September. You watch for insects and use smoke to drive off most pests. When they are full grown, you cut the stalks and let the plants wilt in the field."

"Good, Josiah. Very good. Now that should give you a good crop of leaves, how do you turn those leaves into first quality tobacco for export?

"You can pile them under dried grass and let them cure in the sun, but it is better to gather the leaves in bunches and hang the "hands" inside. Our sweet leaves take about three weeks to dry. When the leaves are dry, you soak them just enough so you can spin them on a spinning wheel into thin ropes which you coil into acorn shaped mounds. Or you can wait for a rainy day, take the hands outside and cover them with cloth to collect moisture. You pack the mounds or leaves as tightly as possible into hogsheads, which we can float from all of our fields except the far field on the south side of the James. Those we cart to the landing at Smith Fort and float from there. To keep the quality high, we take out the stems and keep any inferior leaves to use them for local product."

"Son, you have learned well."

"You have been a fine teacher. Thank you for sharing your knowledge."

"It has been a pleasure, son. Now I have a proposition for you. You know I am leaving for England. I really do not know how long we will be gone. We cannot afford to have anything less than a superior crop this year. I may not even be back in time to plant for next year. I want you to be in charge of all the fields while I am gone."

Josiah was speechless.

"And in exchange for taking that responsibility, I will share the crop with you. You will own one-fifth of the entire product. And I will see to it you are relieved of all your herding duties."

Josiah made a small noise almost a gasp. He took a deep breath and said, "What can I say, sir. Thank you. Thank you so much. I will do my very best … for both of us."

"That is exactly what I had hoped for. I would also like for you to look after our house and direct my Indian servants in working in the fields. You should live there while we are gone. We have a few more days before we leave. Think of any questions you have and ask me anything."

Josiah had one question he had wanted to ask for months.

"Sir, I do have one question, but it is not about tobacco."

"What is it, son?'

"Sir, you know Bridget, Bridget Malone, the Crofts' girl?"

"Yes, an excellent young lady. What about her?"

"Well, sir, we would like to marry. Do you think this would be a good time?"

Rolfe smiled, warmly with a small tinge of sadness.

"Son, I have known both of you for years. I think you are two of the finest young people here and I would be pleased to see you married. You will have a home for many months, maybe a year or more. I think it is the perfect time. Do you need for me to speak to John Croft?"

"Would that be the proper way, sir? I have no idea what arrangements have to be made for Bridget to leave her position."

"I will talk with John. You are sure of the girl?" Josiah nodded eagerly. "I will tell him of our financial arrangement. I think he will agree. I happen to know she has a small dowry."

"I had no idea she had any dowry." He paused. "Sir, I would take her in her shift." And they both laughed fondly as the two adult male friends they had become.

Josiah had one more thought. "Master Rolfe, would you stand up for us?"

Now Rolfe was the one surprised. His emotions ran quickly from surprise, to slight embarrassment, to the tenderness a man feels toward his son. A mist came into his eyes. "That is a great honor, Mister Tucker. I would be proud to stand for you."

Tucker, Josiah, boy. Josiah had been called all those names by gentlemen and men of property but never, never in all his twenty-four years had a fine man called him Mister Tucker.

The Crofts were sad to see Bridget leave them but they were very happy for her to start her own home. Hannah collected a few little things for the new couple and presented them to Bridget at a tea in her honor. One of the ladies provided a length of new cloth and the ladies held a sewing bee to finish a wedding dress in record time.

Pocahontas attended both events, though she stayed in the background. She walked with Bridget on the way back to the Crofts' home after the sewing bee.

"I have a small thing for you. It is a custom of my people, I mean of the Powhatan. Take this seed corn. Put it on a wet cloth until it sprouts. Tuck the sprouted seed in your dress on your wedding day and your union will be fruitful as the blessed corn."

Bridget was a strictly raised Catholic. She had learned to survive in the Anglican colony of Virginia, but she had had little contact with Indians. This custom at first struck her as some Indian sorcery and she was about to refuse the gift when she looked straight into Rebecca's face. The girl was her age. She had been married twice, so the tale went, and had born a child. Her face was open and her look was earnest. Bridget saw no witchcraft there, no evil. She saw a sister wishing her many children. She smiled, opened her hand to accept the little kernel, and then hugged Rebecca.

The day before the ship was to depart, the wedding was held in what was still called the new church. All of the squad attended as well as the Crofts, John Rolfe and all of the women who had feted Bridget. John Croft gave the bride away. After the wedding party was assembled at the front of the building, John Martin crept in the back and stood in the shadows holding his hat in both hands. Knowing he would never see his son married, he somehow wanted to be here.

CHAPTER 15
England

Finally, on April 14, 1616 they were prepared to depart on Argall's *Treasurer*. By the time all the plans had been made, the passengers stacked in the great and stern cabins included Sir Thomas Dale, John Martin, the Spanish spy Don Diego de Molina and Francis Limbrecke, John Rolfe, Rebecca/Pocahontas, their son Thomas, and an Indian "court." The Powhatan contingent consisted of Tomocomo, Powhatan's trusted observer, one of Pocahontas' sisters named Matachanna, three female attendants and four male escorts. The attendants preferred to stay on deck as much as possible. Being inside the walls of a rocking boat was so foreign to them that the wind and wet was a relief.

New clothes had been made for Rebecca and John, but the rest of the Indians refused to adopt the style of the coat-wearers. Both the women and men remained basically naked wearing only the traditional aprons. Other natives who had been to England advised their friends to take their warmest leggings and moccasins. The best cloaks were provided for all. Powhatan gave Tomocomo a stick to count the English people. He was to cut a mark into the stick for each man he saw who would be capable of fighting. Powhatan also told him to find out all he could about the English God, especially how he looked. And, he was to ask if Smith was really dead.

The seven-week voyage was uneventful, even pleasant, until they were in sight of the Devon coast. Argall called all of his sailors to attention on the deck. Dale took a central position on the poop deck. Two of the junior officers marched a man up from below deck and held him between them facing Dale. Dale made an announcement.

"Francis Limbrecke, late of his Majesty's naval forces, you are charged with treason in that you deserted and acted as a pilot for the Spanish enemy during the invasion by their armada. For this crime against your sovereign you are sentenced to hang until dead. Do you have anything to say?"

He did not wait for the prisoner to speak, but he had nothing to say.

"Gentlemen, perform your duty."

The officers tied the prisoner's hands behind him and marched him to the base of the main mast. The youngest officer put a noose around his neck. The other officer tied off the rope that was thrown over a spar. There was a short drum roll and the senior of the two officers shouted an order causing several sailors to haul on the rope lifting the struggling man higher into the air.

Every civilian on the ship turned their head or quickly went to their cabin. The military men had seen a hanging before so they stood calmly and watched until the struggles stopped. The body was dumped into the sea without ceremony.

When the ship docked at Plymouth on June 3, the passengers got off the ship as quickly as they could. Tomocomo, true to his orders from Powhatan, had his counting stick in his hand. As he walked across the gangplank and down the dock he was counting men who could be warriors. He marked the stick to ten tens and he had only counted those on the wharf. He looked up at the road and saw that many or more. He gave up and threw the stick into the water.

Sir Lewis Stukley greeted Pocahontas and her retinue on behalf of the king. Stukley had arranged for transportation for the group and they all boarded coaches and began the uncomfortable 173-mile trip to London. They had rooms at the Belle Sauvage Inn near St. Paul's Cathedral, a tavern and inn that had existed since 1453.

All ranks of people wandered by the Inn to have a look at the curiosity. Notables sometimes were granted a short visit. Commoners simply stared as the members of the party entered or left the building. The comments ranged from complimentary to disbelieving to derogatory.

"That must be her, Harold. She has the arm of the fine gentleman who must be Rolfe. So she is supposed to be an Indian. Well, I think she is nothing but a Cornish woman. I have seen girls from Cornwall who are that dark of skin. I think it is a hoax."

"I can hardly look at 'em, Rob. Can you imagine taking a heathen to your bed? The man is living in sin. He must feel filthy every morning."

"He is not living in sin. I hear she is a Christian now, man. There is no reason he should not take her to his bed, unless it is because he cannot stand to look at her. I cannot say I would want her. "

John Smith, like the rest of London, had heard the Rolfe's were coming. He still remembered Pocahontas fondly as the young girl who had saved his life. He was concerned that she would be viewed as a freak rather than a princess. He thought for some time of ways he might help ensure that she would be received properly. Finally, he decided to use his association with Queen Anne, whom he had come to know in his earlier travels. He considered asking for an audience, but instead chose to write a long letter praising Pocahontas and the many services she had provided to the crown. He mentioned the two times she had saved his own life and the food she had helped provide to save the settlers after the big fire. He also took some pains to remind the Queen of his own importance in the founding and preservation of Jamestown.

At every opportunity, Smith promoted himself as a captain of a ship bound for America. He never married. He spent all of his energy either writing about America or planning to go there. All he wanted out of life was to be part of the growth of America.

Smith had enlisted his friend John Tradescant, Senior to edit his journals and publish them. John Senior was raising his son and namesake, who was but eight years old, to join the business. The first book, *A True Relation of Virginia,* was published in 1616 while the Rolfes were in England. Smith thought of sending a copy to the Queen along with his letter, but decided the letter should stand on its own to get exclusive attention.

The Virginia Company gave the Rolfes four pounds sterling per week for the maintenance of the Lady Rebecca and the baby. Nothing was provided for Rolfe himself. Cash money was not used in the colony, but the sale of his tobacco had given him some funds in a London bank. Staying at the Belle Savauge Inn fit his budget well. Those accommodations were a great deal more elegant than a Powhatan hut, but the Rolfes were entertained in much greater splendor by Lady De La Warr, their hostess in London, and other aristocrats.

Sir Walter Raleigh, who had just recently been released from the Tower of London, even hosted the princess. Oddly, he took her to visit the brother of Sir George Percy, the Earl of Northumberland, who was then being held in the Tower under suspicion of supporting his cousin, a Catholic, who was charged as the ringleader in the recent Gunpowder Plot. The Earl was under lock and key, but in comfortable rooms. There were only two guards to pass, one at the main gates, and one just outside the door of his suite. The guard held the door for Raleigh and the princess as they entered.

Northumberland stood and took Sir Walter's hand. "Raleigh! It is good to see you."

"And you, my Lord Earl. Are you treated well?"

"I miss my freedom, but as a prison, these rooms are satisfactory. But let us not speak of these things when we have this lovely lady in our presence." Making a gracious leg, he continued, "Good day to you, Mistress Rolfe, or should I call you Princess Pocahontas?"

"My Lord Earl, I am now your countrywoman and very proud of my name, Mistress Rebecca Rolfe. I am glad your rooms are pleasing to you."

"Walter, thank you for bringing this delightful lady to me."

"Her husband has done me a great service. He is the man who managed to get the South American tobacco seeds and give England her own source of sweet leaves. I just had to meet him and thank him personally. Then I met this fine lady and she asked to pay you her respects."

Rebecca was looking around the room and, as she moved her head, part of an earring fell off. Henry Percy, Earl of Northumberland, swooped down to retrieve the fallen stone.

"Mistress Rolfe, I fear this pearl has fallen from its setting. I would be most pleased to repair it for you."

Rebecca instinctively touched her ear and did feel an empty setting. She had been around the gentlemen and aristocrats of the Virginia colony for two years and had met a dozen or more peers since arriving in England. To a man, they had all been interested in matters of society and court and occasionally money, but here was one of the most powerful men in England offering to be her jeweler.

"My Lord, I would not presume to have you do such a menial task. I will find a jeweler or dispose of the earrings."

"Please, no, Mistress Rolfe. It would truly give me pleasure to do something useful with my hands and it doubles the pleasure to do a small service for you. Please."

With such a heartfelt plea, what could she do? She unfastened the earbob and handed it to the Earl. He bowed with earnest gratitude and move to a small desk where he withdrew a leather-bound kit of small tools. He moved to the sill of the brightest window to have the best light and a working surface.

"Please, Mistress Rolfe, have a seat while I attend to this."

Raleigh took her elbow gently and guided her to a chair near the desk. She sat and folded her hands in her lap.

"Mistress, did you have a particular purpose in wanting to meet with me?" Percy asked. Rebecca had prepared a little speech to explain her visit, one she hoped would obscure her personal interest in John Smith.

"I did, sir. In my youth, when I visited James Fort, I met with your brother, Sir George, on several occasions. I have inquired of his whereabouts, but no one seemed to be sure where I might find him. I wanted to speak with him about Captain John Smith. I was hoping he would be able to tell me of his fate. It is a matter of some concern to my father. Do you know how I might get in touch with your brother, or do you already know the fate of Captain Smith?"

"I believe my brother is at our hunting lodge, but I can save you searching further since I do know something of Captain Smith. He came back to England in 1609. He was severely injured, but with good doctoring and time he healed well. He then started looking for a way to go back to Virginia or at least to America. He did take one voyage to the northern coast, but the Virginia Company no longer considers him as a candidate for a Jamestown supply. Last I heard, he is here in London writing of his adventures."

When Sir Lewis Stukley was first met the Indians, one of the first things Tocomoco asked about was whether John Smith was dead. Stukley had said no, but had given no other information. Rebecca had brought his name up to Lady De La Warr and she too avoided the topic. So when Percy said Smith had recovered, she was not surprised, but she was surprised and shocked, even dismayed, that he was here in London, only a few miles from her at most and yet he had made no attempt to contact her. It was very difficult to keep the emotion from her face. She was very glad both men were concentrating on fixing the earring.

"There!" Percy said triumphantly. "As good as new, maybe better, "as he ceremoniously presented the repaired earring to her. His face fairly beamed with pride in his work. Rebecca liked this aristocrat. Skill with your hands and pride in your work were both valued highly in her culture. Yes, this man would be easily accepted by her people - her former people, she reminded herself. She rewarded him with a rare smile, something that transformed her average face into a thing a beauty.

There was a light knock on the door and the guard opened it for the warden of the Tower.

"Sir Walter," they were obviously old friends, "I am afraid the time allowed for a visit to the Earl is up. Please, come with me."

Raleigh was naturally familiar with these rules having spent many years in the Tower himself, so he demurred readily.

"Henry, it has been good to see you. I will come again as soon as I can."

"Thank you, Walter. Mistress Rolfe, thank you for brightening my day with both your visit and the opportunity to feel useful. I will not ask you to sully your time in England with another visit, but rest assured I will be forever grateful for this one."

"You are most welcome, my Lord. I enjoyed meeting you and thank you for the information." She gave a small curtsey. He gave a formal leg in farewell. Raleigh and Northumberland clapped each other on the shoulder in a military embrace, and the visitors left with the warden. Henry returned to the window and lovingly restored his tools to their case.

Lady De La Warr introduced Pocahontas to London society. She invited many of those involved in the Virginia Company and their wives to a fine dinner. Normally, dancing would have followed dinner, but since neither Rolfe nor Rebecca knew the formal steps, Lady De La Warr engaged a musician and invited the poet Ben Johnson to recite as after dinner entertainment. Even though she had never attended an event like this in her life, Rebecca's natural grace and correct behavior impressed everyone in attendance. Following this triumph, any number of people wanted to have the couple as their guests of honor. Dinners, recitals and parties were arranged for almost every evening.

As soon as he could manage, John Rolfe put and end to the constant social life.

"Rebecca, I know all of this entertainment must be a great pleasure for you, but I really must be attending to business. The Company needs reports from me and we need to be planning our return to Virginia."

"Oh John, I have enjoyed meeting the people and seeing the lovely houses, but I have had quite enough of parties. I have not wanted to bother you about it, but I have not been feeling well. Tomocomo has told me that three of the women who came with us are very ill. Please, is there a way we could be in a more open place, maybe stay outside the city?"

"Are you sure, my dear? We do have several more appointments that we must keep. And I must be able to come in to meet with the Company Council, so we cannot go too far. However, I will ask around to see if there is a suitable place."

"Thank you, John. I truly believe Thomas and I will be much better in a forest." She walked to her husband and he embraced her gently.

Sir Thomas Dale escorted Rolfe, Tomocomo, and the Indian braves to court one day. There were dozens of men standing about in small groups in a large reception room. Tomocomo stood silently and watched the men move from group to group. One man did not move. All of the others eventually moved to talk with this short man. Servants circulated with bits of food and glasses of wine and cider. When the little man raised his right hand, servants broke off from everyone else and attended to him. Sir Thomas walked about with Tomocomo and at one point introduced him to the short man. There was no further conversation and when they walked away from the little man, a stern man in a minister's collar approached. Sir Thomas introduced him as John King, the Bishop of London. He explained that a Bishop was a man of rank who represented his God.

Powhatan had specifically told Tomocomo to find out about this English God, especially what this God looked like, so Tomocomo asked, through Sir Thomas, to see an image of the English God. Had the Bishop been a Roman Catholic, the request would have been simple to grant. Every Catholic Church had many images of God as Father, Son and Holy Spirit. But this was Protestant England, only recently freed from the tyranny of the Catholic Queen Bloody Mary, and no Anglican church dared show an image of any kind lest they be accused of worshiping an idol. So the Bishop tried to describe a spiritual being to a man who had no language to speak of such things. Tomocomo's god was real, a man who had come to be with his people when needed, not a spirit with no face.

Tomocomo asked whether the English god spoke to his people through anyone. The Bishop said, "Our God speaks to us through Gospels."

Tomocomo looked confused and Dale explained the Gospels were writings in a book. Tomocomo had seen Smith's magic writing and now he was to believe that their God used such magic writing to communicate with them. Those in the Powhatan tribes who seemed odd in their mind were often used by Okee to speak for him, so Tomocomo asked if those of strange mind were also used by the English God as well as magic writing.

The Bishop said, "Enlightened medicine says those people should be locked away so they will do no harm to themselves or anyone else. Our benevolent King has provided places of safety, at his own expense, to protect these unfortunates."

Tomocomo was shocked. He was convinced that the English God was weak and commanded no real allegiance. He was certain the English had no idea how to communicate with a god, and that this god was of no help at all to his people. Tomocomo's god, Okee, was always helpful. Okee had come as a real man, not magic writing, and told them how to wear their hair to be most successful in battle. Every Powhatan warrior followed this command to shave the right side of his hair so that the bowstring could fly freely. The

Powhatan warriors were always victorious because their god helped them in their life on earth.

The Bishop invited the Rolfes to dinner. The date was set for one week later. Lady De La Warr and her husband were included as were Sir Lewis and his wife. Dinner was ample yet simple, as befitted a clergyman. After dinner, there was no dancing and no formal entertainment. Any evening at the home of the Bishop was filled with what passed for discussion but was, in fact, a chance for the Bishop to rehearse his latest opinions. This evening varied only slightly in that the Bishop spent the evening lecturing Rebecca on here duty to "her people."

"My dear, Mistress Rolfe, I thank our good Lord that he has given you to us to do his work in the New World. The peace that has followed your marriage to our dear Mister Rolfe has long been hoped for. It is the work of our Lord that the heath…er ah… the natives have finally seen the light and accepted the English as their overlords. I applaud you for setting aside the ways of your youth and becoming English. I feel confident that you will continue to play your part to maintain this proper state. Now you are in the perfect position to return to your native land and support us in bringing the Christian faith to your tribes."

The Bishop's congregations were treated to variation on this theme in his sermons for many weeks to come.

The social high point of the visit to London was being invited to attend the Twelfth Night festival at court. This revel was dedicated to the recently created Earl of Buckingham, George Villiers, an intimate friend of the king. He was a long-legged martinet, but, knowing all eyes were on Pocahontas, he personally sought her out and escorted her to her seat on the platform with the royal party. Her husband, not being of royal birth, was not seated with her but was at a table on the floor close enough that they could clearly see each other. Tocomoco was recognized as the brother of Powhatan, (which he was not) so he was invited to the festival but he chose to occupy no seat preferring to wander though the assembly.

Sir Lewis and the interpreter stayed close to Tomocomo to answer his many questions. At one point he asked when he would meet the king. Sir Lewis explained that he had already met the king many days ago in the palace. Tomocomo said he had met no one who looked like a king. Sir Lewis indicated the man sitting on the platform not far from Pocahontas and said that was the king. Tomocomo recognized the short, little man who the servants paid so much attention to and was indignant. He told Sir Lewis that no one so weak could be a weroance in Powhatan's villages much less a king. Besides, a king knew how to act. Powhatan gave many gifts to his guests and this man had not even spoken with Tomocomo much less given him any gift. If this was England's king, England must not be the strong nation it seemed to be. From such seemingly insignificant events, change grows.

Ben Johnson, playwright, actor, and producer, had arranged the program for the festival entitled "The Vision of Delight." He was a master of theatrical tricks and this program took his genius to new heights. Those who had seen his theatricals before were impressed with this year's effort, the scenic effect being designed by the noted architect, Indigo Jones. Pocahontas, who had never seen so much as a Roman candle, thought she had stepped into a magical world.

Johnson arranged a pantomime celebrating the Court of Misrule. There were many scenes and they were not well connected so that those unfamiliar with theatrical presentations would have had great difficulty in making any sense of it all. There was a monster that bore a slight resemblance to the Bishop of London, a rank of little puppets some hitting each other with paddles, a rising moon into a fake cloud, Italian dancers, loud music, singing, and recitals of poetry, some beautiful and much vulgar. First there were streamers pulled by actors to simulate the trails of rockets while the King of Misrule frolicked around the stage having his betters bring him food and drink. As the "King" nearly passed out from drinking, from both sides of the temporary stage came small rockets streaking across the room. The gentry cheered while Pocahontas looked quickly for a place to hide. John Rolfe rose and came to her side and calmed her, telling her it was only a play something like when she and her friends had played at being warriors and animals in their dances.

Then the great Twelfth Night cake was rolled out. A few years earlier, before Henry, Prince of Wales, had died of typhoid at 18, the cake had been so large that the men and women gathered on opposite sides of the cake and had a mock sea battle with water cannon that were mounted on the cake. Since the death of the Prince, Queen Anne was in deep mourning. In fact, this was the first celebration that had been allowed since his death, so the celebration, though impressive in its uniqueness, was relatively subdued.

The cake was cut and each person took a piece. There were no peasants present to turn the social order completely upside down as the tradition of misrule demanded. However, this year, the bean, the prize baked into the cake that would determine who would be the King of Misrule, was found by a suitably low ranking person, the younger son of a minor baron. The King, knowing there were still many who disputed his right to be king of Scotland, much less England, was not about to foster any further doubts by assuming a subservient role for even a few hours of Twelfth Night. Rather than be seen in any lesser role than King, he dutifully turned over his throne to the Bean King and left the room.

King James' only surviving son, Charles, had no such qualms. He had been born into his father's court in Scotland and was only three years old when James assumed the throne of England upon the death of the Virgin Queen, Elizabeth I. This year was the first Twelfth Night when he was old enough to be fully included in the festivities, so he had worked out a compromise with his parents. He would be allowed to take on the part of a "commoner" and enjoy the celebrating for one hour. He felt no threat in playing a role other than heir apparent. For all of his sixteen years, first as the younger brother of the next King and, for the last two years, as the future King himself, Charles, who would be the first of that name, felt completely secure in his right to the throne. He knew that nothing under God's sky could ever change the fact that would be King of Scotland and England, after his father, for as long as he lived. Thus is the arrogance of youth.

The young King of the Bean caused a small scandal by choosing a young lady for his Queen who was thought to be promised to another man. During the hubbub following this announcement, the Queen surrendered her throne and indicated that all the others on the platform, including Pocahontas, should follow her. The royal entourage having left the festivities, the party degenerated into a typical Twelfth Night debauch.

The Queen stopped in the hallway after leaving the hall and motioned for Pocahontas to approach. Then she motioned to a lady in waiting to bring forth a gift. The gift was a German stoneware jug with a silver rim. The quality of the gift was inferior to that which the Queen would usually give a visiting Princess, but she did present it with her own hands and Pocahontas thought it quite the most beautiful thing she had ever seen.

The Queen then indicated that the lady in waiting should escort Pocahontas to her husband. He was waiting for her, their cloaks were brought to them and their carriage was called. The party had been at the palace of the Bishop, which was only a short way up Ludgate Hill from the Belle Sauvage Inn, but royalty did not walk the lanes of London, even for a few blocks. Once in their carriage, Rebecca showed him the jug.

"Look, John, the Queen herself gave me this gift. Is it not lovely?"

"Indeed it is, wife. A fine gift. I must ask Sir Lewis if we need to send one in return."

"Yes, please, I would not want to offend her. She was very gracious tonight. The bright lights tonight, they sounded like guns but the lights were so bright and colorful. What is the name of these lights?"

"They come from the Far East, from Cathay, and are called fireworks. Normally, they are sent into the night sky where the lights appear even brighter. Perhaps there will be another festival when the weather is warmer and you will see that spectacle."

"That I would very much like to see, my husband. Very much...,"and the exhaustion of the overwhelming evening overcame her and she dropped off to sleep.

Whenever she could, Pocahontas brought up the idea of leaving the city and finding a place to stay in a forest. Rolfe made inquiries and found that they could stay at Brentford, a house a short distance west of London, directly across the river Brent from an estate of the Earl of Northumberland, Pocahontas' jeweler in the Tower. He may have made the arrangements at the request of Raleigh who was grateful for Rolfe's ingenuity in growing English tobacco or he may have done it simply as a favor to the lady who had allowed him the pleasure of useful work during his imprisonment.

The timing of their move was fortuitous since the cold and rain of deep winter had not yet come to London. Two of the Indian women who had been ill and one of the warriors had already died of lung illness. Staying in the ugly, dirty, smelly, disease ridden city with the bad air and fogs of winter would threaten the lives of all those who had no experience with such conditions.

Just before they left, a young man, just twenty-one, as was Rebecca, was engaged to do her portrait. This would not be a painting but rather an engraving. He had just made a similar engraving of John Smith. This tie again reminded her that John Smith had made no attempt to contact her in the months she had been in England. She was insulted and hurt. The engraving showed her strength of character and, at he insistence, showed her heritage clearly, but the woman in the portrait was not happy.

The winter passed. It had been warm but damp and windy. Everyone had colds and some catarrh. Rebecca developed a cough in the cool, damp stone house, but as the spring came on, the cough lessened. One day in March, John Smith finally made his way the nine miles to Brentford. He did not have the heart to come alone; he brought several friends for moral support. His visit was unannounced and Rebecca herself opened the door.

Neither spoke. Rebecca clung to the edge of the door for support. She thought briefly of slamming the door in his face when one of his companions, thinking she was a servant, said, "Good morrow, is the Lady Rebecca at home?"

"Indeed, sir, she is. I am the Lady Rebecca Rolfe."

"I beg your pardon, my lady, I had no idea. Please accept my apologies."

Then to John, "Smith, perhaps you will introduce us?"

She was giving Smith and the group a civil but cool greeting when Rolfe joined her. He touched her elbow gently and the contact broke the shell of her resolve. She covered her face with her hands and would talk no further. Rolfe accepted the introductions and, to give Rebecca time to collect herself, he invited Smith and the group to see the gardens. After a short while, the two broke off from Smith's friends and walked together.

"I have heard so much about you, Captain Smith, it is good to meet you."

"Your reputation precedes you as well, Master Rolfe. I have tried your tobacco and think as highly of it as the rest of London. Well done, sir."

"Thank you, but I would say that finding your way to a new world and founding a colony is a good deal more important that procuring a few seeds and pulling in a crop. I arrived shortly after you left Jamestown and many who knew you wished you had stayed to help them through that terrible winter of 1609. Did you know that only thirty-eight men survived?"

"I must tell you that no one had the courtesy to give me word directly of any of the events at Jamestown, however, I have my sources and I did hear that number. Do you know who those thirty-eight were and how many still live? I called many of those men friend."

"I am sorry that I cannot give a full accounting. I do know some, however. One is tending my farms while I am here, Josiah Tucker."

"Josiah! I knew he would make something of himself someday. I recommend him to you, Master Rolfe."

"Agree with you. He is a fine lad. He married just before we left. Let me think, he has a number of compatriots who he calls "the squad." He has brought some to work on my land at Henrico, but others are apprenticed in Jamestown."

Rolfe continued listing the squad, Davis, Dods, Herd, Fenton, Thomas and William Cassen, Nate Peacock and James Brumfield, and added the names of Robert Beheathland, William Spencer, and Nathaniel Powell. He mentioned William Ward and Thomas Hope. Smith said those two men had actually come on the December supply, though he was glad to know they were still alive. After about a dozen names Rolfe ran out. Smith, of course, knew Percy, Martin, and Thomas Savage had survived what was already being called "the Starving Time" which meant he could identify almost half of the thirty-eight. Rolfe promised to check into the matter and send Smith a full accounting when he returned to Virginia.

They talked of the Indians, farming, expansion of the settlements, Powhatan, and tobacco. Smith told Rolfe of his dream of returning to America and promised to send him a copy of his recently published book on his adventures there. Rolfe mentioned that he had begun his own treatise on life in Jamestown. He was calling it *A True Relation of the State of Virginia* and intended to dedicate it to William Herbert, Earl of Pembroke, who had sent word that he appreciated Rolfe's variety of tobacco. It was a few hours later that Rebecca joined them in the parlor of Brentford.

She had collected herself but did not trust that she would not break out and reveal her anger and hurt, so she assumed the demeanor of a princess. She was exactly correct in the level of formality, every inch the daughter of the king.

"Captain Smith, my brother and father, it is kind of you to come all this distance to see my husband and I. Thank you for bringing your companions as well."

She paused expecting the proper reply. Smith did not have the courtly instincts of this Virginia bred native, but he did have the self-preservation instincts of a successful soldier. He defended himself against the meaning of her words rather than the text.

"I have been indisposed until lately and my friends wished to meet the famous Princess Pocahontas. I fear they will not understand why you call me father as I am not your father, nor truly your brother."

"You are my brother and father, whether this embarrasses you in front of your friends or not, I will call you so." In one of her first attempts at sarcasm in English, she asked, "Tell me, have you been alive all these years? Many ships have come from England to Jamestown, but you have sent no word to Chief Powhatan to tell him you are well. He has thought you dead, you who are his son and weroance. Why have you hurt him so? Why would you deceive him so?"

"My intention was not to deceive or hurt the great Powhatan. I did not know he thought me dead. Who told him this thing?"

"Archer, Martin, Newport, Percy, all of those who were in charge after you left. Each told him you were dead. It will please him to know you are alive. Now I read your English. Now you can write news to him and I will read your letter. Now we are countrymen, you and I, both English."

Having vented her fright, sadness and anger, the lady became quiet again. She stayed with the group, but the men took up the conversation. The visit lasted only a short while more. Smith never contacted Pocahontas or Rolfe again.

As spring came into full bloom, John began planning their trip home. Pocahontas wanted to stay in England in the country house where she had been happy with her English life, living in an English home with her English husband and raising her English child. The lecture, disguised as after dinner conversation, at the Bishop's house had frightened her. She knew that if she returned to Jamestown, she would be expected to betray her father and his people. She would be expected to convince them to give up their god, their way, their very Indian-ness. If she did, her first people would hate her. If she did not, the English would hate her. Either way she would be caught in the middle and her fine English life would become a constant sadness.

John, on the other hand, wanted to get back to Jamestown as quickly as possible. He had been made Secretary to the new governor of the colony, Captain Samuel Argall. As the date to depart approached, the tension began to take its toll on Rebecca's health. She was weak and coughed frequently. Little Thomas was showing signs of chronic illness too. But either John did not notice how his family was failing or else he thought getting back to Virginia would be the best thing for them all. He forged ahead with his plans and on May 19, 1617, they embarked on an open barge to travel the twenty-five miles down the Thames to Gravesend where Argall waited on his ship the *George*.

Even in May, a twenty-five mile journey in the wind and spray of an open barge is uncomfortable, especially for a woman and child who are already ill. As the hours passed, she became sicker and when they reached Gravesend, she could bear it no longer and asked to be taken ashore rather than to board the ship.

She was so weak that she could not walk. John attempted to pick her up, but Tomocomo intervened. He indicated that Rolfe should take the child and that he, Tomocomo, would take the Princess. With ceremony and great deference, he picked her up as if she were light as a fawn and walked in a slow and stately manner to an inn where he placed her gently on the bed in the best room. Then he went and stood outside the door of the room as a sentry.

John, holding Thomas, went to her side and reached down to brush her hair off of her face. When he touched her skin, he recoiled at the heat, and Thomas cried in response. The goodwife of the Inn had entered the room with a basin of water and a cloth. She had raised many children and had instantly recognized the flush of a high fever. John dithered for a moment, not knowing whether he should tend his wife and have the goodwife tend to Thomas or the other way around. The Goodwife stood impatiently waiting to be allowed to minister to her guest. She knew that with raging fever, minutes could count.

Finally, Rolfe said, "Please do what you can for my wife. Is there a doctor in this town?"

"There is, though he is not always available depending on how long the party lasted the night before, but if you tell my man you want the doctor, he will send for him."

"Yes, good, I will do that." Still John shuffled around the room at a loss as to what to do at that moment. A strong whimper from the bundle in his arms brought him around and he hurried to find the innkeeper.

The goodwife addressed Pocahontas, "Lady, lady, do you hear me?"

Pocahontas rolled her head back and forth on the pillow and muttered incomprehensibly. The goodwife shook her head sadly. She had seen this before and the outlook was grim.

John did find the innkeeper. He was hovering over a man slumped in the far corner of the taproom. John demanded his attention.

"Innkeeper. Your wife said you could send for the doctor. My wife is desperately ill and my boy is fevered too. Please send for the doctor at once."

"No use to send for him, sir."

"Why, on earth, not?"

"This is the doctor. Wake up, you old sot!" he yelled at the slumped figure.

Rolfe had reached a dead end. He returned to the room and met the goodwife as she was leaving to get more cool water.

"How is she?" he asked quietly.

"Not good, sir. She babbles in a language I have never heard. She is delirious. The fever is very high and if we do not bring it down soon, I fear the worst." And she rushed on.

John was dumbfounded. She had said she was not well. She had said she wanted to stay. But he had charged onward and now here she lay in a strange inn, delirious, maybe dying. He crept into the room and put Thomas down on the bed. The little boy curled up in a spot near the foot of the bed. Rolfe put a knit coverlet over him. He was asleep in minutes.

When the goodwife returned with fresh water, having left orders for more to brought to the room every half hour, she loosened the fasteners on Rebecca's clothing and instructed John in the best places to bathe her with the cool water. As he stroked her neck, forehead and wrists with the cloth, she swung between being unconscious and babbling in her native tongue. Tomocomo had not left his post outside the door. During one rather louder run of words, he stepped inside the door. He knew some English and he asked Rolfe, "Do you understand her?"

"No, very little. Do you?"

"Most. She speaks of forests and warm days, of happy times and of you. She is ready to go to Okee."

Rolfe's first reaction was to chastise the warrior for presuming she would revert to the old god, but he caught himself. Perhaps Tomocomo was mistaken and she called out to Christ or perhaps in her fever dreams, she was only a child again. She was not responsible for what she was saying and he was grateful to Tomocomo for volunteering to translate. Then it hit him that she was preparing to go to her Maker. He was loosing her. And he started to sob. With tears in his eyes, he turned to look at the tall, straight, strong brave and saw tears there too.

He kept vigil at the bedside of his family all night. There was no improvement. With the dawn, she seemed quieter, hopefully better. Thomas had slept well and, though he was not lively in the morning, he was at least interested in going with the goodwife to find his breakfast. Shortly after the little boy left the room, Pocahontas, favored daughter of the great chief Powhatan, sighed, smiled a bit and breathed her last.

Tomocomo, took matters in hand and went to fetch the goodwife saying merely, "You come." She took in the situation in one look. She gave John a few minutes to say his farewells and then ushered him out of the room assuring him that she would do all that was needful to prepare his wife. She instructed him to go to St. George Church and tell the pastor what had happened. John was grateful to be moving and to have something purposeful to do. As he stepped out of the inn, a cabin boy approached him and said that Captain Argall had sent him to await word of the Lady. John said simply, "Tell Captain Argall that the princess is dead."

The funeral was held the following day. St. George Church did well by the princess from the new world. There was a high Anglican service, well attended, by Captain Argall and everyone of note in the neighborhood. She was buried in the chancel under a stone slab as befit a royal personage. The inscription, which was added a short time later, read, "Rebecca Wrothe wyff of Thomas Wrothe gent. A Virginia lady borne, here was buried in ye Chauncell." How they confused the Christian name of John Rolfe and his son Thomas was a mystery. The same confusion extended to the church register that read, "– today buried Rebecca Wolfe, wiff of Thomas Wolfe, gent. A lady of Virginia."

CHAPTER 16
Growing Real Gold

The ship *George* had already been at Gravesend almost nine weeks. Argall's first mate had brought it there on January 18th. After the funeral, Ralph Hamor re-provisioned the ship while Argall helped his new secretary arrange his affairs. Thomas was not as ill as his mother, but John feared for his health, so he asked his brother Henry to let Thomas foster with him for a time. Henry was not able to come right away. Argall waited for two weeks and finally asked Rolfe to prepare to depart.

Rolfe carried Thomas aboard the *George*. John walked to the bow port rail. He stared at the inn where he had last spoken with his wife. He gazed up the Thames envisioning Brentford house where his family had been healthy and happy. He consciously captured each memory and locked them in his heart. Then, putting this tragedy behind him, he turned and watched as the ship moved down the river and toward America.

On April 10, the *George* met the *Treasurer* at the port of Plymouth. Thomas' health had not improved, so Rolfe put his still-ailing son in the charge of Sir Lewis Stuckley until Uncle Henry could come for him. A pinnacle, captained by the ever-present John Martin, would accompany the *George* to Jamestown.

To distract himself from the loss of both members of his family, Rolfe threw himself into his work. He wrote a letter to Sir Edwin Sandys, the Earl of Southampton and the Treasurer of the Virginia Company, to tell him about the death of Rebecca. He called Sandys "father to me, my wife and child." He wrote again to tell Sandys his view of the status of Jamestown. He wrote letters to the council of the Virginia Company, all of which he would send back to England with the next vessel leaving Jamestown. Rolfe mentioned these letters to Argall and the Captain became uneasy and suspicious that Rolfe would have a personal relationship with the powerful Sandys. At that moment, a small fear that Rolfe might report negatively on Argall was planted.

Argall sailed by his new shorter northern route and was in Cape Cod in four weeks. It was six days from there to Point Comfort and another day up to Jamestown. May of 1617 was another amazing season. Anyone arriving in Virginia in May would think they had found paradise. May had seduced the original settlers and it was equally intoxicating to those on the *George* and *Treasurer*.

When Dale sailed for England, he left the colony in good shape and appointed George Yeardley as Deputy Governor. Yeardley was determined to give the Virginia Company the largest profit it had seen yet. The Company had allowed free men to be granted their own land since 1614. As the price for tobacco rose, more men requested more land. Yeardley's focus and the accelerating price of tobacco encouraged the colonists to neglect everything but their tobacco crop. This left them dependent on the natives for food just as they had been in the first years.

The Chickahominie had been valued friends since the time of the Rolfe's marriage. Yeardley realized that the concentration on tobacco meant that the corn needed to survive had to come from somewhere, so, for the first time since the treaty was signed, he demanded the elders provide the agreed corn tribute. The elders sent a return message to Yeardley that they would send nothing and that he would have to come and get the corn if he dared. He went with a hundred men who killed a dozen braves and took a dozen more as prisoners including two of the eight elders. They were striped of their badges of loyalty and pushed into boats along with the allotted corn tribute and more. One boat capsized losing the looted grain and drowning eleven including some of the prisoners.

Yeardley treated two of the prisoners in a way that made them assume they had been adopted. He trained them to shoot muskets and be bird hunters for the colony. To get food during the tobacco mania, the settlers ate the livestock. When Dale left there were 144 cattle. Within a year, the number was down to 16 and few were having calves. The goat heard was reduced from 216 to only 88. Even with the help of the braves and easy fishing, the colony was on the verge of being at risk of starvation again.

The answer seemed to be to leave the island. With the Indians at bay, the settlers seriously moved to the mainland, parceling out farm lots and planting more tobacco. Knowing they were expected to provide for themselves on their own farmsteads, they did plant gardens and some corn.

At its peak, James Fort had fifty houses and over 200 people. A year after Dale left, there were only five or six houses occupied and the fort's defenses had deteriorated to nearly nothing.

The Jamestown Rolfe left was not the Jamestown he now saw. Yeardley, devoted to profit for the Company, had promoted planting only tobacco. Tobacco plants were everywhere, in front yards, in the cornfields, even in the streets of the fort.

The Deputy Governor Yeardley had been given notice by his sentries of the arrival of the non-cargo ship, so he assembled a court of guard to meet these dignitaries. An armed Indian led the right hand line. Argall was most upset at seeing, not just one, but many Indians armed in and around the fort. He knew through John Martin that Smith, whose views Argall admired, had never allowed any native to have guns or tempered blades.

Argall took in the state of the community. He walked all over the island, crossed over to the mainland, and talked to everyone he could. He made note that there were only half a dozen usable houses, the piers of the bridge had no cover and were beginning to rot, part of the palisades were down, the first well was no longer usable, the church had been damaged in a storm and had not been repaired, and everywhere there was a foot of ground, there was a tobacco plant. Then he went in search of Yeardley.

"I have been looking around the settlement, Mister Yeardley. I see a large crop of tobacco, but little else. Where are the food crops for this year? And why am I seeing Indians with guns?"

"It is all about profit, Captain. Tobacco is better than gold, and the company wants all it can get. I brought in the friendly braves to hunt for us while we tend the tobacco. We will be able to get all the corn we need from those tribes too."

"An interesting approach, Mister Yeardley. Were you informed that I would be coming?"

"No, I was pleasantly surprised to see you."

"Actually, I have been sent as Governor and I have some very specific instructions which will change things somewhat. "

Yeardley looked shocked. He stared for a moment, then his eyes darted around the room as if to evaluate the effort it would take to move from the Governor's residence. Argall, a very observant man, noticed.

"No need to think of relocating just yet. I will be staying onboard the *Treasurer*. I will be visiting all the settlements, so let us leave things as they are for now. I will announce my role presently."

True to his word, Argall sent word to all those who were within a half a day's walk of the fort to attend him. The settlers gathered about noon on his third day in the colony. He announced that he was taking over the Governorship from Yeardley. At first, he seemed to be a godsend.

As commissioned, Argall divided the land into plantations. There were only fifty people living on the island itself when he arrived. Most were elsewhere in James City, Bermuda City, Henrico, and Kecoughton. He was personally granted 2400 acres on Mar 20 (just as he sailed) at Paspahegh, which became called Argall's Gift.

Argall mitigated some of Dale's harsh laws, but not all. He pardoned some men who would have been executed. He commissioned able men rather than only those of rank. He laid out good timing for voyages and he and Rolfe documented the effective handling of tobacco. Lessening some of the severe punishments and making what had been exclusive knowledge available to all planters were all steps in the direction of a more egalitarian society.

But though he showed republican tendencies, Argall was at heart a soldier and dedicated to performance of his duty to the council of the Virginia Company, as he saw it. One of those duties was to subdue the Indians in one way or the other. To that end, he sent Tomocomo, who had returned with him, to tell Powhatan he was back. Powhatan, however, had gone to stay with the king of another confederation on the Potomac leaving his brother in charge. Tomocomo turned against the English and filled Powhatan's brother, Opechancanough, with anger and doubts about the abilities of these interlopers. Tomocomo particularly poisoned his mind against Thomas Dale who had become a friend to Powhatan.

Argall heard of this and took it upon himself to speak with Opechancanough to counter Tomocomo's influence. He visited his village and testified against the words of Tomocomo to the chief and his councilors. They believed Argall, leaving Tomocomo in disgrace. Having established his credentials, Argall felt safe in informing the tribe of the death of Pocahontas. Death brought the same sadness to all men, Indian, Christian, city-bound or forest dwelling. Opechancanough said he would get word to his brother Powhatan. The news that her son was alive, though in England, brought some relief to the sorrow of her death.

After many actions in the direction of liberalizing the colony, Argall began to show another side of his character. He became concerned with having more consistent attendance at church and eventually made it a crime to miss Sunday services more than twice. To this end of strengthening the Christian center of the colony, on June 9th, Argall wrote that spiritual leadership in the colony was at a low ebb. Reverend Buck was on leave and Pocahontas' mentor Reverend Whitaker had accidentally drowned. Argall asked Sir Dudley Digges to find a bishop who would give Master Wickham, then filling in as minister to the settlers basic needs, the power to administer the sacrament. This required a special dispensation since Wickham was not ordained.

In the same letter he asked that De La Warr appoint a different Governor, or at best, to return himself. Argall was an excellent ship's captain, but the strain of managing the entire far-flung colony and the international relations with the Indians seemed to be wearing on Argall from the first.

Powhatan was aging. Smith and Percy had estimated his age in 1607 at sixty or more. Eleven years later, he had attained the age at which death would be expected if not welcomed. Powhatan chose to take one last tour of the lands he had united in his lifetime. Travel was fairly easy in the winter months except during snowstorms. The ground along the forest paths was not frozen, but neither was it muddy. The waterways were at normal depth, not raging as they could be in the spring. So Powhatan and a small retinue struck out from his village on the Pamunkey River to go on a tour.

He stayed with each major village for a day or two, being entertained by the weroance. A part of this tour was to reconfirm these men in their positions as tribal leaders. Powhatan knew that when he died, there could be power struggles that could undo much of the unification he had managed. To forestall such deterioration as much as he could, he renewed his commissions to these chiefs and spoke to them of maintaining the confederation for their common good. After several weeks of travel, Powhatan was tired, more tired than he had felt in memory. He cut his tour short and returned to his main camp.

On a day in March that promised the coming of spring, Powhatan did not awake. The most powerful chief of the Southeastern tribes was no more.

Argall heard of his death from Indians who had come to the fort to trade. Not knowing what direction Powhatan's successor would take, Argall took the precaution of banning all trade with Indians and closing Jamestown Island to them.

Whether it was specifically due to curtailing contact with the Indians or whether Argall simply had enemies in the colony, someone had been sending messages to London accusing Argall of being dictatorial toward both the colonists and Indians and that he was making choices to line his own pockets, not the coffers of the Company. The quicksilver council of the Virginia Company chose to believe the negative reports rather than the positive ones sent by John Rolfe and made plans to replace their choice of only the year before.

One of those sending bad news back to England might have been the man Argall replaced, George Yeardley. He felt he had done a very good job in his short tenure, meeting the company's demands and pleasing the colonists, a combination no one had achieved since John Smith. No word had been sent with Argall that the Company was displeased with his work. On the other hand, there had been no word at all from the Virginia Company to George Yeardley. It was as if he had not existed as a Governor, deputy or not.

In spite of being disgruntled about his treatment by the Company, Yeardley moved on with his personal life. A lovely lady with the improbable name of Temperance Flowerdew had come to Jamestown with one of the early supplies. She had survived the Starving Time and had made a place for herself as a single woman for many years. When Yeardley arrived, he had taken note of this independent lady. Over the months, he courted her. They made plans to marry and to be the ranking couple of the Virginia Colony. They decided the political setback would not interfere with their marriage.

The plans for a grand wedding were scaled back. There was a simple ceremony in the Jamestown church with only a few close friends. The newlyweds took up residence in a home Temperance had built on land she had acquired about twenty miles up the James River. His marriage brought him the thousand acres belonging to his wife. Independently, he acquired 2200 acres at Weyanoke Point. He now had a large personal investment in the prosperity of the colony.

John Rolfe was very busy being secretary to the colony. With both Governor Argall and Deputy Governor Ralph Hamor to handle the business of the colony, Rolfe had thought his duties would be limited to occasional reports back to England. He expected he would be able to return to tobacco farming. However, the two men generated a great deal of correspondence and demanded a daily journal be kept. For example, on June 8, 1617, Rolfe's daily report include a passage to help gather Company support for more clothing supplies. He spoke of "All men cheerfully labor, though many have scarcely rags to cover their naked bodies." On the very next day's entry, he wrote about the condition of the fort, but he did not mention anything about the dilapidated fort or the overplanting of tobacco.

John found himself unable to go to Henrico. He visited his fields in Jamestown only once in the first two weeks home. Clearly, he still needed his foreman, Josiah.

A week later, Josiah came for his monthly visit to Jamestown. As soon as he landed, he heard that Rolfe had returned, but without his wife and son. He made a quick tour of the fields and checked with his men who tended them. All was well. Then he went to the statehouse building to find John.

"Master Rolfe, it is good to see you. I have just come from your Jamestown fields and the crop is drying well. I believe we will have an extraordinarily large yield this year."

"Greetings, Josiah. I was able to go by the property last week and saw what you have reported. You have done very well, Josiah, very well indeed. I received word of the excellent shipment you sent last year too. I am very pleased with your work.

I think we have a long future together, if you are interested. But first, tell me everything I have missed."

"Two years is a long time, sir, but I will do my best to remember.

First, let me tell you of my own history. Bridget and I have had such a blessed life in your home. We have had two lovely children. Our daughter Hannah was born just a year after you left and our new son John is now only a month old."

"John, you named your son John?'

"Yes, sir, we proudly named him for you. I hope you are pleased."

"Pleased, yes certainly, and honored. When he is christened, may I be among his godfathers?"

"We had planned on that. We hoped you would return soon enough, but if you had not, we would have had someone stand proxy. You, sir, have been central to our happiness. We owe you everything."

"Josiah, we have a good partnership. I may have been in a position to get you started, but you have certainly done your part. Let us hear no more of this. Pray, continue your tale."

Josiah told him of the planting, drying and shipping. He gave a rough accounting of the profits and offered to bring a detailed report on his next visit. He told of Yeardley's program of growing tobacco on all available land and of his having to defend Rolfe's land against poachers.

"We had prepared all the fields for last year's planting. You know you have to make a special effort to go to the outlying fields and no one had been there since the preparation work. A few days before we were going to plant that field, Nate went out first to see that everything was ready. As he approached, he heard men talking. He hid and watched as some planted the field and others were constructing a wall. I gathered the men and went to reclaim the field.

There was a battle and one of the poachers was mortally wounded and two of my men were also injured. We ran off the poachers and I posted a guard on that field until we cut the leaves. We brought those leaves into the barn to dry. We got an unusually good yield from that cutting."

That unintentional use of the barn for drying sparked an idea with John Rolfe. He instructed Josiah to move half of the current crop into barns to see if the yield would increase again.

Josiah returned to his tale of the next year, 1617. Josiah told of the smallpox epidemic that had hit both the Indians and the settlers. So many died. Besides the little graveyard inside the fort, there were now three hundred graves in a cemetery on the island about seven hundred feet from the fort wall.

More died from an illness that killed the deer. Some deer were taken and used for food before the illness was discovered. Those who ate the poisoned deer became ill and some died. Once the illness was identified, deer was off the list of available provisions and that reduced the meat intake of the settlers. Since none of the English had been growing corn and the corn crop at the Indian villages were much reduced due to the epidemic, the absence of venison made starvation a real threat once again.

Josiah explained that he had not joined the stampede to plant only tobacco. He had continued to plant enough acres in food to feed all of those who worked on Rolfe's land, so the famine did not affect them. Josiah explained that he had to bring supplies to his Jamestown people in secret so that no one would steal the food or expect it to be shared. Since their workers were better fed, the crop was well tended and the shipment about to go to England would be among the only first quality leaves of the season. Rolfe could demand a premium price.

"I have talked with the few others who have quality crops this year," said Josiah, "and we have been thinking about joining our shipments under one name. That way, this year, only the leaves under our common name would be recognized as top quality. What do you think?"

"That is a clever idea. Do you think we could ask a higher price?"

"We hope so. Part of this crop belongs to the Company, but the rest belongs to each planter. Since we took greater care with our tobacco, we feel we deserve a better price. But, no one was certain if we could set the price or if the Company Council controls that."

"I will talk to Governor Argall. There is little point in letting men farm for themselves if their hard work does not result in a good profit."

After more discussion, the planters decided to export their portion of the crop together under the label of simply, Jamestown. They had lead tags made to label each hogshead. The blacksmith who made the tags did not read well and he mistakenly used a Y instead of a J, so the tags actually said Yamestowne.

Former Deputy Governor Yeardley, having settled all the deeds to his lands, prepared to leave Virginia. What he saw as the ingratitude of the Company ate at him until he felt he had to return to England to see to his reputation. He and his bride quietly left in the fall.

That fall John Rolfe also married. Eight years before, a child named Jane Pierce had accompanied her parents on the Third Supply. She and her mother, also Jane, arrived safely but her father had been with John Rolfe on the ill-fated *Sea Venture* that ran aground in Bermuda. John and Jane's father, William, had stayed close over the years. John did not confide in Josiah whether his proposal to young Jane, now nineteen, was one of caring and convenience or real love. In a small colony, having your only daughter married to a successful planter and member of the ruling class would be a good match. Perhaps Mother Jane wanted to see her daughter well settled. Perhaps young Jane had fallen in love with the one man of whom her father approved. Perhaps it was mutual. Whatever the case, John and Jane were married in the church at Jamestown and took up residence in the Statehouse with a second home at Henrico.

Winter brought yet another change to the colony when the Virginia Company chose to support a new sentiment in London. Social reformers and judges in the overcrowded city thought transporting convicts to the new world would relieve the pressure on the penal system and give the prisoners a life outside farming rather than walled up in dank cells. Just before Christmas that year, London magistrates put a ship full of men who had committed minor crimes that carried large sentences to Virginia. This was only the beginning of a pattern that would continue for centuries.

Argall had enemies in London and Jamestown. Letters to the Virginia Company Council continued and charged him with everything from being too lenient to being too harsh. They claimed he favored the natives and that he was cruel to them. The smear campaigned was fierce and a man named Brewster was particularly vitriolic. It was true that Argall had made an edict that anyone who missed church would be jailed, but this was an extension of a long-standing custom in England that a man who did not attend church at least once a month would be fined.

Governor for life De La Warr heard of Argall's tactics and the resulting state of Jamestown's morale and decided to return as Argall had suggested some month before. Just before leaving England, De La Warr had a dream in which he sailed up to the loading dock that had been built and stepped off his ship directly onto solid footing.

He stocked a ship intending to make Virginia his home. His wife, the lovely lady who had hosted Pocahontas in England, emigrated with him. The trip was uneventful but midway across the Atlantic, De La Warr suddenly died. They were closer to America than Europe, so it was decided that his body would be preserved with salt for the rest of the trip to Jamestown.

When his ship dropped anchor, his dream of walking proudly onto the dock of Jamestown was not to be. There was no place to step out. The dock had fallen in and all that remained were the posts that were rotting in the sun. De La Warr's widow came ashore in a small boat to the same spot where Gosnold and Smith had landed eleven years before.

The widow De La Warr went directly to the fort and identified the statehouse building by the two guards at the door. She first encountered Ralph Hamor and asked for the Governor. He apologized and said that Argall was out on a short expedition but was expected back in a day or two. Lady De La Warr stoically told of her husband's death. Before she could say more, Hamor offered to take complete charge of the situation, to lay the body in state, and to arrange for their earliest return to England. The lady smiled slightly appreciating the care and efficiency of this man in such a primitive place.

He offered her the Governor's quarters for her use as long as she was in Jamestown, which she accepted as her due. "Master Hamor, perhaps you are not aware that my late husband had these quarters built, in fact this entire statehouse. He has described them to me many times and I am sure I will feel very much at home in them."

Hamor called a guard in and ordered that Argall's personal belongings be moved immediately to another room in the statehouse and that Lady Argall's things be brought from the ship. Then he offered her tea and they sat in the Governor's office talking of small things to pass the time.

Lady De La Warr, feeling she should take her husband's place, inquired about the state of the fort. "We expected a fine dock as a landing but we found rotting piers. What has happened here?"

"I apologize, my Lady. When Governor Argall and I arrived, the entire settlement had been given over to the planting of tobacco. All else had been left to ruin. We are just now getting the buildings back into reasonable repair and have not yet dealt with the landing."

"So, I suppose Governor Argall's expedition is in support of these repairs?"

Now Hamor was stuck. Argall traveled because Argall liked to travel. He often returned having built up good will with neighboring tribes or with provisions, but none of that directly helped refurbish the settlement. He had not actually given orders as to what should be done and the men continued to grow their tobacco knowing that was their only cash crop. Hamor had been working on a plan to engage men in the repairs needed and in expanding the community to accommodate new settlers, but he and Rolfe were both administrators, not dynamic leaders, so little had been accomplished.

He did what he could to put a good face on it, but Lady De La Warr was not fooled.

"When the good Governor returns, I will want to have a talk with him on my husband's behalf. When I return to England, I am sure the Company investors will expect a full accounting from me." The threat could not have been more obvious.

Argall returned and Hamor apprised him of Lady De La Warr's interest. Under her watchful eye, Argall spent the next several weeks organizing repair crews. There was not a great need for housing on the island, but the public buildings were put in good repair and by the time she left, there was a partially rebuilt dock from which she could board her ship.

The body of Lord De La Warr had been secluded for some days until the salt had had its full effect. Once the body was dried out and no longer had a strong odor, the coffin was set on a bier in a room of the statehouse and guarded by two men night and day as was befitting the Governor for Life of this colony. When it came time to carry the coffin to the ship, it was done with as full military honors as Argall, an old soldier, could manage. There were cadenced drums and keening fifes and every gun that could be found was shot off as a salute. Not since the burial of Bartholomew Gosnold had their been such a ceremony.

In spite of the fact that the Governor himself was dead, the visit of the De La Warrs had brought much greater order to the settlement. Argall was still Governor, but he understood from lady De La Warr's opinions that he would not be in that position for long.

As a reward for Josiah's excellent stewardship, Rolfe now offered Josiah 100 acres of his own site at Jordan's Journey near Henrico.

Grants of land were ostensibly done through the Governor. Since Powhatan had offered this land, Rolfe thought it would be a good idea to file a paper with the Governor declaring Josiah's right to it. Rolfe had finally made a trip to Henrico so Rolfe and Josiah rode down to Jamestown together on a barge that often ran between Jamestown and Henrico, stopping along the way at other townships and marked spots as a sort of public transport for people and goods.

When they reached the Statehouse, Rolfe went to his secretary's desk and wrote out a deed for the land near Henrico. Governor Argall had put his Deputy, Rolfe's old friend Ralph Hamor, in charge of filing the land grants. John took the paper to Hamor whose office space was in another part of the Statehouse.

"Hello, Ralph."

"Ah, John, welcome back. How are things in Henrico?"

"Very good, Ralph, very good indeed and my good fortune is in great part due to this young man, my foreman, Josiah Tucker."

Hamor stood and bowed slightly to Josiah who returned the courtesy.

"In fact, I am giving Master Tucker some of my land. Here is a deed of transfer for the land adjacent to mine in Henrico." He handed Hamor the paper.

"Next to you, you say. West or east?"

"West," said Rolfe looking proudly at his protégé.

"Just a moment ... I seem to recall another claim on that land." Hamor went to a shelf and pulled down a roll of papers. He turned them over slowly and when he got to the third one, he stopped and looked at Rolfe with a combination of regret and embarrassment.

"Here it is, John. Just last month a gentleman, a George Warrington, filed a grant from Governor Yeardley. Odd, I wonder why he would wait to file it. Yeardley has been out of office for months. I had not really studied the details of this. There has never been a question of any land granted by a Governor before."

"There is certainly something odd here, Ralph, and I am going to get to the bottom of it right now. Is the Governor in?"

"He was out and about. I will send a runner to find him."

Hamor shouted, "Charles!" and a tow-headed boy of about seven popped his head around the doorframe. "Find the Governor, boy, and tell him we need him here as soon as possible."

The boy's head disappeared and the sound of bare feet running on a wood floor took its place.

Not more than ten minutes later, the bare feet sounded again. The boy stood in the doorway and said, "He is coming, sir," just as Argall himself entered the room.

Hamor explained the situation. Rolfe added the history of Powhatan and Smith and himself. Argall paced in an open space of ten feet and then stood at the window with his hands clasped behind his back. Hamor, Rolfe and Josiah exchanged puzzled looks. Argall spun on his heel and addressed the three.

"I think what has happened here is plain. Governor Yeardley, in his haste to leave us, accepted this man's request without taking time to check the facts. He was in error. The land is most certainly in your prevue to give to this fine young man. Hamor, throw out ... who is the other man?"

"Warrington, Your Honor."

"Throw out Warrington's grant and record the land as the property of ..."

"Josiah Tucker, Your Honor."

"... Josiah Tucker. Congratulations, young man."

Argall then addressed himself only to Hamor on another topic and Rolfe and Josiah were dismissed without further word.

Bridget and the children were waiting anxiously for Josiah to return. Having their own land meant that she would finally have her own home. She looked around their little cabin and took stock of the few possessions they had. To move to their own home would mean packing three pouches and carrying two chairs Josiah had made. Everything else in the cabin belonged to John Rolfe. She sighed deeply at starting from scratch, but then smiled at the thought of being mistress of her own home. Baby John squirmed in her arms and she could feel the milk rising in her breasts. Addressing her toddler daughter, she said, "Hannah, love, your brother is after wanting his dinner." Hannah pulled her mother toward the better chair and said two of her dozen words, "Eat, momma, eat."

Bridget's vigil had lasted almost long enough for just as she finished feeding John, Josiah appeared at the door. He paused to take in the precious scene of his wife holding his son and his daughter standing with her head on her mother's lap. Bridget's black hair was echoed in both of the children. Hannah had the same curls but Johnny's fluff held the promise of soft waves like his father. The sunlight caught all three bowed heads. It was one of those images he would hold in his memory for life. Josiah walked the few steps to stand in front of her and then knelt and embraced his family in one huge hug.

After a long, lovely minute, he sat on the floor and Hannah crawled onto his lap. Then he told Bridget the story of the other claim on their land and that the Governor had decided against the gentleman and in his favor. The land now belonged to them and Rolfe had given him a fair copy of the deed paper so he would have proof of his ownership in case anyone challenged him.

Then he told Bridget his big surprise.

"Love, I know we planned to build a house and be done by winter, but that is not going to happen."

He saw her delightful lower lip come out into a little pout. He knew he was saying this to first disappoint her so that the good news would be that much more exciting.

"No, we should have the house built in a month."

The pout switched to a broad smile and she exclaimed, "A month! How on earth can we build a house in a month?"

"We are going to have help. John Herd is coming to lay the foundation and build us a fine brick chimney. Rob Fenton is coming to help and then he will be staying on to help work the land. And the two Cassen brothers asked for time off from their jobs to fell the trees and saw the lumber for us."

The news was so overwhelming Bridget did not know how to react, so she did what women have done for all time, she cried. Josiah picked Hannah up in one arm and held Bridget to his strong shoulder with the other. She surrendered herself to the protection of this fine man she had come half way around the world to find. What could be better than this?

True to their word, the five men arrived the following week all piled into a wagon with the saws and tools. Bridget had worried about how she would feed all these hard-working men but as part of their gift, they brought extra provisions. When she had the right ingredients, Bridget was an excellent cook. She enjoyed making meals the men could take with them and eat at the building site. It was too far for them to come back every day, but Rob and Josiah came back every third day to take care of the heavy chores at the Rolfe farm.

Exactly four weeks later, Josiah took Bridget and the children to see the new house. It was positioned on a rise twenty yards behind the earth rampart Smith had constructed giving a clear view of the river and a defensible position. The house had a center door and four windows on the side toward the river. There were two more windows on each of the other sides and a center back door. It was made of tightly fitting sawed logs notched at the corners with a pitched roof of split cedar shingles. There were shutters with z-shaped braces on all the windows.

The floor plan was unusual. The two doors opened into a large room with a large fireplace on the sidewall. The other part of the house was divided into two rooms with paneled doors and molding surrounding them. The front room was to be their private bedroom and the back room would be for the two children. In the back corner of the big room was a permanent staircase that led to a trap door. Under the pitched roof was an open space with a floor that could be used as more sleeping space as the family grew. With the doors and windows open, the breezes kept the house very livable. Herd, the bricklayer, and Cassens, the lumbermen, had used all of their skills for their friend's home. It was a showplace.

Josiah took Bridget back to the Rolfe's place for another week while the men completed the necessary outbuildings. Only Josiah returned to pack up his family and bring them to live in their new home. When he arrived, Bridget had wonderful news of her own. A letter had arrived from John Rolfe carried by the regular barge captain. She could read enough now to be able to tell him that Rolfe had written to say they should take any furnishings they needed with them from the Henrico house, save one table and chairs and one set of bedroom furniture. Since he and Jane were primarily living in Jamestown, they would only be visiting at Henrico and

371

would not need the rest. They would be starting out with a houseful of furniture and goods, as well set up as the richest family in the colony.

While he was gone, the men added a final touch by transplanting one red and one yellow maple tree on the west and south sides of the house. When grown these would give excellent shade in the summer and drop their leaves to allow the warmth of the sun to hit the house in winter. William Cassen made a special contribution by transplanting a small flowering dogwood on one side of the front yard and a redbud on the other side. He also put sprouts of red columbine and purple coneflowers under the front windows. There was no purpose for these spots of color but he knew Mistress Bridget would enjoy them.

The fairytale house became well known in the colony and, after having built a small jetty and dock the following year, the place became known as Fairy Landing.

The Cassens had to go back to work at the sawpit at Jamestown, but John and Rob stayed to prepare the fields for the next year's planting. They made a snug one-room cabin for Rob, also with a brick chimney. John was able to take the barge downriver and as he and Josiah were saying goodbye, Richard Dixon and Nate Peacock, who had been living in Jamestown tending Rolfe's land there, stepped off the barge.

"Woo, woo, woo!" they shouted in unison. The others on the barge stared at this odd behavior as the four men engaged in much backslapping.

Dixon spoke first, as usual, "Josiah, your place is perfect, just perfect."

"That is due to the talents of John, here, and the Cassen brothers and the hard work of Rob Fenton. But surely you did not come all this way to admire my house?"

Nate, no longer the shy youngster from the days of the Squad, teased, "Of course not, we came to see if Bridget has gotten prettier, and to be sure that new heir of yours looks like you." Again there was shoving and backslapping. By this time Rob, Bridget and the children had come out to see what all the commotion was about.

Dixon added, "And we heard you had four hundred acres to plant. Though you could use some help with that. Not now, of course. We will be back in the spring for that. Right now I want to see how much my best girl Hannah has grown." On cue, little Hannah ran to her "Unca Rich" and jumped with abandon trusting he would catch her in midair.

John decided he could stay one more night and the five comrades spent a fine evening eating Bridget's delicious dinner and telling tales of the old days.

Josiah sat comfortably in his own house surrounded by his family and friends. He looked at the little boy sleeping in his mother's arms and thought of the man he would become. He dreamed a bit of that young man extending his land and turning this into a fine plantation, that is, if the boy stayed on the land. And that made him think of his own father.

For all these years, he had not tried to contact his family in England. There had been a brief conversation with William Strachey as he prepared to leave in which Strachey had offered to get word to the Tuckers that Josiah was alive and well, but now Josiah had a compelling urge to tell his father of his life in America, of his children and of his good fortune. One thing he had worried over whether to take from John Rolfe's house was paper, pen and ink. Knowing John typically carried these with him, he had taken them and now he went to locate them and start a letter to his father.

True, his father could not read. That was one reason he had never try to contact him. People left the country all the time to go to war or to work elsewhere or to the cities and they were never heard from again. It was not unusual. He could not write to his father, but he could write to the parish minister and hope that man would take the letter to the farm and read it to the family.

Outside of Josiah's idyllic world, long-planned change that would affect all of Virginia was underway. In 1618, Edwin Sandys and the Earl of Southampton took control of the Virginia Company. Sandys, in particular, was a forward thinking man, a strong supporter of the Parliamentary Party in England that favored a powerful elected government body to advise the king. These men believed in the intelligence and dignity of everyman and spoke out against autocratic rule. Having had reports of Argall's harsh and self-serving methods, they decided to repeat De La Warr's orders and recall him. They also decided to repeal the harsh code under which the colony had been ruled since the leadership of Thomas Dale. Getting control of the Company was only the first step. It would take many months to put their plan completely into action.

The arrival of a ship bearing the body of Lord De La Warr gave increased impetus to their plans. Lady De La Warr sent formal notice of the death of the Governor for Life to the Company Council along with a personal letter to Sir Edwin Sandys of her observations at Jamestown. Then she arranged for her husband's coffin to be taken to the town of Argall, ironically, where a new church was being built. He was buried in the aisle there with all the ceremony due a fallen, noble hero of the realm.

Yeardley had been busy since his return to London. He had courted many of those who were invested heavily in the Virginia Company and particularly Edwin Sandys. Overlooking all the devastating policies of his time as Governor, when Sandys had the opening to appoint a new Governor, he picked Yeardley. To reinforce his status, Sandys worked though some of his contacts at court and arranged for the king to knight Yeardley so he would return to Virginia with a noble rank.

On November 18th, the reappointed Governor, Sir George Yeardley, took four ships and three hundred men and departed for his colony. Among those who went with him were his wife Temperance Flowerdew Yeardley and her cousin, John Pory. Pory was a formally educated man of forty-seven who would serve as Yeardley's secretary. Also with the new Governor went the Great Charter. The Great Charter was to replace all charters and laws that had come before. It named Yeardley as Governor, but only for three years and, most portentously, created an elected General Assembly.

Other changes were afoot. Just three weeks before Yeardley set sail, Raleigh, the "father" of Virginia was beheaded. When he had been released from the Tower of London during Rolfe's visit to England, Sir Walter Raleigh took up some of his old adventurous ways. He returned to the sea traveling to Guiana, South America. Among his other exploits, he attacked a Spanish garrison against orders expressly given by King James. This disrupted peace negotiations between the two rival counties and James came to the end of his tolerance of this larger-than-life figure. Raleigh was tried for treason and taken back to the Tower.

There were many tales of Raleigh's death, but one of the most intriguing was that when the minister and guard came to escort him to the block, he demanded the privilege of one last pipe of tobacco. This was granted and one of the guards had sent out the word that henceforth any prisoner of rank should be offered this privilege. Word also went out that Raleigh specifically requested sweet-leaf tobacco grown by John Rolfe. This one act increased the general demand for Virginia tobacco more than any promotional campaign of the Company.

Raleigh was not the only unreformed adventurer. Governor Argall, knowing he was likely to be replaced, decided to add to his fortune while he could. He commissioned Captain Elfrid to take the *Treasurer* to the Caribbean as privateer. He was supported in this by his friend and partner in England, Sir Robert Rich. This type of free-lance pirating also upset the balance of power between Spain and England and Argall knew it would not be looked upon favorably, so support from a powerful ally at court was essential. Elfrid did well and returned to England with valuable cargo stolen from the Spanish.

Argall thought it best that he go back to England of his own accord rather than wait to be dismissed. Being in London would also let him put his own story forward about the treasure on the *Treasurer* before his detractors put out their versions.

With little fanfare, he left, putting Nathaniel Powell in charge with the various titles of Temporary Governor, Lieutenant Governor, Captain of the Guard and Commander of Jamestown. Powell was among the longest residents of Jamestown having arrived in the first supply of 1607. Anyone who had survived both the famine of 1607 and the Starving Time of 1609 was held in high esteem, so he was a good choice as a man who would have instant credibility with the community.

In fact, the sense of continuity engendered by Powell's leadership along with the influence of more than thirty-five women who were now among the settlers, resulted in some of the quietest time the settlement had enjoyed in years. The women were more interested in making homes as comfortable as in England. In fact, Jane Pierce said that her home was better than any she could have had in England.

That year a distance relative Richard Pierce and his wife Elizabeth arrived on the *Neptune*. The early settlers were told that the Company would provide for their needs, but these later settlers were mostly more wealthy and brought more of their own goods with them. When Jane went to call on her husband's relations, Elizabeth proudly unpacked a large pewter measure, big enough to hold a gallon of ale. Jane showed Richard where the common stores were kept and they filled the measure, closed the lid and started back to the house.

Just outside the front yard, three young boys came dashing out from around the neighboring building and ran right into Jane and Richard. Richard lost hold of the handle and in a heroic juggling act, managed to catch the measure before it hit the ground. Sadly, the lid flew up and the force broke it free. The two were doused with ale and looked much the losers when they appeared at in the doorway sheepishly presenting the damaged measure to Elizabeth.

Eliza, as she was called, was not known for her gentle temperament. She flew into a red rage grabbing the expensive container and the broken lid from her cowering husband. Alternately screaming and sobbing she roared, "Look at that, Cousin Jane, my best measure. And look here, under the thumb lever. I even had our initials engraved, PRE. It is ruined, simply ruined. I do not know why I bothered to pack it so well and get it safely to this New World just to have my fumble-fingered husband destroy it. There is no use in keeping it, no use at all. Might as well throw it in the trash heap." And with that she stormed out of the house and marched around casting for the trash heap. All the trash was put outside the fort palisades so, seeing no trash pile, she chose instead to toss measure, lid, ale and all into the nearby well.

With a few exceptions, like Eliza Pierce, peace and prosperity reigned in Jamestown in the fall of 1618.

CHAPTER 17
A Chink in the Armor

With the new settlers brought by the *Neptune* and other ships, the English population on the James-York peninsula reached 2000, more than the entire native population had been when the first fleet arrived in 1607. The Indians had been driven away from many of their traditional campsites, moving upriver, inland or to a different river. Convicts and slum children were coming with almost every supply. The Virginia Company still sent many goods that could not be made in Virginia, but, with their first crop of wheat in 1618, the colony had become mostly self-sufficient for food. Delicacies like sugar, tea, citrus fruit, and chocolate were imported and would be for centuries. But with having domestic animals and a source of bread, the settlers could now live much as they had in England.

The spring of 1619 brought big changes back home in England. When Yeardley arrived in April, he brought the sad news of the death of Queen Anne. King James had been devoted to his wife and the court was in deep mourning. The court had been in mourning often since seven of the king's nine children had died between being born and the age of sixteen. Only one daughter, Elizabeth, who had married the Elector of the Palatine in Germany, and one son, Charles, who would be the next king, had survived.

There had been further changes in the Virginia Company as well. Sir Edwin Sandys had been appointed as Treasurer, essentially giving him full control over the Company. With his mentor in charge, Yeardley was very secure in his position and had no fear that the sweeping changes he was about to make, at Sandys' direction, would be supported.

Among his first acts was to formally create four political unit or boroughs, named James Town, Charles City, Henrico, and Kiccowtan. He created a parcel called the Governor's land, 3000 acres to be farmed by freed servants with them retaining half the profits and the other half going equally to the Governor and the Virginia Company. The Governor now had substantial and legitimate financial support from the colony.

Then he called for a General Assembly to be held. The Assembly would consist of two delegates from each of the boroughs and two from each granted plantation. The Governor and his council of six would also be part of the Assembly.

Elections for representatives of each James River and Eastern Shore settlement were held. The candidates had to meet specific qualifications: they had to hold at least 100 acres of land, they had to reside in the colony for at least the last three years, they, of course, had to be male, and they had to have received their land from the Virginia Company. How the elections were held was up to each township.

As expected, the largest landowner in each locale was one of the delegates in almost all cases. The second delegate varied. For Henrico, Thomas Dowse was the primary delegate, though Rolfe owned more land, and Josiah's popularity made him the second delegate.

As the elections were held, word of the new Assemblymen's names circulated via the colonial grapevine. The few people who still lived on Jamestown Island took special note of the names. Since the meeting was to be held at the church, the delegates would find it most convenient to find food and lodging on the island. Small cottage industries sprang up to accommodate the Assemblymen and their parties.

Mistress Norton, the former Tomasina Cawsey, who had been widowed in 1617 when her husband died of pneumonia, was the first to send word to each delegate that she would be letting rooms in her two-story home just outside the old fort. Rolfe, seeing the wisdom of having Josiah staying close to the meeting place, immediately reserved a room. Rolfe had not yet shown his bride the property at Henrico. He arranged for some time off from his secretarial duties, now that John Pory was available, and made a visit to Henrico in July, partly as a delayed honeymoon and partly so he and Josiah could travel down river together and have some time to talk about the Assembly.

Jane and Bridget were both expecting before the end of the year. Jane had loved spending time with baby John, practicing for her new role as mother. Hannah had been a bit jealous at first, feeling that she was Johnny's second mother, but the bedtime stories Jane told her won her over completely. Josiah asked about John's son in England.

"Do you hear often of Thomas, John?

"Henry encourages him to write a line at the end of each letter. He actually spelled "Papa" correctly last time. I do miss him so, Josh."

The two men, so different in their beginnings, had become close, even intimate, friends. Neither had a brother or other male relative in the colony, so they became older and younger brothers for each other, much as Smith and Josiah had been.

"Now that you have a wife, will he come to live here, do you think?"

"It is my dearest wish, but I think it best that Jane and I have some time together first and then some time with our little one. Perhaps in a couple of years, before he starts his formal schooling." Picking up the subject of schooling, he continued, "Hannah is a bright child. Will you teach her to read and write? I remember how keen you were to learn."

"I will. I have been teaching Bridget. She has been teaching Hannah her letters already. It is like a drawing game for her, but in a few months it will start to make sense to her. Ann Laydon stopped by last week so her youngest could play with Hannah and the three older girls could spend some time with Bridget on their letters. Do you think it is because I know how to read that the neighbors voted for me? I though for sure one of the largest planters would be the delegate to get the most votes, not Dowse or me."

They wandered off into discussion about experiments in tobacco growing and drying for the next year as they passed Bermuda Hundred and finally got back around to talking of the Assembly just as they came upon Shirley Plantation.

"So two men from each of the four cities and two from each plantation. That should be twenty-four, right, John?"

"That is how I count it, and the six councilmen, including me, and the Governor. That is twenty-four and six and one, eh thirty-one. Do you think we will be voting on anything? I mean, would each man get one vote, even the Governor?"

"John, I am sure you know much more about the workings of a General Assembly than I do." John looked a little embarrassed. "I wish they would have told us more, " Josiah finished, to ease John's discomposure.

"I did see great rolls of paper with formal seals on them spread out on Yeardley's desk. Perhaps it is more of a meeting where he will tell us what instructions the Company has sent."

"If that is so, I hope it is some extension of the 'headright' system. Since it was Captain Smith who paid my fare, I got no part of the 50 acres for anyone who would pay a fare or the 50 additional acres for each person brought with him. The Cap'n would have gotten 100 acres, if he were still here, for himself and me and more for the others he brought. If they asked me what I think should be different, I would say that if you have been here since the beginning, no matter who paid your fare, you should have land of your own."

"Well, now you have 400 acres."

"I do, and I thank you for it, good friend. But did I not tell you that I granted a bit of it to Rob? I have the paper with me now to file to give him fifty acres on the south end of my land." He felt strange calling it "my land" to the man who had given it to him. "That way he can claim the adjoining fifty acres as his headright and be able to vote the next time there is an election."

"Josh, you amaze me with how you think ahead, not just for yourself but for all the men in your old Squad. They still see you as their leader."

"It just comes to me ... to think about the future. And, yes, I still think of them as the men Captain Smith left me in charge of. I feel responsible for them."

They passed Flowerdew Hundred when John asked an odd question, "Josh, what do you think would surprise Smith if he came back today?"

Josiah took a moment to think, but the answers were fairly obvious to him, "First, it would be the very size of the place. We have passed three large plantations and will soon pass more long before we see Jamestown. Martin's land is even further down river. We are so spread out and there are so many people here now. And I am sure he would marvel at the road. We used to trek along Indian paths to get up and down the river. With the Great Road coming right to the Neck, travel is much easier. Then I think he would be surprised at the peace we have now with the Indians. Since you married Rebecca, " John frowned at this reminder, "we have had little disturbance."

"That is true," John said, "but I fear that could change so quickly. If there is an incident or even if a strong leader takes charge in one of the tribes, travelers could be threatened or even worse."

'I am glad to hear you talk that way, John. I am afraid Yeardley and the recent settlers have no idea what could happen if we let our guard down. Say, look there, someone at the next landing is signaling the barge to stop."

Two men came onto the barge with satchels. They were John and William Russell, bothers who had headright land just north of this landing. They had sponsored several boys on their voyage in 1609 and so had land from those headrights as well. Apparently, they had both been elected delegates.

"Good Day, Master Rolfe," they said courteously. "Hello, Josiah." Word of Josiah's land holdings had spread but not to everyone in the colony. They presumed that he was traveling as a servant for Rolfe. Rolfe felt awkward for a moment and then decided this would be happening often. He tried for a short explanation. "Gentlemen, my friend, Master Tucker, is a delegate from Henrico. He has 400 acres there now."

They both looked astonished. The last they knew of Josiah, he was Rolfe's foreman. Good manners won out. "Master Tucker, congratulations, I had not heard of your change in circumstance. We also are delegates to the Assembly," offered William. "Rolfe, are you also a delegate?"

"Not from Henrico. As a member of the Council I will be part of the Assembly, however."

"Ah, good," said John Russell, "I have long found you to have a voice of reason."

Rolfe said the appropriate thank yous and the conversation ranged. William remembered to congratulate Rolfe on his recent marriage and that brought up the subject of women.

John, the more outspoken brother, told of a rumor. "I have heard from some recent newcomers that the Company is looking for two hundred young women to sign up to come to Virginia for the purpose of marrying. You gentlemen are among the lucky few who have found wives here. I, for one, would welcome more of the fairer sex."

Josiah, recalling the earlier conversation about headrights, asked, "how would they determine who they would marry. My Bridget, thank the Lord above, chose me. Do you suppose these women would also be allowed to choose or would someone have to repay their passage to marry one?

"I had not thought of that," mused John, "but I have enough spare tobacco to be able to pay one's fare I am sure." The two brothers laughed and congratulated each other's fortune with some manly backslapping.

"That would limit their choice of husband to someone with extra cash or tobacco which would eliminate most of the laborers and tradesmen. Seems a bit unfair," suggested Josiah.

With the specter of unequal classes raised again, the moment became awkward. Luckily, Jamestown came into view and everyone busied themselves with collecting their baggage and readying to debark.

The four men said a quick farewell and Rolfe and Josiah headed for the house where Rolfe had reserved a room. They arrived two days before the Assembly was to commence, but Mistress Norton was ready for them and met them at her door.

"Gentlemen, welcome. I hope your voyage down river was pleasant. The weather has been so dreadfully hot here. Is it the same at Henrico?"

"Not quite so extreme, Mistress, but hot enough. The river is low. The banks were barren for more than a foot in some places even when the tide was in. The backwaters are foul and the mosquitoes swarm by the hundreds. Please tell us there is at least some breath of air in the room you have for us?"

"Since you were first to reserve space with me, I have assigned you the best room, sirs. Come I will show you."

She led them through a short center hallway from which steps led to the second floor. At the back of the hallway was a door that opened onto a small porch. A door opposite was the entrance to the "best room." This room was a freestanding structure set on foundation pillars of stones, shaded by heavy-leaved tulip poplars. Wonder of wonders, it had two windows, one on a southwest wall and the other on the northeast giving excellent cross-ventilation. With the door open onto the breezeway, the twelve by twelve foot space was deliciously cool. There was also a peaked roof that allowed space for the hot air to rise above the heads of the occupants. In winter, the room could probably be used for cold storage, but, in July, it was a little heaven.

The furnishings were simple yet adequate. There was a rope bed (a box frame with ropes worked crisscross to support a mattress), a stand with a wash bowl and pitcher, pegs long one wall for clothes, and an arrangement of two small benches and a table. Except for not having a place to cook, it was a complete cabin.

"This is most certainly a fine room, Mistress," said Rolfe. "Thank you for your thoughtfulness, but I have my room at the Statehouse. Master Tucker will be using this room."

"Oh, well this is meant for at least two to stay, sirs, but nothing is too good for our Assemblymen. " Then she addressed Josiah directly, "Breakfast is served at seven, dinner at two, and if you need supper, let me know and I will find something for you. I will bring towels and a cover for the bed if you will be wanting one?"

"I doubt there will be need for a cover, mum, but the towels will be welcome. Where may I fill the pitcher?" asked Josiah.

"Oh, here now, you must not be used to hiring a room, young sir. Fetching the water is part of the service. If you will be so kind as to pass me the ewer, I will have it filled and brought back straight away. Get yourself settled, now. I will be back with the water and, when you have freshened up, you come to the parlor and I will have refreshments ready." Holding the pitcher like a trophy, the landlady waddled onto the porch and down two steps toward the well for water.

"What do you think of that, Master Rolfe? Did you know the Mistress of the house would do all the fetching and cooking and such?"

"I gather you have not stayed in a tavern or inn before, lad? I have not stayed in many, but when we were in England, my dear Rebecca and I, there were servants at the inn and the country house. Neither of us did any of the chores for that whole year. I can tell you, it was pleasant for a while, but then I got bored with nothing to fill my time. For these few days you should take advantage, though, and enjoy the service."

"I will try, sir, I will try."

The men rested until the day of the Assembly finally arrived. It was Friday, July 30th, and everyone was up early and turned out in their very best clothes. The day promised to be a typical high summer day in coastal Virginia, hot, humid, and airless, so the heavy formal English clothing was wildly inappropriate. By the time Rolfe walked the short distance from the Statehouse to the churchyard, his velvet suit was already soaked with sweat under the arms and along his spine. His silk stockings were wilting and beginning to sag at the ankles. Josiah fared better. All of his clothing was made of linen so the perspiration wicked into the linen and evaporated actually cooling the skin. Bridget had been embarrassed that she had not had time to create sleeves for his best jerkin, but Josiah was thankful for their absence. Each time they encountered another delegate, the first topic of conversation was the heat.

Davis and Stacy, the two men sent to the Assembly from Martin's Hundred, greeted Rolfe but only nodded to Josiah. This was to be the first of many such encounters and Rolfe was ready.

"Gentlemen, perhaps you do not know our delegate from Henrico, Master Josiah Tucker. He owns land adjacent to my own as well as a significant plot on the river."

This news immediately changed the men's attitude toward Josiah. With his rough dress, they, like the Russell brothers, had assumed he was a servant to Rolfe, not a landholder. Now they were most cordial.

"Tucker, is it?" Stacy began, "Pleasure to make your acquaintance."

Davis moved next to Josiah and picked up the conversation with a political question, "How do you stand, Tucker, on the question of selling guns to the natives?"

Before Josiah could answer, Rolfe interrupted with greetings for Thomas Dowse. Dowse, the same Thomas Dowse who had been the dancer and drummer used to lure out the Indians so many years ago, now had 400 acres. He knew Josiah's story. The older settlers, especially those who had come over as penniless commoners, kept track of those among them who had acquired land. They shared a warm handshake and Thomas took the place of Davis next to Josiah.

"Where are you staying, Thomas," asked Josiah.

"Over on the mainland, with friends. I came a week ago. How about you?"

"Master Rolfe arranged a rented room for me here in town. There is plenty of room if you want to stay over for a night or for the entire time."

"Thank you for the offer. I may need to take you up on it if some of these fellows get long-winded. How does this work anyway? Have you any idea?"

"Not really. It is all very new. Master Rolfe said it would be something like Parliament, but I have no idea how Parliament works, do you?"

By this time, they had reached the churchyard, which was filling up with delegates and a few servants. John Pory, the Secretary to the Governor, strode toward the group with purpose. He made his way to the center of the group and slowly opened a large journal.

"Good morning, gentlemen. I have the honor to be the Speaker for this Assembly. In that capacity, I will announce some points of protocol. Please gather round and listen closely."

Staring straight at Josiah, he said, "Only duly elected delegates may enter the church. Servants are to remain outside. The Assemblymen may move to a window and summon his servant as needs be."

Rolfe moved closer to Josiah with the intention of delivering his standing introduction again, but Pory plowed ahead.

"The Governor and his staff will arrive shortly and lead the delegation into the church. The Governor and his staff will be seated in their customary stall. The delegates may take their places in the choir. The proceedings will be opened with a prayer and the next order of business will be to check the credentials of each man before he takes his seat, so please have your papers ready."

Then he said more loudly, so anyone near the church could hear, "These proceedings are to be private and privileged so all who are not a part of the Assembly are to stay at a distance from the church and take no part in the meeting. Anyone interrupting the business of this Assembly will be dealt with accordingly. Do I make myself clear?"

No one responded. No response was expected. After a short pause, he continued, "Please settle your business and keep this path clear. The Governor will be coming shortly." With that he snapped shut his journal and fairly marched back to the statehouse.

"Excuse me, Josiah, I must join the other council members now. You and Dowse do Henrico township proud." With that, Rolfe followed in Pory's wake.

Robert Beheathland and his friend William Spencer, both of whom had arrived with the original fleet, were in the churchyard to see old friends. Neither had yet become landholders and therefore they were not eligible to stand for election. They were, however, both doing quite well, one having a storehouse for tobacco and the other running the old trading post as a general store. Both had married widows with children and added to their families with sons recently born. Taking Pory at his word, they closed their conversations, accepted a few final paternal congratulations and headed back to their businesses.

Others had also left the area, so that when the Governor made his appearance, the crowd consisted of only the twenty-four delegates and a handful of servants. Yeardley made a great show of his arrival. The Reverend Buck led the procession. The six council members, in their finest clothes and hats with fresh plumes, preceded the Governor. They carried their swords raised in front of them as a sort of honor guard. Captain Francis West and former-Governor Captain Nathaniel Powell in their military dress came first followed by William Wickham and Samuel Maycock. John Pory and John Rolfe were the last pair and two paces behind came Governor Yeardley himself in a brand new suit of green brocade in the latest English fashion.

The delegates parted to allow the honor guard to pass and enter the church first. Only half-jokingly, Josiah leaned close to Dowse and whispered, "There should be music."

Governor Yeardley and his council took their usual places in the special choir stall built for the Governor. The delegates found seats across the aisle or in the choir stall next to the council. The Reverend Buck had gone ahead to the steps of the altar and turned to face the gathering, prayer book in hand. When the group was settled, the Reverend motioned them to stand, closed his eyes and lifted his face to heaven and prayed.

"Dear Lord, our God, we are gathered here to do good service to the colony of Virginia. For as much as men's affairs doth little prosper unless blessed by your grace, we humbly beseech You to guide the thoughts and hearts of these men in their speech and deliberations. Open their ears to the directives of their leaders and grant them wisdom in all things. Dear Lord, guide and sanctify these proceedings to the glory of Your name and the good of this plantation."

Thirty-two voices joined in the, "Amen."

John Pory, as he would throughout the Assembly, called the meeting to order and recognized Governor Yeardley.

Yeardley was clearly quoting from a script as he opened the meeting, "As the duly appointed Governor of the Colony of Virginia and the representative of its founders, the Virginia Company, I hereby open this first Assembly of Burgesses of the Colony of Virginia. God save the King."

Everyone responded as expected, "God save the King."

This was the first time the delegates had heard the term Assembly of Burgesses and they were whispering about it when Pory reclaimed the floor.

"The first order of business is the verification of credentials of each Burgess. As I call the name of the township, step forward and present your certification of election."

Pory began with the city of Jamestown itself and worked his way outward. Two by two, each pair of delegates, now called Burgesses, brought a paper showing that they were residents of the township they represented, that they owned land there, and the voting results of the election.

Henrico was the eleventh and last township called. When it was clear that Pory had come to the end of his list, Davis stood and politely addressed the speaker.

"Mister Pory, you have not called for the credential of the Burgesses from Martin's Brandon. May I offer you the credentials of myself and my fellow delegate Master Stacy?"

Pory was prepared for this challenge. "Mister Davis, John Martin chose to make his own contract with the Virginia Company separate from the common contract under which this body now meets. Martin's Brandon will not be represented in this Assembly."

A general hubbub ensued. Stacy jumped out of his place to stand beside Davis. Others muttered to their neighbors or moved to where they could speak to another friend. The Governor nodded to Captain West who stuck a stout pole on the wooden dais on which the Governors chair was placed. This abrupt noise silenced the crowd as intended.

Yeardley spoke quietly and with finality, "These men cannot take part in this Assembly as seated and voting members. In deference to Captain John Martin, who has done this colony great service, they will be allowed to stay and observe if they so wish."

Stacy, the more hot-tempered of the two, said, "No, Your Honor, I will not stay where I am not an equal. I will take this news to Captain Martin." He grabbed his hat and stomped out. Davis took the opposite view, "I thank you, Your Honor, I will stay at least until I receive further word from Captain Martin." Davis was already seated at the far end of the stalls across from the Governor's chair. There was nowhere farther away for him to be seated, so he simply stayed, silently, in his place. Many sympathetic eyes turned his way, but no one spoke to him.

This bald exercise of power set the stage perfectly for the next act of the drama, the taking of the Oath of Supremacy.

Over a century before, King Henry the Eighth, caused this oath to be written to ensure that every adult in the kingdom would abide by his choice of heir and recognize his right to be the head of the Church of England. As every Englishman knew, those were serious issues during the reign of the Tutors. Catholic Queen Mary had repealed the oath, but Protestant Queen Elizabeth had rewritten it slightly and reinstated it. At the end of her reign, having never married and having no direct heirs, her choice of James Stuart of Scotland, son of her cousin, was upheld by this oath.

Since the Stuarts had taken the throne upon the death of Elizabeth in 1603 and since King James had a living adult son, the oath seemed less important. It was also less controversial since King James was a Protestant. However, there were still enough powerful families who were either professed Catholics or who had shown Catholic leanings that the oath was still administered to *"every temporal judge, justice, mayor and other lay or temporal officer and minister, and every other person having your Highness's fee or wages, within this realm or any your Highness's dominions"* which included the new Burgesses. One by one, each seated Burgess, stood before the Governor with his hand on the Bible, and repeated the words of the oath to this agent of the King.

" I, ..., do utterly testify and declare in my conscience that the King's Highness is the only supreme governor of this realm, and of all other his Highness's dominions and countries, as well in all spiritual or ecclesiastical things or causes, as temporal, and that no foreign prince, person, prelate, state or potentate hath or ought to have any jurisdiction, power, superiority, pre-eminence or authority ecclesiastical or spiritual within this realm; and therefore I do utterly renounce and forsake all foreign jurisdictions, powers, superiorities and authorities, and do promise that from henceforth I shall bear faith and true allegiance to the King's Highness, his heirs and lawful successors, and to my power shall assist and defend all jurisdictions, pre-eminences, privileges and authorities granted or belonging to the King's Highness, his heirs or successors, or united or annexed to the imperial crown of this realm. So help me God, and by the contents of this Book."

This tedious ritual was follow by Pory reading the documents from the Virginia Company. There was a brief statement commissioning the establishment of the general Assembly and their duties. Then he read in full the new charter, called by its author, Sir Edwin Sandy, the Great Charter.

The provisions of this Great Charter amazed the Assembly. The predecessors of Yeardley had been hard, autocratic types who imposed severe and even cruel penalties for serious and minor infractions of a set of laws designed to bring all settlers into one mold. This Charter abolished that strict martial law and went even farther to abolish Company ownership of all the land and tools. Some colonists had indeed been given land either through the headright or an outright grant from the Governor and they had been allowed to make some personal profit from it, but this was far from universal.

Now, in this Great Charter "ancient planters", those who paid their way over and lived there for at least 3 years before 1616, got 100 acres for each man and family member and another 100 acres when the first acreage was plowed. Later comers got 50 acres plus 50 for each person they brought with them. This accounted for thousands of acres of land. Since Jamestown island consisted of only 1500 acres all together with less than half of that being arable land, a lot of that grant land would be along the river or inland. The condition of having paid your own way over was still there, but this was better than the first headright. Josiah was happy for his friends and saddened for himself.

Now individuals would actually own their land. This would naturally encourage their ambitions to grow their holdings and provide crops that would generate a profit. It would allow them to make the most of their abilities and interests. It was a legalization of the individual spirit that had grown of its own accord for the last twelve years.

The quick thinkers were already planning which land they would try to claim. Indian clearings known as "old fields" would be the most desirable because they were already cleared. Land fronting on any water over twelve feet deep, the draw of the largest trading vessels, would also be in demand to be landing sites. Part of Josiah's river frontage was that deep and more. He was glad he would not have to be in the rush for the prime land.

The Great Charter said that the Company would continue to choose the Governor and Council, but it also establish the rule of law as had been the tradition in England for generations and permitted the heads of households to elect representatives who would partner with the Virginia Company to establish and enforce laws for the whole colony equally.

Except for a few gasps and the occasional, "Did you hear that?" whispered to a neighbor, the Burgesses were silent for this entire recitation. It was a silence of wonder.

Then Pory announced, "We will now divide into four groups. Each group will consider one area of the Great Charter just read and propose laws in support of these instructions. We will reconvene tomorrow to hear a report of your progress."

Dowse pulled at Josiah's arm, "So this is what an Assembly, … no wait, an Assembly of Burgesses does. We take a broad instruction and craft our own laws. Can you believe it, Josiah? The rules are no longer given to us, we make them!"

"So it seems, Thomas, so it seems. Have you any idea how to write a law?"

"Well, no, but we can figure it out. How hard can it be? You describe a situation and then say what should happen and what penalty there is if it does not."

"That sounds simple enough. Which committee of eight will you join?"

"I am very interested in the how the land will be granted to those who bring new settlers. I hope to have more of my family join me here eventually. What about you, Josiah?"

"I would like to work on how the plantations will be defined. This business of contiguous land may prove an issue for some of us. And not being within five miles of a borough or ten miles of one another could be very difficult for those of us already working granted land. I see Reverend Buck is gathering a select group to work on the definition of lands to support the clergy."

Thomas chuckled and paraphrasing the Bible joked, "Give unto Caesar the things that are Caesar's, but give unto Buck anything he can get."

Yet another committee considered the founding of a university for teaching Indian children. The groups mostly moved outside where there was a small breeze and the servants who had stayed nearby brought some refreshments. Some groups worked for two or three hours and disbanded for the day. Others worked long into the evening.

George Thorpe, an Episcopal priest, had recently come to the colony. He had been interested in distilling all his adult life and so, naturally, he tried his hand at distilling liquor from the American grain, corn. He had some success and had brought samples of his attempt to Jamestown in hopes of getting some notice. The long evening meetings were either helped or hindered by this new drink for the new country called bourbon.

When they reconvened the next day, it was clear that each group had discovered that writing a sound, fair, and comprehensive law was no easy task. There were many details and special circumstances to be considered. The conversations inevitably raised related issues, some of which the groups brought back to the Assembly to be considered in addition to the laws they were sent to construct. One after the other, individuals asked to be recognized to propose a law.

The first law proposed was that tobacco be sold for no less than three pence per pound. It passed unanimously.

Next Captain Thomas Graves stood and said, "Gentlemen, we appreciate the 100 acres to be granted to those who suffered the hardships of the early years of this colony. However, some of those "ancient Planters", and others outside that definition, now have more than 100 acres under cultivation. We propose that land grants by former Governors be reconfirmed so that these men may retain what they already work."

There was some open discussion, all favorable, and then a member of the committee on cities proposed that the Company rush settlers to Virginia specifically to build up the four burgeoning towns. There was little discussion of this proposal.

Then Graves again took the floor and added to his first request, "I would amend my first proposal to include that any "ancient Planter" who has come to Virginia, at his own expense, at anytime before this year, be assured of land grants for himself and his children." Josiah had hoped the committee would extend the grant to anyone who had survived those early years, but the restriction on having paid your own fare remained.

The University committee proposed that the Company send workmen assigned to build the proposed University at Henrico since the current settlers had their hands full with their own tasks.

Yeardley had sat quietly and listened to all the proposals. During a lull, he spoke up to say, "You have considered well, gentlemen. I find all of these proposals to be fit to be sent to England for consideration. Master Pory, note that I personally endorse these proposals."

Pory nodded to the Governor and added a notation to the sheet on which he had been recording the proposals. Josiah noticed that the stack of Pory's papers was already growing. That second day, Saturday, was spent as a committee of the whole in the church. By two o'clock, the heat had become so unbearable that the meeting was dismissed for the day.

Normally, Sunday would not have been a meeting day, but because they could not work full days in the heat, they did convene after Sunday service was concluded and they had taken a short time to eat. Only an hour into the session, Burgess Walter Shelley of Smith's Hundred, began to show signs of succumbing to the heat. He stood and wandered aimlessly around the room. He was confused and disoriented. He seemed to be speaking to a woman and his breathing became increasingly labored. Someone called out, "It is his heart. I have seen this before." Shelley turned to stare at the speaker and collapsed.

Four men carried him out into a shady spot and called for water. They loosened his stock and jerkin and bathed his fevered skin with water. It cooled rapidly, not because the treatment was effective, but because Shelley was dead.

The Governor's wife, Flowerdew, was called to the scene and, after a few private words with her husband, she took charge of the situation. She sent for other women, asked four servants to carry the body to the Statehouse, and followed along to take care of the necessities. The Governor spoke quietly to Pory and, without returning to the church, he dismissed the session for the day and set six in the morning as the time to reconvene so as to make the most of the cool of the day.

Both the heat and the need to return to their tobacco farms encouraged the Burgesses to keep their discussion of laws to a minimum. In quick order they passed laws against injuring an Indian, against idleness and gaming, against drunkenness and against "excess in apparel" meaning dressing above one's station. These men wanted an orderly and moral community at peace with the Indians. The penalty for violation of these laws was a fine to be paid in church.

The Burgesses ordered that four viewers examine tobacco before shipment and that the worst be destroyed to keep quality and prices high. This did cause some argument as to how the determination would be fairly made. No details were added to the law itself, but the idea that such inspection could be corrupt was planted in everyone's mind.

Admonitions to the settlers were put into the record but not given the force of law. They were to keep the Indians at arms length, neither rejecting them nor inviting them into the settlements. It was recognized that Indians could be of service in hunting and fishing and even in working the corn crop provided they were closely watched. The settlers were directed to begin to find ways to educate the young Indians in preparation for attending the would-be University. Christianizing the Indians had been, and would remain, an underlying goal for the colony.

Somewhere between a directive and a law sat some proposals about diversifying farming. The Company would provide the materials to start new crops, but the settlers were to take on the task of ensuring their success. Specifically, every planter was to set out at least six mulberry trees for the next seven years to provide food for silkworms who would, theoretically, provide silk for a textile industry. Each planter would be given a hundred flax plants, ten grape vines and some aniseed to make flavoring. This would require that some land that might be used for tobacco be put to these new crops. This caused more discussion than any other proposition because the men could see the direct effect on their profits. Since the measure did not hold the power of a law, those who felt the heat prevailed upon the debaters to accept the directive as stated.

The next day, the floor was opened to proposals from individuals. These could be new laws, but, in effect, it became a tribunal hearing accusations against individuals. Josiah was not aware that this would be a part of the Assembly or he might have brought charges against the men who tried to poach Rolfe's land. But someone must had gotten wind of the option for several men were charged, some found guilty and some not. The most serious punishment was given to one Thomas Garnett. His ear was to be nailed to the pillory for four days and each day he was to be whipped. So ended the fifth day of the Assembly.

Wednesday, August 4th was overwhelmingly hot and the Governor himself became ill early in the day. The Assembly, having passed the laws suggested by the Great Charter and those the committees had proposed, voted to dismiss for the day.

The next day, Speaker Pory read over all the laws and orders and asked for any amendments. There were none. However, members originated eighteen additional proposals and all were passed with little deliberation. The need for these laws was apparent to those who had lived in this rough and challenging land. They forbade the sale of guns (and dogs) to Indians, they limited travel to twenty miles from home (the distance of a good day's walk) and never to an Indian village without authorization, they prohibited the killing of cattle (a key food for survival) and the theft of boats (essential for travel and transportation of goods). Curiously, they also took time to prescribe the duties of ministers and churchwardens. Since they left the judging of "enormous sins" to these churchwardens with the penalty being repentance or else the sinner would be excommunicated and his property seized, putting limits on this key office was a critical piece of business.

Pory wrote furiously, especially on this last day and ended with twenty-six pages of Proceedings ending with the sentence, "Here ends the laws."

But there was one more bit of business for the Assembly. The colony, not an individual, brought charges against the famous, or infamous, Henry Spelman who had attained the rank of Captain. As a boy he had been sent or sold to the Indians to learn their language and, having learned it well, had acted as an interpreter for years, sometimes living with the Indians and sometimes with the settlers. Now he was being charged with alienating the mind of the Powhatan chief, Openchancanough. Why the rulers of the colony wanted Spelman punished was not clear. Little evidence was presented, but clearly the council wanted a guilty verdict.

The matter of how to fund the government officers, Pory and clerks, had to be covered. The group quickly agreed to tax every male Virginian over the age of 16 one pound of tobacco per year. They had had enough, enough talk, enough heat, enough of good clothes, and enough time away from their farms. They apologized to the Speaker for wanting to quit so abruptly, but he had also had enough and was happy to accept a motion for adjournment. He dutifully sent a fully accounting of the Proceeding back to the Virginia Company officers, meaning Sir Edwin Sandys.

All the Burgesses left for home before nightfall. While Rolfe went to settle their bill with Mistress Norton, Josiah sought out all of the squad who were on the island. He did this each time he came down from Henrico.

Congratulations were in order for several new sons and daughters born since his last visit. Davis had finally gotten married. Dods had gotten land of his own and was moving to the middle part of the peninsula. Fenton was going with him to help work the place. They would, of course, be growing tobacco. Josiah shared the crop rotation plan he and Rolfe had been trying and gave him some ideas on how to diversify his planting to feed his family as well as gain a fair profit.

Josiah and Rolfe met at dusk at the boat landing. The barge was full and it took some time for the ferry owner to arrange all the cargo and baggage. They would leave as the tide was moving upstream to make the poling easier. While they stood waiting for the loading to finish, they shared some thoughts on the landmark events of the Assembly. After a bit, they both went quiet as if, by mutual agreement, they had decided to talk of something else. Rolfe opened a new subject.

"As I said farewell to the statehouse clerk, he handed me a letter from my cousin, Richard, the one who writes to me occasionally of family matters in Herefordshire. Let me see what he has to say." John unfolded the thin paper and began to read to himself.

"I trust everything is well with your family in England?" Josiah offered. Does he speak of Thomas?"

"He does. Richard says he has been to see my brother Henry and that he is impressed with my son. He does not say in what way he is impressed," John said with a chuckle. "That may be good or bad."

CHAPTER EIGHTEEN
New Beginnings

It was well into harvest time. The crops, tobacco and otherwise, were good this year. Since the assembly of Burgesses, Josiah's standing in the colony had risen. Other planters now greeted him cordially. Bridget had little benefit from his new status since she stayed at home but she enjoyed hearing his stories about his new friends.

John Rolfe was in Jamestown most of the time now. His role as Secretary to the Governor kept him very busy. Josiah kept an eye on John's holdings in and near Henrico. It seemed he was going down river regularly to see to his own interests and to report to John. Once more he had gotten a ride on a downriver barge.

When Josiah got to the statehouse, he noticed a dozen or more Africans. He had seen African sailors, but these people looked more like families of colonists, though colonists dumped on the beach with nothing. Some were doing simple menial tasks like moving firewood or raking pathways. Others were just sitting huddled by the side of the building. Once inside the building, his first question to Rolfe was, "Who are those people?"

John's tone was oddly official. "They are servants, recently acquired by the Company, for the use of the Governor and our Cape Merchant, Abraham Peirsey."

Josiah caught the tone in John's voice and understood this was a touchy subject, but his curiosity got the better of his judgement.

"And where did the Company acquire these folks?"

John fairly exploded, "Peirsey arranged a trade with a Dutchman John Jope who is captaining the English ship *White Lion*. Jope needed provisions to continue his voyage to Bermuda and Peirsey decided the Company needed these extra mouths to feed more than the supplies we had! No one can speak to them or understand them. We have no way to determine if they have any skills. I suppose they will end up tending tobacco fields on Company land or Governor Yeardley's land. They debarked at Point Comfort on the seventeenth of this month and arrived here just yesterday. Right now they are nothing but another nuisance for me!"

"You say the captain was Dutch? And on an English ship? Why would an English owner use a Dutch captain? It would be like hiring a spy."

"I agree with you, Josiah. Some worry about being invaded by the Spanish from Florida. In fact, the captain of the *White Lion's* consort *Treasurer*, Daniel Elfrith, warned the authority at Hampton Roads that Governor Yardley should install cannon at Point Comfort since the Spanish had plans to attack Virginia. Since he was among those commissioned to stir up the Spanish, his intelligence was likely good. You know we have cannon and a fort but with no gun carriages and no trained gunners, our cannon are of no use. But I think it is much more likely we would lose our trade to the Dutch than our lives to the Spanish."

"Not to mention involving us in the African trade. How many of these people are there, John?"

"I count twenty men, women, and useful boys and girls. I believe there is a babe hidden in a sling on one of the women and another might be with child. There are two or three younger children. I am not sure how many or if they are boys are girls since they hide among the women and I can barely tell them apart anyway."

"What am I to do with them, Josiah? Are they servants? Do they have terms of indenture? Heaven forbid that we should list them as slaves. Englishmen do not keep slaves. It has been part of our understood constitution for generations."

John's irritation and concern were personal. He seemed to be affronted by the presence of these unspecified persons. Josiah was not sure if his issue was philosophical or administrative or both. Whatever the case, his friend John was as upset as Josiah had ever seen him.

"As if this were not enough, the latest packet from the Company says that the rumors about a ship of women is true. Let me read you this. They say 'a fit hundredth might be sent of women, maids young and uncorrupt, to make wives to the inhabitants and by that means to make the men there more settled and less movable.' A hundred unattached women! No instructions on how these women are to be matched with husbands. No specific timing. Nothing! I suppose I will be the one who will have to sort that out too."

"Is the job of Secretary not what you thought it would be?"

"Sometimes it is exactly as I expected. I enjoy keeping records and doing the correspondence for the Governor. It is these unexpected and undefined tasks that irritate me. I truly believe the decisions belong to the Governor or his assistant. I am happy to document all of it, but I do not have or want the authority to make decisions."

"And listen to this! Also in this packet is mention of a new company sending a ship of colonists. It says three men from one Gloucestershire family William Throckmorton, Richard Berkeley, and George Thorpe and a man named John Smyth intend to make a settlement here on the James River. It will be named for the home castle and be called Berkeley Hundred. John Woodlief is to be their leader."

"John Smith! Do you suppose that is our John Smith?"

"Not likely. Your, not my, Captain John Smith has not been in good favor with the Virginia Company for some years. And this man's name is spelled with a "y", though spelling is always doubtful.

"I would so like to meet with my John Smith again. And did you say Woodlief?"

"Yes, John Woodief. Do you know the name?"

"I knew the man. He arrived just before the terrible winter of 09, if it is the same man. He did survive, but like all those who returned to England after living through that hell, he vowed never to return. I wonder if it is the same man?"

"Well, Josiah, this is quite a different place than it was ten years ago. Maybe tobacco has lured him back."

"Possibly, but speaking of tobacco, I had best be about the business that brought me to Jamestown. Fascinating to talk with you Master Secretary, as always. My best to Jane."

"Good to see you, friend. And my best to your lovely wife."

Captain John Woodlief was indeed the same man who had endured the starving and depredations of the winter of 1609 and 1610. From his experience at Jamestown, he had learned not to bring colonists of quality but to enlist men of crafts -- journeymen, joyners, carpenters, smiths, fowlers and turners -- men comfortable with doing the work required to establish a colony.

The owners of the Berkeley Company had given him broad powers in matters concerning both the voyage and the settlement. Knowing the breadth of work to be done, he had five assistants, Ferdinando Yate, John Blanchard, Richard Godfry, Rowland Painter and Thomas Coopy. He hired an accomplished pilot for the "Good Ship *Margaret*" and filled it with appropriate supplies and provisions including 8,000 biscuits and bread, 160 pounds of butter, 127 pounds of bacon and horsemeat, 60 bushels of peas, 20 bushels of wheat, 6 tons of cider, 15 gallons of aqua vitae and 5 ½ tons of beer. Looking toward the first year in the new colony he also brought clothes, kitchen utensils, construction and agricultural tools, weapons, Bibles and 6,000 beads for Indian trade.

On September 16, 1619, twelve days after he was commissioned, Captain Woodlief and thirty-five hand-picked men departed Kingrode, Bristol, England. Two and half months later, on Sunday November 28, 1619, the ship entered the mouth of Chesapeake Bay. They stayed at anchor through a bad storm on the 29th, but moved to land at Hampton Roads on November 30. The Captain went ashore briefly to get the most recent news of the colony. Hearing nothing to change his mind, he proceeded up the river and arrived at the Berkeley site on December 4.

The men were rowed ashore along with their personal belongings. They, like many before them, were awed by the size of the trees and stillness of the landscape.

Instruction from the Company in London had been thorough and precise. The first instruction was that upon landing they would offer a prayer of thanksgiving for a safe voyage and that this custom should be repeated yearly on the same day. So, along with Captain Woodlief, all the men gladly knelt on solid land as he prayed, "We ordaine that this day of our ships arrival, at the place assigned for plantacon, in the land of Virginia, shall be yearly and perpetually kept holy as a day of Thanksgiving to Almighty God."

There was little to eat at hand, but the men assembled some scraps of food from the ship and found some oysters in the bay where they came ashore. On December 4, 1619, thirty-six Englishmen and no Indians, held a prayerful and meager feast of Thanksgiving.

Completing the voyage was only the beginning. Another of the specific instructions was that the Captain would assign a parcel of land to each man and a length of time that each man would be indentured to the Company. The five assistants received the shortest terms of three years and the promise of the largest land holdings of 30 acres at the end of the three years of service to the Company. The least skilled of the men received eight years of indenture and the promise of only 15 acres of land. Owning any land in England was a dream beyond imagining for any of these men. Now they would spend a few years working land they would eventually own. Since they had not paid their own passage, this was much better terms than other colonists who came as indentured could expect.

John and Jane Rolfe and their daughter came to their home at Varina Farm near Henrico in late December. The twelve days of Christmas would begin on the twenty-fifth and John wanted to avoid official duties and spend that time peacefully with his family. They invited Josiah and his family to spend the last days with them. Naturally, then would stay overnight.

Josiah and Bridget had spent precious hours making small but special items for their children to mark the holidays. They had agreed on the gifts for Hannah and John and worked together to create them.

Hannah was nearly old enough to begin instruction in spinning and sewing. As soon as a girl was coordinated enough to control a spindle and work a needle, she would begin her training. Bridget assembled a sewing kit for Hannah that included two needles, a small pair of scissors, a dozen pins, a small bit of beeswax, three feet of twine and a pin cushion, all wrapped in a bound layers of cloth with a ribbon to tie up the bundle. Hannah would learn to coat the needles with beeswax to make them slide more easily, to coat the thread with beeswax so it would move through cloth without knotting and to coat the pins with beeswax to keep them from rusting. She would learn to knot the twine as a measure for cutting cloth and knitting. Bridget collected all the bits of cloth it would take to make a doll. For the last two years, Bridget had made a doll for Hannah. This year, with all the tools at hand, Hannah would be encouraged to learn the skills to make her own doll. Bridget spend several hours embroidering the outside of the bundle with small vines and flowers and Hannah's name.

Josiah added to Hannah's gift by carving a drop spindle that would fit her small hand. It looked like rather like a spinning top with a long handle but with a hook cut into the wood. Hannah had already learned about carding wool where she would take a fluff of clean wool and put it on one of two paddles filled with tiny stiff wires. As she moved the two paddles against each other, long fibers of the wool would be pulled straight. Now her hands were ready to do the more detailed task of leading the fibers onto the spindle where they would twist into useable yarn. The spindle had to be very smooth so as not to snag the yarn. Josiah spent a long time rubbing the carved wood with sand to be sure it was smooth but he could not resist carving an H on the bottom of the disc where it would not interfere with the spinning.

At only two, John was not ready for any major chores, though he already enjoyed throwing feed to the chickens and gathering kindling as his father chopped wood. John was fascinated by the river so Josiah carved him a boat. It was more of a barge than a ship. He also carved various blocks in various sizes, blocks that John could stack on the boat like cargo. Bridget had lobbied for an ark with pairs of animals but Josiah thought that was more than he could manage with his carving skills. Bridget used a bit of ink to write the name "John T" on the side of the boat. This nice a toy should last for many years so eventually John would be able to read his name on the boat.

Gifts were wrapped only if the wrapping could be put to some good use later on. Bridget found some pieces of cloth she was saving to repair worn clothes and wrapped each gift tying the folds closed with strips of cloth. She hid the gifts in her sewing basket knowing she would take it with her to Rolfe's.

Giving gifts among adults was not common. A husband might purchase some pretty thing like a bit of ribbon for his wife or he might make a useful tool and, perhaps, put extra effort into decorating it. Likewise a wife might embellish a shirt for her husband. But giving a gift to others outside the family was rare. However, Josiah felt he wanted to do something for the man who had been their benefactor. Josiah did not know enough about animals in the ark to carve them, but one thing he did know was tobacco. So for John he carved a perfect tobacco leaf, one that would lay on John's table, with a depression along the center stem meant to fit John's quill.

Though all of Catholic Europe had adopted the new Gregorian calendar thirty-seven years ago in 1582, the protestant nations, like England, clung to the old Julian calendar. The Julian calendar had an extra day every four years, or leap years, including all century years. But over 1600 years, those extra hours had added up to ten days. So at the winter solstice, the shortest daylight of the year, the English calendar said the date was December 11 not December 21. By the tenth day of Christmas 1619, the night was at its longest.

So January 4th dawned late but the weather was crisp and perfect. An hour after dawn, breakfast was over, the fire was banked and everyone was ready for the two-mile walk. Little John insisted on walking at first but his mother wrapped the carrying sling around her anyway knowing that he would be asking to be carried soon. Hannah was accustomed to walking a mile or even two, but Josiah was prepared to carry her on his back if needed.

Being situated about midway on the river frontage of each property, the two homesteads were less than a mile apart and Josiah had made enough trips back and forth that he had created an indirect though discernable path. But that path was far from straight and not an easy walk for a family carrying baskets and children. None the less, and even with a short morning, the little family arrived at the Rolfe's place before noon. Rolfe greeted them with open arms, "Ah, Josiah, you made good time."

"We did. It helped that young John slept half the way." But little John was awake now and squirming his way out of the sling on his mother's side.

Jane had a large meal planned for midday. She put the biscuits on to cook as soon as she heard voices in the yard. Then she went outside cleaning her hands on her apron. Little Jane followed her.

"Bridget, Josiah, how delightful!"

Jane helped Hannah climb down from her father's back. "And Hannah, you have grown since I saw you at harvest."

"Yes, mam, I have. Mama puts marks on the side of the fireplace and I have grown a whole inch."

Jane smiled and hugged Hannah. "Do let's go in. Food is ready and I must check the biscuits."

Hannah and little Jane hugged so hard they nearly fell over but they were still the first inside. They huddled on the floor in a corner near the fireplace chattering quietly.

With the increased heat and the lack of movement, little John began to stir. He had always been a child to wake up slowly. Bridget was glad he was completely weaned. It would make this journey much easier.

Jane and Bridget began to lay out a huge meal.

When the meal was done, the girls returned to their favorite corner and included little John in their play. The women dealt with the extra food and the dishes. The men pulled out pipes and settled in at the cleared table.

John went to a shelf and retrieved a letter. "Josiah, I have another letter from my cousin, Richard. He brings me up to date on other family members … and here is an interesting note. He says our cousin Walter in Plymouth has hired on as a carpenter with a group taking ship for America. Many of those on the voyage are part of a conservative religious group who call themselves Pilgrims. Their leader is a John Winthrop. He says the published destination is the northern part of the Virginia Colony somewhere on Hudson's Bay. They are to sail in winter or early spring."

He raised his eyes up from the letter and grinned at Josiah with a hopeful look on his face. "Perhaps I will be able to meet up with Walter someday."

"That would truly be a blessing, John. Did I tell you that Richard's first letter inspired me to write home to my family? No one there can read or write and they may all have moved on or be dead by now, but I made the effort."

"What with the new people at Berkeley Hundred and this group headed north, it makes you wonder how many more people will come here from England. Does it say anything about who will captain the ship?"

"Let me see. Not exactly. It says that Walter heard that Winthrop was impressed with the books of your friend Captain Smith and had contacted him to be their captain, but that Smith's price was too high."

Both men laughed, Rolfe to think that a captain would price himself out of job and Josiah to think how foolish these Pilgrims were not to willingly pay the price his hero demanded.

Josiah asked, "So they do have a ship, then?"

"Yes, Walter says they will be sailing in about six months on an old wine carrack named *Mayflower*."

Epilogue

William Shakespeare moved back to his hometown of Stratford on Avon in 1612. It was there that he wrote his final two plays, *The Tempest* and *Henry VIII*. He died on April 23, 1613 at the age of 49. No collection of his plays was published until 1623. The story of the shipwreck in the Tempest, is remarkably close to Strachey's notes on which he wrote an account of the adventure to an unknown lady on July 15, 1610.

In 1622, Openchancanough, the chief of the Powhatan did rise up against the settlers. On March 22, his assembled tribes attacked all the outlying settlements and killed over 300 people. Jamestown had been warned by a friendly Indian and escaped the devastation.

John Rolfe died in1622 about the same time as the Indian massacre, but probably not in the massacre. Rolfe's family line in America is second oldest only to two settlers from 1607, Robert Beheathland and William Spencer who, as of today, have living descendants.

John Rolfe's son, Thomas, was educated in England and returned to Virginia as a grown man in 1632 to claim his inheritance. It is presumed he then met his half-sister, Elizabeth. He stayed in Virginia in the military.

Samuel Argall was eventually cleared of piracy charges, knighted in 1622, and proposed as governor again.

In 1624, King James revoked the charter of the Virginia Company and made Virginia a Royal Colony as it remained until the American Revolution.

Governor Yeardley had extensive land holdings including acres that bordered on the Back River where a landing was created. By 1624 he had a fleet of five boats and a stable of twenty-one horses.

John Martin returned to Virginia to found Martin's Hundred and lived there until his death in 1632.

John Smith published three accounts of his adventures in Virginia, all somewhat different and his editor selected passages and then lost or destroyed the originals. He did captain ships to New England three times but never returned to Virginia. He died in England in 1631.

Study Guide

1. What do you think of the type of people who came with the first fleet in 1607? Were they fit to be settlers?

2. At what point do you think Josiah came into his own?

3. Which of the women in this story do you think were most suited to live in Virginia?

4. What do you think made Pocahontas want to stay with the English?

5. Which of the Governors of Jamestown did the best job? The worst job? Why do you think this?

6. Why do you think the Virginia Company council kept returning the same ineffectual Governors to Virginia?

Made in the USA
Columbia, SC
01 October 2024